Reading, Writing, and R........

Lucy Newlyn's important new book . . . marks a culminating moment in Romantic studies. . . . Newlyn is alert to the theoretical issues–from reader-response criticism to hermeneutics, from deconstruction to feminism–which necessarily frame any discussion of author-audience relations. . . . This is historicism of a fine-grained, rigorous and precisely documented kind. But it is a historicism which allows for the aleatory, for a certain undergrounding of the historical determinism that so pervades contemporary criticism of Romantic poetry.

Andrew Bennett, *Romanticism on the Net*

Lucy Newlyn's fascinating study . . . is rich in its range of material and suggestiveness. She rarely fails to say something new and challenging about even the most well-known of poems. . . . Her book is intelligently and illuminatingly responsive to the dynamics of the writer-reader relationship.

Michael O'Neill, *Review of English Studies*

Splendid. . . . The magisterial first chapter should by itself be required reading for any advanced student of this literary period. Newlyn provides a richly illustrated and radically transforming context for the growth of 'high' Romanticism. Building on recent historical and materialist criticism, but based also on fresh research in the primary literature, this chapter models the approach taken in the book as a whole. . . . Lucy Newlyn need have no anxiety about the reception of this career-defining book, which deserves a wide, sympathetic, and critically engaged audience.

Robin Jarvis, *The Coleridge Bulletin*

Newlyn's remarkably rich and wide-ranging study takes in battles along generic and gender lines, struggles between critics and poets about the relative values of poetry and prose, debates in the campaign for reform of copyright legislation, and the relationship of the spoken to the written word vis-a-vis the poetics of reception. . . . She persuasively argues that the creation of literary texts is inseparable from an author's conception of how–and by whom–their texts will be read.

Jacqueline Belanger, *British Association for Romantic Studies*

Lucy Newlyn's fascinating new study reconsiders and historicises the theory of poetic influence, shifting the focus away from antecedents towards posterity.

She brilliantly analyses the relations of fantasy, fear, and anticipation in the mind of the poet when confronted with the idea of an audience. In an impressively wide-ranging discussion, Newlyn shows how the rise of the reader as a figure of both allure and chastisement shaped the poetic projects of significant Romantic poets. The claims of the reader are, Newlyn argues, woven into poems, as both symptoms and defences. Newlyn tells a story of poetic identity which engages with both social life and literary tradition.

Anne Janowitz

Lucy Newlyn's lucid and eloquent new book shows just how crude–and therefore symptomatic–our idea of literary influence has been. What is inspired about Newlyn's approach is that the newly emerging complicities between readers and writers that she traces in Romanticism begin to seem like the most illuminating paradigm for our distinctively modern relationships with ourselves and others. It is clear, after reading this book, that we have been living in the age of the anxiety of reception.

Adam Philips

Reading, Writing, and Romanticism:

The Anxiety of Reception

LUCY NEWLYN

OXFORD
UNIVERSITY PRESS

OXFORD
UNIVERSITY PRESS

Great Clarendon Street, Oxford OX2 6DP

Oxford University Press is a department of the University of Oxford.
It furthers the University's objective of excellence in research, scholarship,
and education by publishing worldwide in

Oxford New York

Auckland Bangkok Buenos Aires Cape Town Chennai
Dar es Salaam Delhi Hong Kong Istanbul Karachi Kolkata
Kuala Lumpur Madrid Melbourne Mexico City Mumbai Nairobi
São Paulo Shanghai Taipei Tokyo Toronto

Oxford is a registered trade mark of Oxford University Press
in the UK and in certain other countries

Published in the United States
by Oxford University Press Inc., New York

British Library Cataloguing in Publication Data

Data available

Library of Congress Cataloging in Publication Data

Data available

ISBN   0 19 818710 6 (hbk)
ISBN   0 19 818711 4 (pbk)

1 3 5 7 9 10 8 6 4 2

Typeset by Kolam Information Services Pvt. Ltd., Pondicherry, India
Printed in Great Britain
on acid-free paper by
Biddles Ltd.,
Guildford and King's Lynn

Some solace thus I strive to gain,
Making a kind of secret chain,
If so I may, betwixt us twain
In memory of the past.

(Wordsworth)

Preface

This book sets out to explore a problem with perennial manifestations and implications, which takes on a special colouring in the English Romantic tradition. Broadly speaking, it is a problem concerning the precarious status of subjecthood. In Romantic hermeneutics, this becomes a question of how writers and readers imagine each other—the difficult balance of identification and differentiation involved in the processes of communicating or understanding. In Romantic literature, it leads into a more complicated series of intersecting questions. How was the relationship between writers and readers affected by the rise of professional criticism? On what terms was authorial identity negotiated? How could writers construct an authentic identity for themselves, either from an unstable present, or from a past whose authority was under question? How was it possible to accommodate authorial rights alongside interpretative freedoms at a time when the emerging power of the subject was seen as both desirable and contentious? English Romantic writers, who negotiated these problems at both a theoretical and a practical level, were especially interested in how they affected the transmission of authority and tradition— subjects that provide a focus for what I have to say throughout.

Authority, tradition, and canon-formation have been Harold Bloom's subject-matter too, but Bloom's celebrated theory of the 'anxiety of influence' lays all its emphasis on one side of the polarity, writer–reader, and works in a single temporal direction only. In doing this, it risks ignoring the duality of the writing–reading subject, who looks both 'before and after'. All writers are also readers, and many readers also write. Anxieties experienced by writers centre as much on the future as on the past—not just because an author's status, authority, and posthumous life are dependent on readers, but because writing exists in dialogue with others whose sympathies it hopes to engage. Readers are as important to writers as their precursors, when it comes to constructing or defending literary identity; and whether they are named, invoked, figured, or idealized, their presence is just as discernible within a given text as are the traces of earlier writings. Moreover, writers are peculiarly alive to their own status as readers, and as often as not this leads to an awareness of their revisionary relationship to the materials they read. Such awareness brings with it, as an inevitable cost, the apprehension that all writing—including their own—is contingent, provisional, open to reconstruction. Potentially, then, the writing–reading subject is divided in its response to the release of subjectivity which occurs in acts of interpretation. Writers who are robustly revisionary in relation to past authors can be prescriptive when it comes to imagining their own reception; and this equivocation with respect to interpretative freedom is sometimes reflected in the way they imagine or theorize the reader's role. Such internal division becomes particularly apparent wherever there is an acknowledged confluence of writer and reader, as there is for instance rhetorically in poetic allusion, methodologically in literary criticism, or generically in parody. An allusive poet will be conscious of the implicitly critical or secondary activity involved in creativity; in the same way that a critic will be aware of a potential in criticism to claim creativity or 'primariness' on its own behalf. Poets who are also critics often attempt to mediate between these respective roles, perceiving them as rivalrous but not ultimately incompatible.

When the duality of the writing–reading subject gives rise to anxiety, the subject may betray symptoms which R. D. Laing attributed to a 'divided self'. Laing describes the divided self as the product of 'a basic ontological insecurity', which, when developed to an extreme, can cause an individual's personality to be 'profoundly modified even to the point of threatened loss of... identity'.[1] One of the major threats to a sense of unified identity comes from what Laing calls 'engulfment by... an alien sub-identity' who is frequently an authority figure, or an other on whom the self depends. The subject becomes sick when this sub-identity is internalized, or when the authentic self is sacrificed 'in compliance with the intentions or expectations of the other, or what are imagined to be the other's intentions or expectations'. At this point the insecurity that is a fairly normal feature of human behaviour may be said to have intensified into a schizoid condition.[2] What I am calling the 'anxiety of reception' resembles that condition, and appears in many shapes and

---

[1] *The Divided Self: An Existential Study in Sanity and Madness* (Harmondsworth, Middlesex: Penguin, 1959), 59.

[2] 'In the schizoid person', Laing continues, 'the whole of his being does not conform and comply... The basic split in his being is along the line of cleavage between his outward compliance and his inner witholding of compliance' (ibid. 99).

literary trends. Chapter 5 deals with the dialogues and crossings which took place between creativity and criticism in the early nineteenth century; and Chapter 6 with the place of women's poetry alongside and in the writing–reading dialectic. Chapters 7 and 8 examine the texture of Romantic rhetoric, especially critical rhetoric, as a complex mediation between authorial and interpretative claims to importance. Models of canon-formation, intertextuality, and reader-response are here considered in relation to ideas of personal and communal property which proliferated in copyright discourse and political debate. My study of the defences which underpin Romantic rhetoric allows me to reach some conclusions about the emergence of a Romantic poetics of reception, its peculiar power to survive. Finally, Chapter 9 casts back over the entire period under discussion—from the mid-eighteenth century to the 1820s—and sees it as a momentous phase in the history of reading. Hazlitt's pivotal essay, 'My First Acquaintance with Poets' is used to frame an investigation of the symbolic relation between spoken and written discourse in the performance and reception of literary texts.

Although the complex historical phenomenon which we term Romanticism can be understood as a species of 'reaction-formation'—a system of defences against the new power of reading—the overall picture that emerges in this study is more complicated, less embattled. In the periodical culture of the 1800s, when there was a running battle not only between authors and reviewers but between poets and writers of prose, most of the major English Romantic authors found themselves in several camps at once. The rise of criticism, by which poets were at one level deeply threatened, was at the same time a phenomenon on which they were dependent, and to which they contributed: the claim of criticism to be considered as itself creative was indeed significantly advanced by some of their number. While the tension between poetry and criticism persisted as the expression of divided allegiances that proved difficult to reconcile, it also turned out to be a valuable resource. Rhetorically, it enabled poet-critics to play sophisticated games with generic hierarchies, thus negotiating or contesting literary authority in ways appropriate to a given occasion. At a more fundamental level, it proved a crucial component in the evolution and endurance of a Romantic poetics of reception. This dialectic is played out at both theoretical and practical levels. It is reflected in the rhetorical complexity of debates about the respective merits of poetry and prose; and across processes of reading and writing. As is the case with the structure of most complex pathologies, it can prove difficult in practice to distinguish between the symptoms which evince anxiety and the defences which, at different levels—cultural, linguistic, and behavioural—evolve to keep that anxiety under control. Although defence mechanisms are clearly visible, both in theories of interpretation and in the practices of individual writers, they are not confined to the workings of literary language. They are also evident in a range of authorial strategies with respect to readers and audiences (both contemporary and posthumous); in the hermeneutic models which writers adopt; and in the inflections given to writing and reading practices by the personal, political, and psychological circumstances of individuals. Rhetoric and figuration are important aspects of the anxiety of reception, but they are reflective of wider paradigm-shifts in the way that authors and readers are understood. For this reason, *Reading, Writing, and Romanticism* is necessarily eclectic in its methodology, combining the psychological and the hermeneutic with the historical in an attempt to bridge materialist and idealist approaches to the reader.

My main concern throughout is with authorial anxiety as it manifested itself in the Romantic era, and specifically with the threatened status of poetry as it dealt with the challenges posed by the rise of the reader. The book is intended to offer a new reading of Romanticism by reversing the temporal direction of Bloom's model of influence and applying it to a particular nexus of personal circumstances and historical conditions. Far from being oppressed by the burden of the past, I argue, Romantic writers were intensely preoccupied with the combined threats of modernity and futurity. This preoccupation can be discerned not only in their ambivalent and sometimes hostile reactions to the growth of literacy, the reading-public, and the rise of criticism (as well as to the emergence of a new readership for the novel and women's poetry) but also in their more intricate and occluded devices for pre-empting misinterpretation. In the first part of the book, I trace the circumstances which exacerbated authorial anxiety in the late eighteenth and early nineteenth centuries. There follow three individual 'case studies', of Coleridge, Wordsworth, and Barbauld, three of the most important poet-critics of first-generation Romanticism. Part II then fans out into a series of wide ranging thematic chapters, concerning issues of canon-formation and reception. My intention here is to show how the private anxieties of individual writers were reflected in much broader literary trends. Chapter 5 deals with the dialogues and crossings which took place between creativity and criticism in the early nineteenth century; and Chapter 6 with the place of women's poetry alongside and in the writing-reading dialectic. Chapters 7 and 8 examine the texture of Romantic rhetoric, especially critical rhetoric, as a complex mediation between authorial and interpretative claims to importance. Models of canon-formation, intertextuality, and reader-response are here considered in relation to ideas of personal and communal property which proliferated in copyright discourse and political debate. My study of the defences which underpin Romantic rhetoric allows me to reach some conclusions about the emergence of a Romantic poetics of reception, its peculiar power to survive. Finally, Chapter 9 casts back over the entire period under discussion—from the mid-eighteenth century to the 1820s—and sees it as a momentous phase in the history of reading. Hazlitt's pivotal essay, 'My First Acquaintance with Poets' is used to frame an investigation of the symbolic relation between spoken and written discourse in the performance and reception of literary texts.

Although the complex historical phenomenon which we term Romanticism can be understood as a species of 'reaction-formation'—a system of defences against the new power of reading—the overall picture that emerges in this study is more complicated, less embattled. In the periodical culture of the 1800s, when there was a running battle not only between authors and reviewers but between poets and writers of prose, most of the major English Romantic authors found themselves in several camps at once. The rise of criticism, by which poets were at one level deeply threatened, was at the same time a phenomenon on which they were dependent, and to which they contributed: the claim of criticism to be considered as itself creative was indeed significantly advanced by some of their number. While the tension between poetry and criticism persisted as the expression of divided allegiances that proved difficult to reconcile, it also turned out to be a valuable resource. Rhetorically, it enabled poet-critics to play sophisticated games with generic hierarchies, thus negotiating or contesting literary authority in ways appropriate to a given occasion. At a more fundamental level, it proved a crucial component in the evolution and endurance of a Romantic poetics of reception. This dialectic is played out at both theoretical and practical levels. It is reflected in the rhetorical complexity of debates about the respective merits of poetry and prose; and across the full discursive range in this period, it allows crossings to take place on the creative–critical divide.

The 'anxiety of reception' thus involves not only the rivalry between individual writers and their readers, as they attempt to maintain purchase on their joint and several identities, but the symbiotic development of creativity and criticism, as writing- and reading-subjects cross into each other and merge. For this reason, in interrogating the significance for Romantic culture of a series of binary oppositions—private–public; creation–reception; poetry–prose; masculine–feminine; active–passive; voice–echo; writing–speech—I have sought at all times to deconstruct them. The concepts of crossing, mediation, and hybridity have proved crucial, not only to the book's temporal logic but to the poetics of reception which it describes and reaffirms.

First and foremost, then, this is a book about the competitive–collaborative relationship between creativity and criticism in the Romantic period. But it is concerned with a question that has further-reaching theoretical implications: what happens when literary criticism declares its status equal or even superior to that of creation, as it has done in some branches of twentieth-century literary theory? Is there evidence of an anxiety of reception in Barthes's triumphant announcement that 'the birth of the reader must be at the cost of the death of the author'? Or in Bloom's belief that critics become honorary poets through the strength of their misreading? Or in the thought that, as Geoffrey Hartman puts it, 'literary criticism is now crossing over into literature'?[5] These critics, for all their championing of the reader's freedom, remain writing-subjects themselves, with the perennial anxieties that this involves; and their defence strategies (like the Romantics') are visible in the models of canon-formation, intertextuality, and reader-response which they propose. An analysis of the continuing place of Romanticism in recent definitions of the reader extends far beyond the range of this book; but I hope that the need for such analysis is here established.

[5] 'Literary Commentary as Literature', in *Criticism in the Wilderness: The Study of Literature Today* (New Haven: Yale University Press, 1980), 213.

Acknowledgements

This book could not have gone to press without the assistance of Graeme Stones, who worked with enormous energy and concentration to check the typescript through at the end. It is an honour to have had the help of so careful a scholar, and he has saved me from numerous errors: any that remain are of course my own responsibility.

I would like to record my immense gratitude to Nicky Trott, Tim Fulford, and Nicholas Roe for taking the time and trouble to give detailed feedback on a first draft of the book; and to Fiona Stafford and Tom Paulin for their generous comments on a large portion of my argument. Anne Janowitz, Paul Hamilton, and Seamus Perry have provided valuable advice on my work at various stages. Andrew Bennett kindly allowed me to read in manuscript parts of his book, *Romantic Poets and the Culture of Posterity* (Cambridge University Press, 1999), and our dialogue has been a productive one. The reports of Michael O'Neill and John Strachan (who acted as readers for Oxford University Press) have been immensely helpful in the process of revision. I have also benefited from conversations with Kelvin Everest, Duncan Wu, Jon Mee, Uttara Natarajan, Timothy Webb, Graeme Stones, Mina Gorji, Luisa Calé, and Chris Koenig-Woodyard. Sophie Goldsworthy has been a wonderfully supportive and efficient commissioning editor and Rowena Anketell has provided copy-editing of the very highest quality. Matthew Hollis has seen the book through the Press with great friendliness and speed. I am grateful to the Principal and fellows of St Edmund Hall for two terms of sabbatical leave, which enabled me to complete a first draft. I owe special thanks to Geoffrey Hartman for the occasion that initiated the book, and for helping me believe the project was worthwhile. A more personal thank-you to Martin, Paul, Fiona, and Emma for being so long-suffering; to Peter Avis for help with the title; and to Ann McPherson and Jenny Harrison for their support. I dedicate the book to my parents, Doreen and Walter Newlyn in memory of my sister Sally. Sally's enthusiasm for ideas about reading and writing, as well as her hands-on experience of their implications, were always an inspiration. My parents taught me the 'three R's'—and a whole lot else besides.

A shorter version of Chapter 2 first appeared as 'Coleridge and the Anxiety of Reception' in *Romanticism*. As this book goes to Press, sections from Chapters 3 and 9 are due to appear in the Proceedings of the Bars Conference 1995, edited by Peter Kitson and Nicholas Roe; and in a volume edited by Seamus Perry and Nicola Trott. My thanks, in both cases, for permission to reuse material.

L. N.

Contents

PART II: CROSSINGS ON THE CREATIVE–CRITICAL DIVIDE

Abbreviations

BL Coleridge, S. T., *Biographia Literaria*, ed. James Engell and W. Jackson Bate (Bollingen Series; 2 vols., Princeton: Princeton University Press, 1983).

CC *The Collected Works of Samuel Taylor Coleridge*, gen. ed. Kathleen Coburn (Bollingen Series; Princeton University Press). See further abbreviations for individual volumes in the series.

CPW *The Complete Poetical Works of Samuel Taylor Coleridge*, ed. Ernest Hartley Coleridge (2 vols., Oxford: Clarendon Press, 1975).

EY *The Letters of William and Dorothy Wordsworth: The Early Years, 1787–1805*, ed. Ernest de Selincourt, 2nd edn. rev. Chester Shaver (Oxford: Clarendon Press, 1967).

Friend Coleridge, S. T., *The Friend* (Bollinger series; 2 vols., Princeton: Princeton University Press, 1969).

Gill Gill, Stephen, *William Wordsworth: A Life* (Oxford: Clarendon Press, 1989).

Godwin Works Godwin, William, *Political and Philosophical Writings of William Godwin*, gen. ed. Mark Philp (7 vols., London: William Pickering, 1993).

Griggs *The Collected Letters of Samuel Taylor Coleridge*, ed. E. L. Griggs (6 vols., Oxford and New York: Oxford University Press 1956–71).

Howe Hazlitt, William, *Complete Works*, ed. P. P. Howe (21 vols., London: J. M. Dent and Sons, 1930–4).

Lectures Coleridge, S. T., *Lectures 1808–1819 On Literature*, ed. R. A. Foakes (Bollingen Series; 2 vols., Princeton: Princeton University Press, 1987).

LY *The Letters of William and Dorothy Wordsworth: The Later Years 1821–1853* ed. Ernest de Selincourt, rev. Alan G. Hill (4 vols., Oxford: Clarendon Press, 1978–88).

Marrs *The Letters of Charles and Mary Lamb*, ed. Edwin W. Marrs, Jr. (Ithaca, NY: Cornell University Press, 1975).

Masson *De Quincey's Collected Writings* ed. David Masson (14 vols., Edinburgh: Adam and Charles Black, 1890).

MY *The Letters of William and Dorothy Wordsworth: The Middle Years, 1806–1811*, ed. Ernest de Selincourt, 2nd edn. rev. Chester Shaver (Oxford: Clarendon Press, 1967).

Notebooks	*The Notebooks of Samuel Taylor Coleridge*, ed. Kathleen Coburn, (Bollingen Series; Princeton: Princeton University Press, 1957–).
Peacock Works	Peacock, Thomas Love, *The Works of Thomas Love Peacock*, ed. H. F. B. Brett-Smith and C. E. Jones (10 vols., London: Constable and Co., New York: Gabriel Wells, 1934).
Prelude	Wordsworth, William, *The Prelude: The Four Texts (1798, 1799, 1805, 1850)*, ed. Jonathan Wordsworth (Harmondsworth, Middlesex: Penguin, 1995). Year will follow title in italics.
Reynolds Prose	Reynolds, John Hamilton, *Selected Prose of John Hamilton Reynolds*, ed. Leonidas M. Jones (Cambridge, Mass.: Harvard University Press, 1966).
SM	Coleridge, S. T., *The Statesman's Manual, Lay Sermons*, ed. R. J. White (Bollingen Series; Princeton: Princeton University Press, 1993).
Wordsworth Prose	*The Prose Works of William Wordsworth*, ed. W. J. B. Owen and J. W. Smyser (3 vols., Oxford: Clarendon Press, 1974).

Note to the Reader

All quotations from Wordsworth's poetry (unless otherwise specified) refer to the Oxford Authors edition, ed. Stephen Gill (Oxford: Oxford University Press, 1984).

Art subsists by communication, not by exclusion. The light of art, like that light of nature, shines on all alike; and its benefit, like that of the sun, is in being seen and felt. The spirit of art is not the spirit of trade: it is not a question between the grower or consumer of some perishable and personal commodity: but it is a question between human genius and human taste, how much the one can produce for the benefit of mankind, and how much the other can enjoy. It is 'the link of peaceful commerce 'twixt dividable shores.' To take from it this character is to take from it its best privilege, its humanity.

William Hazlitt

Part I

The Anxiety of Reception

CHAPTER 1

The Sense of an Audience

We have become a reading, and of course a critical nation. A refined writer is now certain of finding readers who can comprehend him.

> Isaac D'Israeli, *An Essay on the Manners and Genius of the Literary Character*, 1795

We are born in too late an age, and too chilly a climate. Worst of all, we are born in an age of criticism, where the boldest of us dares not let himself loose to be all that he might have been capable of being.

> William Godwin, Appendix to *The Enquirer*, 1797

Surely no one will deny the propriety of distinguishing the present as an age of books! of book making! book reading! book reviewing! and book forgetting!

> Maria Jane Jewsbury, *Phantasmagoria*, 1825

I. LITERACY, THE READING-PUBLIC, AND ANONYMOUS CRITICISM

Early nineteenth-century England marks the rise of the reader in a number of distinctive ways. 'Understood in a non-generic sense', Wai-Chee Dimmock argues, 'reading might be said to be a phenomenon peculiar to modernity':

Unlike the medieval preoccupation with exegesis and the Puritan preoccupation with typology, reading in its modern guise is not centered on or authorized by one particular text, least of all the Bible. Modern society is a society of interpretation, interpretation at once deregulated and *de rigueur*, for in this world, a world increasingly acted upon by forces unknown and unseen, and increasingly removed from our immediate comprehension, all of us, whether or not we accept the label, have to become readers of sorts.[1]

---

[1] 'Feminism, New Historicism and the Reader', in Andrew Bennett (ed.), *Readers and Reading* (London: Longman, 1995), 114.

Something of the same combined sense of compulsion, exhilaration, and alienation is conveyed in Coleridge's remark that 'Events...have made us a World of Readers' (*Lectures*, i. 186), or in Wordsworth's less global evocation of London, in Book VII of *The Prelude*, as a vast and overwhelming system of indecipherable signs—an excess of signifiers (*1805*, ll. 625–740). For Dimmock, one of the outstanding characteristics of modernity is that an apparent universalization of reading-practices is accompanied by an increasing dependency on expertise—on the *professionalization* of interpretative activity—and thus by a widening gap between the common reader and the expert. This, too, was a feature of modernity apprehended by English writers at the turn of the eighteenth century, when increasing literacy created a mass-reading audience, but when the rise of professional criticism registered the emergence of a new race of specialist readers. The mutual pressures exerted on writers and their critics, which mounted under the increasingly competitive conditions of periodical culture in the early nineteenth century, were further intensified by this dual consciousness. More potential readers of literature existed than ever before, but fewer and fewer, it was feared, were genuinely qualified to understand what they were reading. Those, meanwhile, who did understand—the professionals, or experts—were often perceived as threatening. In some cases, as we shall see, this produced a kind of paranoia. Across the full discursive range in the Romantic period, there is a tendency to dismiss audiences as either mindlessly passive or voraciously appetitive; to demonize reviewers as an army of talentless upstarts, concealing their various envies behind the shield of collective anonymity; and to caricature novelists—especially female novelists—as passive readers turned would-be writers, purveying sentimental and sensationalist narratives to an audience all too ready to receive them.

The circumstances which led to the widespread hostility of authors towards their readerships were many and diverse; but they can be understood in the light of dramatic developments taking place during the latter years of the eighteenth century, whose repercussions were felt equally in England and on the Continent. Hazlitt—provocative as always—identified the most important of these developments, and their symbolic interconnection, when he observed that 'The French Revolution might be described as a remote but inevitable result of the invention of the art of printing' (Howe, xiii. 38). As a staunch defender of the liberty of the press, he celebrated recent advances in printing-technology and the rapid growth of literacy as the agents of enlightenment and reform. '[O]ur present opinions and the prevailing tone of society are the result of light and conviction, of the free communication of mind with mind', he wrote in 'The Influence of Books on the Progress of Manners': 'Our institutions ... are the result of darkness and force, of systematic wrong and individual aggrandisement.' Books had already 'battered down so many strongholds of prejudice and power, and must everlastingly militate against violence and wrong', for, as he saw it, books are ' "a discipline of humanity" ... a kind of public monitor, a written conscience, from which nothing is hid'. Although ambivalent towards the reading-public himself, Hazlitt had no truck with those who ana-thematized it. He saw reading as an act that empowered the individual and promoted the progress of society as a whole:

Public opinion ... is the atmosphere of liberal sentiment and equitable conclu-sions; books are the scale in which right and wrong are fairly tried. ... The reading-public—laugh at it as we will, abuse it as we will—is after all (depend upon it), a very rational animal, compared with a feudal lord and his horde of vassals. ... Formerly, neither the vassal nor his lord could read or write, and knew nothing but what they suffered or inflicted: now the meanest mechanic can both read and write, and the only danger seems to be that every one, high and low, rich and poor, should turn author, and the whole world be converted into waste paper. (Howe, xvii. 325–8)

Among Hazlitt's less liberal contemporaries, however, the same sym-bolic association between literacy, print culture, and revolution led to very different conclusions. Much of the antipathy towards readers and reading in the 1790s and onwards had an anti-Jacobin flavour. It was expressed as an anxiety about the blunting of sensibility and taste which was believed to occur under the repeated impact of shocking news. But it usually translates into a fear of the responsiveness of the British reading-public to political events as they unfolded in France and were reported in the popular press. The conviction that these events had a momentous influence on readers—one that could be neither resisted nor properly assimilated—is borne out in the use of theatrical meta-phors which reduced readers to passive observers, as here in Burke: 'In viewing this monstrous tragi-comic scene', Burke wrote in *Reflections on the Revolution in France*, 'the most opposite passions necessarily succeed, and sometimes mix with each other in the mind; alternate contempt and indignation; alternate laughter and tears; alternate scorn and horror'.[2] In Romantic rhetoric, the French Revolution often figured as the root cause of an addiction to sensational incidents, novels, and news, together with an excessive engendering of spectators. When Wordsworth, writing in 1800, inveighed against the 'craving for extraordinary incident which the rapid communication of intelligence hourly gratifies',[3] he was registering what he believed to be a deterioration in the reading-public's taste that followed as a consequence of the Revolution. He connected this hunger for sensational incidents with a more pervasive 'communication of intelligence' which derived from an ability to read, and from increased access to all kinds of reading-matter, including (pre-eminently) newspapers.

'The spirit of Antichrist is abroad', wrote Thomas Love Peacock, in an amusing parody of the spirit of the age: 'the people read!—nay, they think!! the people read and think!!! The public, the public in general, the swinish multitude, the many-headed monster, actually reads and thinks!!! Horrible in thought, but in fact most horrible!'[4] Literacy was understood by some as not only the cause of revolution, but a revolution in its own right; and the statistics support contemporary accounts of its momentous transforming implications. An increase in literacy accelerated from the 1780s onward with the establishment of Sunday schools, where a diet of 'histories, romances, stories, poems' helped in diffusing 'a general taste for reading among all ranks of people' at an early age.[5] According to Lee Erickson's calculations, the production of books rose gradually in England from about 1,800 items of all kinds in 1740 to 3,000 items in 1780, with a further sudden rise in 1792, when they doubled to 6,000.[6] James Lackington, a London bookseller, noticed that four times as many books were sold in the year 1791 as twenty years earlier:

The poorer sort of farmers, and even the poor country people in general, who before that period spent their winter evenings in relating stories of witches, ghosts, hobgoblins, etc. now shorten the winter nights by hearing their sons and

[2]   *Reflections on the Revolution in France*, ed. with introd. Connor Cruise O'Brien (Harmondsworth, Middlesex: Penguin, 1986), 92–3.

[3]   *Wordsworth Prose*, i. 128.

[4]   *Melincourt*, ch. xxxi: 'Cimmerian Lodge', in *Peacock Works*, ii. 339; cited and discussed by Marilyn Butler, *Peacock Displayed: A Satirist in his Context* (London: Routledge and Kegan Paul, 1979), 89.

[5]   The words are James Lackington's. See John Tinnon Taylor, *Early Opposition to the English Novel: The Popular Reaction from 1760–1830* (1943; New York: King's Crown Press, 1970), 3.

[6]   *The Economy of Literary Form: English Literature and the Industrialisation of Publishing, 1800–1850* (Baltimore: Johns Hopkins University Press, 1996), 7.

daughters read tales, romances, etc. and on entering their houses you may see *Tom Jones*, *Roderick Random* and other entertaining books, stuck up on their bacon racks.[7]

Literacy further increased in the first two decades of the nineteenth century when, as a result of technological changes—the first hand-operated iron-frame printing-press, the Fourdrinier papermaking machine, and stereotyping—cheaper books became possible, allowing more people to read than ever before. The consequent shift from a literature written for an elite audience to one written for the public at large promoted a rapidly expanding publishing industry, and, as both Jon Klancher and Kathryn Sutherland have emphasized, a 'questioning and attempted re-ordering of the relations between kinds of reading-matter and classes of readers'.[8]

While an unprecedented proliferation of reviews, essays, magazines, newspapers, literary annuals, anthologies, abridgements, and miscellanies confirmed that reading of all kinds was in the ascendancy, it was not always reading of a kind approved by the defenders of high culture. As Erickson puts it, 'the expansion of the publishing market precipitates a crisis for literature, because the most profitable work is no longer that which appeals to the most sophisticated and literary taste'.[9] The novel was rapidly cornering the market as the most popular literary genre; and poetry, if it was to appeal to the same kind of reader, had to be written in narrative form. Female novelists were successfully establishing their own readership in a competitive literary market, while female readers were gaining increased access, through circulating-libraries, to this now fashionable (though still expensive) commodity. In 1801, there were said to be 1,000 circulating-libraries in England, 'flourishing businesses to be found in every major English city and town' which (like booksellers' shops) served as 'daytime lounges where ladies could see others and be seen', and where books were 'only one of several kinds of merchandise available'.[10]

---

[7] *Memoirs of the Forty-Five First Years of the Life of James Lackington* (London: James Lackington, 1795), 420–1; cited in Taylor, *Early Opposition to the English Novel*, 3–4.

[8] See Klancher, *The Making of English Reading Audiences, 1790–1832* (Madison, Wisc.: University of Wisconsin Press, 1978); and Sutherland, ' "Events have made us a World of Readers": Reader Relations, 1780–1730', in David Pirie (ed.), *The Penguin History of the Romantic Period* (Harmondsworth, Middlesex: Penguin, 1994), 1–48: quotation from p. 2. See also Erickson, *Economy of Literary Form*, 5.

[9] *Economy of Literary Form*, 15.

[10] Ibid. 126, 129.

The generation of English writers establishing their reputations in the second decade of the nineteenth century inhabited a more perilously competitive culture than their forebears; and many of them experienced a sense of alienation as relatively secure systems of recognition gave way to a dependency on unknown readers, whose numerical power and anonymity were felt to be threatening. The decline of patronage, accompanied by the rise of criticism as a profession, meant that writers (who could no longer regulate or predetermine their reception) looked increasingly to the public for their hopes of survival. In a period which saw a rapid expansion in the book-market, success was measured in terms of the number of books sold, with writers such as Byron, Scott, Rogers, Bloomfield, Campbell, and Moore topping the list of best-selling authors. Six thousand copies of Scott's *The Bride of Abydos* were sold in a month, and ten thousand copies of Byron's *The Corsair* on the day of publication.[11] According to the *Dictionary of National Biography*, an estimated twenty-six thousand copies of Bloomfield's *The Farmer's Boy* were consumed in less than three years. It was a buyer's market, and popular tastes dictated the price at which the copyright on books was sold. Longman paid £80 for the second edition of *Lyrical Ballads*, the very same year that Vernor and Hood paid £4,000 for the copyright of *The Farmer's Boy*. Even Scott and Byron never matched the popularity of Bloomfield, but at £2,000 for *Rokeby* in 1812, and £1,000 per poem for *The Bride of Abydos* and *The Giaour*, they were doing nicely by comparison with Wordsworth.[12]

It is not difficult, under these economic circumstances, to understand why a certain bitterness crept into the Lake Poets' response to the British reading-public, or why they became the butt of jibes directed against their defensiveness. In a typically even-handed remark, which measured Byron's success alongside Wordsworth's aloofness, Hazlitt managed to poke fun both at the prevailing ethos of popularity and at the Lake School's pretended immunity to it:

When a certain poet was asked if he thought Lord Byron's name would live three years after he was dead, he answered, 'Not three days, Sir!' This was premature: it has lasted above a year. His works have been translated into

[11] For a discussion of the semi-antagonistic relation between Romanticism and the popularity of narrative, see Andrew Bennett, *Keats, Narrative and Audience: The Posthumous Life of Writing* (Cambridge: Cambridge University Press, 1994).

[12] My information is drawn from John Strachan's article ' "That is true fame": A Few Words about Thomson's Romantic Period Popularity', in Richard Terry (ed.), *James Thomson: Essays for the Tercentenary* (Liverpool: Liverpool University Press, 1999).

French, and there is a *Caffè Byron* on the Boulevards. Think of a *Caffè Wordsworth* on the Boulevards! (Howe, xvii. 209 n.)

For poets such as Wordsworth and Coleridge, the financial necessity of engineering their own success went hand in hand with a desire to mould public taste in a direction they themselves found palatable. Their double objective, of becoming canonical while distancing themselves from the popularity enjoyed by the likes of Byron, made it the task of a lifetime to 'create the taste by which they were to be enjoyed'. The seriousness of that task—its centrality to their status as 'fellow-labourers', engaged in the aesthetic enlightenment of their readers—cannot be overstated. This project was hindered, in their view, by the periodical press, which aimed to reflect rather than transform the preferences of the reading-public. The story of Wordsworth's and Coleridge's sustained ambivalence towards the press (for which, at various times, they worked, and on which they were always dependent) discloses, in epitome, the conditions under which 'high' Romanticism emerged.

Periodical criticism did not spring up from nowhere. Its roots went back into the coffee-house culture which thrived from the beginning of the eighteenth century onwards; and many of the established journals, such as the *Gentleman's Magazine*, continued well into the period with which we are concerned. But there was, at the turn of the century, a sudden and astonishing rise in the number of journals available, each with an ideological inflection designed to cater to the tastes of a specific audience. The emergence of the essay as (by the 1820s) the most popular and profitable literary format showed 'the needs of an educated pub-lic . . . for organized information delivered in a manageable length and pleasing variety'.[13] Two periodicals in particular emerged as near monopolists in the second decade of the nineteenth century: Marilyn Butler claims that 'At the height of its success, in 1814, the *Edinburgh* was printing 13,000 copies, and the *Quarterly* about the same',[14] while Erick-son puts the *Edinburgh*'s figure higher, with 'a peak sale of 13,500 copies in 1818 before the stiff competition of the monthly magazines began'.[15] Approximate numbers, however, convey no notion of the influence of these journals over their readers, since as Butler points out, 'Jeffrey estimated that at least three people saw every copy, so that the journals had a readership of several times their actual circulation.'[16]

[13] Erickson, *Economy of Literary Form*, 102.   [14] *Peacock Displayed*, 273.
[15] *Economy of Literary Form*, 32.   [16] *Peacock Displayed*, 273.

As the vulnerability of writers to the whims of their audiences increased, so did the crucial role of reviewers in the making and marring of reputations. This was an age in which anecdote was fashionable and biography an increasingly popular genre.[17] Reviewers were not slow to cash in on public interest in the foibles and eccentricities of authors. 'What is the prevailing spirit of modern literature?' Hazlitt asked (in a rare moment of affinity with Coleridge, who anathematized the 'age of personality'): 'To defame men of letters. What are the publications that succeed? Those that pretend to teach the public that the persons they have been accustomed unwittingly to look up to as the lights of the earth are no better than themselves' (Howe, xvii. 211). The private lives of Wordsworth, Coleridge, and Hazlitt himself were all at various times subjected to public scrutiny; and since all of them had something either personal or political to hide, it is not surprising that they developed an antipathy to the invasiveness of the press. Their antipathy was further intensified by the practice of anonymous reviewing, which enabled the circulation of scurrilous gossip to take place without fear of repercussions.

Bedevilled though they were by political infighting and advocacy, reviewing-bodies were seen as steadily acquiring an authority which legislated arbitrarily over the tastes of the reading-public: 'Jeffrey, Croker and Hazlitt may not have slain with a review', Butler writes, 'but it is not surprising that contemporaries thought them capable of it.'[18] The capriciousness and anonymity of reviewers became the standard complaint of writers as diverse as Coleridge, Wordsworth, J. H. Reynolds, Godwin, Peacock, Shelley, and Keats, all of whom strove to define artistic success in terms other than popular acclaim. Hazlitt himself on more than one occasion joined the ranks of those who condemned the partisanship of contemporary reviewing-practices: 'Whether this state of the press is not a serious abuse and a violent encroachment in the republic of letters, is more than I shall pretend to determine', he wrote in his 'Essay on Criticism' (Howe, viii. 215). Complaining that anonymous reviewers naturally grow 'arbitrary with the exercise of power', he identified the 'decided and paramount tone in criticism' as the 'growth of the present century' (Howe, viii. 215–16), and anathematized the party-political complexion of the periodical press: 'political' (as distinct from disinterested) criticism he defined as 'a *caput mortuum* of impotent

---

[17] See Annette Wheeler Cafarelli, *Prose in the Age of Poets: Romanticism and Biographical Narrative from Johnson to De Quincey* (Philadelphia: University of Pennsylvania Press, 1990).
[18] *Peacock Displayed*, 273.

spite and dulness... varnished over with the slime of servility, and thrown into a state of unnatural activity by the venom of the most rancorous bigotry' (Howe, viii. 220).

Ideological and party-political differences account for much of the personal animosity which pervaded critical rhetoric in the period, and a great deal of it was directed at rival periodicals. Hazlitt's unpublished 'Reply to Z' was written in a spirit of inspired rage as a riposte to a scurrilous article by Keats's enemy, Lockhart, entitled 'Hazlitt Cross-Questioned'. Lockhart's article had appeared in *Blackwood's Edinburgh Magazine* (August 1818) over the anonymous signature of 'an Old Friend with a New Face'. It had exposed Hazlitt as 'a writer of third-rate books, and a lounger in third-rate bookshops', a 'self-taught interloper', 'an essay, criticism, review and lecture manufacturer', and (this was the last straw) 'pimpled' despite his clear complexion. Hazlitt's answering abuse rose splendidly to the occasion: 'I think then that you are a person of little understanding, with great impudence, a total want of principle, an utter disregard to truth or even to the character of common veracity' (Howe, ix. 3). Driven by political rage, but motivated by the principle of a disinterested attachment to truth, Hazlitt's greatest writing was directed forcefully at rivals for whom he felt nothing but contempt. His anger was of a piece with his disinterestedness.

As the fury here indicates, essayists were just as exercised by the problematics of reception as poets. Even the staunchest advocates of journalistic enterprise felt defensive, at a time when critical activity was constructed as parasitic; and the mutual antagonisms that arose between poets and critics came about largely because each saw their own status as marginalized in relation to the other. By virtue of a generic hierarchy which had been in place for centuries, poetry had a higher cultural status than prose, even when the poets concerned were struggling to make ends meet. Prose writers, by contrast—and this applied particularly to reviewers—were considered hacks. They struggled alongside poets for recognition of their value in an increasingly utilitarian culture; but they competed against poets for a higher place in the pecking-order of writers. 'Even more than the author', writes Annette Wheeler Cafarelli in her appropriately titled book, *Prose in the Age of Poets*, 'the critic is destined to find an ungrateful audience, and more likely to sink into oblivion.'[19] The Grub Street Romantics—who included (alongside

---

[19] *Prose in the Age of Poets*, 69.

Hazlitt) Lamb, De Quincey, Reynolds, and Hunt—led a life of insecurity as freelance writers, in the pay of journals whose own status was precarious. The more successful among them found ways of turning the deadline pressures of serial publication to aesthetic advantage; but they laboured incessantly under a sense of their undervalued status in society, and were acutely conscious of the supposed inferiority of prose.

In his 'Essay on the Periodical Press' (1823), Hazlitt provided one of the earliest attempts to account for the emergence of professional criticism as a socio-economic as well as a literary phenomenon. His analysis probed the circumstances that lay behind this unique historical moment, when advances in printing-technology meant that books and periodicals were becoming available to all classes of readers. At the same time, with a different kind of historical purpose, he implicitly defended and dignified the periodical press by providing evidence that its origins—although recent—were as much a part of history as the older genres whose status was widely respected. This explains the prominence given in his account to *St James's Chronicle*, where he had first encountered the writings of his political anti-hero, Burke. Honouring him with a generous tribute, Hazlitt went on to suggest that, although there was no one in the current climate of quite his quality, 'we have a host of writers, working for their bread on the spur of the occasion, and whose names are not known, formed upon the model of the best writers who have gone before them, and reflecting many of their graces' (Howe, xvi. 222). If journalism, like the novel, had no 'imposing family tree',[20] then Hazlitt's contextualization supplied it with historical roots. Burke's stature, combined with his deeply conservative brand of Englishness, was admirably suited to give his 'scribbling' successors the lineage they needed.

As performed by Hazlitt, this elevation of the journalist's role in relation to contemporary authors—and particularly poets—takes on a political colouring: one which has significant implications for the rivalry between genres which characterized early nineteenth-century England. The inferiority complex of prose gave criticism at this time both its animus and its potential for rhetorical sophistication. Critics saw it as one of their missions to redeem the downtrodden status of prose, and when they were not using a mode of direct attack on generic hierarchies, they were often using irony or sarcasm. Hazlitt meant it literally as well

---

[20] Taylor, *Early Opposition to the English Novel,* 12.

as metaphorically when he observed that 'The language of poetry naturally falls in with the language of power' (Howe, iv. 214). We should not underestimate the class-consciousness that informed that remark, or the personal bitterness that motivated it. Nor should we overlook the significance of envy as a pervasive phenomenon in early nineteenth-century culture.

II. AUTHORSHIP AND THE PUBLIC SPHERE

In a competitive cultural climate, when the sheer numerical weight of books daily produced obliged authors to distinguish themselves from scribblers, ownership-claims on ideas became crucially important. The reforms in copyright law which took place in the course of the eighteenth century bore witness both to a new commercial premium placed on originality, and to an awareness of words as property (to be either shared or hoarded) which consolidated the transition from oral to print culture. Print, as Walter Ong claims, had been 'a major factor in the development of the sense of personal privacy that marks modern society. It produced books smaller and more portable than those common in a manuscript culture, setting the stage psychologically for solo reading in a quiet corner, and eventually for completely silent reading'.[21] This sense of personal privacy was accentuated by the commercialization of publishing, which ensured that more books found their way into more homes than ever before. But ambiguities about the ownership of words nonetheless persisted; for although 'The old communal world had split up into privately claimed freeholdings', words were 'still shared property to a degree'.[22] The repercussions of these ambiguities may be seen in the concern of many nineteenth-century writers with issues of authenticity and originality, imitation and plagiarism, as well as in individual acts of self-authorization, designed to reinforce authorial status. Wordsworth, who published *Lyrical Ballads* as a collaborative and anonymous publication in 1798, decided to reissue the volume's second edition under his own name, and seriously considered changing its title, to safeguard himself against the volume's confusion with Mary Robinson's *Lyrical Tales*. In this act of proprietorship, one may see a significantly self-protective manoeuvre: identity itself appeared to be

---

[21] *Orality and Literacy: The Technologizing of the Word* (London: Routledge, 1982), 131.
[22] Ibid.

under threat, when the title of an anonymous publication could become common property, or be used to constitute another's claim to fame.[23]

For journalists, there was an even more acute sense that their identity was defined by (or subject to) powers beyond their control. This came about because, unlike poets (who on the whole published their works as single, named authors), they were subservient to the journal who employed them, and their identities were often not revealed. Just as their livelihood was dependent on editors who might replace them without notice, so their copy was not their own, but the property of the journal and controlled by its views and aims. Editors were not above making major revisions to their work, and even minor changes were keenly felt as a diminution of the journalist's autonomy. 'Any thing to preserve the form and appearance of power', Hazlitt complained, in a vengeful essay 'On Editors',

> to make the work their own by mental stratagem, to stamp it by some fiction of criticism with their personal identity, to enable them to run away with the credit, and look upon themselves as the master-spirits of the work and of the age! (Howe, xvii. 362).

Sometimes prose writers experienced extreme anxieties in relation to the machinery of production. For De Quincey (whose relationship with his publisher, William Tait, was fraught) the experience of revising material for publication under pressure became a metaphor of the 'hack' writer's powerlessness, his alienation from his own labour. He was acutely conscious that errors might creep into his work through the carelessness of compositors; and he lived 'in terror of . . . mutual misunderstandings' from both his publishers and his readers. He revised his prose with minute care so as to maintain for as long as possible the authorial control that he feared would slip away from him the moment his manuscript was delivered to the press. As Edmund Baxter has shown, he figured the author as a victim, reduced to 'utter insignificance' by the conditions under which he was obliged to work.[24]

The defensive nature of Romanticism's sacralization of the author— and, more particularly, the poet—may be seen as arising reactively, out of a resistance to the consumerism and anonymity which characterized the publishing-world. This is exemplified in a little-known lyric of

---

[23] See Susan Eilenberg, *Strange Power of Speech: Wordsworth, Coleridge, and Literary Possession* (Oxford: Oxford University Press, 1992), 7.

[24] *De Quincey's Art of Autobiography* (Edinburgh: Edinburgh University Press, 1990), 18.

Wordsworth's, composed in 1807. The poem, featuring an urban crowd scene, shows his anxieties with respect to his audience and his prospects of achieving fame. It deals with Wordsworth's fear that poetry was being marginalized by a readership avid for the kinds of 'cheap thrill' that poets such as himself were reluctant to provide. Queueing by night to see through a showman's telescope, members of a crowd of 'Star-Gazers' excitedly anticipate their private glimpse of the heavens; but instead of rapt wonderment, each in turn experiences a sense of anti-climax and disappointment:

> Whatever be the cause, 'tis sure that they who pry and pore
> Seem to meet with little gain, seem less happy than before:
> One after One they take their turns, nor have I one espied
> That doth not slackly go away, as if dissatisfied.

> ll. 29–32

Stars appear frequently in Romantic literature as metaphors for poetic genius. Coleridge claimed in the *Biographia* that 'the great works of past ages seem to a young man things of another race, in respect to which his faculties must remain passive and submiss, even as to the stars and to the mountains' (*BL* i. 12). And Hazlitt, in his essay 'Whether Genius is conscious of its powers?' wrote wistfully, perhaps with Keats's 'Bright Star' in mind: 'A name "fast-anchored in the deep abyss of time" is like a star twinkling in the firmament, cold, silent, distant, but eternal and sublime; and our transmitting one to posterity is as if we should con-template our translation to the skies' (Howe, xii. 125). Wordsworth's poem, by contrast, suggests the impossibility of sustaining the mystery of genius in an age that takes poetry for granted. The activity of stargazing may be read as a wishful metaphor, signifying his need to compensate for the public's indifference by ascribing a mysterious distance to poetic discourse, but the conventional rhyme on name/fame suggests a more personal longing to achieve the lasting recognition which Coleridge and Hazlitt attach to great works of the past: 'The silver Moon with all her Vales, and Hills of mightiest fame, | Do they betray us when they're seen? and are they but a name?' (ll. 15–16). The twin fears of disappointing and being disappointed are seen to arise from a con-cern with the threatened status of poetry in an age of utility, and its reception by an audience progressively desensitized to poetic power. Just as Wordsworth feared that technology might lead to a demystifica-tion of Nature's secrets, so he lamented the passing of wonderment (in the way that Keats would later lament the destruction of beauty by Newtonian physics) as a process of gradual and deadening habituation.

Wordsworth held the commodification of culture by middlemen (here tellingly figured in the showman) ultimately responsible for the blunting of readers' sensibilities; and he blamed the fickleness of popular taste for the neglect of original geniuses such as himself. His confusions and anxieties in relation to his potential readership included the reluctant admission that an uneducated population might be resistant to the kind of power his own poetry embodied, and therefore (implicitly) to the legitimacy of his entitlement to a 'name' and 'fame':

> must we be constrained to think that these Spectators rude,
> Poor in estate, of manners base, men of the multitude,
> Have souls which never yet have ris'n, and therefore prostrate lie?
> No, no, this cannot be—Men thirst for power and majesty!
>
> (ll. 21–4)

Torn between a despairing dismissal of the crowd's vulgarity and an implicit faith in the universality of imagination, Wordsworth clung to the democratic convictions underpinning the *Lyrical Ballads*—namely, that ordinary people have a capacity for deep feeling which is undermined by the culture to which they are daily exposed. But the specifically urban nature of the audience here depicted suggests how alienating he found the idea of a mass readership, and how awesomely difficult he viewed the task of unifying its anonymous members.

'Star-Gazers' may be read as an exemplary expression of the anxieties with which this book is concerned—anxieties that centre not just on the writer's subjection to the invasive gaze of anonymous readers, but on the nature of reception itself, as it became divorced from oral culture: 'listening to spoken words forms hearers into a group, a true audience', writes Walter Ong, 'just as reading written or printed texts turns individuals in on themselves.'[25] At the centre of Wordsworth's poem is a fear that the rise of literacy and the apparent democratization of writing might bring with them, not an enhanced collective access to poetry but the diminishment of shared appreciation. Whereas the rural folk gathered in to listen to the tale of 'Peter Bell' are drawn together by shared experience, the queue in 'Star-Gazers' remain faceless and occupation-less members of a disparate crowd. Each in turn pays his fee then silently

---

[25] *Orality and Literacy*, 136.

disappears, figuring the solitariness of the act of reading when it becomes disconnected from community values.

Communal reading-scenes, of the kind featured in Wordsworth's 'Peter Bell', played an important role in eighteenth- and nineteenth-century life and literature. But did they do so anachronistically? In a suggestive passage from *The Practice of Everyday Life*, Michel De Certeau claims that from the seventeenth century onward, reading aloud occurred less and less frequently; and that its decline carried a charge of cultural significance:

reading has become, over the past three centuries, a visual poem. It is no longer accompanied, as it used to be, by the murmur of vocal articulation.... To read without uttering the words aloud or at least mumbling them is a 'modern' experience, unknown for millennia. In earlier times, the reader interiorized the text; he made his voice the body of the other; he was its actor. Today, the text no longer imposes its own rhythm on the subject, it no longer manifests itself through the reader's voice.[26]

De Certeau is concerned in the first instance with the practice of *sotto voce* reading, to which I shall be returning later. But he is also making a broader generalization about the demise of orality, which includes the communal activity of reading aloud; and in this respect, his chronology is dubious. One need only recall the practice—widely documented by eighteenth- and nineteenth-century writers—of reading aloud at public meetings, in pubs and clubs; or the family custom of reading novels by the fireside; or the tradition of giving recitals from published works. As John Tinnon Taylor has observed, 'the appeal of this new form, the novel' was precisely that it 'found its root in one of the oldest of social customs'.[27] It was only with the coming of radio and television that the tradition of reading aloud began to die out; but it still persists in most schools and homes, as well as in the popular spoken-word cassettes available in bookshops all over the country. In their recent collection of essays, *The Practice and Representation of Reading in England*, James Raven, Helen Small, and Naomi Tadmor have enriched our sense of the overlap between 'public' and 'private' scenes of reading which the habit of oral delivery highlights. Raven draws attention to the ways in which the arrangement of library space in the eighteenth century allowed both

---

[26] *The Practice of Everyday Life* (Berkeley and Los Angeles: University of California Press, 1988), 175–6.

[27] *Early Opposition to the English Novel*, 4.

solitary study and communal reading, reinforcing what he calls 'the select social intimacy of the library'.[28] Tadmor's account of the reading-habits of Peggy and Thomas Turner, alongside those of Samuel Richardson and family, shows how 'in both households reading was a private experience in the sense that it was done in the home', but also 'that it was often a sociable rather than a solitary experience and this was especially manifested in the regular habit of reading aloud'.[29] Anyone familiar with Dorothy Wordsworth's Grasmere Journals will know how persistently reading aloud featured, both indoors and in the open air, as a practice signifying the centrality of literature to the daily activities of the Wordsworth household.

In the same way, the educational practice of learning by heart (which was widely prevalent throughout the eighteenth and nineteenth centuries, and still persists to this day in some schools) invariably entailed reading aloud the text to be memorized. As Walter Ong puts it,

Until the past few generations in the west, and still in perhaps most of the world today, academic practice has demanded that students in class 'recite', that is, feed back orally to the teacher statements (formulas—the oral heritage) that they had memorized from classroom instruction or from textbooks.[30]

This activity brings to mind earlier epochs, when what George Steiner calls 'the availability of total recall and reiteration of massive bodies of texts—epic, ritual, liturgical, historical, taxonomic'—was a purely routine matter. 'Commitment to memory is, in the first place, an individual phenomenon. . . . But active remembrance is also a collective, a cultural agency. It initiates and preserves a communion of shared echo, of participatory reflex, pertinent to the notion of canon.'[31] For this reason, oral communication is often seen as the appropriate model of an art that is concerned with relationship, whereas an art of visual imagery turns the audience into mere spectators, witnesses from a distance.[32]

Notwithstanding the inaccuracy of De Certeau's claim that reading has 'become a visual poem', his comment provides a useful stimulus to

---

[28] *The Practice and Representation of Reading in England* (Cambridge: Cambridge University Press, 1996), 199.

[29] Ibid. 165.

[30] *Orality and Literacy*, 56.

[31] 'Critic/Reader', in Philip Davis (ed.), *Real Voices on Reading* (Houndmills, Basingstoke: Macmillan Press, 1997), 26.

[32] Ong, *Orality and Literacy*, 69.

consider the significance of customs so deeply embedded in cultural life that they persist despite the larger historical trends that will eventually overtake them. If the preference for a discourse that is oral and performative is a throwback to earlier traditions of reception—and presumably De Certeau has in mind the oral and bardic traditions that mark the ancient model of poetic composition described by Steiner and Ong—this raises the question of why reading aloud was so important, as both a social practice and a figure, in the eighteenth and early nineteenth centuries. Silent reading is the sign of literature's commodification, in the sense that reading as a private act of consumption came about with the mass production of printed books. Reading aloud, by contrast, provides a reassuring continuity between creation and reception through the mediating figure of the voice.

For Wordsworth and Coleridge, who shared a mistrust of the 'despotism of the eye', the 'murmur of vocal articulation' that De Certeau mentions served as a bodily guarantee of connectiveness with the otherwise silent and visual act of reading. Their own most significant scenes of reception, frequently framed and highlighted in their letters and poems as crucial biographical moments, were those in which they read their own work aloud to each other. One thinks of Wordsworth's valedictory recitation of the (as yet incomplete) *Prelude*, which took place 'in the highest & outermost of Grasmere' in January 1804, just before Coleridge's departure for Malta.[33] Or of Coleridge's reading of 'Dejection', poignantly recorded by Dorothy in a journal entry for 1802:

William and I sauntered a little in the garden. Coleridge came to us, and repeated the verses he wrote to Sara. I was affected with them and was on the whole, not being well, in miserable spirits. The sunshine, the green fields, and the fair sky made me sadder; even the little happy, sporting lambs seemed but sorrowful to me.[34]

Or of the momentous occasion in 1807, when Coleridge, now returned from Malta, listened to *The Prelude* in its entirety, and found himself, as he recorded in 'To William Wordsworth', in a state of rapt passivity resembling worship: 'Scarce conscious, and yet conscious of its close | I

[33] Coleridge's Notebook entry for Wednesday 4 Jan. 1804 reads: 'in the highest & outermost of Grasmere Wordsworth read to me the second Part of his divine Self-biography' (*Notebooks*, i. 1801).

[34] Grasmere Journal, Wednesday 21 Apr. 1802: *Journals of Dorothy Wordsworth*, ed. E. de Selincourt (London: Macmillan and Co., 1941), i. 135–6.

sate, my being blended in one thought | ... And when I rose, I found myself in prayer' (ll. 108–9, 112). In these models of creation–reception, the reader is sensitively attuned to the voice in which poetry is rendered, and the line separating recitation from listening becomes blurred. Dorothy uses an allusive language that merges her own mood as receiver with Coleridge's as giver, bearing out Coleridge's testimony that she is a 'perfect electrometer' in her feelings;[35] while Coleridge accentuates an ideal continuity between himself and Wordsworth through a series of figurative crossings or hoverings between one identity and the other: 'Strong in thyself and powerful to give strength'; 'Scarce conscious, and yet conscious of its close'; 'Absorbed yet hanging still upon the sound'. Scenes of reception such as these offered the perfect antidote to reading as it was figured in Wordsworth's 'Star-Gazers' where solitude, distance, and the despotism of the eye are negatively registered as signals of the withdrawal of readerly sympathy.

The coterie practice of reading aloud acquired a symbolic status which emerged reactively, in response to the rise of criticism and the reading-public. We can catch a glimpse of the beginnings of its complex role as a protective or defensive strategy by backtracking as far as 1710, to Shaftesbury's *Advice to an Author*. Shaftesbury recommended the practice of reading aloud in private, as one of the preparations which an author could make for his public reception. He believed that internal dialogue was intellectually beneficial. He referred to the 'frothy distemper' of some writers, who 'discharge' their thoughts in public rather than in private, and claimed that 'it is the hardest thing in the world to be a good thinker, without being a strong self-examiner, and thorough-paced dialogist, in this solitary way'.[36] A projected or imagined reception was thus a crucial component of thoughts as they were formulated and written: the 'public' crossed over into the 'private' at the very moment that an address was made. Just as 'a passionate lover, whatever solitude he may affect, can never be truly by himself', so an author, who had begun his 'courtship to the public', was never alone: 'Whatever he meditates alone, is interrupted still by the imagined presence of the

---

[35] See Coleridge's description of Dorothy, 3 July 1797: 'Her information various—her eye watchful in minutest observation of nature—and her taste a perfect electrometer—it bends, protrudes, and draws in, at subtlest beauties & most recondite faults.' (Letter to Joseph Cottle, in Griggs, i. 330–1.)

[36] *Soliloquy, or, Advice to an Author*, in *Characteristics of Men, Manners, Opinions, Times* (3 vols., London, Basil: J. J. Tourneisan and J. L. Legrand, 1790) i. 145–6. Page refs. will be given in the text.

mistress he pursues. Not a thought, not an expression, not a sigh, which is purely for himself' (pp. 151–2).

Shaftesbury's ambivalence towards the professionalization of letters emerged as much in his description of the coquetry of the would-be author, whose 'epistles dedicatory, prefaces, and addresses to the reader, are so many affected graces, designed to draw the attention from the subject towards himself' (p. 173), as it did in his heavily ironic caricature of the fears produced in authors by the rise of criticism:

To judge ... of the circumstances of a modern author, by the pattern of his prefaces, dedications, and introductions, one would think, that, at the moment when a piece of his was in hand, some conjuration was forming against him, some diabolical powers drawing together to blast his work, and cross his generous design. He therefore rouses his indignation, hardens his forehead, and with many furious defiances and Avaunt-Satans! enters on his business. (p. 200)

Shaftesbury's own response to the anxiety of reception was one of resolute denial: 'I am no wise more an Author, for being in print. I am conscious of no additional virtue, or dangerous quality, from having lain at any time under the weight of that alphabetic engine called the press' (p. 263). The best way to deal with imagined criticism was to internalize it in an unthreatening form: to anticipate it by means of internal dialogue, or to make it familiar, in the shape of a listening friend. Shaftesbury referred to the 'mirror-faculty' which writers possess in respect of themselves (p. 172), and he believed that dialogue encouraged the process of self-reflection. Enhanced by the presence of an imagined listener, who was figured as both the other and the double of the writer–speaker, his model of reception closed the gap between 'private' and 'public'. Crucially, the audience was thus tamed, and made benign.

'Mirror-writing', the term we shall use for this dialogic medium, anticipates the figure of friendship as it was deployed in Coleridge's 'conversation poems' (and their Wordsworthian analogues), as well as the 'ideal reader' as it has been defined by reader-response criticism. Symbolized by the practice of reading aloud, it exemplified an intimacy between writer and reader that was beginning to come under threat from the expansion of the reading-public, and a practical method for keeping consumerist constructions of reading at bay. In this sense, it embodied a significantly private version of the cultures of sociability and

enthusiasm. It was to a similarly convivial model of reception that Lamb
turned, a century later than Shaftesbury, in his 'Detached Thoughts on
Books and Reading', when attempting to explain why he would always
read Shakespeare or Milton aloud, but never a newspaper or novel.
'Books of quick interest, that hurry on for incidents, are for the eye to
glide over only', Elia asserts: 'It will not do to read them out. I could
never listen to even the better kind of modern novels without extreme
irksomeness ... [and] A newspaper, read out, is intolerable.' Shakespeare
or Milton, on the other hand, 'you cannot avoid reading aloud—to
yourself, or (as it chances) to some single person listening. More than
one—and it degenerates into an audience.'[37] The preferences voiced in
this passage—for an aural model of reading, as distinct from a visual
one; for Shakespeare and Milton, rather than newpapers and novels;
for poetry rather than prose; for leisurely rather than hurried reading; for
reflection rather than incident; for a single listener (presumably a friend
or family member) rather than an audience—are all expressions of an
allegiance that can be characterized as Romantic, even if their occurrence in Lamb's essay is complicated by irony. The crucial distinction
made, between a dialogue with oneself (or a single other person) and the
addressing of an audience, allows sociability to enter the act of reception
in ways that are unthreatening. Lamb's specification that reading aloud
should not 'degenerate' into performance contains an implicit acknowledgement of the threat that wider audiences posed. It embodies a
withdrawal from the public sphere, whose defensiveness is camouflaged
by its appearance of sociability.

One of the surest indications that a defence strategy has become
established is that it gets into parodies by contemporary writers. It is
significant that critics of the Lake School were not slow to anatomize the
act of withdrawal signified by reading aloud. Lamb, through his Elian
persona, showed himself to be partly ironic and partly sympathetic
towards this mode of reception/performance. But the anonymous
writer of *Benjamin the Waggoner* (1819) took a different view. In a long
note, he satirized the cosy storytelling scene which Wordsworth had
used to frame the story of 'Peter Bell'. Adopting a Wordsworthian
persona, he reassures himself that his listeners 'were exceedingly delighted' with its recitation, then continues:

---

[37] 'Detached Thoughts on Books and Reading', in *Elia and The Last Essays of Elia*, ed.
Jonathan Bate (Oxford: Oxford University Press, World's Classics, 1987), 198.

I could not help remarking, how like it was to the Romans of old, as mentioned by Pliny ... my being surrounded by my friends, and reciting to them my works before they issued to the public—my requesting their remarks and animadversions, and meeting with nothing but bursts of applause. O! that one's friends were the sole critics upon our works, how smoothly and unobstructedly we should proceed.[38]

Wordsworth's practice of reading aloud is here presented, not in the terms he would himself have approved—namely, as a sign of his allegiance to the collaborative oral tradition which the publication of *Lyrical Ballads* had strengthened—but in terms of his perpetuation of a Roman custom, strongly patrician in tone, and comically at odds with the homely idiom of 'Peter Bell'. High Romanticism, in this critique, is exposed as an anachronism; coterie reading-circles a method of self-defence; and the poet as a narcissist unable to face his critics. The anonymous parodist has put his finger on the main ingredients of the anxiety of reception as it was evinced by first-generation English Romantic writers.

III. CRITICS AS JUDGES, ADVOCATES, AND PATRONS

The survival of poets and critics in the early nineteenth century involved a rather more complex negotiation between public and private spheres of reception than is often remembered. It is the tendency of hindsight to concentrate either on the high points of a writer's rejection or acceptance by the reading-public, or on the more embattled aspects of the relationship between poetry and criticism. Even contemporary accounts can be misleading. Hannah More once complained that 'Literary patronage is so much *shorn of its beams*, that it can no longer enlighten bodies which are in themselves opake; so much abridged of its power that it cannot force into notice a work which is not able to recommend itself'.[39] But just as literary coteries of a kind survived long after the demise of the coffee-house culture—in the Bluestocking group of which More was herself a member; in families such as the Wordsworths and

---

[38] Graeme Stones and John Strachan (eds.), *Parodies of the Romantic Age* (5 vols., London: Pickering and Chatto, 1999), ii. *Collected Verse Parody* ed. John Strachan, 244.

[39] *The Complete Works* (2 vols., New York: Harper and Brothers, 1835), vol. i, p. vii; quoted in Marlon B. Ross, *The Contours of Masculine Desire: Romanticism and the Rise of Poetry* (Oxford: Oxford University Press, 1989), 229.

Coleridges or the Wollstonecraft-Godwin-Shelleys; in groupings such as the 'Lake School' and the 'Cockney School'; and in Dissenting circles like the Warrington Academy—so the traces of a system of patronage were observable in the dependence of writers such as the young Coleridge on private annuities; in the persistence of subscription methods of publication; in various methods of advocacy, whether they took place in public or behind the scenes; in the active promotional role played by influential booksellers; and in the relation between established literary figures and their young protégés. An example of the last occurs in Hannah More's befriending of Ann Yearsley, by whom she was later rejected. In the slanted account offered by Polwhele of their estrangement, Yearsley is seen as the ungrateful recipient of More's protection:

Mrs Yearseley's [sic] Poems, as the product of an untutored milk-woman, certainly entitled her to patronage: and patronage she received, from Miss H. More, liberal beyond example. Yet, such is the depravity of the human heart, that this milk-woman had no sooner her hut cheered by the warmth of benevolence, than she spurned her benefactor from her door.[40]

With the evidence suggesting that, on the contrary, More was overprotective (and that Yearsley rightly strove to achieve financial independence), this episode survives as a record of the gulf between writers of different class origins. It also demonstrates an uncomfortable transition between one generation and the next with respect to the role played by patronage in establishing a successful literary career.

Despite the difficulties to which they sometimes gave rise, the persistence of anachronistic systems of reception was a crucial component in the protective armoury of authorship at this time. Not only did the existence of coteries allow writers to circulate their work before it appeared in print (thus delaying and pre-empting its public reception), it also helped them to establish common aims, intentions, and prejudices; a shared and inevitably exclusive language; and strongly cohesive loyalties. As members of clans, writers were better able to confront what Marilyn Butler calls the 'dire inveterate partisanship' of the reviewing culture (where, as Peacock puts it, 'The *legatur* of corruption must be stamped upon a work before it can be admitted into fashionable circulation');[41] and to maintain a privacy of address despite emerging

---

[40] Richard Polwhele, *The Unsex'd Females: A Poem, Addressed to the Author of the Pursuits of Literature* (London: Cadell and Davies, 1798), 19 n.

[41] *Peacock Displayed*, 277; 'An Essay on Fashionable Literature', in *Peacock Works*, viii. 273. Professor Butler observes that 'Especially in the second decade of the century, party feeling

into the public domain. It is for this reason that, as Jeffrey Cox has recently argued in respect of Keats, we should consider writers in relation to the immediate circle of colleagues by whom their creativity was sustained, rather than in isolation:

We need to affirm in general terms the importance of groups in establishing the social nature of cultural objects and in representing the living ground upon which individuals come to share in a more widely diffused ideology.... we need to (re-)place second generation Romanticism, and the work of Keats in particular, as Cockney poetry, poetry produced within a circle of writers with a communal cultural project.[42]

In the absence of patronage proper, favourable critical interventions became increasingly important for ensuring the lasting recognition of writers. Such rites of passage were overseen by public acts of recognition between authors; by the plaudits of reviewing bodies; and by private recommendations between colleagues and friends. In all cases, they could be mutually beneficial to author and critic. Made by a named and recognized writer, such interventions frequently stood out as acts of politesse, solidarity, or proprietorial guardianship. When Anna Barbauld, for instance, allocated eight lines in *Eighteen Hundred and Eleven* to the contemporary dramatist Joanna Baillie—by comparison with a couplet devoted to Shakespeare—she risked being accused of a disproportionate imbalance of praise by her contemporary readers. Doubtless it was one to which she gave careful thought, both as a woman with an interest in promoting women's writing, and as a British writer concerned to warn her readers that London—still considered the thriving centre of European culture it had been in Shakespeare's day—might yet lose its reputation. Of similar political import, but unsigned, was Leigh Hunt's review of Keats in the *Examiner* (1817), a journal with distinctly liberal politics and avant-garde tastes. Hunt found it necessary to include the disclaimer that his reception of Keats's poems preceded their friendship, before going on to establish cockney Keats as the direct successor to Wordsworth, Coleridge, and Southey. The effects of this review were to be material and lasting, so far as a long-term adjustment in what Jauss has called the audience's 'horizon of expectations' was concerned; but as Butler points out, the effect of Hunt's support was generally counter-

---

leads to automatic pre-judgement, and to spiteful assaults on individuals' (*Peacock Displayed*, 277).

[42] 'Keats in the Cockney School', *Romanticism*, 2/1 (1996), 27–39: 28.

productive: although grateful for his sympathy, it was unfortunate for Keats that 'a favourable mention by Hunt tended to bring down on a writer the much more influential disfavour of the [Tory] *Quarterly*'.[43]

Hazlitt was the most powerful writer of his age when it came to anatomizing the politics of reception with a satirical eye. Educated in early life at a Dissenting academy, and therefore debarred from a university education, his stance was that of an embittered outsider to what he called the 'Aristocracy of Letters'. His principled resistance to all forms of patronage derived from his fierce independence, and from a growing resentment towards the privileged institutions from which he was excluded. He felt there was a deep injustice in the affairs of writers, and denounced the practices of puffing and coterie insularity which he saw as discredited anachronisms. Editors he saw as patrons in disguise, borrowing dignity from their situations as arbiters and judges, and increasing their sense of self-importance by abusing the little power they had: 'It is utterly impossible', he lamented, 'to persuade an Editor that he is nobody' (Howe, xvii. 361). Critics who ought to have been allowed their status as impartial judges were, he argued, coerced by the internal power structure of the journals for which they worked into promoting the editor's patrons or friends:

A poem is dedicated to the son of the Muses:—can the critic do other than praise it? A tragedy is brought out by a noble friend and patron:—the severe rules of the drama must yield in some measure to the amenities of private life.... Mr.——is a garetteer—a person that nobody knows; his work has nothing but the *contents* to recommend it; it sinks into obscurity, or addresses itself to the *canaille*. (Howe, xvii. 365)

Whereas the 'man of letters' survived in a form acceptable to polite society, the hack writer was seen as less than nothing:

Unless an author has an establishment of his own, or is entered on that of some other person, he will hardly be allowed to write English or to spell his own name. To be well-spoken of, he must enlist under some standard; he must belong to some *coterie*.... You must commence toad-eater to have your observations attended to; if you are independent, unconnected, you will be regarded as a poor creature. (Howe, viii. 211–12)

To Hazlitt's eye, the scurrilous treatment Keats had endured at the hands of *Blackwood's Magazine* was self-evidently the consequence of

---

[43]   *Peacock Displayed*, 273.

his cockney origins. The injustice of this treatment came sharply into focus when Keats's abortive career was considered alongside the success of his noble contemporary, Byron. In his essay 'On the Aristocracy of Letters', Hazlitt's anger against this disequity of treatment reaches its pitch. The real butt of his satire is not Byron himself, however, but the spirit of privileged dilettantism for which Byron is a symbolic figure-head:

Look in, and there, amidst silver services and shining chandeliers, you will see the man of genius at his proper post, picking his teeth and mincing an opinion, sheltered by rank, bowing to wealth—a poet framed, glazed, and hung in a striking light: not a straggling weed, torn and trampled on; not a poor *Kit-run-the-street*, but a powdered beau, a sycophant plant, an exotic reared in a glass-case, hermetically sealed. . . . The poet Keats had not this sort of protection for his person—he lay bare to weather—the serpent stung him, and the poison-tree dropped upon this little western flower:—when the mercenary servile crew approached him, he had no pedigree to show them, no rent-roll to hold out in reversion for their praise: he was not in any great man's train, nor the butt and puppet of a lord. (Howe, viii. 211)

Hazlitt's prose is full of moments of insight such as this, which reveal the persistence—alongside the Grub Street conditions under which he himself worked—of an outmoded model of gentlemanly authorship. Hazlitt anathematized belletrism of this kind, seeing it as a throwback to an earlier age, when writers were either of independent means or supported by a wealthy patron. The genius as 'man of letters' features in Isaac D'Israeli's *An Essay on the Manners and Genius of the Literary Character* (1795), and is possibly the source of Hazlitt's caricature here.[44]

Hazlitt was right in his analysis of the structure and abuse of power. The role of the critic was complicated, at this historical juncture, by being required to fulfil an outmoded role alongside a new one. Criticism rose as patronage fell, yet some of the features of a system of patronage were still discernible in the practices of reviewers, who acquired the status of disinterested judges from their position of anonymity.[45] As a consequence of the realities which lay behind this pretence, the relation

[44] D'Israeli's book went through numerous revised editions, and was widely read. Among its many admirers was the author's idol, Byron. Hazlitt referred disparagingly to D'Israeli in a passage arguing that 'spurious reputation, like false argument, runs in a circle'. See 'The Aristocracy of Letters' (Howe, viii. 212).

[45] For Byron's interactions with his anonymous reviewers, and a broader theoretical placing of the practice of anonymity, see Jerome Christensen, *Lord Byron's Strength: Romantic Writing and Commercial Society* (Baltimore: Johns Hopkins University Press, 1993).

between creativity and criticism was in fact a mutual dependency, some-times collaborative and sometimes competitive, but more often than not a combination of the two.

Consequently, the rhetoric of reviewers reflected a confusion be-tween the roles of judgement and patronage. Summing up the case against Wordsworth's *Poems* (1807) to the 'jury' of the British public, Francis Jeffrey clearly enjoyed his self-arrogated status as the arbiter of public taste: 'Putting ourselves thus upon our country, we certainly look for a verdict against this publication; and have little doubt indeed of the result, upon a fair consideration of the evidence contained in these volumes'.[46] According to Carlyle, Jeffrey 'was always as if speaking to a jury', and Lee Erickson has observed that his 'lawyerly' manner was widely recognized.[47] Less established reviewers, however, found the mantle of authority uncomfortable. When Barry Cornwall (who signed himself 'L' in the *London Magazine* (April 1821)) intervened in the posthumous reception of Keats, he drew attention to the unsettling transition between old and new sytems of public recognition, as well as to his own unease within them:

The public is fond of patronizing poets: they are considered in the light of an almost helpless race; they are bright as stars, but like meteors

Short lived and self-consuming.

We do not claim the *patronage* of the public for Mr. Keats, but we hope that it will now cast aside every little and unworthy prejudice, and do justice to the high memory of a young but undoubted poet.[48]

In much the same way, the rhetoric used by writers in their dealings with reviewers came to reflect a divided expectation, of sympathy and im-partiality, as we see in the letter Byron wrote to Thomas Moore in 1815, attempting to engineer a favourable review for a poet who is represented simultaneously as victim and genius:

By the way, if C**e [Coleridge]—who is a man of wonderful talent, and in distress, and about to publish two vols. of Poesy and Biography, and who has been worse used by the critics than ever we were—will you, if he comes out,

---

[46] *Edinburgh Review* (11 Oct. 1807); repr. in *Jeffrey's Criticism: A Selection*, ed. with introd. Peter F. Morgan (Edinburgh: Scottish Academic Press, 1983), 55.

[47] Carlyle, *Reminiscences*, ed. Charles Eliot Norton (London: J. M. Dent & Sons, 1932, repr. 1972), 328; Erickson, *The Economy of Literary Form*, 79.

[48] Quoted by Susan Wolfson, 'Keats enters History: Autopsy, *Adonais*, and the Fame of Keats', in Nicholas Roe (ed.), *Keats and History* (Cambridge: Cambridge University Press, 1995), 22.

promise me to review him favourably in the E[dinburgh] R[eview]? Praise him, I think you must, but you will also praise him *well*,—of all things the most difficult. It will be the making of him.[49]

If the advocacy of writers was frequently complicated by private motivations, so there was sometimes a resistance to being publicly acclaimed for personal reasons. When Coleridge included advance praise for *The Prelude* in *Biographia Literaria* as part of a bid to establish Wordsworth's reputation for philosophical poetry, he did so expressly against his friend's own wishes. Wordsworth was wary of receiving praise before it was due, and did not wish *The Prelude* to be retrospectively associated with *Biographia* by this kind of cross-marketing. Nor, one suspects, did he relish the thought that Coleridge might draw sustenance for his criticism from a creative identity that was still in the making—which is how *The Prelude* was regarded until the end of Wordsworth's life. Conversely, Coleridge himself came to regret the way in which 'Christabel' had been systematically promoted by Lord Byron. This behind-the-scenes 'puffing' by a fellow-poet proved ineffectual in the end, and may even have contributed to the reviewers' hostility. Certainly, in the notice of the volume that appeared in the *Edinburgh Review* (September 1816), it was to Byron's recommendation of this 'wild and singularly original and beautiful poem' that the reviewer drew attention, with the dismissive remark that 'his judgement is not absolutely to be relied on'.[50] The review was for some years attributed to Hazlitt, perhaps on the grounds that it so openly revealed its prejudice against Byron.

Whereas anxieties of reception focus in the first instance on the author's ownership, authority, and control of the text he or she has written, they take on a more symbolic significance in the public domain after that text has been circulated in manuscript or published in print, when it becomes subject to political appropriations, themselves reflective of wider struggles for power. As we shall later see, in a more detailed examination of the case of 'Christabel', the friction between two systems—of public judgement and private patronage—sometimes caused a radical split in the reception of a volume, which may be read as paradigmatic of the defensive and embattled culture of the early nineteenth

[49] *Letters and Journals*, ed. Leslie A. Marchand (12 vols. and suppl., London: William Clowes and Sons, 1975), iv. 324.

[50] The review, which appeared anonymously, was understood by Coleridge (and a number of 20th-cent. scholars) to have been written by Hazlitt; but its true provenance has since been established beyond reasonable doubt.

century. The further case of 'poor Keats' has provided a number of recent critics with an instance of the party-political allegiances clearly discernible in acts of critical reception.[51] Interactions of this kind, in which authorial identity was negotiated at the crossing between private and public spheres—or in a sphere where private and political concerns became jumbled—were in all probability widespread. But even where they concerned major canonical authors they are rarely documented, and more often they involved the fortunes of writers whose lasting place in the canon was never secured. Such interactions were, however, the site for successive struggles between authorial and interpretative authority in the Romantic period; and in them we see the ways in which anxieties of reception were reactively produced by the upward mobility of professional criticism.

IV. POETRY, NEGLECT, AND THE PURSUIT OF POSTHUMOUS REPUTATION

Under conditions of dependency on readers who were constructed as hostile others, the question of what constituted the writing-subject's identity became increasingly ambiguous; and a recurrence of the figure of death in the mythology of reception shows that when identity crises were caused by loss of self-esteem, anxieties tended to focus on the threat of extinction. In glamorized images such as those of Chatterton's suicide and Burns's poverty-stricken death, writers found their own worst fears both reflected and sublimated into viable self-exonerating narratives, in which the public's hostility was figurally and causally connected with the poet's demise. These graphic instances of the 'birth of the reader' being at the cost of the 'death of the author' register both the deep hermeneutic anxieties which underlay attitudes to audience at this time, and the defensive strategies which evolved to keep them at bay.

When Wordsworth wrote, in his career-crisis poem, 'Resolution and Independence',

> I thought of Chatterton, the marvellous Boy,
> The sleepless Soul that perished in its pride;

[51] The phrase 'poor Keats' was common currency in contemporary periodicals. It is used by Hazlitt in his essay 'On the Periodical Press' (Howe, xvii. 237). The most recent study of Keats's politics, and the politics of his reception, is Nicholas Roe, *John Keats and the Culture of Dissent* (Oxford: Clarendon Press, 1998).

> Of Him who walked in glory and in joy
> Behind his plough, upon the mountain-side
>
> (ll. 43–6)

he bought into popular myth, at the same time investing it with his own particular brand of wishfulness. Chatterton the temperamental forger, who spent most of his life doing hack work, then killed himself at 17, and Burns, whose drunken debauchery and domestic unhappiness became notorious after the publication of James Currie's *Life*, are here endowed with heroic attributes—made to triumph posthumously over adversity and the public taste for scandal. Fearing that his own talent would go to waste unless he established a successful reputation, that his own private life was open to investigation as theirs had been, and that poverty and death might similarly cut him down in his prime, Wordsworth made these poets into figures of what Bloom has called 'capable imagination'. As a corollary to this idealization of creative genius, the public is associatively likened to the leeches whose dwindling numbers are reported by the poet's rustic double, in his turn apotheosized as a kind of surrogate poet. A subliminal connection is made between readers as parasites (sucking the lifeblood out of poets) and readers as a dwindling source of remuneration. Wordsworth here registered how acutely conscious he was of his failure to engage the public's attention as fully as Bloomfield or Burns. Elsewhere it is the largeness, remoteness, and anonymity of the reading-public that overwhelms him; here the increasing scarcity of leeches works as a complex metaphor of his resentful dependence on an audience by whom he was neglected.

Burns and Chatterton were appropriate figures to appear as part of Wordsworth's myth-making, not just because of their sensational deaths, but because in important ways they challenged preconceptions about the relation between a poet's identity and his hold over his readers. Fleshed out later, in his *Letter To A Friend of Robert Burns*, Wordsworth's admiration for Burns centred on his ability to speak to and for the *people* (as distinct from the public) in the ordinary language of men. His representativeness ran so deep and was so pervasive that it almost negated personality altogether, turning the poet into a spokesman—an everyman figure—whose poems might just as easily be signed ANON as 'Rabbie Burns'. This was the kind of popularity Wordsworth craved, and in his critical prose he defensively sought to distinguish it from the approval of a fickle reading-public. Chatterton, on the other hand, challenged the cult of personality by the more daring route of tricking his publishers and readers into believing in a false identity. He perished 'in his pride' for this act of fraudulence, but his reputation for genius survived nonetheless; and it was this paradox which held Wordsworth's attention.

In Shelley's *Adonais*, Keats's death is blamed directly on Croker's review of *Endymion*. Andrew Bennett has recently claimed that 'The story has the virtue of a certain dramatic pathos and its apparent implausibility... most neatly summed up in... Byron's idea of the poet "snuffed out by an article" in *Don Juan*—is reduced by the suggestion that Keats was already suffering from tuberculosis and the reviews simply weakened his will to live'.[52] Whether or not it contains elements of truth, the story has an extraordinary and enduring potency, as a myth of this particular poet's (feminine) sensitivity to the views of others, and of creativity's vulnerability to criticism. Shelley here successfully packaged Keats's posthumous reception for an audience attuned to the conventions of sensibility, making death at the hands of hostile re-viewers the signifier of eternal life at the hands of sympathetic readers. As a piece of defensive marketing, this bore a remarkable resemblance to Keats's own poetic strategies, which involved an emptying out of personality and identity as an inversion of the egotistical sublime. If the poet had 'no identity'—if his genius was characterized by its character-lessness—then perhaps, in this position of impersonality, he could successfully undermine the powerful anonymity of his reviewers.

A complementary myth is to be found in Byron's (masculine) im-perviousness to his own popularity. The opening sequence of Ken Russell's film, *Gothic*, presents the poet as something akin to a pop star—gazed at from a distance, through a telescope, by a crowd of admiring tourists. Their main interest is Byron's scandalous sex life, and the poet remains supremely and aristocratically indifferent to their presence. In this powerful filmic representation, Russell summarizes the main ingredients of the Byron myth as it was constructed jointly by the poet himself and his reviewers. If Keats triumphed over the cult of personality by its negation, Byron's was the opposite course. As John Scott observed in his article on Byron in 'Living Authors' (1821), his unprecedented literary success was almost entirely due to 'adventitious' and 'surreptitious' advantages, 'derived from being considered as too

[52] *Keats, Narrative and Audience*, 40.

bad for repentance, and too desperate to be pitied'.[53] 'He looks upon [his readers] as sentient existences that are important in his poetic existence', wrote John Wilson, in his review of *Childe Harold*:

—so that he command their feelings and passions, he cares not for their censure or their praise,—for his fame is more than mere literary fame; and he aims in poetry, like the fallen chief whose image is so often before him, at universal dominion, we had almost said, universal tyranny, over the minds of men.[54]

This view was shared by Hazlitt, who wrote in May 1818, 'Byron would persuade us that the universe itself is not worth his or our notice; and yet he would expect us to be occupied with him';[55] and whose subsequent exposure of Byron in *Table Talk* (1821) focused on the appeal of his class origins to a public eager to claim 'acquaintance with the Lord':

Is he dull, or does he put off some trashy production on the public? It is not charged to his account, as a deficiency which he must make good at the peril of his admirers. His Lordship is not answerable for the negligence or extravagances of his Muse. He 'bears a charmed reputation, which must not yield' like one of vulgar birth. The Noble Bard is for this reason scarcely vulnerable to the critics. The double barrier of his pretensions baffles their puny, timid efforts. (Howe, viii. 210)

Hazlitt's judgement of Byron brings into focus some of the animosities (and perhaps envies?) of a writer with stronger allegiances to criticism than to poetry, but with a deep conviction that each is answerable to the other. But it also bears contemporary witness to the successful management of what Jerome Christensen has called 'the literary system of Byronism', which was the collaborative invention of 'a gifted poet, a canny publisher, eager reviewers, and rapt readers', and which worked by selling Byron to the public on the strength of his aristocratic glamour. Furthermore, as Christensen conclusively proves, the commodity 'Lord Byron' was produced *reactively*: first in *English Bards and Scotch Reviewers*, as a belated revenge for Brougham's hostile review of *Hours of Idleness*, and subsequently in *Childe Harold*, where the Byronic persona first appeared. If the first of these poems belonged 'as much to the history of English

---

[53] Unsigned article in the series 'Living Authors', *London Magazine*, 2 (Jan. 1821); extract in Theodore Redpath, *The Young Romantics and Literary Opinion, 1807–1824* (London: George G. Harrap and Co., 1973), 262–75.
[54] Unsigned review of *Childe Harold*, canto iv, *Edinburgh Review* (June 1818); quoted in Redpath, *Young Romantics*, 31.
[55] *The Yellow Dwarf*, 2 May 1818; quoted in Redpath, *Young Romantics*, 183.

dueling as to the history of English literature',[56] the third disclosed a subtler mode of counter-attack on hostile reviewers. Constructing 'Lord Byron' first as a persona, and subsequently as an entity indistinguishable from the writing-subject himself, Byron vanished into his charismatic and untouchable disguise, to the delight of his spellbound readers.

The Bloomian category of 'strength' which Christensen resuscitates as the primary characteristic of Byron's self-image is appropriate to the atmosphere of embattled personalities on which the periodical culture of the 1800s thrived: Hazlitt drew on a similar terminology when he referred to 'the defensive and offensive armour of criticism' (Howe, viii. 217), a phrase which updated the courtly language of pugilism used fifty years earlier by Samuel Johnson in *The Rambler*:

he that writes may be considered as a kind of general challenger, whom every one has a right to attack; since he quits the common rank of life, steps forward beyond the lists, and offers his merit to the publick judgement. To commence author is to claim praise, and no man can justly aspire to honour, but at the hazard of disgrace.[57]

Marlon Ross has shown how metaphors of quest and conquest pervaded critical and poetic discourse at the turn of the eighteenth century:

As the contest moves from the court and the patronage of gentlemen to the publishing house and the market of the common reader, the poet's success becomes literally more dependent on the power of self-possession, the potency of his individual vision, his ability to captivate and rule a diverse, saturated and fickle public[58]

Under these conditions, the language of chivalry had come to seem inadequate to describe the sinister conduct of writers who sold their souls to the periodical press. To John Hamilton Reynolds, reviewers were 'creatures that stab men in the dark'—'young and enthusiastic spirits are their dearest prey',[59] and John Clare complained, in a letter of 1821, 'is the cold hearted butchers of annonymous Critics to ⟨ blast a ⟩ cut up everything that escapes their bribery or thinks contrary to them is

---

[56] *Lord Byron's Strength*, 33.

[57] In *The Yale Edition of the Works of Samuel Johnson*, ed. W. J. Bate and Albrecht B. Strauss (New Haven: Yale University Press, 1969), 133–4; quoted in Mary Poovey, *The Proper Lady and the Woman Writer: Ideology as Style in the Works of Mary Wollstonecraft, Mary Shelley, and Jane Austen* (Chicago: Chicago University Press, 1984), 35.

[58] *Contours of Masculine Desire*, 27.

[59] Review from *The Alfred* on 'The Quarterly Review—Mr Keats' (6 Oct. 1818), in *Reynolds Prose*, 225.

polotics [*sic*] to rule genius'.[60] The demonization of reviewers by authors—and particularly by poets—was in some cases well founded; but paranoia was so widespread as to appear almost indiscriminate; and for this reason it became a source of parody. James Hogg, in *The Poetic Mirror, or Living Bards of Britain* (1816), was one of a sequence of writers who made fun of Wordsworth as an over-anxious poet, his eye always on the critics, whose most fervent hope was that he might survive their scorn. In the closing lines of 'The Flying Taylor', Wordsworth is over-heard prophesying his immortality. He speaks with the complacent but anxious tone of solemnity which, to an audience sceptical of his objectives, seemed the hallmark of his Prefaces and notes:

> eternally my name
> Shall last on earth, conspicuous like a star
> 'Mid that bright galaxy of favour'd spirits,
> Who, laugh'd at constantly, whene'er they publish'd,
> Survived the impotent scorn of base Reviews,
> Monthly or Quarterly, or that accursed
> Journal, the Edinburgh Review, that lives
> On tears, and sighs, and groans, and brains, and blood.[61]

In an environment of attack and counter-attack, survival was the key enterprise, but not everyone survived, and martyrdom became a recurrent defensive figure in a reception mythology designed to keep the professional reviewers at bay. In an anonymous letter published in the *Alfred*, J. H. Reynolds wrote that 'The Monthly Reviewers...endeavoured...to crush the rising heart of young Kirk White; and indeed they in part generated that melancholy which ultimately destroyed him.'[62] Susan Wolfson observes that 'the role-call of martyrs had become so routine by the mid-1830s that the *Metropolitan* could invoke it ritualistically, unquestioningly associating Keats with Shelley's mythology'.[63] She quotes the list of sacrificial victims provided by the reviewer, in what is seen as a systematic and vindictive purge of poetry:

There was Chatterton . . . There was Kirke White . . . and lastly there was 'Adonais', the sensitive Keats, who might have prospered, though his birth

---

[60] *The Letters of John Clare*, ed. Mark Storey (Oxford: Clarendon Press, 1985), 188–9.

[61] In Stones and Strachan (eds.), *Parodies of the Romantic Age*, ii. 134. See also George Darley's use of the term 'literary fratricide' in 1836; discussed by Erickson, *Economy of Literary Form*, 91.

[62] Repr. by Hunt in the *Examiner* (11 Oct. 1818), 648–9; quoted in Wolfson, 'Keats enters History', 21.

[63] Wolfson, 'Keats enters History', 21.

was humble, and his means straitened, had not an enmity, as gratuitous as it was wanton, as cruel in act as it was malignant in spirit, met, tore and trampled him to the earth![64]

Just as the language of victimization was applied to authors who received critical treatment in the press, so vicarious anxieties were frequently expressed by means of interventions on behalf of an author who was seen to be underrated or wilfully marginalized. The hagiographical prefaces and notes which Mary Shelley as editor attached to Shelley's poetry were a retrospective attempt to put the record straight—to show that, 'Shelley did not expect sympathy and approbation from the public; but the want of it took away a portion of the ardour that ought to have sustained him while writing.'[65] In recuperating his reputation for posterity, Mary echoed her husband's stance of proud detachment, while at the same time suggesting the extent to which this very pride was a defence against the cruelty of critics:

I had not the most distant wish that he should truckle in opinion, or submit his lofty aspirations for the human race to the low ambition and pride of the many, but, I felt sure, that if his poems were more addressed to the common feelings of men, his proper rank among the writers of the day would be acknowledged; and that popularity as a poet, would enable his countrymen to do justice to his character and virtues; which, in those days, it was the mode to attack with the most flagitious calumnies and insulting abuse. That he felt these things deeply cannot be doubted, though he armed himself with the consciousness of acting from a lofty and heroic sense of right.[66]

John Wilson detected an underlying hypocrisy in this mythology of victimization. In an essay entitled 'An Hour's Talk about Poetry' (first published in *Blackwood's Edinburgh Magazine* in October 1831, then later revised and enlarged for *The Recreations of Christopher North* in 1842), he brought this sharply into focus by contrasting a double standard in the attitudes of English readers towards two figures, Bloomfield and Burns. Both these writers were 'self-taught' poets whose 'native wood-notes wild' earned them the label of genius, and whose popularity brought them a legendary status in their own lifetimes. As Wilson observed, English readers were much readier to sentimentalize Burns as a figure who suffered neglect at the hands of his readers than they were to take

---

[64]   *Metropolitan*, 14 (Sept. 1815), 61; quoted in Wolfson, 'Keats enters History', 21–2.

[65]   *The Novels and Selected Works of Mary Shelley*, gen. ed. Nora Crook, with Pamela Clemit; ii, ed. Pamela Clemit (London: William Pickering, 1996), 316.

[66]   Ibid. 316–17.

responsibility for Bloomfield, a genius of comparable status their own soil had produced. The reception of Burns, in the wake of Currie's *Life*, provoked loyal and impassioned defence; but Bloomfield 'dropt into the grave with no other lament we ever heard of but a few copies of poorish verses in some of the Annuals, and seldom or never does one hear a whisper of his name'.[67] Wilson was not slow to expose the mythology of victimization as a species of scapegoating. There was a veneer of patronizing sentimentality, he implied, which distanced the reader from the grim realities of a poet's occupation: 'Let England then leave Scotland to her shame about Burns; and, thinking of her own treatment of Bloomfield, cover her own face with both her hands, and confess that it was pitiful.'[68] The inwardness and sophistication of Wilson's rhetoric in this essay serves as a reminder of how well developed the mythology of victimization had become by the 1830s. It could be used to reflect ironically on the reading-habits of a nation determined to construct the poet as a figure on the margins of society, but blind to the implications of that construction.

It is notable, in this period, that many critical interventions on others' behalf were rendered less powerful by failing to appear in print, by coming too late, by misjudging the audience for whom they were intended, or by using terminology which further marginalized the author concerned. In an essay on 'Fashionable Poetry' in 1818, Peacock launched a spirited counter-attack on the *Edinburgh Review* for its pillorying of Coleridge's 'Christabel', subjecting contemporary standards of reviewing to reasoned and prolonged critique. But he neither finished nor published the essay, and his defence of Coleridge survives to this day as a puzzling anomaly in his largely anti-Romantic output. Wordsworth's concern for Burns, or Shelley's for Keats, were expressed through elegiac homages, designed to redirect these poets' posthumous reputation, and Godwin's vindication of Mary Wollstonecraft was an attempt—drastically ill-conceived, as it turned out—to offer a candid retrospective account of her life as the best possible context for the proper reception of her work. In adopting a confessional mode, Godwin defeated his own purposes: appearing as advocate instead of detached biographer, he succeeded in further alienating an audience that was still not ready for his enlightened and liberal views.

---

[67] *The Recreations of Christopher North* (3 vols., William Blackwood: Edinburgh and London, 1842), i. 326.
[68] Ibid.

Godwin's notorious intervention on Wollstonecraft's behalf is a reminder that protective advocacy was even more fraught with difficulties where women writers were concerned than in the case of men, and that it continued to be so, even in a climate which ostensibly accepted and fostered the literary productions of women. Looking back on a century that had seen the rise of the professional woman writer, Richard Polwhele (whose misogynist poem, *The Unsex'd Females* appeared in the same year as Wollstonecraft's posthumous works) reflected on the dramatic changes which had taken place during that time in the reception of women's writing:

In this country, a female author was formerly esteemed a Phenomenon in Literature: and she was sure of a favourable reception among the critics, in consideration of her sex. This species of gallantry, however, conveyed no compliment to her understanding. It implied such an inferiority of woman in the scale of intellect as was justly humiliating: and critical forbearance was mortifying to female vanity. At the present day, indeed, our literary women are so numerous, that their judges, waving [*sic*] all complimentary civilities, decide upon their merits with the same rigid impartiality as it seems right to exercise towards the men. The tribunal of criticism is no longer charmed into complacence by the blushes of modest apprehension. It no longer imagines the pleading eye of feminine diffidence that speaks a consciousness of comparative imbecility, or a fearfulness of having offended by intrusion.[69]

Invoking the notion of 'gallantry' as a species of anachronistic indulgence which women are only too ready to exploit, Polwhele was both sarcastic and inaccurate in claiming that women are judged impartially, on their own merits. So pervasive was the spirit of patronization in contemporary reviewing rhetoric that those seeking actively to defend or promote women's writing were caught in a double bind. When Maria Edgeworth condemned Croker's review of *Eighteen Hundred and Eleven*—'so ungentlemanlike, so unjust, so insolent a review I never read'—she did so privately, and therefore ineffectually, to Barbauld herself.[70] But even in a public forum, these words might be seen as

---

[69]   *Unsex'd Females*, 16–17. For a discussion of the various strategies of modesty deployed by women writers in the late 18th and early 19th cents., see Poovey, *The Proper Lady and the Woman Writers*. For a useful general discussion of the strategies used to exclude women from the world of publishing, see Stephen Behrendt, 'Mary Shelley, Frankenstein, and the Woman Writer's Fate', in Paula Feldman and Theresa Kelly (eds.), *Romantic Women-Writers: Voices and Counter-Voices* (Hanover, NH: University Press of New England, 1995), 74.

[70]   Quoted in Betsy Rodgers, *Georgian Chronicle: Mrs Barbauld and her Family* (London: Methuen and Co., 1958), 142.

playing into the hands of a species of gender-stereotyping, which disallowed women success unless it was couched in the language of chivalry. In much the same way, when Henry Crabb Robinson leapt gallantly to Barbauld's defence against Coleridge—whose criticisms are dismissed in similar terms, as 'unhandsome and unmanly'—he unwittingly entered into what appeared to be a form of special pleading;[71] as did John Hamilton Reynolds when he complained, with respect to the unethical practices of contemporary reviewers, that 'Party knows no distinctions,—no proprieties,—and a woman is the best prey for its malignity, because it is the gentlest and the most undefended.'[72]

V. THE THREAT OF MODERNITY: READING, CONSUMPTION, AND OVERPOPULATION

Anxiety, which thrives in incestuous conditions, is given a particular inflection by the competitive–collaborative relationship between poets, reviewers, and critics. But its figurative expressions tend to repeat themselves from context to context, transcending specific circumstances even as they powerfully articulate them. These repetitions help to explain the uncanny way in which Romantic texts sound 'modern'—sound, indeed, as if they speak prophetically of the fate of reading in the 1990s—as when Coleridge complains that the enormous stimulant power of events makes the desire to be stimulated almost an appetite; or when he condemns 'general and indiscriminate reading', and 'the habit consequently induced of requiring instantaneous intelligibility'.[73] Such accusations have an all-too-familiar resonance in our multimedia culture, where we are assaulted at every level by unassimilable information. Similarly, De Quincey's 'On the Poetry of Pope', haunted as it is by the twin fears of multiplication and repetition, strikes a chord in our electronic age. The book, some believe, is rapidly being replaced, but fear of an equivalent reduplication has persisted in relation to electronic text, on a scale that De Quincey almost anticipated:

As books multiply to an unmanageable excess, selection becomes more and more a necessity for readers, and the power of selection more and more a

---

[71] Crabb Robinson, who attended a lecture given by Coleridge on 27 Jan. 1812, reported that 'there were some excrescences in the lecture, and he offended me by an unhandsome and unmanly attack upon Mrs Barbauld'. In a letter to Mrs Clarkson (28 Jan. 1812) he said that he could not forgive Coleridge for this attack (*Lectures*, i. 406, 407).

[72] *Selected Prose*, 225.

[73] *Lectures*, i. 195–6. These observations are discussed in detail in Ch. 2, below.

desperate problem for the busy part of readers. The possibility of selecting wisely is becoming continually more hopeless as the necessity for selection is becoming continually more pressing. Exactly as the growing weight of books overlays and stifles the power of comparison, *pari passu* is the call for comparison the more clamorous.[74]

This awareness of 'information overload'—of an incommensurability between the amount of data received and the ability to process it—is recognizable as a species of what Kant called the 'mathematical sublime', which involves an overwhelming sense of awe in relation to a magnitude that cannot be comprehended. In one sense, the sublime might be said aesthetically to frame the complex Romantic phenomenon I am terming the 'anxiety of reception'.

Wherever the expansion of reading-matter is at issue, in late eighteenth- and early nineteenth-century discourse, it is figured as having the power to annihilate human capacities of retention and organization. As early as 1795—three years, that is, before the idea of exponential growth took on political topicality, with the publication of Malthus's *Essay on Population*—Isaac D'Israeli wrote the following passage:

When I reflect that every literary journal consists of 50 or 60 publications, and that of these, 5 or 6 at least are capital performances, and the greater part not contemptible, when I take the pen and attempt to calculate, by these given sums, the number of volumes which the next century must infallibly produce, my feeble faculties wander in a perplexed series, and as I lose myself among billions, trillions, and quartillions, I am obliged to lay down my pen, and stop at infinity.[75]

It was a cry of alarm that periodical essayists over the next century were to echo; and in the context of debates about whether literary standards were improving or on the decline it acquired a note of increasing urgency. Francis Jeffrey, writing in the *Edinburgh Review* in 1819, complained that 'The very multiplication of works of amusement, necessarily withdraws many from notice that deserve to be kept in remembrance ... As the materials of enjoyment and instruction accumulate around us, more and more must thus be daily rejected, and left to waste. ... many poets, worthy of eternal remembrance, have been forgotten, merely because there was not room in our memories for all.'[76] The insistence

---

[74] In Masson, xi. 52.
[75] Preface to *An Essay on the Manners and Genius of the Literary Character* (London: T. Cadell and W. Davies, 1795), pp. xviii–xix.
[76] Review of Campbell's *Specimens of the British Poets*, *Edinburgh Review* (Mar. 1819), 471.

with which the question of numbers and standards was raised gave a particularly demographic flavour to nineteenth-century discussions of canon-formation and the poetics of survival.

Harold Bloom has recently claimed in *The Western Canon* that 'Over-population, Malthusian repletion, is the authentic context for canonical anxieties'.[77] There is much that bears this out in the metaphorical language that nineteenth-century writers used to figure the reader and the reading-public. It is a discourse characterized by doom-laden pro-phecy with respect to numerical expansion, and by an almost hysterical sense of unstoppability: 'There never was an age so prolific of popular poetry as that in which we now live', Jeffrey claimed; 'and as wealth, population, and education extend, the produce is likely to go on increas-ing.... if we continue to write and rhyme at the present rate for 200 years longer, there must be some new art of short-hand reading invented—or all reading will be given up in despair'.[78] The playwright Robert Brinsley Sheridan compared life as a theatre manager to 'the constant super-intendence of executions' at Newgate prison:

The number of authors whom he was forced to extinguish, was, he said, 'a perpetual literary massacre, that made St. Bartholomew's altogether shrink in comparison.... He had counted plays until calculation sank under the number; and every rejected play of them all seemed, like the clothes of a Spanish beggar, to turn into a living, restless, merciless, indefatigable progeny.'[79]

Thomas Carlyle wrote in his *Characteristics* that 'all Literature has become one boundless self-devouring Review', his metaphor recalling Shake-speare's evocation of chaos as 'appetite, an universal wolf', which 'last eat up himself'.[80] In his essay on 'Biography' (1832) the image of a devouring mouth recurs again, as part of a semi-comedic tirade against the whole wasteful industry of book production and circulation. Literat-ure is seen, here, as feeding the voracious appetite of the reading-public, but destined ultimately to perish in its own excess:

Ship-loads of Fashionable Novels, Sentimental Rhymes, Tragedies, Farces, Diaries of Travel, Tales by flood and field, are swallowed monthly into the

[77] *The Western Canon: The Books and School of the Ages* (New York: Harcourt Brace and Company, 1995), 15.

[78] *Edinburgh Review* (Mar. 1819), 471–2.

[79] *Sheridaniana; or, Anecdotes of Robert Brinsley Sheridan; His Table-Talk, and Bon Mots* (London: Henry Colburn, 1826), 285. I am grateful to Nick Roe for bringing this passage to my attention.

[80] In *The Collected Works of Thomas Carlyle*, ed. H. D. Traill (30 vols., London: Chapman and Hall, 1896–9), xxviii. 25; quoted in Erickson, *Economy of Literary Form*, 90. For the Shakespear-ian allusion, see Ulysses' famous speech on order in *Troilus and Cressida*, III. iii. 119–24.

bottomless Pool: still does the Press toil; innumerable Paper-makers, Compositors, Printers' Devils, Book-binders, and Hawkers grown hoarse with loud proclaiming, rest not from their labour; and still, in torrents, rushes on the great array of Publications, unpausing, to their final home and still Oblivion, like the Grave! cries Give! Give![81]

Perhaps the fear of proliferation, of 'unmanageable excess' that we share as an urgent concern with our forebears is played out in a metonymic connection between books and people. This associative link would give a powerfully specific resonance to Coleridge's condemnation of 'promiscuous' reading habits, as well as to Wordsworth's preoccupation with removing readers from the 'gross and violent stimulants' to which they are unhealthily addicted, thereby establishing a modest and manly health in the poetry-reading public.[82] It would also explain the recurrent gendering of novel-readers as feminine, and the association between women's reading-habits and a species of guilty, excessive consumption. In the conduct-book rhetoric of Thomas Gisborne's *An Enquiry into the Duties of the Female Sex* (1799), for instance, excessive reading is the index of greed and corruption that begin in the female mind: 'The appetite becomes too keen to be denied . . . the contents of the circulating library, are devoured with indisciminate and insatiable avidity. Hence the mind is secretly corrupted.'[83] In Germany, a connection between excessive reading and over-indulgence leading to self-destruction was expressed in an exactly contemporaneous book by the popular philosopher Bergk, whose writings have recently been resuscitated by Martha Woodmansee:

Never has there been as much reading in Germany as today! But the majority of readers devour the most wretched and tasteless novels with a voracious appetite that spoils head and heart. By reading such worthless material people get used to idleness that only the greatest exertion can overcome again. . . . The consequences of such tasteless and mindless reading are thus senseless waste, an insurmountable fear of any kind of exertion, a boundless bent for luxury, repression of the voices of conscience, ennui, and an early death.[84]

---

[81] *Fraser's Magazine* (Apr. 1832), repr. in *Collected Works*, xxvii. 62; quoted in Erickson, *Economy of Literary Form*, 106.

[82] See Coleridge, *BL* ii. 142, discussed in Ch. 3, below; and Wordsworth, Preface to the *Lyrical Ballads* (*Wordsworth Prose*, i. 128).

[83] *An Enquiry into the Duties of the Female Sex* (1799), 122–3; quoted in Poovey, *The Proper Lady and the Woman Writer*, 20.

[84] *The Art of Reading Books* (1799), 411–12; quoted in Woodmansee, *The Author, Art, and the Market: Rereading the History of Aesthetics* (New York: Columbia University Press, 1994), 89.

There was a widespread and explicit association of excessive writing with women whose reproductive capacities were seen to be out of control. 'Who are those ever multiplying authors, that with unparalleled fecundity are overstocking the world with their quick-succeeding progeny?', wrote Hannah More, in her *Strictures on the Modern System of Female Education* (1799): 'They are novel-writers; the easiness of whose production is at once the cause of their own fruitfulness, and of the almost infinitely numerous race of imitators to whom they give birth.'[85] The novel, in particular, became the focus for fears of reduplication, in which biological metaphors frequently recurred: 'The press daily teems with these publications which are the trash of the circulating libraries', wrote Burton, in his *Lectures on Female Education and Manners*: 'A perusal of them in rapid succession is in fact a misemployment of time; as, in most novels there is a similarity in the incidents and characters; and these perhaps are unnatural'.[86]

Even Mary Wollstonecraft, a talented novelist herself, shared with her contemporaries an intense disenchantment with the contemporary novel: 'From reading to writing novels the transition is very easy', she complained, in an early and characteristically acerbic review: 'and the ladies, of course, take care to supply the circulating libraries with ever varying still the same productions. "Of making many books there is no end," when talents and knowledge are out of the question'.[87] Typical of this cultural moment was Wollstonecraft's fear that readers were usurping the place of writers, rather than improving their capacity to reflect on what they read. Her use of the circulating-library to symbolize the ceaselessly repetitive pumping of literature through the system was also a recurrent contemporary motif, in which monetary and medical preoccupations converged—for the health of the nation was brought under question when the amount of reading-matter was seen to increase in inverse proportion to the capacity for reflective reading. Novels and novel-reading continued to be the site for ideologically motivated anxieties about women's reproduction and health throughout the nineteenth

[85] *Strictures on the Modern System of Female Education. With a view of the principles and conduct prevalent among women of rank and fortune* (2 vols.; London: Cadell and Davies, 1799), i. 184.

[86] *Lectures on Female Education and Manners* (New York: Samuel Campbell, 1794). Note esp. the recurrence of metaphors relating novels to reproduction (the word 'teeming'; and also the ideas of rapid succession and sameness).

[87] *Analytical Review*, 1 (June 1788), article 33. Wollstonecraft is reviewing *Edward and Harriet, or the Happy Recovery: a Sentimental Novel. By a Lady.* See *The Works of Mary Wollstonecraft*, ed. Janet Todd and Marilyn Butler (7 vols., London: William Pickering, 1989), vii. 20.

century, as Kate Flint has demonstrated in her book on the woman reader.[88] Poetry has tended to provide the focus for more masculine preoccupations with heredity, succession, and selection—explaining the strong Darwinian undercurrent, for instance, in this warning from Harold Bloom: 'Who reads must choose, since there is literally not enough time to read everything, even if one does nothing but read.... The Canon...has become a choice among texts struggling with one another for survival'.[89]

If the excessive multiplication of literature was metonymically connected with fear of overpopulation, the anonymity of audiences (and of reviewers) was a figurative displacement for more troubling anxieties about loss of self-identity consequent on industrial expansion and the overcrowding of England's great cities. As Charles Rzepka puts it, describing these larger phenomena,

Greater social mobility, mass urbanization...had the general effect of making England an island of strangers. It became increasingly difficult for the self to find a recognizable place in English society, harder to tell if what others saw was the true self, or if the self was being compromised, made false, taken away from its 'owner' by more fluid and less dependable categories of public identification.[90]

In addition, Romantic writers experienced Anglocentric fears that the infiltration of foreign literary tastes into national culture might threaten identity on a larger and more pervasive scale. These fears were most famously brought together, in a loosely associative cluster of prejudices, in a passage from the Preface to *Lyrical Ballads* (1800) which would not be out of place in Malthus's 'Essay on Population'. Complaining that 'a multitude of causes, unknown to former times, are now acting with combined force to blunt the mind, and, unfitting it for all voluntary exertion, to reduce it to a state of almost savage torpor', Wordsworth identified the foremost of these as 'the great national events which are daily taking place, and the encreasing accumulation of men in cities, where the uniformity of their occupations produces a craving for extraordinary incident which the rapid communication of intelligence hourly gratifies'. Setting the tone for a subsequent (high Romantic) dissociation of genius from urban conditions, Wordsworth posited a connection

---

[88] *The Woman Reader: 1837–1914* (Oxford: Clarendon Press, 1993).
[89] *Western Canon*, 15, 20.
[90] *The Self as Mind: Vision and Identity in Wordsworth, Coleridge, and Keats* (Cambridge, Mass.: Harvard University Press, 1986), 23; quoted in Ross, *Contours of Masculine Desire*, 24.

between the overcrowding of cities, poverty of intellect, and addiction to stimulants. He also discovered a malignant influence in the 'frantic novels, sickly and stupid German Tragedies, and deluges of idle and extravagant stories in verse' which, he asserted, were driving 'the invaluable works of our elder writers' into neglect.[91] The fears of overpopulation and overstimulation which he associated with contemporary living conditions were thus exacerbated by a xenophobic anxiety with respect to continental literature, which threatened to flood and drown England's treasured national heritage.

Later in the century, De Quincey related an incident in his *Suspiria De Profundis* which gives a special twist to the twin fears of anonymity and overpopulation, amalgamated in a childhood fantasy of literature's endless self-reduplication. Typically, as well as appropriately, the episode is itself prolix—running to six or seven pages, and incorporating a number of digressions and overlapping time-segments to narrate events whose cumulative and associative significance is only gradually disclosed.[92] But the salient narrative features are as follows: when quite a young child, De Quincey claims to have experienced a 'craving' for the 'gratification' supplied by books, much as he would later be addicted to opium. This craving led to his contracting a debt with his local bookseller—a debt which caused him a disproportionate degree of guilt and dread because he had agreed to purchase two books (a History of Great Britain and a History of Navigation), the first of which would appear in sixty or eighty parts, the second in an unspecified number of volumes. He was thus contracted (as he saw it) to infinity:

Now, when I considered with myself what a huge thing the sea was, and that so many thousands of captains, commodores, admirals, were eternally running up and down it, and scoring lines upon its face so rankly, that in some of the main 'streets' and 'squares' (as one might call them) their tracks would blend into one undistinguishable blot,—I began to fear that such a work tended to infinity. What was little England to the universal sea? (p. 131)

De Quincey figures his own humiliation in the face of an overwhelming magnitude of yet-to-be-discovered knowledge by way of analogy with England's minuscule size on a globe that is criss-crossed to the point of opacity by voyagers intent on discovery and imperialist expansion. At

[91] *Wordsworth Prose*, i. 128.

[92] In *Confessions of an English Opium Eater and Other Writings*, ed. with introd. Grevel Lindop (Oxford: Oxford University Press, 1989), 129–35; page refs. will be included in the text.

this stage in the narrative, his anxieties are still relatively controlled by the thought that the volume will run to 'perhaps fourscore parts'; and he is able to diminish the globe's size by imagining it as a city with streets and squares. But as the fantasy develops, his fear amplifies; and when he is told (teasingly, by the bookseller's assistant) that the book might run to 15,000 or so volumes, he reaches a point of crisis in the thought that 'there might be supplements to supplements—the work might positively *never* end. On one pretence or another, if an author or publisher might add 500 volumes, he might add another 15,000' (p. 133). Significantly, at this stage, the image of the city returns, with a new and sinister significance, to reinforce his impression of inconceivable power:

> I saw by the imprint, and I heard, that this work emanated from London, a vast centre of mystery to me, and the more so, as a thing unseen at any time by my eyes, and nearly 200 miles distant. I felt the fatal truth, that here was a ghostly cobweb radiating into all the provinces from the mighty metropolis. I secretly had trodden upon the outer circumference, had damaged or deranged the fine threads and links,—concealment or reparation there could be none. Slowly perhaps, but surely, the vibration would travel back to London. The ancient spider that sat there at the centre, would rush along the network through all longitudes and latitudes, until he found the responsible caitiff, author of so much mischief. (pp. 133–4)

Where the globe had earlier been likened to a city, the city is now likened to the globe, its web of streets becoming the lines of 'longitude and latitude' that extend out into the provinces, allowing the spider to exact punishment on the terrified child. Significantly, in this arachnophobic fantasy, London is shrouded in 'mystery', its cobweb is 'ghostly' and the spider at its centre is 'ancient': De Quincey here articulates, from a child's perspective, all the terrors that attach to the written book as an embodiment of sacred authority and patriarchal power. The 'dim terrors' he remembers experiencing in connection with the Stationers' Company are not amplified, but are presumably caused by injunctions against copying—as though, by upsetting the balance of power between authors and their readers even minutely, the child is found guilty of a secret desire to plagiarize material he wishes merely to read. Conflating the fears of readers with those of writers, De Quincey here transforms the whole system of authorship, printing, production, and circulation into an image which hauntingly embodies his sense of persecution by mysterious powers-that-be:

Even, with less ignorance than mine, there *was* something to appal a child's imagination in the vast systematic machinery by which any elaborate work could disperse itself, could levy money, could put questions and get answers—all in profound silence, nay, even in darkness—searching every nook of every town, and of every hamlet in so populous a kingdom. (p. 134)

De Quincey's rhetorical mode might be characterized as ironically sublime—the ironic dimension being supplied by an overlaying of adult 'diminutio' on the child's credulous exaggerations. But when, in the denouement of this extended nightmare, De Quincey imagines the delivery of his books to his very doorstep, the sublime meets the ridiculous in a comic climax worthy of Swift or Sterne:

Looking out, I should perceive a procession of carts and waggons, all advancing in measured movements; each in turn would present its rear, deliver its cargo of volumes, by shooting them, like a load of coals, on the lawn and wheel off to the rear, by way of clearing the road for its successors. Then the impossibility of even asking the servants to cover with sheets, or counter-panes, or table-cloths, such a mountainous, such a 'star-y-pointing' record of my past offences lying in so conspicuous a situation! Men would not know my guilt merely, they would see it. (pp. 134–5)

Ostensibly, De Quincey's simile likens the deposit of his order of books to the delivery of coal. But it also suggests, through a series of scato-logical associations—the repetition of the word 'rear', the undignified 'shooting' of cargo onto the lawn, the allusion to a mountainous pile in a conspicuous situation, the frightened child's anxiety to have his servants cover this 'record of his past offences' with sheets and counterpanes—a subliminal likeness between books and excrement, this latter the end product of his guilty and secret indulgence. Perhaps echoing Swift's pun on 'order'/'ordure',[93] the interconnection between books, coal, and excreta in De Quincey's evolving simile suggests a habit of conspicuous consumption over which the child himself has no control.

Taken as an integrated narrative, De Quincey's fantasy figures the reader as the helpless consumer of books and as the humiliated victim of a powerful machinery of literary production designed precisely to re-mind him of his anonymous unimportance. This nightmare—of liter-ature wrested from the hands of writers and readers, delivered over to

---

[93] See the closing couplet of Swift's poem, 'The Lady's Dressing Room', ll. 143–4: 'Such Order from Confusion sprung, | Such gaudy Tulips rais'd from Dung.' References are to *The Poems of Alexander Pope*, ed. John Butt (Bungay, Suffolk: Methuen, 1965).

the forces of the market place, divested of spirit and reduced to mere waste-matter in a culture of commodities—characterizes many of the ingredients of the anxiety of reception as it was experienced by high Romantic writers. But although it has elements that are historically determined and specific (the imperialist metaphor of navigation, the parochial emphasis given to De Quincey's fear of the metropolis, and the reference to the Stationers' Company) it can also be seen to prefigure twentieth-century nightmares of centralized power and consumerism, in which the individual's identity and agency are extinguished. Crucially, as I hope to show, this is a nightmare for which high Romanticism is itself partly responsible. In considering the historical emergence of Romanticism as a species of reaction-formation against the new power of reading, we shall see how writers weave their own 'ghostly web' from the materials of the past, seeking to consolidate their diminishing sense of authority through strategies of mystification. Just as De Quincey's fantasy turns on a significant inversion—articulating its terror of futurity as a fear of the past and its terror of reading as a fear of the vast authoritative machinery by which books are reproduced—so we shall see that the system of defences which characterizes high Romanticism turns on a similar dialectic, in which writers and readers figure each other as reflexes of themselves.

CHAPTER 2

Case Study (1): Coleridge

Every censure, every sarcasm...which the critic...can make good, is the critic's right. The writer is authorised to reply, but not to complain.

Coleridge, *Biographia Literaria*, 1817

Whom should I choose for my Judge? the earnest, impersonal reader,
 Who, in the work, forgets me and the world and himself!
You who have eyes to detect, and Gall to Chastise the imperfect,
 Have you the heart, too, that loves,—feels and rewards the Compleat?

Coleridge, MS Fragment, 1805

I. COLERIDGE'S SEARCH FOR SYMPATHY

In the opening lecture of his 1811 series on Shakespeare and Milton, Coleridge makes a connection between the occurrence of powerful or extraordinary events and the engendering of interpreters. Momentous happenings, he suggests, are inevitably productive of witnesses; but we should beware of their proliferation. With evident distaste, he argues that 'the enormous stimulant power of Events' makes the desire to be strongly stimulated 'almost an appetite'. He refers to the 'enormous multiplication of Authors & Books'; to the expansion of reviews, magazines and selections, newspapers and novels; and he complains that the ready availability of so much reading-matter has a damaging effect on powers of judgement and evaluation (*Lectures*, i. 186). Crabb Robinson, reporting on the lecture in *The Times*, referred to the speaker's disapproval of 'general and indiscriminate reading; the rage for public speaking, and the habit consequently induced of requiring instantaneous intelligibility' (*Lectures*, i. 195). A report in the *Sun* picked out his condemnation of 'the rage for violent excitement from extraordinary events' (*Lectures*, i. 196). In *The Statesman's Manual*, Coleridge laments that the nation, 'dieted at the two public *ordinaries* of Literature, the circulating libraries and the periodical press', has given itself over to 'the frivolous craving for novelty' (*SM* 25); while in *The Friend*, he objects that amusement is the main criterion of periodical literature, and sensation the object of readers in general. About novels he is even more dismissive: 'the habit of receiving pleasure without any exertion of thought, by the mere excitement of curiosity and sensibility, may be justly ranked among the worst effects of habitual novel reading' (*Friend*, i. 20). Sustaining his conservative disapprobation of reading-as-consumption, he complains in *Biographia Literaria* of a lowering of standards in the general reader (*BL* i. 39); of the debilitating effect of reviews on the powers of discrimination (*BL* i. 48); of the superficiality of the reading-public, ever-growing with the diffusion of literature (*BL* i. 57); and even of the 'depravation of the public mind' (*BL* ii. 229). A reference to 'promiscuous authorship, and reading not promiscuous only because it is disproportionally most conversant with the compositions of the day' (*BL* ii. 142–3) is echoed in the Prospectus to his Lectures of 1818, where he condemns the '*mischief* of unconnected and promiscuous reading' (*Lectures*, ii. 40).

Coleridge's contempt for the reading-public differs from other eighteenth- and nineteenth-century diatribes in the sustained forcefulness of its invective. That his anxiety of reception was acute—more so, perhaps, than any other writer's in the period—is well attested, both in a recurrent nervousness about how his writings would be received, and in his lifelong struggle to establish and sustain a sympathetic readership. Several recent commentators, in showing how significantly his writing was shaped by these concerns, have observed an incommensurability between his expectations of readers—how he imagined and projected his ideal audience—and what, in practice, he understood to be their intellectual habits and capacities. His struggle as journalist and prose writer was marked by the double bind of needing to create 'the taste by which he is to be enjoyed'[1]—or rather, of having to induce the faculty by which he was to be understood. *The Friend*, for Paul Hamilton, is a huge essay in communication of this kind: it tries to 'make public and common currency of difficult philosophical ideas';[2] while for Stephen

---

[1] See Wordsworth's 'Essay Supplementary to the Preface', 1815, in *Wordsworth Prose* iii. 80.

[2] *Coleridge's Poetics* (Oxford: Basil Blackwell, 1983), 114.

Bygrave, Coleridge is 'at the time of the *Biographia*... addressing an audience he has not yet invented'.[3]

To some extent, the intensity of Coleridge's anxiety was due to the ambitiousness of his projects, and the frustration of talking (or rather writing) into a void. Tim Fulford has seen how closely the need for a sympathetic audience was linked to Coleridge's search for spiritual community; and why he preferred the immediacy of spoken communication, 'with its possibility of intimate unity between speaker and listener', to more distanced forms of connectiveness. Striving for 'a relationship with his audience in which... religious and emotional enchantment united all in one conviction', Coleridge replaced unknown readers whose tastes he could not anticipate with intimate reading-circles, frequently made up of family and friends.[4] In literary dialogues with receptive readers, he temporarily fulfilled his craving for acceptance and validation; while in the genre of the 'conversation poem' he found his surest guarantee of sympathy. In both modes of discourse, an 'implausible public' was replaced by a 'like-minded coterie',[5] so that Coleridge was assured of his audience in advance, rather than having to induce sympathy rhetorically.

This was the constructive side of Coleridge's anxiety; but he was not always so resourceful. 'To be beloved is all I need', he once wrote ('The Pains of Sleep', l. 51); and the urgency of this need is apparent in the disclaimers that frequently preface his poems, as in the defensive remarks that punctuate his publications.[6] Even in lecturing, where he had the opportunity for immediate and inspired communication, and where he reputedly mesmerized his audience, confidence was often lacking. In the third of his 1808 lecture series, he publicly confessed to feeling a 'self-dissatisfaction bordering on self-reproach' at his own lecturing performance (*Lectures*, i. 64); and one of his audience complained of 'the vice of apologising, anticipating & repeating' (*Lectures*, i. 259) which betrayed his unconfidence. So worried was he by the thought of causing offence amongst his listeners that he restrained himself, in an 1811 lecture, from commenting on the poetry of his

[3] 'Land of the Giants: Gaps, Limits and Audiences in Coleridge's *Biographia Literaria*', in Stephen Copley and John Whale (eds.), *Beyond Romanticism* (London: Routledge, 1992), 42.

[4] *Coleridge's Figurative Language* (Houndmills, Basingstoke: Macmillan, 1991), 2, 5.

[5] Paul Hamilton, 'Coleridge', in David Pirie (ed.), *The Penguin History of the Romantic Period* (Harmondsworth, Middlesex: Penguin, 1994), 198.

[6] Most famously, the Preface to 'Kubla Khan' and the letter 'from a friend' included in *BL*, ch. 13.

own day (*Lectures*, i. 159): as he later explained, in *Biographia*, he wished to 'furnish no possible pretext for the unthinking to misconstrue, or the malignant to misapply [his] words, and having stampt their own meaning on them, to pass them as current coin in the marts of garrulity or detraction' (*BL* i. 54).

As the metaphor of false coining suggests, Coleridge's anxiety was at base about the devaluation of literature, and the demise of the author as vehicle of truth. In one of his 1811 lectures, he lamented the fact that the authority of the author had been successively destabilized through history: authors were 'At first Oracles, then preceptors, then agreeable Companions, but now Culprits by anticipation' (*Lectures*, i. 186–7). Coleridge blamed the rise of criticism for this demotion; books and authors lost ground as readers gained it; or, as he put it, the critic was 'still rising' as the author sank (*BL* i. 59). Although he acknowledged the dangers of bardolatry, he nonetheless professed a belief that the praise of authors was far more productive than criticism (*Lectures*, i. 268); and that very few readers were in a position to judge the works they read. The word 'public', he claimed, was 'of pernicious effect by habituating every Reader to consider himself as the Judge & therefore the Superior of the Writer who yet if he has any justifiable claim to write ought to be his Superior' (*Lectures*, i. 187). The inadequacies of individual readers were hidden by giving readers in general the right to put authors on trial. Readers were currently flattered, he complained in *The Friend*, by being appealed to as an infallible judge: he dismissed them himself, sweepingly, as 'the half-instructed Many' (*Friend*, i. 126).

Coleridge's sense of a debasement in the value of literature became particularly intense where reviewers were concerned. On the surface, his grudge was that reviewers lacked fixed canons of criticism, substituting for them 'arbitrary dictation and petulant sneers' (*BL* i. 62). He complained of the carelessness of critics—their disregard for truth, and their tendency to fragment, misquote, or otherwise misrepresent the materials they read. In his *Morning Post* squib 'To a Critic' (1801), he attacks a reviewer who had 'extracted a passage from a poem without adding a word respecting the context, and then derided it as unintelligible'. The physical mutilation of the critic is an appropriate revenge, graphically literalizing Coleridge's need to answer violence with violence:

> Most candid critic, what if I,
> By way of joke, pull out your eye,

> And holding up the fragment, cry,
> 'Ha ha! that men such fools should be!
> Behold this shapeless Dab!—and he
> Who own'd it, fancied it could *see!*'
> The joke were mighty analytic,
> But should you like it, candid critic?

> (*CPW* ii. 962)

This poem provides a witty reversal of the language of victimization usually applied to poets; and it draws on contemporary constructions of the critic as wilfully cruel and destructive.

Coleridge refers repeatedly to the arbitrary nature of current criticism (*BL* ii. 113); and in the second volume of *Biographia* he attempts to introduce standards of evaluative judgement, which would educate and transform public taste. His definition of the ideal critic, at the beginning of chapter 21, is a constructive attempt to establish common ground between critical and creative authority, and to set up a code of practice for criticism in general. It is important, he says, for individual reviewers 'to administer judgement according to a constitution and code of laws' (*BL* ii. 110). But behind the quest for consistent critical values there lay a disproportionate feeling of personal and symbolic threat. The opening pages of *Biographia* explore the fragile status of the author in face of his detractors (*BL* i. 5–13); and although later claiming that his original sin was a 'careless indifference to public opinion', Coleridge's vulnerability in the opposite direction is only too apparent (*BL* i. 44). He refers to the 'dirty passions and impudence, of anonymous criticism' (*BL* i. 13); to the personal malice of reviewers (*BL* ii. 157); and to the malignity of reviewing by anticipation (*BL* ii. 241). In an epigram entitled 'Modern Critics', first published in the *Biographia*, he anathematizes the spirit of defamation which he sees as a pervasive feature of the age of personality—and all the more so for taking place under the guise of impersonal detachment or disinterestedness:

> No private grudge they need, no personal spite,
> The *viva sectio* is its own delight!
> All enmity, all envy, they disclaim,
> Disinterested thieves of our good name—
> Cool, sober murderers of their neighbours' fame!

> (*CPW* ii. 972)

When he quotes Jeremy Taylor, on two separate occasions in his lectures, it is to suggest not just the powers of misrepresentation which readers may have, but their invasiveness, and their ability to appropriate: 'no other Patron, but Providence, can defend him, that writes, from him that reads and understands either too much or too little' (*Lectures*, i. 123); and, later, 'the breath of the people is like the voice of an exterminating Angel, not so killing but so secret' (*Lectures*, i. 190 n.). What is at stake, here, is the writing-subject as a personal identity, with the right either to preserve its own privacy or to make public its inner world. The impertinence of reviewers is that, under protection from their own anonymity, they invade private space.[7] As Coleridge puts it, of the reviewer who turns gossip,

> he steals the unquiet, the deforming passions of the World into the Museum; into the very place which, next to the chapel and oratory, should be our sanctuary, and secure place of refuge; offers abominations on the altar of the muses; and makes its sacred paling the very circle in which he conjures up the lying and prophane spirit. (*BL* ii. 109–10)

For Coleridge, the pernicious effects of uncomprehending readers were not to be underestimated. But beyond this there was a much deeper threat posed by the anonymity of reviewers, and of the reading public in general. Anonymity is used, Coleridge claimed, to authorize opinions: reviewers are 'no longer to be questioned without exposing the complainant to ridicule, because, forsooth, they are *anonymous* critics, and authorised as "synodical individuals" to speak of themselves plurali majestatico' (*BL* i. 42). Since Coleridge's own belief in authority worked the other way—in terms of its attachment to authorial identity—there was something especially affronting in the notion that these two functions might become separated. The transferral of authority from authors with identities to readers with none may be read symbolically, as a frightening reminder of the unstable status of identity, at a time when authority is under question. More suggestively, it may also be read as an uncanny premonition of Roland Barthes's claim, that 'the birth of the reader must be at the cost of the death of the author'.[8]

---

[7] Coleridge's personal grudge in this respect was towards Francis Jeffrey, whom he accused of having been 'unwarrant[ab]ly, severe on my morals and Understanding'. See Griggs, iii. 116–17. For discussion of Coleridge's fate at the hand of reviewers, see *BL* i. 50 n. 1.

[8] 'The Death of the Author', in David Lodge (ed.), *Modern Criticism and Theory: A Reader* (London: Longman, 1988), 172.

II. FIGURATIONS OF THE READING-PUBLIC

Coleridge's anxiety focused on the erosion of that sacred authority which attaches to the writing-subject, and which found itself under threat, for reasons outlined in Chapter 1, at the beginning of the nineteenth century. Taken together, and in the wake of the French Revolution, the material and spiritual embodiments of a levelling Zeitgeist had profound implications for this always theocentric writer; who responded, not just as though he were among the few surviving members of an endangered species, but as though (in a kind of Malthusian nightmare) the nation were about to be overrun by a new race of unreflecting, unspiritual readers.[9] Combining a number of different ingredients, his metaphors for the reading-public evince his revulsion at the threat which reading posed for writing; and they frequently take on a political colouring. The new power of reading is not only associated with current events and news; it is figured in terms of rampant activity, and seen as either sexually or politically questionable. 'The multitudinous PUBLIC, shaped into personal unity by the magic of abstraction, sits nominal despot on the throne of criticism' (*BL* i. 59): this and other such metaphors are a reminder that Coleridge's understanding of literary history is heavily inflected by his response to the French Revolution, taking its anti-revisionary flavour from there. Literary (like monarchical) power must, in his view, be legitimately inherited; if it is violently overthrown or wrongfully appropriated, chaos will ensue. Anonymous critics are imagined usurping the throne of criticism, in the same way that Satan, Cromwell, Robespierre, all gave themselves kingly powers. This is upstart republicanism, writ large. Coleridge saw the 'multitudinous public' (shaped not by the Logos, but by the 'magic of abstraction') as a parodic version of the multeity-in-unity which was his personal creed; and as a mockery of the monarchical values he held dear ('sits nominal despot on the throne of criticism'). Yet the parody works against itself; for is there not also, in the development of his regal metaphor, a suggestion that monarchs themselves might be vulnerable, their status nominal, and their power dependent on mystification? Some of the mistrust towards regal power which Coleridge had felt during his radical phase (1795–6) emerges implicitly in the vehicle of this

---

[9] For a literary/anthropological survey of the idea of endangered species, see Fiona Stafford, *The Last of the Race: The Growth of a Myth from Milton to Darwin* (Oxford: Clarendon Press, 1994); and for the Romantics' concern with the population crisis as a species of the sublime, see Frances Ferguson, *Solitude and the Sublime* (New York: Routledge, 1992), 114–28.

metaphor, as well as being openly stated in its tenor. This ambivalence suggests that while upholding the sanctity of tradition, Coleridge also perceived how his cherished values might be undermined from within; and how responsibility for the erosion of authority could be a two-way process.

Coleridge's figurative language may associate the reading-public, in Burkean fashion, with arbitrary dictators and unruly, faceless mobs— both of them, by implication, the monstrous products of Revolution. But there are also more subtle suggestions that he saw indiscriminate reading as the by-product of a creeping laxity in the nation's morals. He refers scathingly to 'that restless craving for the wonders of the day, which in conjunction with the appetite for publicity is spreading like an efflorescence on the surface of our national character' (*SM* 8); and reading-habits are frequently condemned by him as 'promiscuous'—a word which Milton had used, in an educational context, in *Areopagitica*.[10] But where Milton had used it paradoxically, to suggest that a diet of indiscriminate reading fostered the liberty to choose (and so eventually to choose with wisdom), Coleridge uses the word without irony, as a term of abuse which carried the fullest sexual connotations. Furthermore, a subliminal Malthusian allusion links the allegation of 'promiscuity' in readers with the dread of an overpopulous reading-public. In the chain of metonymies which connect indiscriminate reading-habits with excessive reproduction on the one hand and wasteful consumption on the other, there appears to be a topical explanation for the nation's depleted literary resources.

The charge of promiscuity extends even to those whose responsibility it was to uphold tradition. Describing the burgeoning power of readers as 'the misgrowth of *our luxuriant activity*' (*SM* 36), Coleridge suggests that the energies of writers (here represented by the royal 'we') have become misdirected, or run riot. Their empty and unspiritual productivity (Pope was similarly eloquent about scribblers in *The Dunciad*) had produced a 'misgrowth'—cancerous perhaps, or at least malformed—in the shape of an amorphous appetitive reading-parasite, preying on the nation. Since botanical images at this time were sometimes complex symbols in moral, social, and political discourse, it may be the case that Coleridge's metaphor carries a specific political resonance. Alan Bewell, examining the role played by botany in the sexual debates of the 1790s,

---

[10] *Areopagitica* (London, 1644), in *The Complete Prose Works of John Milton*, gen. ed. D. Wolfe (8 vols. in 10, 1953–82), ii, ed. E. Sirluck (New Haven: Yale University Press, 1959), 514–15.

has shown how, in popular conservatism, plants were thought to have a 'democratic bent', and could be 'enlisted as a threatening fifth column of a "New Morality"'. More specifically, luxuriants were often viewed as 'the monsters of the floral world', and the horticultural discourse on luxuriants could be adapted to social critique: 'The "wild" flower could be associated with health, the "luxuriant" with the degeneration ushered in by human society.' In a footnote, Bewell further observes that 'Sebastian Vaillant, in his discourse on luxuriants, equated them with cannibalistic castrating females, monsters who devour the testicles of the male'.[11]

If luxuriance was the signifier of a conservative revulsion against the reading-public, might it not also be associated with Regency indulgence in luxury and sexual excess?[12] Just as the monarchy was endangered by its failure to preserve the chivalrous and family ideals which were the cornerstone of Coleridge's (as of Burke's) conservatism, so the symbiotic organism of writer–reader had become sick or unbalanced through the 'luxuriant activity' of writers, whose function—unless it was spiritual—Coleridge saw as otiose. His critique did not limit itself to the unworthiness of readers, then, but applied to the literary scene as a whole, which he saw as subject to a more pervasive moral and spiritual degeneracy. He insisted that the 'habitual unreflectingness' which characterized the nation at large, could 'in this country be deemed blameless in none' (*SM* 6–7).

Some responsibility for lazy reading is thus accorded to authors themselves; but not to authors such as Coleridge, whose prime endeavour was to encourage the spiritual growth of an elect audience. At a time when literacy was on the increase, and, in particular, the female reader was becoming empowered, it is difficult to avoid the elitism (and with it the anti-democratic, anti-feminist implications) of Coleridge's reading-theory. Hardly coincidental is the fact that his most condemnatory

---

[11] '"Jacobin Plants": Botany as Social Theory in the 1790's', *Wordsworth Circle*, 20/3 (Summer 1989), 132–9, see esp. p. 138.

[12] For Coleridge's views on the conduct of the royal family, and esp. his condemnation of the Prince Regent's hypocritical and unchivalrous response to Princess Caroline's alleged promiscuity, see Tim Fulford, 'Coleridge and the Royal Family: The Politics of Androgyny', in id and Morton D. Paley (eds.), *Coleridge's Visionary Languages: Essays in Honour of John Beer* (Cambridge: Boydell and Brewer, 1993), 67–82. Coleridge's critique of lax morals is discernible also in a passage from *SM* ascribing 'the causes of the revolution and fearful chastisement of France' to 'restlessness, presumption, sensual indulgence, and the idolatrous reliance on false philosophy in the whole domestic, social, and political life of the stirring and effective part of the community' (*SM* 33–4). In context, a parallel with Regency Britain is strongly implied.

remarks about lazy reading-habits are reserved for readers of contempory novels and members of circulating-libraries. Nor is it chance that the figures he deploys for the lazy reader are frequently gendered: witness his use of Mistress Quickly's speech to exemplify that 'absence of Method, which characterises the uneducated', and is 'occasioned by an habitual submission of the understanding to mere events and images as such' (*Friend*, i. 451). Or his condemnation of habitual novel-reading, which, he claims, encourages a taste for short and unconnected sentences—a Frenchified style he likens to a woman at home, receiving guests:

> Like idle morning visitors, the brisk and breathless periods hurry in and hurry off in quick and profitless succession; each indeed for the moments of its stay prevents the pain of vacancy, while it indulges the love of sloth; but all together they leave the mistress of the house...flat and exhausted, incapable of attending to her own concerns, and unfitted for the conversation of more rational guests. (*Friend*, i. 21)

This critique of restless passivity has been ingeniously described by Jerome Christensen as 'metaphor become fantasy—a fantasy of masturbation';[13] but more significant is its explicitly gendered tenor. Coleridge repeatedly and pointedly linked the feminine with what he calls the 'epigrammatic unconnected periods of the fashionable *Anglo-gallican taste*' (*Friend*, i. 20). Just as, a decade or so earlier, it had seemed to Wordsworth that the nation's craving for 'gross and violent stimulants' was exacerbated by newspapers, Gothic novels, and 'sickly and stupid German tragedies',[14] so Coleridge associated the female fashion for novel-reading and the French language with cheap sensationalism. As Christensen points out, 'The hurried, inadequate communication of the truth' is seen by Coleridge as 'the vice of the Enlightenment, the *French* Enlightenment, whose ideology and whose very style incur the *Friend's* unremitting hostility'.[15]

The consistency with which Coleridge denounced the reading-public has led Paul Hamilton to conclude that he was incapable of a generous

---

[13] The ingredients of this fantasy are, as Christensen describes them, 'solitary habits; involuntary visitations; breathless, hurrying thoughts; sudden exhaustion; and the superstitious fear of...imbecility'. See *Coleridge's Blessed Machine of Language* (Ithaca, NY: Cornell University Press, 1981), 206.

[14] See the Preface to *Lyrical Ballads* (1800), discussed in Ch. 1, above.

[15] *Coleridge's Blessed Machine of Language*, 205. Conversely, for Coleridge's ideas on what constitutes 'manliness' of style, see n. 54, below.

engagement with his audience. This meant, Hamilton argues, that he was also unlikely to have entered into the kinds of sophisticated ironic play which critics such as Kathleen Wheeler (and, more recently, Tilottama Rajan) have seen as crucial to his hermeneutic enterprise.[16] 'We must remember that he conceived of his reader as a member of the reading public, and not as an ideal figure', says Hamilton: 'To idealize this figure is to put history on one side and ignore the entire political dimension of his discussion of reader-response.'[17] My own position is different from Hamilton's, and arises from the belief that historical and hermeneutic approaches to the reader may have important things to say to each other, even if these cannot be heard from either side of the materialist–idealist divide. Coleridge's ideal reader bears a significant relation to his views on readers and the reading-public; and the apparent contradictions which Hamilton detects may well be explicable (even resolvable) in terms of Coleridge's dual function as poet-critic.

At a historical moment when reading was in the ascendancy, and criticism was beginning to lose its secondary status, Coleridge found himself playing what appears at first sight to be a double game. This doubleness does not work simply, according to a binary opposition between poet and critic; but rather finds itself redoubled, across (and partly so as to interrogate) the critical–creative divide. As poet, responding to the new and urgent pressure to be original, Coleridge evolved subtle revisionary strategies in relation to poetic authority, which show the adventurousness of his reading-practices, and of the role he envisaged for readers as writers.[18] Moreover, in the use of framing devices (prefaces, footnotes, marginal comments) around his poems, as well as in the inclusion of model readers within them, he elaborately foregrounds the reader's role in constructing meaning.[19] Yet at the same time, he attempts to place constraints on the reader's activity, so as to preserve his own authority as poet: indeed those same devices which are

---

[16] See Wheeler, *Sources, Processes and Methods in Coleridge's Biographia Literaria* (Cambridge: Cambridge University Press, 1980) and Rajan, *The Supplement of Reading: Figures of Understanding in Romantic Theory and Practice* (Ithaca, NY: Cornell University Press, 1990).

[17] *Coleridge's Poetics*, 21.

[18] See e.g. my accounts of Coleridge's allusive language in *Coleridge, Wordsworth, and the Language of Allusion* (Oxford: Clarendon Press, 1986) and *'Paradise Lost' and the Romantic Reader* (Oxford: Clarendon Press, 1993).

[19] The gloss attached to 'The Ancient Mariner' provides the most famous example of Coleridge's framing devices; while the intervening figure of Sara Coleridge in 'The Aeolian Harp' and the mediation of the wedding guest in 'The Ancient Mariner' are two obvious examples of his use of model readers.

taken by some to be the registers of 'Romantic irony' have been used by others to demonstrate Coleridge's consolidation of his 'oracular' authority.[20]

Conversely, in his role as critic, he saw it as his mission to protect the sanctity and authority of poetic genius from would-be usurpers, whom he chose to figure as readers, rather than as writers. Yet the mode of criticism he proposed was one which singularly collapsed the distinctions between creative and critical practices, thus elevating the status of reading. Indeed *Biographia*, of all other Romantic texts, began the process whereby, as Geoffrey Hartman puts it in a very different context, 'literary criticism [crosses over] into literature'.[21] One only has to glance at Coleridge's *Marginalia* to see how extensive that crossing is: how very unmarginal, in other words, were the insights of a reader whose commentaries and 'asides' encroached on the texts he was reading, as though to proclaim a spirit of independent creativity, actively at work in the reading-process.[22]

Complexities and contradictions of the kind described above arise partly from the duality of the writing–reading subject, whose perennial condition I outlined in the Preface to this book. But they became particularly evident at a pivotal moment in the history of reading, when ideas of authorship and original genius were under construction, and the roles of poet and critic were seen as mutually antagonistic. It would be interesting, in Coleridge's case, to pursue these contradictions into the arena of psychobiography. Particularly striking is the consistency with which he refers to the reading-public in metaphors of violence, promiscuity, appetite, and rage—this despite the fact that his main objection to contemporary reading-habits is their inactivity. It is also striking that so many of these figurations of the reading-public are themselves paradoxical. Just as Pope's Dulness was prolifically

[20] For a compelling argument in favour of Coleridge as Romantic ironist, see Kathleen Wheeler, *The Creative Mind in Coleridge's Poetry* (London: Heinemann, 1981). The opposite view is put by David Riede, in *Oracles and Hierophants: Constructions of Romantic Authority* (Ithaca, NY: Cornell University Press, 1991).

[21] See 'Literary Commentary as Literature', in *Criticism in the Wilderness: The Study of Literature Today* (New Haven: Yale University Press, 1980), 213.

[22] Kathleen Wheeler argues that in reading Coleridge's *Marginalia*, one 'has the most extraordinary sense of being in Coleridge's presence, hearing him speaking as if alive, partly because he himself seems to feel the corresponding vividness of the author's personality, and directs himself as if in speech to a living writer instead of a book. (Or to the owner of the book, who was sure to read his notes?)' See 'Coleridge's Notebook Scribblings', in Peter Kitson and Thomas Corns (eds.), *Coleridge and the Armoury of the Human Mind: Essays on his Prose Writings* (London: Frank Cass, 1991), 31.

decreative,[23] so the public, for Coleridge, is belligerently passive in temperament; anonymously personal in its methods of abuse; and amorphously unified in the judgmental power it arrogated to itself. Such paradoxes may well tell us something about Coleridge's individual pathology, but more to the point are their significance for the status of reading at this historical moment, and for a theory of reading in general. What I want to suggest is that they bear a figurative relation to the larger paradox in which writers are implicated, by virtue of being also readers: the paradox, that is, of being vehicles for production and consumption, at one and the same time.

III. PUBLIC ENEMIES, PRIVATE FRIENDS

The paradoxical implications of Coleridge's anxiety are brought sharply into focus by the reception of 'Christabel', a poem which was recited and circulated in manuscript over a period of sixteen years before its eventual publication. Coleridge's anger at the discrepancy between its private and public reception gives us an insight into his divided allegiance to two alternative traditions of circulation which coexisted at the beginning of the nineteenth century. As we shall see, the dichotomy between private and public lay at the heart of Coleridge's theory of reading, and proved crucial to the system of defences he evolved to keep his anxiety under control. The 'Christabel' incident, and the narratives that surround it—particularly those offered by Coleridge himself—remind us of the inseparability of symptoms and defences in the anxiety of reception.

Charles Lamb, on hearing that 'Christabel' was about to be published along with 'Kubla Khan', described hearing the latter read by Coleridge 'so enchantingly that it irradiates & brings heaven & Elysian bowers into my parlour while he sings or says it'. But, he goes on, 'there is an observation Never tell thy dreams, and I am almost afraid that Kubla Khan is an owl that wont bear daylight'.[24] Lamb's fears proved prophetic: 'discovered by the lantern of typography & clear reducting to letters, to be no better than non-sense' (as he put it) the 'Christabel' volume was vilified in the periodical press. Coleridge referred to this episode when accusing anonymous reviewers of malice in *Biographia*

---

[23] See esp. 'The Dunciad Variorum', bk. iii, ll. 335–56.
[24] Lamb to Wordsworth, 26 Apr. 1816 (Marrs, iii. 215).

Literaria, and Peacock rose to the poem's defence in his 'Essay on Fashionable Literature' (1818) in exposing contemporary reviewing practices to sustained critique. 'Christabel' became the centre of a critical debate whose repercussions were significant and lasting. The details of its reception provide an example of the wider issues at stake when authors were reluctant to exchange the relative security of private patronage for the more fickle demands of the reading-public; and when reviewers were under simultaneous pressure to act as both judges and advocates or friends.

In his embittered attack on the standards of reviewing-bodies in *Biographia*, the public vilification of 'Christabel' provided a focus for the poet's sense of betrayal by readers, one of whom (allegedly Hazlitt) praised the poem on hearing it recited, then subsequently demolished it in the *Edinburgh Review*. 'During the many years which intervened between the composition and the publication of the Christabel', Coleridge explained, 'it became almost as well known among literary men as if it had been on common sale, the same references were made to it, and the same liberties taken with it, even to the very names of the imaginary persons in the poem' (*BL* ii. 238). He went on to boast of the 'celebrated Poets' who praised it, and of the effects it had produced 'in societies of the most different kinds' (*BL* ii. 238) when it was recited—all this, to be subjected to abuse, and to a 'malignity and a spirit of personal hatred' when it finally appeared in print (*BL* ii. 239). Coleridge's angry conviction that private panegyric ought by rights to have earned him public success, and that friends should remain friends, whichever journal they wrote for, expresses itself by way of an attempt to understand the poem's private recitation and circulation as though they were *analogous* to publication. In the language used to elide these stages of reception, Coleridge describes 'Christabel' being passed around 'as if it had been on common sale'. The metaphor carries more than a hint of prostitution, to be amplified in the accusation that readers 'took liberties' with the poem by borrowing and plagiarism. In this symbolic and revealing narrative of persecution, Coleridge's sense of the public humiliation caused by a bad review is projected out onto the reviewing-body itself, then back onto his private audience, who are retrospectively accused of exploiting the poem as though it were an available woman. His own sense of ill-treatment is disclosed as a chivalrous desire to protect the poem's honour, combined with a half-guilty regret that he had touted the poem around in the first place.

Framed and placed in a position of prominence, Coleridge's account of the circulation and reception of 'Christabel' closely resembles that given by Hugh Blair, in the Preface to his *Lectures on Rhetoric and Belles Lettres*. Blair's text was a locus classicus in all discussions of orality in the period, and a symbolic source of authority for writers declaring their allegiance to oral traditions. I quote the whole paragraph, in which Blair explains that the publication of his lectures 'was not altogether a matter of choice', since he had first circulated them amongst his students, whose promiscuous borrowings from them endangered his own claim to originality:

Imperfect Copies of them, in Manuscript, from notes taken by Students who heard them read, were first privately handed about; and afterwards frequently exposed to public sale. When the Author saw them circulate so currently, as even to be quoted in print, and found himself often threatened with surreptitious publications of them, he judged it to be high time that they should proceed from his own hand, rather than come into public view under some very defective and erroneous form.[25]

Both writers were acutely aware of the ironies involved for the oral tradition as it negotiated a place for itself in the market place. But Coleridge's narrative was further embittered by the sense that his generosity towards listeners who were also friends (as opposed, in Blair's case, to students) had been repaid with ingratitude and exploitation. Scott, who allegedly plagiarized from his poem, and Hazlitt, whom he held responsible for its unfavourable reception, both figure in Coleridge's demonology as the representatives of a cut-throat world of publishing, at odds with the vanishing world of orality to which he himself belonged, and which his comradely allusion to Blair confirms.

Coleridge used his hard-won experience in this instance as a warning against calculating on 'the probable reception of a poem' by the applause of friends (*BL* ii. 239). But friendship still provided his model for the ideal bond between poet and reader; and if it was an absence of 'friends behind the scenes' that most damaged a poem's chances of sympathetic reception, this was thought by Coleridge to reflect badly on reading-practices in the public domain, not on the credentials and tastes of his private audience. Clearly discernible behind his muddled rhetoric of self-exoneration is a poetics of reception centred on the oratorical skills of a performer whom Coleridge covertly identified as a version of himself. In describing the 'excitement and temporary sympathy of feeling, which the recitation of the poem by an admirer, especially if he be at once a warm admirer and a man of acknowledged celebrity, calls forth in the audience' (*BL* ii. 239), Coleridge expressed both his yearning for a public advocate and his nostalgia for the coterie audiences which had, over the years, listened with such reliable raptness to recitations of 'Christabel'.

The lessons learnt from the 'Christabel' episode were summed up as early as 1805 in a letter of Dorothy Wordsworth's complaining of Scott's alleged plagiarisms: 'circumstance shews how cautious Poets ought to be in lending their manuscripts, or even *reading* them to Authors. If they came refreshed out of the Imitator's brain it would not be so grievous, but they are in general like faded impressions, or as the wrong side of a piece of the Tapestry to the right'.[26] In trusting his listeners, Coleridge had learned the hard way that his ideals of reception were under threat. But at the same time, he had discovered a tension in his own thinking with respect to the importance of literary ownership. For is there not a contradiction, in his *Biographia* narrative, between the collaborative ideal of sociable diffusion embodied in the practice of 'reading aloud' and the proprietorial model of authorship implied in his resentment that 'Christabel' has been plagiarized?

The confusions in Coleridge's thinking about literary property are registered at a rhetorical level in the defensive preface he attached to 'Christabel' when it first appeared in print. This Preface was designed to protect him from the charge of plagiarizing from Scott's 'Lay of the Last Minstrel' by establishing the prior date of his own poem's composition. But the rhetoric he used in establishing his originality suggests a very different model of creation. Rebuking those critics who 'hold, that every possible thought and image is traditional; who have no notion that there are such things as fountains in the world, small as well as great; and who would therefore charitably derive every rill they behold flowing, from a perforation made in some other man's tank', Coleridge succeeds in denegrating the source-hunting mentality that would seek to track his own writing back to Scott. He then turns the argument round so as to establish himself as the 'fountain' and Scott as the 'rill' by expressing his confidence that Scott will vindicate him from the charge of imitation. Finally, in an even more muddled attempt to reconcile communitarian

---

[26] To Lady Beaumont, 27 Oct. 1805 (*EY* i. 633).

and possessive models of creation–reception, he quotes the following lines of doggerel, translated from Latin:

> 'Tis mine and it is likewise yours;
> But an if this will not do;
> Let it be mine, good friend! for I
> Am the poorer of the two.

> (*CPW* i. 214–15)

With its slippage from economic to intellectual ideas of poverty, the last line struggles to compliment Scott while establishing that Coleridge himself occupies the higher moral ground of generous egalitarianism. There is something uncomfortable, even disingenuous, in making the resolution of a quarrel over ownership rest on the device of false modesty.

At a time when ideas of original genius and of literary property were under construction, the 'Christabel' episode survives as a record of their transitional status. Just as Coleridge's investment in non-possessive models of authorship, reception, and literary influence is undermined from within by the need to establish the boundaries that separate one poet's work from another's, so during the eighteenth and nineteenth centuries the same tensions were played out in the literary discourse of genius (and the legal discourse of copyright) as the modern concept of the author came into being. And in the same way that the supportive role played by patronage and small coteries began to come under threat, as the traditional gentlemanly world of authorship became professionalized, so friendship—when it was used to figure or embody the ideal of unpossessive interaction between writers and their readers—proved an inadequate defence against the commodification of literature. Not only were individual writers placed under strain when obliged to fulfil the role of ideal readers, but the idea of friendship itself proved insufficiently resilient to safeguard writers against competition, in both private and public domains. Friendship, in the words of Godwin, 'requires that the hearts of the persons should, as it were, be amalgamated into one substance, that their thoughts should be transparent to each other, and their communications entire'.[27] But, since writers were able to prove their worth only by demonstrating their originality, this model of amalgamation threatened both individual and communal notions of

---

[27] 'Of Choice in Reading', *Enquirer* (1797); repr. in *Godwin Works*, v, ed. Pamela Clemit, 136.

propriety. The boundaries separating private from public reception were permeable, and even friends could (knowingly or unknowingly) abuse the ambiguous status of a poem that had been 'published' by being read aloud.

IV. MODELS OF READER-RESPONSE

Coleridge's method for allaying his anxiety of reception was to imagine a spirit of friendship that transcended time, place, and person, thereby blurring the distinction between private and public scenes of reading, while also sidestepping the danger that friends in theory might turn out to be no friends at all. His defence mechanisms worked to unify and protect the divided self by mediating between a sequence of polarities on the writing–reading axis. Negotiating the counter-claims of authors and readers (which were often generically encoded in the contest between poetry and prose) he tried to negotiate a diplomatic compromise between such values as antiquity and modernity, originality and imitation, competition and collaboration—all preserved as dichotomies in the prevailing cultural climate. But he did so uncomfortably, and in such a way that his rhetoric is open to deconstruction. Here, for instance, he is writing on the subject of how he reads history in *The Friend*. He is likening it to the activity of listening to music; and his analysis of the successive moments of anticipation and recapitulation tells us much about his approach to literary history, to the individual's engagement with tradition, and to the ideal process of reading:

> Each present movement bringing back, as it were, and embodying the spirit of some melody that had gone before, anticipates and seems trying to overtake something that is to come: and the musician has reached the summit of his art, when having thus modified the Present by the Past, he at the same time weds the Past *in* the Present to some prepared and corresponsive Future. The auditor's thoughts and feelings move under the same influence: retrospection blends with anticipation, and Hope and Memory (a female Janus) become one power with a double aspect. (*Friend*, i. 130)

Coleridge's musical analogy is a comforting one, in its transcendence of linguistic barriers and temporal divides. However, the process of mediation is itself envisaged as 'one power with a double aspect'. If we read this passage as an allegory of the writing–reading subject (here interestingly figured as female) we become aware, simultaneously, of the strength of Coleridge's defences and the vulnerability they betray. The process of 'trying to overtake something that is to come' calls up in order to cancel competitive associations; while peaceful and antagonistic elements of the creative–critical process are precariously resolved.

In positing an ideal of connective authority which mediates between the spirit of collaboration and competition, Coleridge congratulates individual writers with respect to their own contributions, allowing them also the comfort of belonging to a community of eternal equals. 'The *Spirit* of Poetry [is] common to all ages', he observes in one of his lectures (*Lectures*, i. 481). In another, he refers to the eternity of 'Works of genuine Fame' (*Lectures*, i. 77); and in *Biographia*, he celebrates 'the authority of works, whose fame is not of ONE country, nor of ONE age' (*BL* ii. 88). Finally, in *On the Constitution of the Church and State*, he describes the clerisy as guardians and coordinators of genius, whose function it was 'to preserve the stores, to guard the treasures, of past civilization, and thus to bind the present with the past; to perfect and add to the same, and thus to connect the present with the future'.[28]

The notion of a connective past with composite authority was especially important in an era when originality was at such a high premium— because it allowed for the possibility that truth was communally produced; that there were no ownership rights on ideas; and that repetition was not necessarily culpable. In this respect, it held a particular appeal for Coleridge, who suffered from a pressing anxiety of priority: 'I always rejo[i]ced & was jubilant when I found my own ideas well expressed already by others', he claimed, as a pre-emptive defence against the charge of plagiarism (*Notebooks*, ii. 2375). And again, in *Biographia*, 'I prefer another's words to my own, partly as a tribute due to priority of publication; but still more from the pleasure of sympathy in a case where *coincidence* only was possible' (*BL* i. 147). If truth was a divine ventriloquist, then not only was the occurrence of plagiarism unlikely, but origins themselves became irrelevant: 'I care not from whose mouth the sounds are supposed to proceed, if only the words are audible and intelligible' (*BL* i. 164). Resources were thus pooled, and an eternal community was established for those capable of uttering truth.

The argument that truth is not a property to which individual writers competitively aspire was one that Coleridge could prove through his own handling of prior authority. Elinor Shaffer has shown how his

---

[28] *On the Constitution of the Church and State*, ed. John Colmer, *CC* x. 43–4.

habits of quotation and allusion—his weaving together of different voices—create an effect of ventriloquism in practice, not just in theory; and she has argued that his much misunderstood and maligned prose style is 'a complex model of Romantic intertextuality in the service of a new, secular hermeneutic dialogism'.[29] Instead of reading *Biographia* as the 'psychological struggle for dominance with his one-time friend and rival' she proposes that we read it as 'a major work of hermeneutic criticism',[30] in which 'dialogism across history . . . is carried out through intertextuality'.[31] This is a thoroughly compelling defence against the charge of competitiveness, both at the theoretical level, and for the allusive style of the poetry, *Biographia*, and also Coleridge's lectures. When, for instance, in the fourth of his 1818 series, he makes a connective sequence of quotations—Milton on Shakespeare, Milton, and Wordsworth—he demonstrates the cohesiveness of the hermeneutic community as a nationalist phenomenon (*Lectures*, ii. 113). More importantly, 'in relating Spenser to Ariosto, Rabelais to Swift, and Dante to Milton', he not only helps to 'establish the comparative study of literature in Britain'[32] but also furthers the hermeneutic community as a European ideal. As a defence, then, the hermeneutic principle is highly successful; but it reduplicates the pattern of Coleridge's own defences, establishing Shaffer as his ideal reader. We should retain some awareness of the anxieties which this connectiveness dispelled, together with some scepticism about the degree to which, in practice, Coleridge's allusive habits were uncompetitive.

For all its allegiance to an ideal of hermeneutic community, Coleridge's vision of literary history has the flavour of anxious conservatism. Shaffer is concerned to establish that the interpretative community proposed in *Biographia* did not signal a withdrawal from politics; and that it had important affiliations with his early pantisocratic ideals.[33] This was clearly the case; since the communal quest for truth that Coleridge was celebrating implied that truth was not to be equated with private property. But equally one should note that when he refers to the existence of '*a tacit compact among the learned as a privileged order*' (*BL* i.

[29] 'The Hermeneutic Community: Coleridge and Schleiermacher' in Richard Gravil and Molly Lefebure (eds.), *The Coleridge Connection: Essays in Honour of Thomas McFarland* (Houndmills, Basingstoke: Macmillan, 1990), 221.
[30] Ibid. 210.
[31] Ibid. 221.
[32] See R. A. Foakes's Introduction, *Lectures*, ii. 33.
[33] 'Hermeneutic Community', 224.

140) the meritocracy he envisions has some affinities with a Burkean aristocracy. If Coleridge's ideas about literary ownership reflected his political ambivalence, more generally, towards the idea of property, they can also be read as paradigmatic of the transitional status of the author at the time *Biographia* was published. The Romantic concept of the author evolved as a complex negotiation between the claim that authorship is a species of ownership, and the counter-claim that its value could only be measured by its collective uses. The eventual success of appeals for perpetual copyright rested on the power and persuasiveness of this chameleon rhetoric (to which I shall be returning in greater detail in Chapter 7). So although Coleridge believed that an author's works might be 'received, retained and prolonged' by analogy with heritable property, this did not cancel his commitment to communitarian ideals. His strongest defence, as a writing-subject, was the number of possible reading-positions he anticipated; and in this respect his anxiety of reception ensured his own survival in future communities of writers.

So far I have considered only how Coleridge's model of connective authority worked to mediate between author and author, protecting the spirit of authorship as a communal or hereditary ideal. But how successfully, if at all, did this model transfer to the relationship between author and reader? In his theorizing of reader-response, as in his conception of an ideal writing–reading community, the effectiveness of Coleridge's defence mechanisms as mediations depended heavily on the notion of sympathetic identification. 'To know that we are in sympathy with others, moderates our feelings as well as strengthens our convictions', he says in *The Friend*; 'and for the mind, which opposes itself to the faith of the multitude, it is more especially desirable, that there should exist an object out of itself, on which it may fix its attention, and thus balance its own energies' (*Friend*, i. 133). Sympathy is established by Coleridge, as it is by Schleiermacher,[34] as the criterion for understanding (*Lectures*, i. 124); and faith in the mutuality of understanding (*Lectures*, i. 126) allows dialogues to take place across history. This is an early (and crudely psychological) version of Gadamer's fusion of horizons.[35]

---

[34] 'In interpretation it is essential that one be able to step out of one's own frame of mind into that of the author': *Hermeneutics: The Handwritten Manuscripts*, ed. Heinz Kimmerle, trans. James Duke and Jack Forstman (Missoula, Mont.: Scholars Press, 1977), 30.

[35] See Hans Georg Gadamer, *Truth and Method* (2nd rev. ed.), trans. rev. Joel Weinsheimer and Donald G. Marshall (London: Sheed and Ward, 1975), 374.

Just as the hermeneutic ideal offered individual readers and authors the comfort of belonging to a like-minded community, so the criterion of sympathy between author and reader collapsed these two functions into each other, thus dispelling rivalry or conflict. Coleridge uses just this argument (implicitly) in the *Notebook* entry in which he justifies his habit of talking so much about himself:

Egoistic Talk *with me* very often the effect of my love of the Persons to whom I am talking / My Heart is talking of them / I cannot talk continuously of them to themselves—so I seem to be putting into their Heart the same continuousness as to me, that is in my Heart as to them. (*Notebooks*, i. 1772)

If he is solipsistic, Coleridge implies, then his is a generous form of solipsism, based on real communicative bonds: hence the emphasis on talking. The 'continuousness' of self, between interlocutor and auditor, or writer and reader, enacts on an interpersonal level that collapse of subject into object which was crucial to Coleridge's philosophical thinking; and which—as we have seen in his model for literary history—was a state devoutly to be wished.

But what limits could be set to the confluence of writer and reader, once the process of sympathetic identification had begun? And how easily did a writing–reading subject maintain its identity, in this two-way mirroring process? Such questions, as we shall see in Chapter 8, were crucial to the development of hermeneutics from Schleiermacher onwards; and recently they have been reformulated in terms of our own critical purchase as readers of the past. Their persistence as questions reminds us that the collapsing of divisions between separate identities is a source of anxiety, whether it takes the form of a subsuming of the written in the read or the read in the written; and that the creative–critical divide performs a special function in preserving these separate realms. This explains why, even though he celebrated the power of sympathy between author and reader, Coleridge had reservations about allowing criticism to move from its secondary status; and why he evolved defence mechanisms that kept authorial imagination somewhat aloof.

A 'consciousness of the Poet's Mind must be diffused over that of the Reader or Spectator', he argues, in the fourth of his 1808 lectures (*Lectures*, i. 86). The reader thus becomes a vessel for the author's spirit, and even a replica of the author, without any reduction of the author's power. In much the same way, the definition Coleridge offers of imaginative reader-response allows roles to be swapped, and poses no threat to the integrity of authorial imagination: 'You feel him to be a poet inasmuch as, for a time, he has made you one—an active creative being'. This is what he says of Shakespeare, in the fourth of his 1811 series (*Lectures*, i. 251). He himself provided a working model of such response when delivering a lecture on Milton in January 1812. According to one listener, he 'described the image impressed on the mind, in language and figure so fugitive and evanescent, that he became the poet he described' (*Lectures*, i. 402). The crossing here suggested, between the separate creative geniuses of Shakespeare and Coleridge, is a difficult one: posing questions about the element of envying identification in mimetic criticism, and therefore—on behalf of both sides of the writing–reading subject—a potential anxiety about the loss of identity.[36] It was, nonetheless, a crossing that involved intense pleasure, and that could be negotiated as an act of homage, not of usurpation.

Coleridge's ideal writers are those who promote the reader's imaginative activity—Shakespeare, who 'provides...for *his readers*—& leaves it to them' (*Lectures*, ii. 315); Milton, whose sublime language encourages in the reader 'an effort in the mind' (*Lectures*, i. 311); Hooker, Bacon, and Jeremy Taylor, whose prose is difficult, and exacts vigilance (*Friend*, i. 20). These writers are not seen as issuing open invitations to the reader to construct meaning—not even Shakespeare, whose imagination provided Coleridge with a heuristic model of interpretation; and whose relativism suggested a generously open method of understanding the human condition. They are seen, instead, as creating obstacles to the path of understanding, which the reader could overcome through imaginative effort. It follows from this that Coleridge's ideal reader is someone always on the alert—working imaginatively, not from competitive motives, but from the desire to enter or receive the spirit in which the works were written.

---

[36] This anxiety is more knowingly confronted elsewhere: see e.g. the 10th lecture of Coleridge's 1818 series, where, in a discussion of Donne, Coleridge distinguishes between reading an author in order to discover fine lines, and reading in order to follow a 'leading thought' through the whole work: 'The former is too much like coveting your neighbour's goods; in the latter you merge yourself in the author, you *become He*'. *Coleridge's Miscellaneous Criticism*, ed. Thomas Middleton Raysor (London: Constable, 1936), 137. For the distinction between 'trivially egotistical' and 'protean' reading-habits, see Stephen Bygrave, *Coleridge and the Self: Romantic Egotism* (Houndmills, Basingstoke: Macmillan, 1986), 139.

V. COMPANIONABLE FORMS: CONVERSATION AS A POETIC IDEAL

A concern with defining the limits of reader-response is discernible not only in the direction of Coleridge's critical theory, but in his selection of discursive and rhetorical modes. The literary model to which he turned, to define his poetic aspirations in the late 1790s, was the 'divine chit chat' of Cowper's *The Task*, with its double allegiance to the sublime and the humdrum; and his own use of conversation as a model for poetry reflected a similarly mixed rhetorical agenda. Although he showed a consistent leaning towards performative discourse, whose origins could be traced back to oral culture, the kind of conversation he advocated had closer affinities with lecturing or sermonizing than with talking. 'Have you ever heard me preach, Charles?', Coleridge is said to have asked Lamb on one occasion. 'N-n-never heard you d-do anything else, C-c-coleridge', Lamb replied.[37] His mythical status as 'Coleridge the Talker' was due to the mesmeric hold he exerted over his auditors, most of whom described the experience of listening to him as one in which the entire personality of the man held them enchanted. If Coleridge's ideal recital was a form of hypnotism, his ideal scene of reception was something between the witnessing of a performance and the succumbing to a spell. This feature of his poetics may have had some connection with the theories of mesmerism and animal magnetism to which he was attracted in the 1790s, briefly mentioned in the *Biographia*:

For this is really a species of Animal Magnetism, in which the enkindling Reciter, by perpetual comment of looks and tones, lends his own will and apprehensive faculty to his Auditors. They *live* for the time within the dilated sphere of his intellectual Being. (*BL* ii. 239–40)

Coleridge's allegiance was to a model of reading which preserved the reader at a distance from the poet, inspiring him or her with awe. But this model was complicated (perhaps even disguised) in the 'conversation poems' by the urbane intimacy of their poetic register, as well as by the ideals of sympathy and community to which they aspired. Rhetorical and figurative mediations are closely connected in the shifting modes of address which these poems deploy. 'The Aeolian Harp' uses a honeymoon setting to mount its philosophical enquiry into the origin of creativity, but the intimate tenderness of its opening is soon displaced

---

[37] Quoted in the 'Editor's Introduction' to *Lay Sermons*, *CC*, vol. vi, p. xxxv.

by a diction appropriate to religious musings. This and other poems disclose a pressing awareness of the intrusion of the public realm into the private, reflecting the poet's divided allegiance to domestic retirement and active life. If, rhetorically, they attempt to occupy a middle ground between the cottage hearth and the lecture podium, their construction of sympathy as a hermeneutic ideal might be seen as similarly negotiatory. Sympathy is figured both in Coleridge's choice of the family unit as a model for social cohesiveness, and in his selection of close friends and family members as auditors. Sara Coleridge in 'The Aeolian Harp', Lamb in 'This Lime Tree Bower my Prison', the child Hartley in 'Frost at Midnight', Sara Hutchinson in 'Dejection'—are all 'companionable forms': sympathetic to the poet by virtue of their connections, and voicelessly acquiescent in the perpetuation of his imaginative vision. As members of a coterie audience on which he can rely, they fend off his anxieties with respect to the public reception of his poetry. But they also embody and enact the domestic communitarianism to which he held allegiance at the time of writing, and which would eventually mature into the hopes he invested in a 'clerisy'. In this sense they indicate, proleptically, the direction of Coleridge's later political thinking.[38]

Although the function of Coleridge's model readers is to mediate between self and other—confirming that the poet needs 'an object out of itself, on which it may fix its attention, and thus balance its own energies' (*Friend*, i. 133)—in practice, these figures seldom move beyond the performance of a surrogate role in relation to the poet's own desires, or a reconciling role in relation to his inner conflicts. Sara, in 'The Aeolian Harp', is used to voice the poet's inhibitions with respect to Unitarianism, to reinforce a proper sense of God's incomprehensibility, and thus to steer the erring Coleridge away from his heretical pantheism. Her admonitory function, as the advocate of God's inscrutable wisdom, serves to underwrite a model of authority which extends by analogy from Coleridge's reading of the divine will to all acts of reading or understanding. In this sense, she speaks not as herself, but as the other in an internal dialogue between the poet's radical Unitarianism and the conservative Anglicanism which was to mark his later writing.

Similarly, the figure of an urban outsider ('Bristowa's citizen') is introduced into 'Reflections on Leaving Place of Retirement' as a reconciling medium between private and public worlds. The citizen,

---

[38] This is the substance of Paul Hamilton's argument in his essay 'Coleridge'.

obsessed with commerce, resembles Satan in his intrusive presence and his declared envy for the 'blessed' pastoral state; and like Satan he is given momentary access to the goodness from which he has fallen. He reassures Coleridge's readers of the social harmony epitomized by the poet's retreat, and suggests the usefulness of domestic tranquillity as an encouragement to philanthropy. But he also allays Coleridge's fears with respect to the Bristol public he was concurrently addressing in his political lectures, whom he worried might be potentially hostile or indifferent to his message. In undergoing a transformation from mis-reader to ideal reader, the visitor from Bristol performatively under-writes the poet's authority. In so doing, he prefigures Coleridge's use of the 'friend' who interrupts *Biographia Literaria*, chapter 13 to question (but ultimately to endorse) his poetic method.

Coleridge's figurations of the reader are at their most evidently self-protective in 'Frost at Midnight'. The 'stranger' who flutters on the poet's low-burnt fire metonymically represents Coleridge's excited ap-prehensiveness with respect to a visitor who will interrupt his solitude—a visitor whose disquieting strangeness is associated with the public world outside his cottage, in much the same way as 'Bristowa's citizen' or the person from Porlock. This 'stranger' is progressively familiarized in the course of the poem by a sequence of associations with members of Coleridge's family—most significantly with his sister 'when they both were cloth'd alike', and his son Hartley, whose 'fluttering' echoes the stranger's in the poem's coda. This transformation of strangeness into familiarity (in its most literal sense) enacts Coleridge's earnest and fearful need that his reader too might become an 'echo or mirror' of himself.

A similar pattern is repeated in the educational and theological tenor of Coleridge's blessing on his son.[39] Hartley learns to interpret the 'shapes and sounds intelligible' of God's language, who 'from eternity doth teach | Himself in all, and all things in himself' (ll. 61–2). The child reflects on and in a landscape which is itself divinely reflective; and his education is encouraged by a universal teacher using Rousseau's her-meneutic methods: 'he shall mould | Thy spirit, and by giving make it ask' (ll. 63–4). Here, as in so many of the liberal educative theories which have preceded and followed it, the adventurous spirit of ques-tioning is guided from above, by one who has already framed the answers, and therefore determines how the questions should be posed.

---

[39] Compare Wordsworth in 'Michael', ll. 341–427.

'Let him always believe that he is the master', Rousseau advises, in *Emile*, 'and let it always be you who are. There is no subjection so perfect as that which keeps the appearance of freedom. Thus the will itself is made captive'.[40]

VI. READING AND ENCHANTMENT

While the 'conversation poems' explore the ways in which sympathy can captivate the reader's will (even while appearing to liberate it), the 'supernatural poems' point to the affinities between sympathy and various forms of enchantment. Their representations of poetic authority by no means endorse the act of possession exerted by writer over reader, but they do return repeatedly to possession as a metaphor for reception. The wedding guest in 'The Ancient Mariner' is held captive by a story he 'cannot choose but hear', delivered by a figure whose 'skinny hand' and 'glittering eye' exert a mesmeric influence over his listeners. His resistance to the mariner's story is overcome, not only by its content, but by a combination between empathy on his part and the mariner's 'strange power of speech'.

This pattern of resistance overcome is a central ingredient in Coleridge's study of the hold that illusion exerts over the imagination in the process of reader-response. A need to distinguish illusion from delusion connects the early poetry with the later prose, but despite the use of a framing device that belittles the storyteller's power, a strong affinity remains between 'The Ancient Mariner' and the Gothic fiction Coleridge finds deeply suspect. Both hinge on the capacity of the supernatural to surmount disbelief (as distinct from the reader's willingness to 'suspend' it), and both depend on holding the reader captive or submissive, in ways that ironically recall Coleridge's castigation of the reading-habits encouraged by sensationalist literature. Coleridge was fascinated by the origins of the mariner's 'strange power of speech' in the primitive storytelling customs of oral culture. As in Wordsworth's 'The Thorn', the mariner's tale is repeated, like a well-worn yarn, to different listeners, who (despite their separation from each other in time and place) are drawn together in the community of feeling shaped by the storyteller's art. In the later version of the text, as it appeared in *Sibylline Leaves*, the addition of the gloss accentuates this sense of a tale that has

---

[40] *Emile or Education*, trans. Allan Bloom (Harmondsworth, Middlesex: Penguin, 1979), 120.

been handed down. The marginal comments represent one historical moment in the successive layerings of the story's reception and mediation. In this sense, they both distance the narrative from the present—containing its supernatural enchantment within acceptable bounds—and concretize its communicative power.

This simultaneous movement of diffusion and containment is also effected in 'Kubla Khan', where Coleridge figures reading as the collective response of an audience at once possessed by and fearful towards poetic genius. Kubla, the poet, and his rapt audience are connected, each to each, through the metaphor of possession. Just as Kubla's act of enclosure is figured as an attempt to restrain disruptive potential, so the poet's desire to create is shown to be an act of volition that echoes Kubla's own. The Khan's appropriative compulsions are displaced onto an imaginary plane—'I would build that dome in air! | That sunny dome, those caves of ice!'—thus partly transcending their negative associations. But the urgency of the poet's compulsion to repeat is seen as threatening; and it is met, in its turn, with an answering need on the part of the poet's audience to enclose and seal off his 'strange power of speech':

> all should cry, Beware! Beware!
> His flashing eyes, his floating hair!
> Weave a circle round him thrice,
> And close your eyes with holy dread,
> For he on honey-dew hath fed,
> And drunk the milk of Paradise.

> (ll. 49–54)

While the presence of a rapt audience bears incontrovertible testimony to the poet's prophetic inspiration, there is some danger, Coleridge suggests, that his enchantment may be contagious. A connection, first observed by Carl Woodring, between the imagery of 'Kubla Khan' and a metaphor later used to describe a debate between Pitt and Fox in the House of Commons, allows us to see one sense in which Coleridge's poem has radical implications:

Mr Pitt built up his periods, as usual, in all the stately order of rhetoric architecture; but they fell away at once before that true eloquence of common-sense and natural feeling which sanctifies, and renders human, the genius of Mr Fox. Like some good genius, he approached in indignation to the spell-built palace of the state-magician, and at the first touch of his wand, it sunk into a ruinous and sordid hovel, tumbling in upon the head of the wizard that had reared it.[41]

Just as Pitt's powers of oratory are rendered powerless by Fox's rougher (more primitive and populist) orality, so the river and caves of ice beneath Kubla's cultivated pleasure garden contain a subversive potential. Akin to the 'ancestral voices prophecying war', their subterranean energies threaten to defy the Khan's act of enclosure, which Coleridge associates with tyrannical rule. In the poem's closing lines, however, Coleridge's poetic discourse moves closer to Pitt's oratorical wizardry than to the authentic energy embodied by Fox. 'The poet and the poem are identified', Tom Paulin concludes: 'the reader must bow down before them.'[42]

In figuring his audience as both resisting and succumbing to the poet-persona's spell, Coleridge dramatizes an ambivalence towards his own powers of oratory. But the tension in these lines also discloses the complexity of his allegiance to the inspired word of prophecy, and to an oral culture which accepted as a matter of course the potency of charms and spells. Coleridge's interest in the power of the word to 'make things happen' is as much anthropological and psychological as political. The notion that a speaker might be possessed of so singular an authority in respect of his listeners that, at his bidding, they could be blighted, frozen, or withered to death, occurs in 'The Ancient Mariner', 'The Wanderings of Cain', and 'Christabel', as well as 'The Three Graves'. The last, which began as a joint venture with Wordsworth, is prefaced by a note explaining that its demonstration of the potency of curses is intended as 'striking proof of the possible effect on the imagination, from an idea suddenly and violently impressed upon it'. The poem was inspired by the effects of '*Oby* witchcraft on the Negroes in the West Indies', and by 'Hearne's deeply interesting anecdotes of similar workings on the imagination of the Copper Indians'. But Coleridge is insistent that 'instances of this kind are not peculiar to savage or barbarous tribes' (*CPW* i. 269). Far from having surmounted its primitivist and animistic beliefs, the civilized western world remained deeply receptive to them. This was one explanation, in Coleridge's thinking, for the powerful hold exerted by Gothic narratives over the reading public,

---

[41] Quoted by Tom Paulin, *Minotaur: Poetry and the Nation State* (London: Faber and Faber, 1992), 10.
[42] Ibid.

as for the tendency of audiences to be 'suddenly and violently impressed' by popular radical enthusiasm.

In the political lectures of 1795, Coleridge's concern to distinguish the patient reflectiveness of his own politics from populist demagoguery had involved a condemnation of sudden and violent rhetorical effects.[43] But just as he believed that the dangerous power of enthusiasm might be channelled in a quietist direction, so he hoped that superstition might be legitimized according to a grand necessitarian design. In *The Destiny of Nations* (1796), Fancy is 'the power | That first unsensualises the dark mind' (ll. 80–1), contributing to human enlightenment through its 'wild activity' (l. 83). Peopling the air 'By obscure fears of Beings invisible' (l. 84), this faculty succeeds in emancipating the mind from 'the grosser thrall | Of the present impulse' through self-control (ll. 85–6). Thus it is that 'Superstition with unconscious hand | Seat[s] Reason on her throne' (ll. 87–8). With this vision of human perfectibility in mind, Coleridge allowed himself to see credulity as imaginative potential, and to find, in the legends of Laplanders, a model of primitive art which served to legitimize his own status as inspired bard:

> Wherefore not vain,
> Nor yet without permitted power impressed,
> I deem those legends terrible, with which
> The polar ancient thrills his uncouth throng.
>
> (ll. 88–91)

If, in laying claim to the prophet's status, the poet taps into primitive beliefs and customs, he must at the same time, Coleridge implies, attempt to control the powers thereby unleashed. Only then is it permissible to be impressed by tales of preternatural agency.

Coleridge's confidence in perfectibility was not to last; and his later studies of supernatural power imply that the potency of spoken words may release uncontrollable forces in those who are sympathetically predisposed. The dark side of his concern with the communicative efficacy of sympathy—his fear that listeners might become demonically possessed by the powerful other, thus rendering it suspect by its violent effects—is nowhere more compellingly conveyed than in the narrative of 'Christabel'. Just as Christabel's hospitality is stimulated in the first instance by her immediate and unquestioning acceptance of Geraldine's

---

[43] See 'A Moral and Political Lecture', in *Lectures 1795 on Politics and Religion*, ed. Lewis Patton and Peter Mann, *CC* i. 5–19.

tale of abduction, so the power which Geraldine goes on exerting over
her is sustained by a steadily strengthening sympathetic identification. In
the climax of Part 2, the innocent Gothic heroine is transformed, by the
intensity of that identification, into the reflex of her experienced or
demonic counterpart:

> The maid, alas! her thoughts are gone,
> She nothing sees—no sight but one!
> The maid, devoid of guile and sin,
> I know not how, in fearful wise,
> So deeply had she drunken in
> That look, those shrunken serpent eyes,
> That all her features were resigned
> To this sole image in her mind:
> And passively did imitate
> That look of dull and treacherous hate!
> And thus she stood, in dizzy trance,
> Still picturing that look askance
> With forced unconscious sympathy
> Full before her father's view—
> As far as such a look could be
> In eyes so innocent and blue!

(ll. 597–612)

Coleridge's choice of the Gothic medium is doubly appropriate to his
subject-matter, not only because the conventions of Gothic involve the
corruption of innocence by experience, but because Gothic is itself
imagined as a form of corruption. More specifically, it is associated in
contemporary critical discourse with women writers, women readers,
and excessive sympathetic identification.[44] Accordingly, the transformation described above is framed by Coleridge as a scene of reading in
which all the traditional shortcomings of women readers are itemized.
Before her father's view, Christabel is shown to be intoxicated, passively
imitative, forced into unconscious sympathy, and finally overwhelmed
by the material she 'reads', in much the same way that indiscriminate
women readers were thought to be possessed by novels.

While drawing specifically on anti-novel discourse, the climactic
scene of 'Christabel' dramatizes Coleridge's more generalized fears
with respect to mimicry, doubling, and the eclipse of one identity by

---

[44] See Ch. 8, below.

another. Just as the closing lines of 'Kubla Khan' suggest both his desire for and fear of the possible outcome of prophetic power, so 'Christabel' figures the nightmare possibility of a world in which identity itself is dissolved in the act of reading. As Susan Eilenberg puts it, 'Geraldine is a thief of identity and voice. She injures Christabel by imitating her so neatly as to make the girl herself seem inauthentic. The original, unable to compete with so wonderful an imitation, becomes derivative herself'.[45] The 'forced unconscious sympathy' which results in this kind of specular doubling applies not only to the novels Coleridge condemned, but to the practice of mimetic criticism he advocated, and the acts of rhetorical and oratorical persuasion which his own poetics performed. In investigating how power came to transfer itself from source to recipient, what he repeatedly encountered was a tendency towards less palatable forms of amalgamation or usurpation. Hence his systematic attempt, in definitions of the reading process, to define the limits of mimetic criticism, the boundaries of sympathy, and the rightful place of prophetic power.

VII. THE CONSTRUCTION OF AN IDEAL READER

When creating his ideal reader, Coleridge's strategies ranged from the bullying to the gently encouraging; but in each case what they promoted was the work of reading. By emphasizing the importance of reflective labour, Coleridge sought to pre-empt the habit of too easy (and, by extension, too lazy and indiscriminate) an identification between reader and author, thus directing his own readers away from the activities encouraged by Gothic narrative and other popular genres. In the opening number of *The Friend*, he describes thought and attention as efforts of the mind. Disparagingly reassuring his audience that he will cut thought down to a minimum, he warns them that attention will be required throughout (*Friend*, i. 17). He goes on to describe the process he demands from his readers as one of 'thinking with the author, not lapsing into lazy half-attention' (*Friend*, i. 25); and he later defines learning in terms of effort: 'how can we gather strength', he asks, 'but by exercise?' (*Friend*, i. 114). The prose style that he adopts both reflects and underwrites this deeply Protestant ethic, as Jerome Christensen has shown:

[45] *Strange Power of Speech: Wordsworth, Coleridge and Literary Possession* (Oxford: Oxford University Press, 1992), 104.

Stately rather than titillating, marching rather than running, difficult rather than facile, evolving rather than exhausting, periodic rather than pointed, intentional rather than willful [*sic*], manly rather than feminine, robust rather than asthmatic, English rather than French—the seventeenth-century style that the Friend adopts (or that has imperceptibly adopted him) requires both attention and thought.[46]

Coleridge's appeals to the value and dignity of labour were sometimes heavy-handed, as when he complained that 'there seems a tendency in the public mind to shun all thought, and to expect help from any quarter rather than from seriousness and reflection: as if some invisible power would think for us, when we gave up the pretence of thinking for ourselves' (*Friend*, i. 123). But even through so contemptuous a caricature of the public mind, Coleridge was attempting to draw the reader into a compact with him, by implying the possibility for improvement. To be a reflective reader could become an energizing possibility—something to be worked for, a goal.

In much the same way, in *Biographia*, Coleridge implies the inadequacy of the readership he is addressing to cope with the depth of his philosophical knowledge (*BL* i. 234–6). Philosophy becomes a higher mode of truth, toward which the reader will have to work; but mystificatory strategies preserve the sense of even further possibilities, as yet ungraspable. Indeed, the Burkean aesthetic of 'judicious obscurity' becomes a central structural principle in chapter 13, where it is used to direct the model reader towards a suspension of ratiocinative processes, and into a poetic frame of mind. As I have argued elsewhere, the inadequacy of Coleridge's philosophical argument comes to suggest as its own defence that logic is insufficient to the grandeur and incommunicability of his subject-matter.[47] Interrupting Coleridge's philosophical

---

[46] *Coleridge's Blessed Machine of Language*, 207. For Tim Fulford, the same passage demonstrates that for Coleridge 'the feminine was dangerous and corrupting when unsupported by masculine self-restraint' ('Coleridge and the Royal Family', 80). See also his discussion of Coleridge's 'manly' prose in ' "Living Words": Coleridge, Christianity and National Renewal', *Prose Studies*, 15/2 (Aug. 1992), 187–207. Kathleen Wheeler touches on the connections between sexuality and Coleridge's prose style when she writes that 'the desire for meaning and clarity must combine with a genial patience and willingness to suspend gratification in order eventually to gain the result' (*Sources, Processes and Methods*, 85). For an extended discussion of Coleridge's ideas about the masculinity of 'a syntax in which the main verb, and so meaning, is deferred', see John Barrell, *Poetry, Language and Politics* (Manchester: Manchester University Press, 1988), 64–77.

[47] *'Paradise Lost' and the Romantic Reader*, 199–200 and 'The Aesthetics of Indeterminacy', in John Beer (ed.), *Questioning Romanticism* (Baltimore: Johns Hopkins University Press, 1995), 221–2.

disquisition, the spoof letter from a friend describes the experience of reading Coleridge's prose as analogous to entering a Gothic cathedral, in which the gloom is so thick that 'substance' and 'shadow' become indistinguishable. The choice of Gothic architecture to figure the sublime is by no means coincidental. Wordsworth had recently used a similar analogy in his Preface to *The Excursion* to justify the apparent fragmentariness of his oeuvre according to a grand overarching design;[48] and Coleridge elsewhere describes Gothic architecture as impressing the beholder 'with the sense of self-annihilation':

he becomes, as it were, a part of the work contemplated. An endless complexity and variety are united into one whole, the plan of which is not distinct from the execution. (*Lectures*, ii. 60)

Gothic architecture thus provides an appropriate vehicle for the spatial representation of Coleridge's sublime aesthetic, which integrates both the reader's initial resistance and his subsequent submission into an appreciation of 'the work contemplated'. Just as the friend's entry into the cathedral enacts a sense of being dwarfed by a grandeur beyond his understanding, so his commentary on Coleridge's method moves from ironic resistance to awe.

The ground is carefully prepared for this sublime turn in chapter 12 of *Biographia*, when Coleridge offers two alternative models of reading in the guise of two alternative explanations for feeling confused. In the first model, he describes how an author's obscurities can sometimes reveal the ignorance of the author; and how the effort to understand can suddenly give way to a sense of victory for the reader:

As when in broad day-light a man tracks the steps of a traveller, who had lost his way in a fog or by treacherous moonshine, even so, and with the same tranquil sense of certainty, can I follow the traces of this bewildered visionary. I UNDERSTAND HIS IGNORANCE. (*BL* i. 233)

In the second model, he describes how, 'utterly baffled in all my attempts to understand the ignorance of Plato', he concludes himself 'IGNORANT OF HIS UNDERSTANDING' (*BL* i. 233). Difficulty is here

---

[48] Wordsworth likens the relation between *The Prelude* and his never-to-be-completed *Recluse* to the relation between antechapel and the body of a gothic church: 'his minor Pieces, when they shall be properly arranged, will be found by the attentive Reader to have such connection with the main Work as may give them claim to be likened to the little cells, oratories, and sepulchral recesses, ordinarily included in those edifices.' See *Wordsworth's Poetical Works*, ed. E. De Selincourt (5 vols., Oxford: Clarendon Press, 1949), v. 2.

envisaged as blockage, giving way to a 'reverential sense of the author's genius', and to humble submission. By implication, it is the second of these models that the reader is meant to follow, in the difficult passage through chapters 12 and 13, so that well before the imagination defini- tions appear, there is a willingness to defer to poetic mystery. In thus encouraging a reverential attitude to the emergence of meaning, Coler- idge claims on his own behalf some of the qualities he attributes to Heraclitus—who, he says in *The Statesman's Manual*, 'was proverbially entitled "the Dark". But it was a darkness which Socrates would not condemn, and which would probably appear to enlightened Christians the darkness of prophecy' (*SM* 97–8).

The sceptical among us are left with a question, which can be asked in two different ways: how is it possible qualitatively to judge the difference between the darkness of sophistry and the darkness of prophecy? And, if it is Coleridge's intention to manipulate his readers towards the religious, awe-inspired passivity of the second model, then how does he distinguish this kind of submission from the lazy passivity he so abhors in current reading-practices? The answer is that he fails to make the grounds of this distinction clear in *Biographia*, although a theory of the sublime can help us to understand it; but that on a number of other occasions, scattered through his lectures, he makes it explicit, in terms of his analysis of stage illusion. In his 'Desultory Remarks on the Stage' for instance, the spectator's activity in surrendering to stage illusion is opposed to the passivity of delusion encouraged by certain kinds of pulp fiction. This 'temporary Half-Faith . . . the Spectator encourages in himself & supports by a voluntary contribution on his own part, because he knows that it is at . . . all times in his power to see . . . the thing as it really is' (*Lectures*, i. 134). This argument is repeated in the first of Coleridge's 1818 series: stage illusion, as distinct from illusions in dream, is willingly entered into by the spectator: 'We *chuse*', Coleridge says, 'to be deceived' (*Lectures*, ii. 266). A similar contrast is drawn between a child's response to *Arabian Nights* (*Lectures*, ii. 191) and the response of the general public to novels (*Lectures*, ii. 193). All of these discussions are closely analogous to the distinction in *Biographia* between illusion and delusion (*BL* ii. 134).

What these passages have in common with a theory of the sublime is that, while apparently hingeing on the distinction between active and passive reading, they serve to demonstrate a willingness on the spec- tator's part to be overwhelmed. It is the component of volition that gives the act of being overwhelmed an aesthetic status. In the case of sublimity, an object or power inconceivably greater than the human subject does the overwhelming; while in stage illusion the spectacle of the play is accorded such power, through the suspension of disbelief. Coleridge stresses the spectator's active participation in this process: an illusion is something the spectator 'encourages in himself and supports by a voluntary contribution'. The separation of active from passive is not possible in a moment of sublimity or stage illusion; since in each case what is involved is (oxymoronically) an act of submission, willingly entered into, from which the subject will re-emerge. Coleridge distinguishes this temporary willed submission from other more permanent states, such as those of delusion or fanaticism. In doing so, he defines a poetics of reception in which the reader's abandonment to the author's spirit can be construed as an act of free will.[49]

Coleridge is interested by the aesthetic frame which mediates these active–passive polarities in the spectator's response to illusion and sublimity. And, for the same reason, he is interested by the oscillation of activity and passivity within the reading process. We know this from the famous, much-discussed metaphor of the water insect, winning its way upstream by 'alternate pulses of active and passive motion, now resisting the current, and now yielding to it in order to gather strength and a momentary *fulcrum* for a further propulsion' (*BL* i. 124); or from the serpent, which 'pauses and half recedes, and from the retrogressive movement collects the force which again carries him onward' (*BL* ii. 14). Such models of reading are later to be amplified by phenomenological accounts of the reading-process, as defined by Georges Poulet or Wolfgang Iser. Compare, for instance, Iser's analysis of the building and breaking of illusions which occurs in reading:

In the oscillation between consistency and 'alien associations', between involvement in and observation of the illusion, the reader is bound to conduct his own balancing operation, and it is this that forms the aesthetic experience offered by the literary text. However, if the reader were to achieve a balance, obviously he would then no longer be engaged in the process of establishing and disrupting consistency. And since it is this very process which gives rise to the balancing operation, we may say that the inherent non-achievement of balance is a prerequisite for the very dynamism of the operation.[50]

---

[49] See *BL* ii. 6 and n., 134.

[50] See 'The Reading Process: A Phenomenological Approach', in Lodge, *Modern Criticism and Theory*, 221.

Coleridge's subject–object fulcrum has in common with Iser's that it allows a carefully negotiatory compromise between granting the text's otherness and allowing that identification of subject with text which verges on delusion. In alternately preserving and collapsing the distinction between subject and object, both writers ensure that the reader maintains sufficient detachment from the text not to be assimilated by it. In this respect, they put into practice the mediations I have been discussing throughout this chapter.

Coleridge's poetics of reception involves an active version of passivity (in the process of reading) which he applauds, just as it rejects a passive version of activity (in the form of the reading-public) which he finds repellent. Might there be a connection between these two versions of the same dichotomy? Is the real source of Coleridge's irritation with readers that they refuse to be passive in the way he wishes; and is the activity he promotes in his ideal reader really just passivity in another guise? Certainly this seems to be the case, if one observes how consistently in his writing the reciprocity of author and reader is underwritten by theism; and how frequently the reader's activity is geared in a revelatory direction. Coleridge quotes Virgil's *Aeneid* to support this aesthetic:

'it is not lawful to enquire from whence it sprang, as if it were a thing subject to place and motion, for it neither approached hither, nor again departs from hence to some other place; but it either appears to us or it does not appear. So that we ought not to pursue it with a view of detecting its secret source, but to watch in quiet till it suddenly shines upon us; preparing ourseves for the blessed spectacle as the eye waits patiently for the rising sun.' (*BL* i. 241)

In the same way that the 'willing suspension of disbelief for the moment' constitutes a 'poetic faith' which for Coleridge is importantly distinct from credulity, so there is a 'wise passiveness' in relation to the sublime tenor of what is written which is distinct from lazy inactivity; and which may in the end be Coleridge's ideal for the reading-process.

VIII. THE RHETORIC OF MYSTERY

If the figure of the ideal reader acts as locus for the mediations I have described, all of which are held in place by the principle of sympathetic identification, it fulfils a number of significant historical/psychological functions. First, it provides a mechanism for negotiating the counter-claims of writers and readers, during a transitional period when they were being considerably unsettled; and second, it makes efforts to protect the writing–reading subject from internal division. Last but not least, it successfully preserves the mystery of the author within a discernible logocentric ideology, while apparently secularizing it as an aesthetic function. So long as we see Coleridge's 'ideal reader' as a figure produced defensively, from a complex of psychological motives, then it is not difficult to reconcile Wheeler's hermeneutic approach and Ha-milton's historical alternative. To read *Biographia*, as Wheeler does, for its complex engagement of reader-response is by no means to accord it the status of Umberto Eco's 'open text' or Barthes's 'writerly' text; any more than to read Coleridge's hermeneutic model of intertextuality, along the lines proposed by Shaffer, is to turn it into a prototype of the 'hyper-text'.[51] Nor is the ideal reader described by Wheeler playfully decon-structive, but rather willingly subservient to the critic's imaginative vision: a co-producer of the text's meaning, certainly, but one who never resists implicit directions from the author. We can of course choose to resist becoming Coleridge's ideal reader; and we can consider the defence mechanisms themselves as points of weakness rather than of strength. As soon as we do this, we begin to exercise what Rajan has called a 'negative' rather than a 'positive' hermeneutic,[52] and the various polarities which are mediated by the defence mechanisms inevitably start to break apart.

Peacock, in his brilliant impersonation of Coleridge's prose style in *Nightmare Abbey*, attacks its elitist defensiveness by way of mocking the philosophical density and obscurantism of its lexical content:

Subtleties! my dear Miss O'Carroll. I am sorry to find you participating in the vulgar error of the *reading public*, to whom an unusual collocation of words, involving a juxtaposition of antiperistastical ideas, immediately suggests the notion of hyperoxysophistical paradoxology.[53]

But it is in Coleridge's coercive rhetoric, not his mystifying vocabulary, that the inconsistencies arising from anxiety become most apparent: 'I must of necessity require the attention of my reader to become my

---

[51] For a description of the 'openness' of hypertexts, see George P. Landow, *Hypertext: The Convergence of Contemporary Critical Theory and Technology* (Baltimore: Johns Hopkins University Press, 1992).

[52] *Supplement of Reading*, 25–6.

[53] *Nightmare Abbey*, ch. 7, in *Peacock Works*, iii. 74.

fellow-labourer' Coleridge writes in *The Friend* (i. 21). Implicit in this egalitarian sharing of the workload was a belief that sympathetic identification was paramount; and that author and reader were working toward the same ends. The dignity of labour was thus granted to the reader; and indeed labour was promoted, as I have shown, through a range of encouraging and belittling strategies; but what was really required was that the reader should be a faithful servant of the text; or of the author as master. Nor was this a problem confined to the journalistic prose. Coleridge's lecturing style, too, evinced the troubling oscillation between authoritarian and egalitarian rhetoric which at every level characterized his engagement with his audience. Sympathy and friendship were expected as part of the intimate bonding between speaker and listener which he wished to establish ('I have made Friends of them all', he says, reporting on the 1813 series at Clifton (*Lectures*, ii. 3)). And the need for mutual trust was made a crucial ingredient of his apologetic style, as when he observed that 'the taedium felt by my hearers cannot be greater than my sympathy with it' (*Lectures*, i. 30); or when he appealed manipulatively to his listeners for 'forbearance with [his] Defects' (*Lectures*, i. 75). Yet, 'Never did any man treat his audience with less respect, or his task with less careful attention' was the judgement of one of his listeners in 1808 (*Lectures*, i. 146).

Obsequious advertisements, flattering his prospective audience (*Lectures*, ii. 4–5), reversed the expectation that Coleridge would be delivering truths from on high; and he gave his listeners the right to stand *in loco parentis*, indulgent and ambitious on his behalf:

> Like affectionate Guardians, you see without disgust the awkwardness, and witness with sympathy the growing-pains, of a youthful Endeavour, & look forward with a Hope which is its own reward, to the contingent results of Practice, to its intellectual Maturity. (*Lectures*, i. 75)

But in practice Coleridge was far from humble toward his audience. His pre-emptive strategies of modesty and self-criticism, designed to draw attention away from the content of his lectures, threw the awesome manner of their delivery into even stronger relief: Coleridge's ability to talk off the cuff, to captivate and mesmerize his audience, preserved intact the separateness of creative genius which he had characterized at the end of 'Kubla Khan'. The 'immethodical rhapsody' of Coleridge's lecturing style could be relied on to keep sublimity as a function of authorial imagination, while at the same time making the reader a co-producer of the sublime tenor. James Gillman, in his *Life of Coleridge*, described his eloquence as 'flowing like some great river, which winds its way majestically at its own "sweet will", though occasionally slightly impeded by a dam formed from its crumbling banks, but over which the accumulated waters pass onward with increased force' (*Lectures*, i. 250). It seems to have been the sense of blockage overcome that 'so arrested his listeners, as to make them feel almost breathless' (*Lectures*, i. 250); and it is not difficult to see significant parallels with the Kantian sublime.[54]

Some of the qualities of Coleridge's lecturing style are carried over into his prose: the use of apology, for instance —'I earnestly solicit the good wishes and friendly patience of my readers' (*BL* i. 105); the demand of sympathy from his audience, who thereby become fit (*BL* i. 69); and the manic digressiveness, which keeps his readers working towards the underlying unity, the overall design. There is, however, a crucial difference between the oral and the written, which Coleridge observes when contrasting the private reception of a book and the public recitation of a poem: that is the hypnotic relation of speaker to audience; the animal magnetism, which at once draws the reader into the circle and sets the author apart (*BL* ii. 239). It is this quality that has to be worked for, in Coleridge's prose, through those moments of metaphorical thickness or complexity which Wheeler describes so well; and which she sees as having the function of blocking the reader's progress, so as to make the emergence of meaning (the sublime tenor) all the more impressive. Her description of how obscurity functions in Coleridge's prose may be compared with Schleiermacher's discussion of the provisionality of understanding:

It becomes more complete as we are able to see each larger section as a coherent unity. But as soon as we turn to a new part we encounter new uncertainties and begin again, as it were, in the dim morning light. It is like starting all over, except that as we push ahead the new material illumines everything we have already

---

[54] See Neil Hertz's essay on 'Blockage and the Sublime', in *The End of the Line: Essays on Psychoanalysis and the Sublime* (New York: Columbia University Press, 1985); but compare also Schleiermacher's analysis of the difficulties experienced 'when something strange in a language blocks our understanding, [and] we must try to overcome the difficulty' (*Hermeneutics: The Handwritten Manuscripts*, 183). N. A. Halmi indirectly comments on the difference between Kant's 'blockage' and Schleiermacher's 'difficulty' when he observes that the sublime involves 'more than a (theoretically) temporary obstacle to comprehending something that has been presented to the mind; it is instead a permanent obstacle, arising from a fundamental disjunction between two mental faculties'. See 'From Hierarchy to Opposition: Allegory and the Sublime', *Comparative Literature*, 4 (Fall 1992), 337–60: 353.

treated, until suddenly at the end every part is clear and the whole work is visible in sharp and definite contours.[55]

And yet, since there is in Coleridge's later prose no 'final illumination' of the kind Schleiermacher describes, it is difficult to know where this leaves the reader's grasp of his meaning. Christensen puts it well when he argues that Coleridge's style 'is meant to be continuously obscure and the reader's understanding is meant to be continuously blocked, thereby continuously provoking the turn inward toward a transcendent entity continuously withheld'.[56]

It is at the point where we start acknowledging the poetic effects of Coleridge's critical discourse that we begin to understand more clearly the element of mystification which prevents his model of the reading-process from being genuinely 'open'. Yet, paradoxically, it is of course these moments which have generated most activity, speculation, and inventiveness on the part of Coleridge's readers. In the same way, it is clear that the model readers Coleridge places in his texts are not active proponents of interpretative liberty, so much as mediators between interpretative freedom and authorial rights. The wedding guest in 'The Ancient Mariner' begins by resisting the power of the mariner's story, but quickly finds that he 'cannot choose but hear'; the sceptical friend intervenes in chapter 13 to complain about the obscurity of Coleridge's argument; and ends by submitting willingly to its mystery (a mystery which is itself underwritten by his intervention, because it gives the chapter permission to reach premature conclusion). These figures are designed to elicit, but at the same time to overcome, disbelief: or rather, to allow the reader just so much critical purchase as to feel that the suspension of disbelief is something freely chosen; but not quite so much freedom as to choose otherwise.[57] It is the function of these figures to guide our own reading-habits; and performatively to underline a reverential attitude to authority. And yet, of course, it is precisely the presence of these figures in the text which has given deconstruction its lever for freeing the reader from the 'problematical logocentrism'[58] of

---

[55] Schleiermacher, *Hermeneutics: The Handwritten Manuscripts*, 198; and see Wheeler, *Sources, Processes, and Methods*, 81–98.

[56] *Coleridge's Blessed Machine of Language*, 215–16.

[57] For a very different reading, not only of the wedding guest's function but of the ironic presence of figures of disbelief in a wider range of texts, see Clayton Koelb, *The Incredulous Reader: Literature and the Function of Disbelief* (Ithaca, NY: Cornell University Press, 1984).

[58] Rajan sees as crucial the 'historical role of hermeneutics as conserver of a continued though problematical logocentric impulse in Romanticism' (*Supplement of Reading*, 29).

Coleridge's hermeneutics; just as it is the reversible hierarchy of 'primary' and 'secondary' imaginations which has allowed Coleridge's theological emphasis to be overturned by his secularizing readers.

One obvious conclusion to draw from this is that, ultimately, all texts are 'open' to the adventurous reader; and no amount of mystification will turn us into the passive recipients of sublime truth, if what we wish to do is to remain 'active creative beings' in our own right. Umberto Eco says as much, in the tantalizing remark that 'Everything can become open as well as closed in the universe of unlimited semiosis'.[59] But I want to conclude with a rather different suggestion. What is interesting about Coleridge's defence mechanisms is their ambivalence: while they evidently work strenuously for the writing side of the writing–reading subject, the levels of pre-emptive anxiety they betray in relation to readers imply an underlying acknowledgement of the reader's creative power. Just as, in a therapeutic situation (or, rather, its transference stage) the analyst begins to act out all the analysand's worst expectations, in response to the very defence mechanisms designed to prevent them, so it is the mystificatory strategies in Coleridge's prose which act as open invitations to the reader, by initiating crossings on the creative–critical divide. Such crossings need to be understood dialogically if individual acts of reading are to be distinguished from the collective menace of readers as Coleridge saw them. Then we can gain a clearer picture of the ascendancy of criticism—that secularizing movement of the 'secondary' into the place of the 'primary'—which Coleridge both resisted and helped to bring about.[60]

---

[59] *The Role of the Reader: Explorations in the Semiotics of Texts* (London: Hutchinson, 1979), 40.

[60] There are as many definitions of Coleridge's primary and secondary imaginations as there are readers. See e.g. Thomas McFarland, *Originality and Imagination* (Baltimore: Johns Hopkins University Press, 1985) and Jonathan Wordsworth, 'The Infinite I AM: Coleridge and the Ascent of Being', in Richard Gravil, Lucy Newlyn, and Nicholas Roe (eds.), *Coleridge's Imagination: Essays in Memory of Pete Laver* (Cambridge: Cambridge University Press, 1986), 22–52.

CHAPTER 3

Case Study (2): Wordsworth

No writer who thinks habitually of the critics, either to tremble at their censures or set them at defiance, can write well. It is the business of reviewers to watch poets, not of poets to watch reviewers.

Hazlitt, *Lectures on the English Poets*, 1818.

I. THE PUBLIC

'There is little need to advise me against publishing; it is a thing which I dread as much as death itself' (*EY*, 211). So Wordsworth wrote to James Tobin in March 1798, when his public reception was still an unknown quantity—at once the focus for long-term ambitions, and the cause of immediate practical concerns. The comment betrays his sense of a deep implicit connection between emergence into the public sphere and loss of personal identity: a connection felt so strongly that it resembles the threat of extinction. Despite the temporal and discursive gap which intervened between this letter and the composition of *The Prelude*, one might read Wordsworth's bald, prosaic acknowledgement of anxiety as a gloss on the famous passage in *The Prelude*, Book VIII where he likens creative process to a 'ferment quiet and sublime | Which, after a short space, works less and less' (ll. 424–5), until finally 'every effort, every motion gone | The scene before him lies in perfect view | Exposed, and lifeless as a written book' (ll. 725–7).[1] In this later passage, the achievement of finality is revealingly associated with a text that lies open to the gaze of passers-by—its creative vitality

---

[1] See *Prelude (1805)*, viii. 724–7. For discussions of this passage in terms of Wordsworth's fear of textuality, see Jonathan Wordsworth, *William Wordsworth: The Borders of Vision* (Oxford: Clarendon Press, 1982), 188–9; Mary Jacobus, *Romanticism, Writing and Sexual Difference* (Oxford: Clarendon Press, 1989), 14–16; and Lucy Newlyn, '"Questionable Shape": The Aesthetics of Indeterminacy', in John Beer (ed.), *Questioning Romanticism* (Baltimore: Johns Hopkins University Press, 1995), 226–9.

drained from it, at the point when it becomes most available to public scrutiny.

At all times in his writing career, Wordsworth disclosed an almost paranoid fear that poets were at the mercy of a hostile reading-public. In his critical writings he expressed the belief that he must transform the taste of his readers before he could be understood. His relations with reviewers were edgy and defensive because he construed them as the representatives and arbiters of public taste, whose capriciousness made them less willing to be transformed than were 'the people' themselves. He also saw in reviewers a threat to the privacy and distance of writers, whose personal and domestic lives were open to the gaze of the public—a threat of exposure which is hinted at in 'Star-Gazers' by a figuration of reading as 'prying and poring' to no happy or useful end. A more fearless revisionary poet than Coleridge, he was also subject to graver doubts about his stability as a writing-subject. He saw that the provisionality of literary tradition—its openness to the modifications and revisions of successive generations of reader-writers—made his own work vulnerable to misreading. Furthermore, he had no overarching system of authority on which to rely. While sharing Coleridge's assumptions about the damaging effects of passive reading, he did not believe that the Bible provided a model for reflective understanding. Nor—despite repeated attempts to establish a communitarian basis for acts of reading and interpreting—did he place an equivalent faith in hermeneutic principles of sympathy and community as the means whereby taste might be transformed. His less theorized, more improvisatory position appears by comparison intensely beleaguered. For him, the task of creating 'the taste by which he [was] to be enjoyed' was one of eliciting the reader's trust and cooperation in his literary endeavour—or, as he put it in 1815, of 'establishing that dominion over the spirits of readers by which they are to be humbled and humanised, in order that they may be purified and exalted'.[2] In this position of maximum dependency on readers, disguised as maximum power over them, the continuity and coherence of poetic self were all that could be relied on to ensure survival.

Wordsworth's anxieties were intensified by an awareness that, however deeply he identified his own voice with that of the people, his poetry would never be popular. The best-selling authors of this

---

[2] See 'Essay Supplementary to the Preface' (1815), in *Wordsworth Prose*, iii. 80–1.

period—Byron, Scott, Bloomfield—had formulas for success that were very different from his own. Wordsworth envied their popularity, but he was also critical of public taste, which he saw as too readily satisfied by narrative stimulants. For this reason, perhaps, Wordsworth's negotiations with his audience showed a mixture of tough-minded pragmatism and vulnerability. Throughout his career, the hope that he might ensure his correct reception involved him in the careful overseeing of how his volumes were produced, advertised, and marketed, as well as in a more theoretical attempt to direct the public's expectations. It was not until the hostile reception of *Poems in Two Volumes* (1807) that he had any genuine cause to feel aggrieved by the reactions of his audience; and yet as early as 1800 the pre-emptive direction of his authorial strategies was visible. The production of *Lyrical Ballads* was seen by him in terms of both commercial viability and the construction of a durable literary identity. Letters to Cottle dictating the shape of the volumes and the appearance of their typeface showed his concern with the minutiae of presentation;[3] while the Preface attempted to frame the volume's critical reception in a semi-apologetic series of directives to the reader. From the beginning, print must be warily supervised if self-image was to be made secure: Wordsworth intervened in both production and reception as a defensive measure.

Defence mechanisms are, however, notorious for eliciting the responses they are designed to pre-empt. Lamb wished the Preface had appeared separately, because it made the ballads look as if they were '*Experiments* on the public taste' (Marrs, i. 266–7)—so provoking Jeffrey's labelling of the Lake Poets as a new sect, to which Wordsworth objected.[4] Coleridge, with the benefit of hindsight, observed in *Biographia Literaria* that the Preface was 'the true origin of the unexampled opposition which Mr Wordsworth's writings have been since doomed to encounter'.[5] There is no doubt that by presenting himself as a theorist Wordsworth laid himself open to attack. Reviewer after reviewer took him to task for the 'system' underlying *Lyrical Ballads*, and went on holding this against him, even in the reception of much later works. ('Wordsworth is eminently, and as we think, faultily, a systematic writer', wrote a reviewer for the *British Critic*, as late as 1821.)[6] It is also clear that

---

[3] See Gill, 185.   [4] Gill, 267.
[5] *BL* i. 70–1. Coleridge has in mind Francis Jeffrey's reviews in the *Edinburgh Review*, i (1802) and 11 (1807).
[6] *British Critic*, 15 (Feb. 1821), 114.

when his exalted claims for the poet appeared in the expanded Preface to *Lyrical Ballads* (1802), he further weakened his standing with the reviewers by clothing himself in a grandeur which conflicted with his claim to be 'a man speaking to men'.[7] But although the defensiveness of his prefatorial material appears to have provoked rather than appeased his critics, this was not how Wordsworth himself saw the matter. The earnestness with which he packaged himself for public consumption increased as a result of attacks on *Poems in Two Volumes*, which he had risked submitting to the public with no theoretical framework. 'It is impossible that any expectations can be lower than mine concerning the immediate effect of this little work upon what is called the Public',[8] he claimed in a letter of May 1807; yet when they were lambasted by Jeffrey his reaction was one of wounded horror. The lesson he chose to learn from this was that the public could be relied on not at all; and that the reception of future volumes must be more tightly controlled than ever.

If hostile reviewers were to discard some of his output as trivial, it was Wordsworth's prerogative to show that underlying principles connected all his works according to a grand predetermined plan: hence the Preface to *The Excursion*, where his autobiographical poem is described as the 'ante-chapel' to a 'gothic Church', with all the minor pieces comprising its 'little cells, oratories, and sepulchral recesses'.[9] When both Jeffrey and Hazlitt proved resistant to these unifying claims, he retaliated with more: *Poems* (1815) had both a directive Preface, explaining the volume's internal categorization of poetic faculties, and an 'Essay Supplementary to the Preface' proclaiming the poet's immunity to hostile reception. Subsequent volumes were even more monolithic, showing an increasing preoccupation with the coherence and organic unity of poetic self. Revising each poem for its new appearance, Wordsworth placed what Stephen Gill has called an 'inordinate' demand on his readers, who must check every poem for its revisions to keep track of the growth of the poet's mind.[10] Determined as he was to keep his great autobiographical poem in reserve, he used the revisionary process as an alternative means of incorporating his life into his works. Nowhere since Milton's

---

[7] See esp. the passage beginning 'Poetry is the breath and finer spirit of all knowledge' (*Wordsworth Prose*, i. 141).

[8] To Lady Beaumont, May 1807 (*MY* i. 145).

[9] *Wordsworth's Poetical Works*, ed. E. De Selincourt (5 vols., Oxford: Clarendon Press, 1949), v. 2. For the intertextual relationship with Coleridge's description of entering a Gothic church, in *BL*, ch. 13, see Ch. 2 above.

[10] Gill, 367.

Defences had self-image, or the illusion of a seamless continuity between public and private identities, been so carefully cultivated.[11]

Nor does the parallel with Milton stop there. Wordsworth's abiding
concern was with finding a worthy audience; and increasingly the label
'fit though few' had an appropriate resonance, given the exacting nature
of his expectations and the extent of his disappointment with the public
at large.[12] As early as 1800, he established the imaginative poverty of
professional critics by referring to them as 'numerous', claiming that the
reader must 'utterly reject' their canon of criticism 'if he wishes to be
pleased with these volumes'.[13] Worthy readers were by inference at once
enlightened and singular—a position of privilege, as far as Wordsworth
was concerned, though not one that always met with gratitude. Crabb
Robinson, writing about *The Convention of Cintra* in the *London Review*
(1809), contrasted the prose of Burke, who 'being schooled in the House
of Commons always laboured to make himself intelligible to the lowest
capacity', with that of Wordsworth himself, who wrote 'from the woods
and lakes', and seemed 'content to be understood and relished by a few
like himself'.[14] A reviewer on the *British Critic*, writing in 1815, took the
poet's reclusiveness as a sign that he was out of kilter with his age:
'whose minds are set upon intrigues and fees, business and bustle, places
and preferments. . . . To such as these the retired poet cannot speak: they
have not learned the alphabet of his language'.[15]

Wordsworth's exclusiveness afforded him little compensation, however, for failing to reach a wider audience: 'remember no poem of mine
will ever be popular', he wrote ruefully to George Beaumont, in 1808,
'. . . I say not this in modest disparagement of the Poem ['Peter Bell'], but
in sorrow for the sickly taste of the Public in verse. The *People* would love
the Poem . . . but the *Public* (a very different Being) will never love it' (*MY*
i. 194). Even less convincing, as a defensive measure, is his slanted
account of literary history in the 'Essay Supplementary' of 1815. Arguing
that all great poets except Thomson had been neglected since their
first appearance, he traces the unreliability of critical taste through the

---

[11] See Dustin Griffin, *Regaining Paradise: Milton and the Eighteenth Century* (Cambridge: Cambridge University Press, 1986), ch. 2; and Lucy Newlyn, *'Paradise Lost' and the Romantic Reader*
(Oxford: Clarendon Press, 1993), 27–8.
[12] See Milton's invocation to Urania, *Paradise Lost*, vii. 30–1; echoed by Wordsworth in his
'Prospectus' to *The Recluse*, which was incorporated into 'Home at Grasmere': see ll. 970–2.
[13] Preface to *Lyrical Ballads* (1800), in *Wordsworth Prose* i. 128.
[14] *London Review* 2/4 (1 Nov. 1809).
[15] Review of *The Excursion*, *British Critic*, 3 (May 1815), 451.

eighteenth century. Special emphasis is given to the ephemerality of the poetic canon, as established by Johnson, and to Johnson's factual error in claiming that Milton was a popular poet during his lifetime. Using the 'slow progress of Milton's fame' and the public's 'unremitting hostility' to his own works as 'pledges and proofs' that 'the products of his industry will endure', Wordsworth brought himself into line with his great precursor.[16] True greatness was seen not only to survive initial unpopularity, but to be confirmed and guaranteed by the purblindness of public and critical opinion.

It was a case of special pleading, made more transparent by Wordsworth's wish (as in the earlier letter to Beaumont) to distinguish 'the people' from 'the public', so keeping open the possibility of becoming a popular poet. And it was immediately seized on by hostile reviewers as a mark of arrogance. 'This prophecy is not merely implied', wrote a reviewer in the *Monthly Review*, of Wordsworth's prediction of immortality: 'it is directly and plainly delivered by the prophet himself, of himself, and for his own benefit'.[17] Taking advantage of a perceived disjunction between the poet's lofty ambitions and the lowly tenor of his poems, the reviewer went on: 'we are so thoroughly overwhelmed by the high and mighty tone of this author's prose, that we really must have immediate recourse to his verse, in order to get rid of the painful humiliation and sense of inferiority which he inflicts on his readers'.[18] The jibes which followed were designed to puncture what were seen as inflated claims to grandeur on the poet's part; and the ease with which the reviewer hit his targets proved how readily Wordsworth's defensiveness played into his readers' hands.

Nor were matters improved when his *Letter to a Friend of Robert Burns* appeared in 1816. Identifying strongly with Burns, as a 'poet of the people' whose private life had been invaded and maligned, Wordsworth rose to the defence. His essay aimed, as one reviewer put it, 'to check ... the exuberant passion in the age for the most injudicious and most injurious exhibition of the faults and follies of departed men of genius'.[19] Its real subject, thinly disguised, was the undeserved vilification of Wordsworth himself at the hands of the periodicals; and its special target was of course the *Edinburgh Review*. 'The world is not to be gulled by his hypocritical zeal in the defense of injured merit', was the

---

[16] 'Essay Supplementary to the Preface' (1815), in *Wordsworth Prose*, iii, esp. 70–84.
[17] *Monthly Review*, 78 (Nov. 1815), 229.   [18] Ibid. 230.
[19] Ibid. 80 (June 1816), 221.

verdict from *Blackwood's* in June 1817: 'It is not Robert Burns for whom he feels,—it is William Wordsworth.'[20] And again, in November of the same year:

Who ... does not at once perceive that the true objects of the author's concern were not Robert Burns and Dr Currie, but himself and Mr Jeffray [*sic*], and those reviews of the *Lyrical Ballads*, the *Excursion*, and the *White Doe*, which he so credibly informs us he has never read? ... Cannot Mr Wordsworth content himself with sitting at home and carping at Mr Jeffray, in the midst of his own little knot of kindred worshippers at Keswick?[21]

Hazlitt, too, was angered by what he saw as the egocentricity of Wordsworth's interest in Burns. '[T]here is no common link of sympathy between them', he asserted: 'Nothing can be more different or hostile than the spirit of their poetry'.[22] Whatever else Wordsworth had hoped to achieve, he had certainly not convinced his critics that he was a man of the people. Lacking the credentials to speak accurately about his subject, he succeeded only in further alienating his detractors.

In cavalier comments such as 'I care little for the praise of any ... professional critic, but as it may help me to my pudding',[23] Wordsworth came to sound increasingly like Coleridge, whose pronouncements on the reading-public were notorious for their stentorian moral tone. Writing to Lady Beaumont in May 1807, apprehensive about the reception of *Poems in Two Volumes*, he complained that 'These people in the senseless hurry of their idle lives, do not *read* books, they merely snatch a glance at them that they may talk about them' (*MY* i. 150). Scott complained that Wordsworth did not do enough to conciliate the public by accommodating himself to their taste, and concluded that his friend cared little for what his readers thought of him. But this was impercipient. Wordsworth remained heavily dependent on the reception of his works by leading periodicals, and looked anxiously to the reviews for signs that he was succeeding in his mission to create the taste by which he was enjoyed: 'for those who dip into books in order to give an opinion', he lamented, '... for this multitude of unhappy, and misguided, and misguiding beings, an entire regeneration must be produced; and if this be possible, it must be a work *of time*' (*MY* i. 150).

[20] *Blackwood's Edinburgh Magazine*, 1 (June 1817), 265.

[21] Ibid. 2 (Nov. 1817), 203–4.

[22] *Lectures on the English Poets*, Lecture VII: 'On Burns, and the Old English Ballads' (Howe, v. 131).

[23] Quoted in Gill, 165.

The yearning to be popular nonetheless remained constant through-out his poetic career, and continued, paradoxically, to inform his most unworldly claims to patient aloofness. Accustomed to thinking of him-self as undervalued—'we shall never grow rich', wrote Dorothy in August 1816, 'for I now perceive clearly that till my dear Brother is laid in his grave, his writings will not produce any profit' (*MY* ii. 247)—Wordsworth went on courting recognition while appearing to accept neglect. 'We want no pensions or reversions for our heirs, and no monuments by public or private Subscription' he wrote proudly to Southey in April 1830: 'We shall have a monument in our works if they survive and if they do not we should not deserve it' (*LY* iii. 566). Well into his later years, after the advent of prosperity and with accolades showering in from all quarters, he adopted the stance of one whose true worth would be known only hereafter. '[I]f it be of God—it must stand' (*MY* ii. 181) has a quiet self-justifying confidence that is again reminis-cent of Milton, the poet with whom he consistently strove to identify himself. In review after review during the 1820's and onwards, Milton's name was coupled with his own, as though in obedience to his prophecy.

Even the awareness that he must look to posterity for lasting fame was bound up with the pragmatics of reception. The poet who cam-paigned concertedly to extend the duration of copyright, and thus to ensure that his family benefited after his death by his growing reputa-tion, can hardly be said to have desensitized himself to public opinion. Equating poetic identity with private property, he strove to keep his in the family, thereby guaranteeing that the select few by whom he was genuinely appreciated in his lifetime would stand to gain, when his true worth finally came to be acknowledged by the fickle many.[24] And by the same token, his strategy of deferring *The Prelude*'s publication until after his death was an act of poetic and economic 'husbandry'. In Erickson's words, its purpose was 'to give his heirs the strongest possible claim on his literary estate for as long as possible'. Wordsworth 'had come to feel that he had triumphed over his critics ... by living long enough to enjoy the financial fruits of his poetic labor and to give his heirs the post-humous benefit of the returns from his collected works for another forty two years'.[25]

---

[24] See Ch. 7, Sect. II, below for my discussion of copyright discourse and Wordsworth's place in it.

[25] *The Economy of Literary Form,: English Literature and the Industrialisation of Publishing, 1800–1850* (Baltimore: Johns Hopkins University Press, 1996), 67–8.

Wordsworth's anxiety with respect to contemporary neglect was always heavily disguised as a trust in future generations of readers. Writing to Sergeant Talfourd, in his 1838 petition to the House of Commons, he explained that the Bill for perpetual copyright had for its main object 'to relieve men of letters from the thraldom of being forced to court the living generation, to aid them in rising above degraded taste and slavish prejudice'.[26] Just as his obsessive habits of poetic revision were evidence of a poet who 'had difficulty in thinking of any work, even published work, as a final statement';[27] so his policy of deferral with respect to successful reception was an attempt to postpone for as long as possible the day of final judgement. By the same token, if publication was metaphorically associated in Wordsworth's imagination with the finality of death, then by a curious twist of logic, death itself became a moment of 'publication', when the poet relinquished self-possession. At a time when to think of the end of copyright was to think of the end of life, its extension became, in Susan Eilenberg's metaphor, a species of 'life-insurance', signifying the need to fix and ensure the durability of poetic self. Perhaps fearing that, in the process of becoming more widely read after his death, his own identity might be dispersed or lost, Wordsworth addressed the government

as if it had jurisdiction over the border between the dead and the living and could repair by legal means the damage death wreaks upon human bonds.... In seeking a way round the limitation on copyright the poet sought to pronounce from beyond the grave a controversion of his own mortality.[28]

II. COTERIE AUDIENCES

If, as Wordsworth himself believed, the public failed him, who were the 'few' on whose fitness he could depend? Stephen Gill, always a generous reader, suggests that while he had little time for the professional reviewer, Wordsworth was responsive to constructive criticism from other creative writers[29] and were it not for both poets' inherent

---

[26] *Wordsworth Prose*, iii. 319. This sentence appears in the 'Appendix' to the Reports of the Select Committee of the House of Commons.

[27] Stephen Gill, '"Affinities Preserved": Poetic Self-Reference in Wordsworth', *Studies in Romanticism*, 24 (1985), 535. 'He let nothing go', Gill claims: 'Of all the great poets he surely practices the most frugal imaginative husbandry' (ibid. 533).

[28] *Strange Power of Speech: Wordsworth, Coleridge, and Literary Possession* (Oxford: Oxford University Press, 1992), 196.

[29] Gill, 81.

competitiveness one might look to the dialogue with Coleridge as paradigmatic of such healthy egalitarian exchange. Coleridge's views were sought and respected by Wordsworth to a degree that no one else's ever were: *The Prelude* remained throughout his lifetime the 'Poem to Coleridge', its subordinate and unpublished position as part of *The Recluse* being largely due to the latter's insistence on his being a philosophical poet—a label which acted for Wordsworth as a kind of moral/aesthetic imperative, dictating the shape of his unfolding career. In respect of other works, too, he hung on Coleridge's approval: the publication of *The White Doe of Rylstone* was deferred for many years as a result of a critical letter; and his friend's much-delayed confession of disappointment with *The Excursion* stung him more keenly than all the reviews put together.

Such dependencies were openly acknowledged in a literary dialogue which thrived for a while on comment, counter-comment, and the readiness to accommodate each other's tastes. But the differences between these two writers outnumbered their similarities; and each cast the other in an equivocal role. Even the centrality of position accorded to Wordsworth in *Biographia Literaria* had its ambivalences. For Coleridge, the challenge of proving his friend to be the greatest living embodiment of the poetic spirit was made more difficult by theoretical disagreements about the nature and function of poetic language, as well as by the suspicion that some of Wordsworth's reviewers had been right. For Wordsworth, the satisfaction of being given so important a place in Coleridge's literary life was marred by anxieties: that some of his friend's mixed reputation might rub off on himself; that Coleridge's estimate of his poetic powers would appear to be further evidence of the complacent inwardness of the Lake School; and that the praise accorded to him as a 'philosophical' poet would further pressurize him to produce the increasingly unlikely 'Recluse'. None of his worries with respect to his public association with Coleridge proved negligible, especially given the haste with which *Biographia* was put together, and the incomprehension with which it was received by contemporary readers.

Although much of the early relationship fostered mutual trust, it later degenerated with the sad acknowledgement that the two writers had gone their separate ways. Recording a conversation with Wordsworth which took place in May 1812, Crabb Robinson wrote in his Diary: 'The approbation he has met with from some superior persons compensates for the loss of popularity, though no man has completely understood him, not excepting Coleridge, who is not happy enough to enter into his

feelings.' Wordsworth went on (with more than a touch of self-decep-
tion) to contrast his own independence with his friend's need for
approval: ' "I am myself...one of the happiest of men; and no man
who does not partake of that happiness, who lives a life of constant
bustle, and whose felicity depends on the opinions of others can
possibly comprehend the best of my poems" '.[30] Falling back for a
moment on old-established patterns of myth-making, Coleridge is
here classified as one of those benighted souls whose restless urban
existence numbs their capacity for deep Wordsworthian feeling.

   Aside from Coleridge, numerous others occupied temporary but
important supportive roles in Wordsworth's literary life: Lamb and
Southey were his longest-standing admirers, their comments on his
work providing a continuous stimulus from the 1790s to the later years;
Crabb Robinson proved a strong ally, when Wordsworth's relations
with the public were at their most embattled; and Scott came to be a
kind of surrogate Coleridge, after the earlier friendship had declined.
Wordsworth also showed a lifelong dependence on coterie audiences,
not all of whom wrote themselves, or were considered to be on his
intellectual level: Talfourd and Field, for instance, whom he met in 1815,
were disciples, rather than friends and equals.[31] In some respects, this
was the kind of literary connection that suited Wordsworth best. W. J.
Fox told Crabb Robinson that his response to Wordsworth's poetry was
less than wholehearted because 'he was not *initiated* or *fraternized*'[32];
while Coleridge's sarcastic description of a poet 'living almost wholly
among *Devotees*'[33] suggests his reliance for self-esteem on an intimate
circle of adoring family and friends. Fraternity in its unfamilial sense was
not part of the picture.

   The animus behind Coleridge's remark was assuredly his growing
sense of exclusion from the Wordsworth household, but there was
much more to their different ideas of an audience than that. Coleridge
saw the bond of sympathy between author and reader in terms of a
communitarian spirit, whose cohesiveness had its roots in Christianity.
The models for his reading-circles can be traced back, as Elinor Shaffer
has shown, to pantisocracy and its seventeenth-century analogues; as

[30] Henry Crabb Robinson, *Diary, Reminiscences and Correspondence*, selected and ed. Thomas
Sadler Ph.D. (3 vols., London: Macmillan and co., 1869), i. 382.
   [31] See Gill, 312.
   [32] *The Correspondence of Henry Crabb Robinson with the Wordsworth Circle*, ed. Edith J. Morley
(2 vols., Oxford: Clarendon Press, 1927), i. 83.
   [33] Coleridge to Tom Poole, 14 Oct. 1803, in Griggs, ii. 1013.

can the principle of friendship, which underwrote both his literary dialogues and publishing ventures including *The Friend* itself.[34] Wordsworth's relations with his readers were both more exclusive and more quarrelsome, depending as they did on personal loyalty and cooperation. When Southey reviewed *Lyrical Ballads* in 1798, Wordsworth complained to Cottle: 'If he could not conscientiously have spoken differently of the volume, he ought to have declined the task of reviewing it'.[35] Southey had clearly overstepped the mark, by allowing his professional role to obscure his private allegiance.

Small interpretative communities were frequently organized in the early nineteenth century to define and constrain the activity of reading; but in Wordsworth's case this was a more than usually systematic practice, linked to his reticence about emerging into the public sphere. The circulation of manuscripts among family and friends was a custom he observed throughout his life. (As early as 1793, Dorothy recorded that she and Christopher amused themselves 'by analysing every Line and prepared a very bulky Criticism . . . to transmit to William'.)[36] So too was the reading aloud of poems just written or as yet incomplete: Hazlitt heard 'Peter Bell' in 1798, and Crabb Robinson was lent it in 1812; but its publication was delayed until 1819. The *White Doe*, composed in 1807, was recited to Hazlitt when he visited the poet in 1808; and Southey, Coleridge, and Lamb each heard it before its final publication in 1815. *The Prelude* had limited circulation among select readers, and was read aloud in its entirety to Coleridge in 1807, but never printed in Wordsworth's lifetime. Even Coleridge's generous acknowledgement of its importance in *Biographia Literaria* met with resistance from its author, who found burdensome this 'precursorship of Praise'; and requested that when it finally came to be published after his death, 'no Copies be sent to any Reviewer or Editor of Magazines or Periodicals whatever.'[37]

Lamenting *The Prelude*'s non-appearance, Southey provided a telling diagnosis of the anxieties which underlay Wordsworth's fear of publica-

---

[34] See 'The Hermeneutic Community: Coleridge and Schleiermacher', in Richard Gravil and Molly Lefebure (eds.), *The Coleridge Connection: Essays in Honour of Thomas McFarland* (Houndmills, Basingstoke: Macmillan, 1990), 41–80.

[35] Wordsworth to Cottle, summer 1799 (*EY* 268).

[36] Dorothy Wordsworth to Jane Pollard, 16 Feb. 1793 (*EY* 89).

[37] In 1815, Wordsworth begged Coleridge not to publish 'To William Wordsworth', judging that 'The commendation would be injurious to us both, and my work when it appears, would labour under a great disadvantage in consequence of such a precursorship of Praise', Wordsworth to Coleridge, 22 May 1815 (*MY* ii. 238). The request that no copies of *The Prelude* be sent for review is quoted and discussed by Erickson, *Economy of Literary Form*, 60.

tion. 'He has a miserly feeling concerning [his poems] as if by being published they would cease to be his own.'[38] Feedback from close associates was naturally more palatable to Wordsworth than the dispersal of self which accompanied public exposure; and especially so given his longstanding battle with the periodical reviewers. But even where associates were concerned, Wordsworth's demands on his readers were considerable. Dorothy came as near as anyone to being his ideal reader, yet on the whole the 'bulky criticism' she and Christopher had provided in 1793 was not what Wordsworth expected of the chosen and trusted few. When Crabb Robinson confessed that he dared not read the lines 'three feet long by two feet wide' etc. in company, Wordsworth observed peremptorily, 'they ought to be liked';[39] and of Lamb's response to *The White Doe* he wrote to Coleridge: 'Let Lamb learn to be ashamed of himself in not taking some pleasure in the contemplation of this picture'.[40] The tone of this remark would have greatly amused Lamb, who in 1801 had received 'a long letter of four sweating pages' telling him why Wordsworth 'was compelled to wish that [his] range of *Sensibility* was more extended' (Marrs, i. 272). Lamb had merely indicated his personal preference for the first edition of the *Lyrical Ballads*.

When Sara Hutchinson complained that 'The Leechgatherer' was tedious, Wordsworth's outraged rejoinder—'everything is tedious when one does not read with the feelings of the Author' (*EY* 367)—suggested the expectation of unconditional empathy from his readers. Nothing less was required than that a person should read this poem with feelings like his (*EY* 366). Similarly, replying to an otherwise unqualified letter of homage from John Wilson, also in 1802, Wordsworth rebuked him for not responding with the poet's own 'exceeding delight and pleasure' to 'The Idiot Boy' (*EY* 355). On such occasions, Wordsworth's directives to members of a coterie audience shaded into the tones of solemn persuasiveness adopted in his Prefaces. Somewhere in-between were instructions of the kind issued to Charles James Fox, in January 1801, about how to read 'The Brothers' and 'Michael' (*EY*, 312–15). In its optimistic reliance on exemplary individuals and reflective reading as a means for political change, this letter came as near as Wordsworth ever did to Coleridge's endeavours to induce a clerisy. But always the key to

---

[38] *Henry Crabb Robinson on Books and their Writers*, ed. Edith J. Morley (London: J. M. Dent and sons, 1938), i. 34.

[39] Id., *Diary*, i. 482.

[40] Wordsworth to Coleridge, 19 Apr. 1808 (*MY* i. 222).

his bond with readers was his power to persuade and their willingness to be persuaded, rather than (as in Coleridge's case) the mutual observance of a religious aesthetic, whose rules had been established by long tradition. It was this that gave Wordsworth's engagement with the reader its querulous egotism, making the transition between 'private' and 'public' audiences problematic. The purpose of his poetry was to extend the range of his audience's feelings; yet, to do this, he depended absolutely on his readers' willingness to enter his own emotional world. John Wilson's resistance to the poetic representation of idiocy, or Sara Hutchinson's to the 'naked simplicity' of 'The Leechgatherer', signified for Wordsworth the breakdown of that implicit trust between author and reader on which his poetic project was founded. That he should go ahead, after receiving Sara's letter, and revise 'The Leechgatherer' in the direction he did, is a measure of the transparency with which his demand for obedience masked his need for approval.[41]

III. THE CONDITIONS OF UNDERSTANDING: CRITICAL PROSE

The problem Wordsworth encountered in his dealings with readers is described in Schleiermacher's *Hermeneutics* as a precondition for all acts of understanding: 'One must already know a man in order to understand what he says, and yet one first becomes acquainted with him by what he says'.[42] In other words, to know an author you have to understand him, but to understand him you have already to know him. Understanding presupposes a dialectic between self and other. Yet, without the readiness to enter the other's imaginative world, no genuine act of understanding can take place; and this entry involves relinquishing one's separateness (and thus, potentially, one's difference) from the other.

Such was the extent of Wordsworth's need for empathy on the part of his readers that it could lead to an erasure of difference; and frequently this appeared to be something striven for rather than accidentally achieved. In his critical prose, for instance, trust had to be carefully established by rhetorical strategies, rather than either relied on as an

---

[41] For the significance of Wordsworth's revisions to 'The Leechgatherer', all of which move the poem away from its balladic origins and matter of fact style, see my *Coleridge, Wordsworth, and the Language of Allusion* (Oxford: Clarendon Press, 1986), 117–37.

[42] *Hermeneutics: The Handwritten Manuscripts*, ed. Heinz Kimmerle, trans. James Duke and Jack Forstman (Missoula, Mont.: Scholars Press, 1977), 99.

emotional given or assumed as a contractual undertaking. Hence the deployment of defensive manoeuvres such as apology and the anticipation of objections, alongside tones ranging from the diplomatically appeasing ('I hope therefore the Reader will not censure me')[43] to the coercive ('there are few persons of good sense, who would not allow...').[44] This latter, as it turned out, was his favoured method for appealing to his readers as though they were already members of the elect. Wordsworth's aim was thus to transform an anonymous public into a sympathetic readership, whose credentials for understanding him were as sound as his family's and friends'. But rhetorically, as well as conceptually, an impasse was produced in the process: 'the understanding of the being to whom we address ourselves, if he be in a healthful state of association, must necessarily be in some degree enlightened':[45] so Wordsworth claimed in the 1800 Preface, without appearing to notice that his capacity to improve his readers' health must therefore depend upon their being already healthy. One wonders whether city-dwellers, readers of newspapers and novels, or any of the other examples he gives of people addicted to 'gross and violent stimulants', were included in the fitness programme he was proposing?

Jon Klancher has argued that Wordsworth saw the middle-class audience as 'consumers of a brutalised popular culture fashioned for urban readers', and that 'he sought to reverse that consumption into a form of reception'.[46] Whereas 'consumption' suggests an activity that is appetitive and mindless, 'reception' is tacitly passive but reflective: Wordsworth's task, then, was to demonstrate that the 'degrading thirst after outrageous stimulation' could evolve into a reflective awareness that action was transitory, and that the capacity for deep feeling might be awakened by 'gentle shocks of mild surprise'.[47] But how was subtlety to be appreciated, except by the subtle? In negotiating the circularity of his own argument, Wordsworth drew the circle ever more tightly; for the model of reading outlined in the Preface did not in fact separate 'reception' from its sensationalist opposite; rather, it proposed what

---

[43] *Wordsworth Prose*, i. 122.
[44] Ibid. 142.
[45] Ibid. 126.
[46] *The Making of English Reading Audiences, 1790–1832* (Madison, Wisc.: University of Wisconsin Press, 1987), 143.
[47] I quote from 'There was a Boy', l. 19. Wordsworth's theory of metre, like his theory of the sublime, works on the principle that our deepest feelings occur at moments when concentration, strained to the utmost, suddenly relaxes, making us acutely receptive.

might be called an erotics of reading, in which receptivity was measured in terms of the extent of pleasure received. 'The Poet writes under one restriction only', Wordsworth claimed, 'namely, the necessity of giving immediate pleasure to a human Being possessed of that information which may be expected of him ... as a Man.'[48] Just as man subsisted on 'the grand elementary principle of pleasure, by which he knows, and feels, and lives, and moves', so 'the end of poetry', in Wordsworth's view, was 'to produce excitement in coexistence with an overbalance of pleasure'. The poet's words 'must raise the reader to a height of desirable excitement'; and his metrical arrangements must give the reader 'small but continual and regular impulses of pleasurable surprise'. Furthermore, 'the Poet ought to ... take care, that whatever passions he communicates to his reader, those passions, *if his Reader's mind be sound and vigorous*, should always be accompanied with an overbalance of pleasure'.[49] None of this makes it clear just how the 'gratification of the reader' produced by poetry was distinct from the gratification produced by a frantic novel or sickly and stupid German tragedy, except (implicitly) in the manliness with which it was administered. (When the style is manly, and the subject important, words would impart pleasure, Wordsworth claimed.) Nor did he suggest how the reader's 'soundness' and 'vigour' were to be tested, other than through their capacity to be excited 'without the application of gross and violent stimulants'. The poet was left giving pleasure only where pleasure was already due, to those fit and few enough to be properly receptive.

The same circularity is shown when discussing the 'endless fluctuations and arbitrary associations' to which language is subject, in his 'Essay Supplementary to the Preface' of 1815. Wordsworth claims that 'The genius of the poet melts these down for his purpose; but they retain their shape and quality to him who is not capable of exerting, within his own mind, a corresponding energy'.[50] The capacity for 'energy' is therefore a prerequisite for healthy reader-response, but it must 'correspond' to the poet's own; and this correspondence depends implicitly on being in a 'healthful state of association'.[51] Wordsworth begs the question of how far associations are in the public domain in the first place, thus evading the issue of whether they are in fact available to be 'melted down' by the poet's genius. Presumably to overcome the Lockian nightmare of a private associationism gone mad, he proposes that there

[48] Preface to *Lyrical Ballads*, in *Wordsworth Prose*, i. 139.   [49] Ibid. 150.
[50] *Wordsworth Prose*, iii. 82.   [51] Ibid. 126.

should be a healthy correspondence between poet and reader; yet the main criterion of a reader's health appears to be the willingness to enter Wordsworth's own associative world—which means, effectively, that one set of private associations wins out over another, not that communication involves entering a shared (and public) domain.

The Shandyan possibilities of this circular theory are humorously exposed by Francis Jeffrey in the passage from his review of *Poems in Two Volumes* dealing with Wordsworth's Note to 'The Thorn'. Quoting the note at length, Jeffrey highlights the pedantry behind Wordsworth's expectation that

> The reader will have a general notion, if he has ever known a man, *a captain of a small trading vessel*, for example, who, *being past the middle age of life*, has retired upon *an annuity, or small independent income*, to some *village*, or country town, of which he was *not a native*, or in which he had not been accustomed to live. [52]

He then goes on, with comical incredulity, to puncture Wordsworth's faith in this shared experience, and to show how vulnerable the poet becomes to the charge of solipsism (or even sheer whimsy), once the expectation of a communicative bond is removed:

> Now, we must be permitted to doubt, whether, among all the readers of Mr Wordsworth, there is a single individual who has had the happiness of knowing a person of this very peculiar description; or who is capable of forming any sort of conjecture of the particular disposition and turn of thinking which such a combination of attributes would be apt to produce. To us, we will confess, the *annonce* appears as ludicrous and absurd, as it would be in the author of an ode or an epic to say, 'Of this piece the reader will necessarily form a very erroneous judgement, unless he is apprised, that it was written by a pale man in a green coat,—sitting cross-legged on an oaken-stool—with a scratch on his nose, and a spelling dictionary on the table.' [53]

Jeffrey catches the solemnity of Wordsworth's tone in preparing his readers for 'The Thorn''s proper reception. As a resistant reader, he also shows how futile is the poet's hope that the 'endless fluctuations and arbitrary associations' of language can be controlled simply by a willed act of imposition. The associationist model within which Wordsworth was working (and which Jeffrey himself shared) in this instance exerts a strain on the bond between poet and reader by assuming too much shared experience. There is only one reader who fulfils the poet's excessive expectations, Jeffrey implies, and that reader is Wordsworth himself.

[52] *Edinburgh Review*, 12/23 (Apr. 1808), 136–7.   [53] Ibid.

Operating from within a circular hermeneutics of identification, Wordsworth betrayed a confusion about the extent to which readers must be active or passive, if they were truly to understand. Kurt Heinzelman has claimed that he 'probed more deeply than his predecessors and contemporaries into the economic status of poeisis', and that his understanding of poetry as 'a socially productive, economically pertinent labour' was reflected in his repeated emphasis on the mutual exertions of poet and reader, as in his definition of the literary work as a form of labour:

In Wordsworth's economy the *reader*, the nominal consumer, must also be a *productive* laborer. Indeed, Wordsworth's labor theory affirms that *only* in the exchange of poetry is 'productive consumption' not an oxymoron...but a powerful transformation and overbalancing of that getting and spending which lay waste our powers.[54]

In practice, however, Wordsworth's understanding of the reader's role was more equivocal than Heinzelman asserts. The 'Essay Supplementary to the Preface' claims that 'without the exertion of a co-operating *power* in the mind of the Reader', there can be no sympathy with pathos or sublimity: indeed, 'without this auxiliary impulse, elevated or profound passion cannot exist'.[55] And yet readers were only nominally exerting themselves, in an interchange where power was seen as auxiliary and cooperative. In much the same way, his rhetorical question—'Is it to be supposed that the Reader can make progress . . . like an Indian Prince or General—stretched on his Palanquin, and borne by his slaves?'— implicitly rebukes his readers for their lack of exercise: 'No, he cannot proceed in quiescence, he cannot be carried like a dead weight'.[56] Such enthusiasm for the reader's activity does not, however, amount to a claim for equality. Wordsworth suggests, rather, that the 'advance made by the soul of a poet' over his readers is akin to a 'conquest', and that the great and original genius is 'in the condition of Hannibal among the Alps'.[57] Such militaristic metaphors take one back to the idea of sublime invulnerability with which he protected his authorial status—ruling out the possibility of dialogue, at least in the critical prose.

---

[54] *The Economics of Imagination* (Amherst, Mass.: University of Massachussetts Press, 1980), 232–3.
[55] *Wordsworth Prose*, iii. 81.
[56] Ibid. 80.
[57] Ibid.

IV. THE IMPLICATED READER: POEMS OF DIALOGUE, WITNESS, AND ENCOUNTER

It is Wordsworth's poetry, not his prose, that has provided the material for all those accounts of his hermeneutics seeking to maximize his generosity to the reader—accounts ranging from the poetics of indeterminacy teased out by Geoffrey Hartman; through Susan Meisenhelder's application of Iser's reader-response theory; to Tilottama Rajan's proposal that the poetry encourages a 'negative hermeneutic'; and on yet further into Don Bialostosky's Bakhtinian emphasis on the 'dialogic', and Michael Baron's recuperation of Wordsworth's poetry of relationship and community.[58] The reasons for this sharp discrepancy in approaches to the poetry and the prose are not hard to discover. If one is looking at Wordsworthian epistemology as a kind of blueprint for creative reciprocity, the poems suggest a more egalitarian analogue for writer–reader relations than anything in the critical prose. (The 'interchangeable supremacy' of mind and nature posited in *The Prelude*, for instance, comes as near as possible to genuine dialectic.) In the sophistication with which they handle subject–object positions, Wordsworth's poems explore the potential for collaboration between poet and reader in terms of a movement to and fro between self and other which is constitutive of hermeneutic consciousness. By showing how readily this movement can turn into absorption or narcissistic reflection, they provide a semi-parodic critique of the impasse we saw operating in the critical prose, where the expectation of readerly sympathy resembles the need for a reflex or echo of authorial self.

Furthermore, it is in the poetry that the bond (or perhaps bondage) of identification between author and reader is acknowledged by Wordsworth to be inadequate protection against the anxiety of reception. As his handling of dialogues between human subjects shows, when self constitutes the other as its own reflex, communication has effectively

[58] For my discussion of Hartman's poetics, see 'Reading After: The Anxiety of the Writing-Subject', first delivered at a conference in Warwick, 'Culture and Critical Form: Reading after Geoffrey Hartman'; and later published in *Studies in Romanticism*, 35/4 (Winter 1996), 609–28. For a less dialectical model of the reading process than Hartman's, see Susan Edwards Meisenhelder, *Wordsworth's Informed Reader: Structures of Experience in his Poetry* (Nashville, Tenn.: Vanderbilt University Press, 1988). For Tilottama Rajan's definition of a 'negative' hermeneutic, see *The Supplement of Reading: Figures of Understanding in Romantic Theory and Practice*, (Ithaca, NY: Cornell University Press, 1990), 5; and for her understanding of Wordsworth's engagement with the reader, see ibid. 141–66. I am particularly indebted to Michael Baron's recent study, *Language and Relationship in Wordsworth's Writing* (London: Longman, 1995).

broken down. One thinks, not just of 'Anecdote for Fathers' or 'We are Seven', where communication problems are considered as aspects of educational theory; but of poems such as 'Old Man Travelling', 'The Discharged Soldier', and 'The Leechgatherer', where the potential mismatch between subjectivities is accepted as a psychological and epistemological given. In these dialogue and encounter poems, Wordsworth exposes the overinterpreting tendencies of narrators whom he closely identifies with his poetic self. The problem of misunderstanding is presented as a problem of misreading, but writers are implicitly akin to readers in their acts of appropriation.

The fact that Wordsworth's concern with the dubiety of interpretation cuts both ways should not blind us, however, to the fact that some of his poetic strategies shared the defensive tendencies of his critical prose. At the same time as implicating the poet in appropriative compulsions which he associated with the reading-public—and more obliquely with the activity of professional criticism, as it was being contemporaneously defined—Wordsworth's dialogue and encounter poems of the late 1790s attempted to suggest what responsible interpretation might be. In doing so, they entered political terrain; for the reading-practices they condemned were of a kind associated with the consumption of sensationalist literature; and the alternative they advocated involved a meditative and reflective quietism, at odds with fashionable literary tastes.

The narrator in 'Old Man Travelling', who describes an old man picking his way along the road as 'insensibly subdued | To settled quiet' (ll. 7–8), may well be guilty of projection. But although his subjectivity is foregrounded, this does not undercut the poem's tranquillizing message. In the ambiguous lines, 'the young behold | With envy, what the old man hardly feels' (ll. 13–14), the word 'hardly' can be read both as a sceptical reference to his misreading and as confirmation of the serene self-oblivion of old age.[59] Similarly, although this sense of possible disturbance behind the façade of tranquillity is later deepened (when the old man responds to the narrator's questions with his brief and blank account of private tragedy), the impression of the old man's serenity is left unretracted. It is as though Wordsworth's resistance to sensational-

---

[59] For a subtle and suggestive reading of 'Old Man Travelling' in which it is argued that 'the poem dramatically questions the whole habit of depicting others as objects of meditation at all', see Heather Glen, *Vision and Disenchantment: Blake's Songs and Wordsworth's* Lyrical Ballads (Cambridge: Cambridge University Press, 1983), 7.

ism—his refusal to hype personal tragedy into theatricality or political commentary—insensibly subdues his readers to a 'settled quiet' resembing the old man's. We are, it seems, being asked to approach the mysterious otherness of human beings with a tact that the narrator himself initially endangers, but which the poem idealizes. In its meditative contemplation of the human losses which occur during times of war, the poem shows us that by becoming more reflective readers, we will become more responsible witnesses.

If the retrospective account offered in *The Prelude* is anything to go by, Wordsworth feared that, like other observers of the French Revolution on this side of the Channel, he was guilty of treating the materials of recent history as though they belonged to a novel of sensibility or partook of the 'spectacle' of theatre: 'I looked for something which I could not find, | Affecting more emotion than I felt', he wrote in Book IX, recalling his visit as a tourist to the Bastille in 1790 (*Prelude (1805)*, ix. 70–1). Running alongside each other two different preoccupations (with epistemological uncertainty, and with the accountability of witnesses) his poetry of 1797–8 atones for the guilt and ambivalence of his response to the Revolution—a 'drama' he narrowly missed experiencing at first hand, but in whose plot he felt himself to be ineluctably implicated. By considering the suffering of marginalized or outcast individuals who were the victims of the protracted war with France, he replaced the sensationalist, action-packed subject-matter of distant revolutionary events with circumstances closer to home. And by foregrounding the uncertain status of eyewitnesses in relation to this subject-matter, he made the issue of accountability one that had implications for both readers and writers.

The impulse that motivated Wordsworth's tales of 'silent suffering', 'by moving accidents uncharactered'[60] was nothing less than a radical modification of public taste. By selecting either the ballad form, with its concentrated and impersonal narratorial style, or a blank-verse idiom that kept action to a minimum, he redefined the genre to which human suffering belonged, rejecting or revising alternative media such as drama, sensibility, and the Gothic, all of which—at least in their contemporary manifestations—he saw as crudely encouraging the tastes he abhorred. (Thus, even when composing his political drama, *The Borderers*, he repudiated the transitoriness of action in favour of the permanence,

---

[60] See 'The Ruined Cottage', ll. 233, 232.

obscurity, and darkness of internal states of mind.)[61] In emptying his own narration of any tendency to pander to the craving for stimulation, he succeeds in turning the reader's attention from extraordinary incidents to the problem of how they are to be assimilated and understood. Sometimes this is done via dramatic monologue (as in the laconic first-person narratives included among the *Lyrical Ballads*), but more often than not, it is explored through the perspectives of those who did not experience hardship at first hand. The pedlar in 'The Ruined Cottage', the sea-captain in 'The Thorn', the narrators in 'Old Man Travelling' or 'The Discharged Soldier', are all distanced from the suffering they observe; and their function as 'implicated readers' is crucial to Wordsworth's revisionary project.

It was only logical that, as part of this project, Wordsworth's own tendency to 'read | The forms of things with an unworthy eye' ('Ruined Cottage', ll. 510–11) should come under scrutiny, as in 'Old Man Travelling'. For there is an incipient danger in all narrative to make aesthetic patterns out of the intractable material of human experience; and this pattern-making can lead to distortion or exploitation. 'The Discharged Soldier' explores the possibility of an imaginative observer being (perhaps by definition) an unreliable witness. As elsewhere, the suffering of an individual, met in a chance encounter, is Wordsworth's theme; but here the mental processes of the observing subject are elaborately foregrounded. There is a strong identification between the narrator's receptive state of mind and the poet's own creative processes, together with a close scrutiny of the ways in which heightened consciousness creates illusions. The poem's long opening sequence establishes the observer's suggestibility—his fictionalizing and specifically Gothicizing tendencies—so that we are inclined to be already sceptical, when the soldier makes his first appearance, of the ways in which he is described. His resemblance to Milton's Death is touched on lightly, to allow us to stand outside the momentary terrors experienced by the poem's Radcliffian narrator; and observations such as 'You might almost think | That his bones wounded him' (ll. 44–5) or 'I think | If but a glove had dangled in his hand | It would have made him more akin to man' (ll. 65–7) are presented as unlikely suppositions, in which the gap between reality and imagination perceptibly widens. Gesturing in the

[61] See *The Borderers*, III. v. 60–5, ed. Robert Osborn (Ithaca, NY: Cornell University Press, 1982), 214.

direction of popular narratorial conventions, Wordsworth registers not only his ironic relation to novels and novel-readers, but his self-ironizing awareness of their powerful hold over his own acts of narration.

Wherever the conventions of Gothic or of sensibility surface in Wordsworth's poetry, they suggest the poet's awareness that he too might be implicated in the exploitative tendencies of sensationalist fiction. Significantly, the disjunction between perceiver and perceived, reader and read, is somewhat lessened as 'The Discharged Soldier' progresses (at least at the level of Wordsworth's didactic tenor) so that the narrator is seen to undergo a kind of hermeneutic education in the course of his encounter. As in 'Old Man Travelling', it is the soldier's dignified habit of understatement that corrects the storyteller's Gothic fantasies. In altering his own narratorial register so that it echoes the soldier's deflated diction ('solemn and sublime | He might have seemed, but that in all he said | There was a strange half-absence . . .', ll. 141–3) he suggests that he has learned something about the necessary process of tact (or self-abstraction) involved in recording human experience. And in the same way, his readiness to receive admonishment from the soldier's refusal of charity implies that he has moved on from the conventional codes of sensibility into which he had attempted to slot this uncomfortable encounter. Mackenzie's Man of Feeling would experience, in a moment of almsgiving such as this, a rush of self-gratification;[62] but the misplaced philanthropy of Wordsworth's narrator is deprived of any reward beyond self-knowledge.

Wordsworth's concern with the compulsion to make narratives of human suffering takes a more subtly dialogic form in 'The Thorn', where he provides a relativist framework from which to consider the responsibilities of interpretation. Instead of focusing exclusively on the workings of a single consciousness, this poem includes the suppositions of village gossips about the circumstances of Martha Ray. These are reported by the sea-captain, in his attempt to construct a narrative, so that two different perspectives on events are indirectly supplied. The narrator's viewpoint is not subjected to so obvious a species of 'reality testing' as in the blank-verse poems, where dialogue is used to suggest the yawning gap that exists between self and other. Instead, Wordsworth allows two different viewpoints to bring each other under question. The unreliability of witnesses is thus suggested implicitly, by way of an

---

[62] See e.g. the end of ch. 20: Henry Mackenzie, *The Man of Feeling*, ed. Brian Vickers (Oxford: Oxford University Press, World's Classics, 1982), 35.

open-ended narrative method which accentuates our own judgements as readers.

It is in the tension between the Gothic sensationalism of the village gossips and the sea-captain's more cautious hints at horror that the narrative is allowed to unfold; and between these two alternative perspectives the reader must either choose or remain undecided. Wordsworth draws, here, on a narratorial technique which had been fully and sophisticatedly developed in the novels of Ann Radcliffe. But he complicates the Radcliffian pattern in several important ways. First, in an apparent reversal, his protagonist (unlike her heroines) appears to be resistant to Gothic possibilities, rather than credulously susceptible to them; so that, as the gruesome details of Martha's seduction, desertion, grief, infanticide, and madness emerge, their verifiability is placed under question by the sea-captain's bewildered refrain: 'I cannot tell, I do not know'. Secondly, Wordsworth offers no authorial closure, no rationalist explanation of events delivered from on high, but leaves his readers to reach their own conclusions about the truth or otherwise of Martha's story. Thus, the poem does not chart an education away from superstition and towards enlightenment, of the kind undergone by Radcliffe's heroines and readers, but remains suspended between belief and disbelief.

As it turns out, this internal division of allegiances is crucial to Wordsworth's characterization of the sea-captain, who may appear at first sight to be empirically rationalist ('I measured it from side to side | 'Tis three feet long and two feet wide'), but whom Wordsworth describes, in his Note to the poem, as a superstitious man, 'of slow faculties and deep feelings'. Paradoxically, the puzzled scepticism of this narrator's refrain registers the degree of his curiosity, just as his resistance to the story he is himself unfolding creates what Susan Wolfson would call a 'questioning presence' in the text,[63] dramatizing the reader's own superstitious excitement. Coleridge uses a similar device in 'The Ancient Mariner', where the wedding guest's interruptions—' "Hold off! unhand me, greybeard loon!" ' (l. 11)—suggest the hypnotic hold of storyteller over listener, drawing the reader more closely into an involvement with the poem's incredible events. In each case, the narrative is propelled forward by an alternation between what Iser (in his account of the reading-process) calls 'illusion-building and illusion-breaking'. The reader's interaction with the text closely resem-

---

[63] See *The Questioning Presence: Wordsworth, Keats, and the Interrogative Mode in Romantic Poetry* (Ithaca, NY: Cornell University Press, 1986).

bles that of the water insect in Coleridge's famous simile, each moment
of resistance to the Gothic storyline acting as a 'momentary *fulcrum* for a
further progression' (*BL* i. 124).

Read in this way, 'The Thorn' may be seen as an elaborate practical
application of Wordsworth's concern (voiced in the Preface to *Lyrical
Ballads*) with reforming the contemporary reader's appetite for Gothic
narrative. It succeeds in exposing the sea-captain's unwilling participation in the story purveyed by the local gossips, just as it parodies our
own incipient sensationalism as readers. By implication, Wordsworth's
audience is thereby reminded of the extent to which it remains steeped
in the superstitions it believes itself to have surmounted; and is invited
to become more reflective by becoming more sceptical. The poet's own
position, as someone to whom sensationalist narrative is an available
option, but who chooses instead to tell his stories in a laconic style, is in
some repects the reverse of the sea-captain's, although he too might on
occasion be charged with complicity in the Gothic medium he parodies.
What he and his persona evidently do share is a potentially invasive
fascination with human suffering. For all the distance he puts between
himself and the sea-captain, Wordsworth does not exempt his own
poetic practices from the charge of exploitation. Preoccupied with the
question of how to combine the qualities of a good storyteller and a
reliable witness, he implicates himself in the hermeneutic responsibilities
to which he alerts his audience.

Four years on from the *Lyrical Ballads*, in the lyric poetry of 1802,
Wordsworth was still preoccupied with the accountability of privileged
onlookers such as himself. In 'Resolution and Independence' the disjunction between reader and read provides a richly comedic undercurrent in the poet's self-presentation. Nowhere else is Wordsworth
so alive to the multiple existence which human beings have as subjects
themselves, but also as objects under the interpretative gaze of other
subjects. Transformed by the preoccupied poet, an old man, stirring a
pond for leeches, undergoes a sequence of metamorphoses—from
stone to sea-beast, to a cloud, to a stream, to a dream figure, to a
messenger from some far region, and then finally to a lonely wanderer,
pacing the moors continually. But at the same time, he is acknowledged
to exist on a different, unmythologized plane, from which he speaks to
the poet about the practicalities and hardships of his daily occupation.
So extreme is the gap between literal and metaphorical that these
different versions of the leechgatherer never touch. Nor do the two

people involved in this encounter at any stage truly communicate; although the leechgatherer makes his best efforts to get through to the poet, from the other side of an unbridgeable gulf:

> The Old Man still stood talking by my side;
> But now his voice to me was like a stream
> Scarce heard; nor word from word could I divide...

(ll. 113–15)

Throughout this encounter, there is a comic resistance on the narrator's part to relinquish his metaphor-making and take in what is being said. His investment is in turning diurnal experience into poetic material; and his fictionalizing tendencies are as much the subject of mockery as they are demonstrations of the vivid transforming power of imagination. Even his wish to carry away a lesson from his experience is made faintly ludicrous, in a couplet whose ambiguities go on resonating beyond the poem's closure:

> I could have laughed myself to scorn, to find
> In that decrepit Man so firm a mind...

(ll. 144–5)

As in the indeterminate lines from 'Old Man Travelling', we are left uncertain whose 'reality' is here affirmed. Is it that the resilience of the old man's mind causes the poet to laugh at himself for his fears about his own future? Or that the poet laughs at himself for finding reassurance in so unlikely a subject? Uneasily, we must acknowledge that the 'firmness' of the old man's mind is pure supposition.

As a study of human interaction, of the relation between reader and read, 'Resolution and Independence' shows that the other can never be truly known; and in this sense it is a poem which accepts the failure of communication as a fact of life. It does not have the cautionary severity of a poem such as 'Point Rash-Judgement', where responsibility for misinterpretation is firmly allocated, after inappropriate surmises are suddenly and shockingly reversed. Nor does it have the enigmatic simplicity of 'We are Seven', where the parental practice of interrogation is belittled, the mystery of childhood riddlingly upheld.[64] But it does nonetheless contain implications, for both author and reader, about the

---

[64] See 'Point Rash-Judgement' (included in *Lyrical Ballads* (1800) as 'A Narrow Girdle of Rough Stones and Crags'), ll. 49–86; and 'We are Seven', esp. ll. 1–40. See also 'Anecdote for Fathers'.

responsibilities involved in the practice of interpretation. Looked at from the leechgatherer's point of view, his encounter with the poet might be said to call attention to the self-preoccupations, personal investments, lapses of concentration, which make for careless listeners and inattentive readers. It reminds us that in all our efforts to interpret we are in danger of missing the point.

V. BROKEN CONTRACTS, DISRUPTED CONTINUITIES: THE *LYRICAL BALLADS* (1800)

A notable feature of the poems so far considered is that they uphold the mystery of otherness—the unknowability of human beings—lamenting, in both poets and readers, any tendency to collapse the difference between self and other through narcissistic identification. It is a potential irony, therefore, that the reversibility of their didactic tenor (by which I mean its even-handed applicability to both sides of any dialogic exchange) should itself involve a species of coalescence, or at least convergence. Jon Klancher has claimed that a major distinction between radical and conservative writers is that the former preserve a sharp sense of differentiation between writing and reading functions, whereas the latter seek to absorb their readers as extensions of themselves.[65] If this is the case, then Wordsworth's poetry approximates most closely to the authoritarianism of his prose at the points where writing and reading collapse into a single function. As we shall see, however, convergences of this kind are never a question of unproblematic cloning. Even when, at his most vulnerable, Wordsworth seeks to guarantee continuity through the construction of a 'second self' (in the shape, for instance, of an ideal or model reader) he is troubled by the thought that misunderstanding could work both ways—as an authorial imposition and as a readerly resistance—and that even contracts might not ensure the fruitful interdependency of self and other.

This problem surfaces in a number of poems published in the 1800 *Lyrical Ballads*, a volume characterized by its intense preoccupation with understanding how the appropriative compulsions of writing and reading might be contained. Wordsworth has recourse, here, to a number of different models for poetic communion: interactions between the mind and nature, in which mutual respect is advocated; acts of naming and

---

[65] *Making of English Reading Audiences*, 111.

memorializing, in which the poet 'possesses' the landscape in a benign sense (by peopling it with familiar associations); witnessed or silent contracts between family members, whereby the poetic spirit is meta-phorically shared with nature or handed down in the family; and forms of what Michael Baron has called 'cultural bequest', whereby the con-tinuity between past and present is understood in terms of conviviality and communal life.[66] In all these attempts to define a form of inter-pretative community in which the hostility of his critical readership is bypassed, Wordsworth appeals to ecological and communitarian values so as to give his modes of possession an ethical grounding. But he thinks through to the other side of his ideals even as he figures them: just as the mind's appropriation of nature can become exploitative, so memorials can be incomplete and contracts broken. The frailty of the poetic spirit is everywhere evidenced as a rebuff to its immortal aspirations, in the same way that Nature's blankness or indifference is the counterpart of its readiness to bear witness, to record, and to memorialize. Thus, what Susan Eilenberg says of the 'Poems on the Naming of Places' is true of the volume as a whole: 'Seen from one perspective, the poems seem to be gestures of affection and compliment, pointing to the continuity of generations and the endurance of communal memory; seen from an-other, they are reminders of the inevitability of oblivion and death.'[67] 'Nutting', a poem in which the act of possession is given a violent and destructive significance, reminds its readers of their obligations to Nature—to the spiritual connections they are in danger of forget-ting—and as such it exemplifies a species of 'Romantic ecology'.[68] But its figurative potential also opens the way for less explicit kinds of ideological closure. As an account of writing, heavily determined by its associations with violation, it reveals a fear about the disfiguring poten-tial of language as acute as Shelley's.[69] This allegorization is invited by the poem's self-reflexive structure, and by a framing device which underlines the gap between experiential past and textual present. How-ever, the duality of the writing-subject, who is reading, but perhaps also 'misreading' his earlier self, allows the admonishment to apply in two directions at once—to his own writing, which threatens to invade or

---

[66] *Language and Relationship in Wordsworth's Writing*, 46.

[67] *Strange Power of Speech*, 69.

[68] Jonathan Bate, *Romantic Ecology: Wordsworth and the Environmental Tradition* (London: Routledge, 1991), 107.

[69] See Paul De Man, 'Shelley Disfigured', in *The Rhetoric of Romanticism* (New York: Columbia University Press, 1984), 93–123.

colonize what is other, and also to reading, which replicates this threat in respect of the texts it seeks to master.[70] In the closing lines of this poem, Wordsworth addresses the reader as a 'dearest Maiden', asking her to 'move along these shades | In gentleness of heart... | —for there is a Spirit in the woods' (ll. 52–4). These words, somewhere between an admonishment, an epitaph, and a blessing, are powerless to protect the bower of hazels, whose 'quiet being' has been 'Deformed and sullied' by 'merciless ravage'. They are uttered as a healing and self-forgiving spell, whose frailty is moving, because it invites us to suspend our post-enlightenment faith in a world where oracles are dumb, and spirits long since fled. If the 'dearest Maiden', whose respect for enchanted nature the poet trusts, is inscribed in his poem as a figure for the reader, she could be said to reinforce Wordsworth's ecological principles in a way that applies not only to nature itself, but to the poem he has written: 'with gentle hand | Touch...' (ll. 53–4). Writing is prey to the random appropriations of readers, just as nature yields itself up to marauding boys, or is abused as textual material by writers. But there is a spirit in the woods: to respect this 'genius loci' demands an ecology of writing which is also an ecology of reading.

Just as nature can be protected by appealing to archaic principles of animism, so the mutual enchantment of writer and reader must be actively conserved if it is to withstand the threat posed by modernity. In this sense the spirit of poetry is closely akin to the spirit of place. But what happens, Wordsworth asks, when enchantment no longer holds, and the fragile bond between author and reader breaks down? 'There was a Boy' figures poetry and its reception in the colloquy between boy and owls, where the owls, instead of obediently hooting back to the boy, make a cacophony of noises that sound uncannily human. Nor are they always responsive to his call. 'Pauses of deep silence' sometimes 'mock his skill', and these moments of resistance or blankness acknowledge the ephemerality of voice, its inability to guarantee response. The pattern of 'To Joanna' is here anticipated, but with a difference. The owls have the power to alienate through mimicry, just as Joanna's laughter becomes amplified by echo into a 'loud uproar' of derision, tossed from one mountain peak to the other, and causing her to seek shelter 'from some

---

[70] As on a number of occasions in *The Prelude*, Wordsworth draws attention to the division between past and present selves, whilst at the same time acknowledging the extent to which the past is readjusted by the present: see esp. 'Nutting', ll. 46–7: 'unless I now | Confound my present feelings with the past'.

object of her fear'.[71] In 'There was a Boy', though, the pauses of silence, as much as the echoes themselves, are imagined as a form of mockery— as if, for one whose vocation is imitation, the ultimate fear is a parody which does not speak, a parody of the expectation that there will be answers. The poem collects itself by allowing tranquillity to remind the boy of the otherness of a world he has attempted to control. It is the unmediated voice of mountain torrents, not of anthropomorphized owls, that is 'carried far into his heart', and it is a visible scene, not a choral accompaniment, that 'enters unawares into his mind'. Sublimity is registered subliminally: the emphasis falls on 'unawares', since at dusk the contours of landscape are darkly visible. In this crepuscular atmosphere, the boy's mind merges with the 'bosom of the steady lake', into which the solemn imagery both 'enters' and is quietly received. The boy is thus recalled from an anxiety about his reception to his own receptive (indeed maternal) powers: he becomes a reader who is responsive to the poetry of place. But this recuperation of self through otherness is only momentarily consoling, for the poem moves abruptly into inscription— a bare stating of the facts of the boy's death; followed by lines in which the silence of the owls is echoed by the muteness of the traveller, looking at the grave in which the boy lies.

If one were reading 'There was a Boy' and 'To Joanna' as allegories of the anxiety of reception, one might say that in the first poem the object of Wordsworth's fear is non-cooperation on the part of his readers, whereas in the second it is their insensitivity; and that in both the threat of mockery is anticipated, only to be replayed and defused. Thus, the child mocking the owls is mocked in turn by their refusal to play his game; but in the silence of non-reception he learns to be himself receptive rather than coercive, gaining thereby an alternative form of (sublime) recuperation. Similarly, the poet-persona's 'ravishment' at Nature's beauty is mocked by Joanna's laughter; but her derision comes back to admonish her in an uncanny echo, confirming that the poet's responsiveness to Nature should be the model for her own. However, Wordsworth's handling of subject–object positions refuses so comfortable an alignment of author–reader roles. If these are allegories at all, they work in two directions at once, turning an implicit rebuke to readers for failing to respond into an admonishment of poets for attempting to predetermine response. Nor does their cautionary neatness succeed in

---

[71] 'To Joanna', ll. 54–76.

holding Wordsworth's deepest anxieties at bay. Joanna's laughter may connote his fear of a female and urban readership, hostile to the claims his poetry makes on behalf of the renovating virtues of Nature. Although her scorn rebounds on her, and although it is she who takes shelter 'as from some object of her fear' (l. 76), the mountains' cacophonous echoing of her mockery is in itself deeply disturbing. If only for a moment, the poet is unsettled by the possibility that Nature too finds him risible: that even she will prove ungrateful for his works. And in the same way, in the bleakness with which 'There was a Boy' concludes, Wordsworth anticipates, hauntingly, not only his own death, but a refusal on the part of readers to be his 'second selves' when he is gone.

Wordsworth had used the 1800 Preface to negotiate a rhetorical contract with his audience, based on mutual trust and shared labour. But if the poetic accompaniments to his Preface showed little confidence that readers would honour their side of the contractual undertaking, they also placed a question mark over the poet's expectation that he could somehow 'possess' his readership, both during his lifetime and after his death. In 'Michael', the centrepiece of this volume, a concern with the tenuousness of authorial possession is played out in terms of the fragility of property itself, and also of the model of inheritance that is used throughout the eighteenth century to underwrite the poet's claim to posterity. Marjorie Levinson has suggested that the poem values aesthetic inheritance more highly than legal inheritance of landed property,[72] but in the suggestive readings offered by David Bromwich, Kurt Heinzelman, Susan Eilenberg, and Michael Baron, these two models of inheritance are not opposed.[73] Wordsworth's intense poetic concern with the idea of an afterlife is graphically literalized in the old man's story, which 'internalizes, in a single life, the idea of a tradition; even as it monumentalizes, for an unnamed audience, a personal idea of memory'.[74] In this respect, the poem confirms a more general Wordsworthian tendency to 'confront the idea that posterity begins now', and to 'explore the future in the very act of remaking the past'.[75]

---

[72] See *Wordsworth's Great Period Poems: Four Essays* (Cambridge: Cambridge University Press, 1986), 58–79.

[73] Bromwich, *A Choice of Inheritance: Self and Community from Edmund Burke to Robert Frost* (Cambridge, Mass.: Harvard University Press, 1989), 65–71; Heinzelman, *Economics of Imagination*, 221; Eilenberg, *Strange Power of Speech*, 92–3; Baron, *Language and Relationship in Wordsworth's Writing*, 70–1.

[74] Bromwich, *Choice of Inheritance*, 70.

[75] Baron, *Language and Relationship in Wordsworth's Writing*, 69.

The story of 'Michael' focuses on an old man's tragic misjudgement in sending his son away from home to work in the city—a measure taken so as to safeguard 'the land, his small inheritance' from dwindling into nothing. For this misjudgement, Michael pays heavily: Luke's dissolute life in the great city causes his betrayal of the filial bond connecting him both to his father and to the patrimonial land. After his symbolic departure for the city has led (suddenly and almost perfunctorily) to disgrace, Michael is left alone—working the land as always, and in that work remaining true to his son's memory, but tragically bereft of his hopes for continuing life in posterity. Wordsworth keeps all overt parallels to a minimum; but a shadowy analogy is suggested with the poet's own predicament by way of a passing reference on the narrator's part to those who will become his 'second selves' when he is gone. As Bromwich observes, Michael's hope of a living posterity is 'bound up with the idea of his name being carried forward, in the patrimonial fields'; just as, more suggestively, 'his piety will come to be shared only if the poet communicates a certain sense of things to his readers'.[76] The narrator, the poet, and Michael are interlinked by their common dependency on future generations who will perpetuate their work, thus validating their contribution to the community. It is by appealing to this communitarian notion of posterity that Michael's intensely possessive relation to private property is given its ethical and political justification. Michael's land is, in Susan Eilenberg's words,

the embodiment of patriarchal authority, received from one's ancestors and to be passed on to one's sons. It sustains the continuity of a way of life, binding generation to generation, an index not of its owner's autonomy so much as of his connection with other people. In this it resembles a story, which is valued not as it is hoarded but as it is shared.[77]

This ethical underpinning does not, however, diminish the pervasive sense of atonement in the poem's tragic finale—as though Michael is working through the guilt of having sacrificed his child to his investment in the future.

Heinzelman argues that 'the basis of poetic value' for Wordsworth is 'a contract which burdens the reader with the need to labor in order to sustain that (poetic) inheritance which is a necessary part of existence'; and that 'The labor bestowed upon Luke prefigures the (poet's) labor

---

[76]   *Choice of Inheritance*, 70.   [77]   *Strange Power of Speech*, 92.

bestowed upon the reader'.[78] But although the poem's central metaphor is a broken labour-contract between father and son (which might be read in terms of the misplaced trust of poets in their readers) there are more troubling, less formally symbolic resonances in the old man's obstinate allegiance to an ideal of inherited property. An intense confusion between Michael's feeling for his land and his feeling for Luke lies at the centre of his tragedy; and one might see a parallel for this 'blind love' in two of Wordsworth's most palpable defences against the anxiety of reception: first, his hope that as a result of his own poetic labour, a readership for his poetry would eventually emerge—that his allegiance to a life in posterity might somehow compensate for present difficulties—and, second, his strong conviction that his family ought to reap the rewards of his labour when he is dead. In both these senses, Wordsworth conflated the hope invested in family with the faith that poetry (as a species of property) would survive; and in each case this implied a suspension of concern for the present, involving sacrifice. 'Michael' could be read as playing out, on a narrative level, issues with respect to the inviolability of authorial property that were later to resurface in the poet's campaign to establish perpetual copyright.

There is a further, rhetorical, sense in which 'Michael' ironizes the poet's urge to possess and control his readership. At the centre of this poem, the moment of contract between Michael and Luke is given a momentous—almost biblical—significance. The father's injunction to his son, that he should remain faithful to the land he is to inherit, is preceded by the telling of a story, solemnized by way of an oath, and consecrated by the symbolic laying of a stone—the first stage in Michael's construction of the sheepfold that is to be a lasting (but also practical) labour of love. From the intensity with which this moment is invested, one might well conclude that Wordsworth shared with Rousseau a conviction that 'the language of signs' exerts a stronger, more authoritative hold over its witnesses than does writing itself. 'I observe that in the modern age men no longer have a hold on one another except by force or by self-interest', Rousseau observes in *Emile*:

the ancients . . . acted much more by persuasion and by the affections of the soul because they did not neglect the language of signs. All their covenants took place with solemnity in order to make them more inviolable. Before force was established, the gods were the magistrates of mankind. It was in their presence

---

[78] *Economics of the Imagination*, 221.

that individuals made their treaties and alliances and uttered their promises. The face of the earth was the book in which their archives were preserved. Stones, trees, heaps of rocks consecrated by these acts and thus made respectable to barbaric men, were the pages of this book, which was constantly open to all eyes.... None would have dared to attack these monuments with a sacrilegious hand, and the faith of men was more assured by the guarantee of these mute witnesses than it is today by all the vain rigour of the laws.[79]

For all its apparent faith in the ancient language of signs, the tragic denouement of 'Michael' suggests that 'Stones, trees, heaps of rocks' cannot themselves be obedient to the binding patriarchal contracts they symbolize. Nor, for that matter, can words invariably take on a persuasive force so irrefutable that they instil obedience in their listeners and readers. The unfinished sheepfold bears witness to a contract that has been wilfully broken, even though it survives beyond Michael's life as a testimony to his enduring love.

Attempting to protect a spot of land as though its 'genius loci' were one and the same as the poetic spirit, Wordsworth reached back (for his models of poetic authority) into a past when no reader would have dared to attack the spirit of authorship 'with sacrilegious hand'. Just as 'Nutting' invokes the power of spells to pre-empt future acts of violation, so 'Michael' seeks to enjoin or afforce a fideistic bond between author and reader; and in this sense, the act of extralinguistic 'consecration' which seals Luke's promise is analogous to a spell of enchantment. After Michael's death, when his property has passed into the hands of a stranger and the ploughshare has been through his land, all that remains of the contract between father and son is a 'straggling heap of unhewn stones'. These stones bear an epitaphic relation to Michael's life, but they are also 'mute witnesses' to the failing power of enchantment in the modern age. As such they memorialize both the coerciveness and the the fragility of Wordsworth's dependence on his readers.

VI. DOUBLES AND SHADOWY INTERPOSITIONS: AN EPITAPHIC THEORY OF READING

Wordsworth's theory of reading is epitaphic, both in the sense that it acknowledges—fearfully, uncannily, persistently—the death of the author, and in the sense that it seeks to accommodate and transcend

---

[79] *Emile or Education*, trans. Allan Bloom (Harmondsworth, Middlesex: Penguin, 1979), 321.

that death by simple acts of remembrance. In providing an 'intimation or assurance within us, that some part of our nature is imperishable', the first requisite of an epitaph is that 'it should speak, in a tone which shall sink into the heart, the general language of humanity as connected with the subject of death'.[80] Just as the dead person's survival depends on a community of readers who bear witness to his death as something towards which they in their turn are moving, so it is this sense of a shared destiny that makes epitaphs universally legible:

an epitaph is not a proud writing shut up for the studious: it is exposed to all— to the wise and the most ignorant; it is condescending, perspicuous, and lovingly solicits regard; its story and admonitions are brief, that the thoughtless, the busy, and indolent, may not be deterred, nor the impatient tired: the stooping old man cons the engraven record like a second horn-book;—the child is proud that he can read it;—and the stranger is introduced through its mediation to the company of a friend: it is concerning all, and for all:—in the church-yard it is open to the day; the sun looks down upon the stone, and the rains of heaven beat against it. (p. 59)

In celebrating death's levelling significance, Wordsworth defines more closely both the 'general language of humanity' which his own poetry seeks to utter and the communality of reading into which it will pass after he has himself deceased. In doing so, he transforms his fear of exposure to public scrutiny into a trust that the act of reception will be as harmless as the gaze of a stooping old man or a child learning to read— as benignant as the warmth of sunshine on stone, as natural as the steady beating of rainwater in a country graveyard.

In this way, Wordsworth's attempt to convey the notion of 'the perfect epitaph' leads almost imperceptibly into a definition of how best to preserve the spirit of the dead in the act of reading, and so to an evocation of the ideal reader. 'To analyse the characters of others, especially of those whom we love, is not a common or natural employment of men at any time . . .', he claims:

We shrink from the thought of placing their merits and defects to be weighed against each other in the nice balance of pure intellect . . . and, least of all, do we incline to these refinements when under the pressure of sorrow, admiration, or regret, or when actuated by any of those feelings which incite men to prolong the memory of their friends and kindred, by records placed in the bosom of the all-uniting and equalising receptacle of the dead. (pp. 56–7)

---

[80] 'Essay Upon Epitaphs' I, in *Wordsworth Prose*, ii. 57. Page refs. will be given in the text.

In arguing that the perfect epitaph must bypass a particularization of the dead person's characteristics, Wordsworth eradicates the invasive act of criticism from his ideal scene of reading. The epitaph-writer 'is not an anatomist, who dissects the internal frame of the mind', but a sympathizer, capable of interpreting the universal significance of mortality even under 'the pressure of sorrow, admiration or regret'. Describing the convention whereby epitaphs 'personate the deceased, and represent him as speaking from his own tomb-stone' (p. 60), Wordsworth draws attention to 'the tender fiction' or 'shadowy interposition' which 'harmoniously unites the two worlds of the living and the dead by their appropriate affections'; this he contrasts with the more credible and flexible epitaphic convention which has the survivors speaking 'in their own persons' (p. 61). In his own poetic practice, these two modes of address are frequently conflated. Wordsworth's model reader speaks as though from both sides of the grave, preserving the fiction of the poet's continuing life while at the same time figuring his ideal reception at the hands of his posthumous public.

'A Poet's Epitaph', published in *Lyrical Ballads* (1800), is spoken in the person of the dead poet himself, and addressed to a sequence of possible readers. The majority of these are judged incapable of empathy with the poetic spirit, and are automatically excluded from communion with the dead. One figure only stands out as capable of responding with sympathy; and he is presented in terms that associate him unmistakably with a poet in the Wordsworthian mould. Onto this figure, Wordsworth projects both his own self-image, and (in a reflexive doubling of that image) his best hopes of being understood by his readers: 'And you must love him, ere to you | He will seem worthy of your love' (ll. 43–4). In a circular pattern of identification, not only is the ideal reader singled out as possessing poetic characteristics, he is also literally conflated with the speaker himself:

> —Come hither in thy hour of strength,
> Come, weak as is a breaking wave!
> Here stretch thy body at full length;
> Or build thy house upon this grave.—
>
> (ll. 57–60)

Just as the curious conjunction of weakness and strength is characteristic of Wordsworth's divided wishes with respect to his readers, so the effacement of difference between reader and read recalls the urgency with which, in his critical prose, he sought to establish his readers as clones of himself. In its poetic context, the 'tender fiction' of continuity that is sought by means of this effacement has a distinctly macabre effect. The reader is invited to lie down in the grave of the poet—literally to swop places with him—as though the poet's continuing life must be at the cost of the death of the reader.

The role of Wordsworth's 'ideal' and 'model' readers was to provide protection against an audience he imagined might prove either hostile or indifferent to his writing. While performing a role similar to that occupied by Coleridge's surrogate selves in the 'conversation poems', they differed markedly from Coleridge's model readers in their intensely compensatory function as mediators between life and death, or community and separation. In this sense, they signified—as did Wordsworth's preoccupation, more generally, with the epitaphic mode—that a persistent and insurmountable fear of dying and being forgotten was connected with an equally persistent fear of being read.

Often, in his poetry, Wordsworth's model readers take the shape of a family member or female companions, like the 'gentle maid' in 'Nutting'—traditionally identified with Dorothy—whose healing presence defends the spirit of place and poetry against future desecration. Here and elsewhere, the credentials of Wordsworth's model readers are established by the confidential and trusting tones in which they are addressed, and by their tacit obedience to the poet's wishes, both of these drawing them sympathetically close to the poet, whose surrogate they are asked to be. Such is the figure of Dorothy, silently prominent at the close of 'Tintern Abbey', and apotheosized with urgent and solemn intimacy as both other than and coextensive with Wordsworth himself. In a bizarre projection of his own death, Wordsworth pleads with his 'dear dear sister' to go on seeing for him—as it were with his vision— after his decease. Dorothy takes on the role of nurse, guide, and guardian to Wordsworth's poetic spirit, a role which had previously been occupied by Nature. Just as his own memories have acted as confirmation that the scene before him is permanent, so Dorothy's will guarantee his continuity of vision. Implicitly, a likeness is thereby suggested between nature's formative influence over him, and the influence his poetry has on the minds of his readers. Mediated by his sister, Wordsworth's poetic spirit becomes 'a power like one of nature's', with the same permanence, and the same inviolable claim to respect.

Such too is Wordsworth's brother John, as he is described in 'When to the Attractions of the Busy World': a poem not included among 'Poems on the Naming of Places' because of its extreme privacy of address.[81] The poet is here presented, in Michael Baron's words, as one 'addressing his silent public: naming, placing, defining human experience without knowing that his formulations will have general acceptance'.[82] In a fantasy of convergence so strong that it can defeat separation—or even, by implication, death—the poet's brother John is imagined pacing the decks with a steady motion, and 'Muttering the verses which I muttered first | Among the mountains' (ll. 106–7), while the poet himself treads the path at home, 'for aught I know, | Timing my steps to thine' (ll. 112–13). This proof of the brothers being 'twinned almost' in their sensibilities and habits (despite their severed lives and occupations) forms the basis for Wordsworth's claim that John is a 'silent poet', possessed of a 'watchful heart | Still couchant, an inevitable ear | And an eye practised like a blind man's touch' (ll. 89–91)—qualities of receptivity that take him remarkably close to the ideal reader, as defined in the 'Essay Supplementary to the Preface' of 1815.

The poem bears witness to Wordsworth's need to figure his ideal reception in terms of a self whose actions mirror his own. Appropriately, since he is the younger sibling, John echoes William; but in all other respects temporal/hierarchical differences between the brothers are elided. As reflexes of each other, they defeat the temporality of reading through an act of repetition in which, paradoxically, they are thought to coincide. We might, with Michael Baron, draw an analogy between the addressee of the poem and Wordsworth's 'putative readership', emphasizing the extremely idealistic nature of that analogy. But the poem resists disclosure of its implied desire to adapt a fraternal model of readership so that it has application to the public at large. Carrying the feelings of community into the 'barren' and 'dreary' world in which John fulfils his occupation as a sailor, the action of 'muttering' is half-private and half-public. Serving a mediatory function between

---

[81] See Michael Baron's excellent discussion of the 'Poems on the Naming of Places', in *Language and Relationship in Wordsworth's Writing*, 55–9.

[82] Ibid. 57. According to a local eyewitness account, recorded by Canon Rawnsley, Wordsworth used to 'set his head a bit forrad and put his hands behint his back. and then he would start a bumming, and it was bum, bum, bum, stop; then bum, bum, bum reet down till t'other end'. See *Reminiscences of Wordsworth among the Peasantry of Westmoreland* (London: Dillons, c.1968), 18.

familiarity and estrangement,[83] it provides relief in the same way that shared memories of the landscape above Tintern Abbey protect Wordsworth and his sister against hours of loneliness in the great city.

There is a tragic sequel to 'When to the Attractions', in which Wordsworth once again figures his brother as a silent poet; but this time that silence betokens death. 'Distressful Gift! this Book receives' was written into the commonplace book which John habitually carried with him on shipboard, but which he left behind on his final fateful voyage.[84] The poem is addressed to the deceased himself; but it hovers between second- and third-person pronouns, as though confusing the line between the living and the dead:

> Oft have I handled, often eyed,
> This book with boyish glee and pride,
> The written page and white:
> How have I turned them o'er and o'er,
> One after one and score by score,
> All filled or to be filled with store
> Of verse for his delight.
>
> He framed the Book which now I see,
> This very Book upon my knee
> He framed with dear intent
> To travel with him night and day,
> And in his private hearing say
> Refreshing things whatever way
> His weary Vessel went.
>
> (ll. 22–35)

By his intense concentration on the book's materiality, Wordsworth recreates and prolongs the sense of a relationship that was fulfilled during John's lifetime through the sharing and repeating of familiar poems. Just as, in the earlier poem, he and his brother had surmounted separation by 'pacing o'er and o'er' their private sanctuaries, in time with each other's thoughts, so here, as he turns the book's pages, Wordsworth incorporates his memory of the earlier repetitive motion of pacing into the memory of reading—'How have I turned them o'er

---

[83] Note the coincidence between Wordsworth's poem and Dorothy's later account of her own habits of composition: 'I have often tried, when I have been walking alone (muttering to myself as is my Brother's custom) to express my feelings in verse' (*MY* i. 25).

[84] *Poems, in Two Volumes and Other Poems, 1800–1807*, ed. Jared Curtis (Ithaca, NY: Cornell University Press, 1983), 617–18.

and o'er, | One after one and score by score' (ll. 25–6)—as if once again finding that shared actions can defeat the curse of time. Refusing to acknowledge that death can obliterate the private bond that connects brother to brother, Wordsworth suggests that there is a communality of writing and reading which takes place in the private memories of his family. Within that community the lines separating poet from reader become blurred, so that Wordsworth swaps places with John, to become the reader of a book his brother has 'framed'. But, as the poet narrows his audience to the single person able to bear the weight of his grief, the fellowship of family members shrinks away, leaving the writing-subject in a secret and lonely dialogue with the dead:

> And so I write what neither Thou
> Must look upon, nor others now
> Their tears would flow too fast;
> Some solace thus I strive to gain,
> Making a kind of secret chain,
> If so I may, betwixt us twain
> In memory of the past.

> (ll. 15–21)

Addressing the dead on behalf of the living (and thus reversing the speaker's situation in 'Tintern Abbey') these lines make painfully literal a theory of writing–reading in which the only reader to be trusted is a version of the poet himself. In keeping with this exclusivity of address, the lines were not published in Wordsworth's lifetime, although family members must indeed have read them and wept.

Not all of Wordsworth's personified 'model readers' were so evidently identified as members of a coterie audience. It is the figures who reside in the interstices of his similes and digressions who provide the most telling indication of what Wordsworth expected (and feared) from his readers; and they do so by enacting the transition from 'public' to 'private' (or uncomprehending to sympathetic) which he wished to effect in his audience at large. Such figures are closer to the 'friend' who writes the spoof letter in *Biographia*, chapter 13, than they are to the silent listeners of the 'conversation poems'. This is because, by occupying a puzzled or semi-resistant stance, which develops into an acquiescent one, they stage a scene of instruction for the reader. In Book IV of *The Prelude*, for instance, Wordsworth provides a meta-commentary on his autobiographical method in the shape of a simile whose central figure (the traveller) is both a persona for the poet himself and a model reader of *The Prelude*:

> As one who hangs down-bending from the side
> Of a slow-moving boat
>
> .   .   .   .
>
> Sees many beauteous sights—weeds, fishes, flowers,
> Grots, pebbles, roots of trees—and fancies more,
> Yet often is perplexed, and cannot part
> The shadow from the substance, rocks and sky,
> Mountains and clouds, from that which is indeed
> The region, and the things which there abide
> In their true dwelling
>
> .   .   .   .
>
> Such pleasant office have we long pursued
> Incumbent o'er the surface of past time...
>
> (*Prelude (1805)* iv. 247–64)

Our initial assumption might be that parting shadow from substance is an act of skill and vigilance, which the narrator laments being unable to perform, and which we as readers unwittingly repeat. But as the simile develops, we learn to recognize the puzzlement of the traveller as a version of the 'judicious obscurity' which Wordsworth associates with the sublime.[85] Confused by the interchangeability of past and present selves, the traveller validates an aesthetic of indeterminacy which is crucial to Wordsworth's narratorial procedures, in that it collapses *The Prelude*'s 'two consciousnesses' into a single, continuous being. The unfolding simile might be said to bridge the duality of the writing–reading subject, and at the same time to identify the 'model reader' as an extension of the poet himself. Wordsworth here recuperates his own past—not as an entity that is separable from the present, but as a vital component in how the present is construed: he inscribes his own continuity into the act of reading.

In *The Prelude*, Book VIII, Wordsworth uses the simile of a traveller to describe the experience of his arrival in London. Once again, the traveller may be read as a figure of the reader, whom Wordsworth envisages, not as an urban tourist visiting the Lake District for the first time, and not as a country-dweller like himself, overwhelmed by his first glimpse of city life; but as someone of unknown origins, who

---

[85] See my discussion of this passage in 'Aesthetics of Indeterminacy', 228.

occupies an intermediate and neutral position between city and country. By transferring a figure from the picturesque tradition into an urban setting, Wordsworth creates an amalgam of readerly expectations, thereby crossing or mediating the boundary between the alien and the familiar. A similar crossing is negotiated by the traveller himself in the course of absorbing the scene before him. This 'crossing' may be read as the rhetorical enactment of a process Wordsworth expects and hopes for in his readers. An expert in the art of reading landscape, the traveller sees the cave (as Wordsworth sees the city) through the medium of Burke's sublime aesthetic. He responds with awe to its 'judicious obscurity', observing that its 'shapes and forms and tendencies to shape', cause the cavern to 'spread and grow, | Widening itself on all sides' (*Prelude (1805)* viii. 715–16). And he is duly disappointed when, habituating himself to the darkness, this 'ferment quiet and sublime' gives way to clarity, and the scene before him lies 'in perfect view, | Exposed, and lifeless as a written book' (ll. 725–6). Burke, similarly, had noticed that visual uncertainty gives sublime objects their overwhelming grandeur; and that 'a clear idea is ... another name for a little idea'. He too had alluded to Milton's description of Death as a touchstone of sublimity, just as Wordsworth's traveller does, when he sees 'substance and shadow' changing and interchanging like spectral forms.[86] The Burkean affinities of Wordsworth's traveller clearly establish his credentials as a model reader, indicating the respect for mystery which Wordsworth thinks crucial to the reading-process. Furthermore, the simile provides a Burkean scene of instruction in how to read Wordsworth himself. Like Coleridge, Wordsworth invokes a sublime aesthetic when his own authority comes under threat, or when mystery needs to be reaffirmed. It does so, in this unfolding simile, at the point where imaginative activity winds down towards lifeless closure, a point which Wordsworth significantly associates with the experience of completing 'a written book', and thereby becoming 'exposed' to the threat of extinction (ll. 715–18). The finality of this moment is awesome. But, after a significant pause—a pause, that is, signifying the interval between publication and reception—a secondary stage of imaginative activity takes place under the gaze of the traveller:

---

[86] Ibid. 226–7. Quotation from Burke in *A Philosophical Enquiry into the Origin of our Ideas of the Sublime and Beautiful*, ed. James T. Boulton (1958; Oxford: Blackwell, 1987), 63.

... let him pause awhile and look again,
And a new quickening shall succeed, at first Beginning timidly,
   then creeping fast
Through all which he beholds ...

                          (ll. 728–31)

Just as the indeterminate 'tendencies to shape' on the cavern wall are replaced with a train of more distinct images drawn from the world of fantasy and romance, so, Wordsworth suggests, the reading-process may reactivate imaginative process in 'a spectacle to which there is no end'. Overseeing the transition between death and rebirth, the traveller becomes a figure of continuity and recuperation, as well as of understanding. He defends the writing-subject from oblivion.

We have seen how Wordsworth's poems unsettle that authoritative bond between author and reader which elsewhere he asserts repeatedly—in his attempts to frame his public reception, in his relations with individual readers, and in his theory of reading—and that they do so by acknowledging the dependencies and anxieties which the critical prose holds at bay. We might be tempted to conclude from this that (contrary to Hazlitt's belief) the language of poetry is more democratic than the language of prose. On closer inspection, however, it becomes apparent that these binaries can be broken down, or at least shown to be operating across as well as between generic categories. It might be said in conclusion that the authoritative voice of Wordsworth's criticism masks a deep uncertainty about the direction in which he wishes to move his theory of interpretation—towards the hermeticism on which he over-insists, or towards the hermeneutics of collaboration which implicitly contradicts it. Further, that while his poems more readily acknowledge a division of allegiances within the writing–reading subject, they do not relinquish the hope that a hiatus between 'creation' and 'reception' might be bridged, and the poet's authority thereby preserved. Figures such as the 'gentle maid' in 'Nutting', Dorothy in 'Tintern Abbey', and the traveller in the 'Cave of Yordas' simile provide reassurance that books are by no means 'exposed and lifeless' after publication, but are subject to a vivid continuing life in their readers' minds. The author dies, perhaps—but only perhaps, because a 'new quickening' soon succeeds.

CHAPTER 4

Case Study (3): Anna Barbauld

Your business chiefly is to read Men, in order to make yourselves agreeable and useful. It is not the argumentative but the sentimental talents, which give you that insight and those openings into the human heart, that lead to your principal ends as women.... Men who understand the domestic Science know that its first principle is ease.... But we cannot be easy, when we are not safe. We are never safe in the company of a critic; and almost every wit is a critic by profession. In such company we are not at liberty to unbend ourselves. All must be the straining of study, or the anxiety of apprehension.

James Fordyce, *Sermons To Young Women*, 1766

INTRODUCTION

In a poem of 1815, written to celebrate the newly discovered comforts of a coal-fire, Anna Laetitia Barbauld used a topos that would have been familiar to her audience as an allusion to Cowper's *The Task*. Like Cowper, she describes a contemplative poet, sitting comfortably at his fireside, safe from the demands and responsibilities of public life:

> ——Nor less the bashful poet loves to sit
> Snug, at the midnight hour, with only thee
> Of his lone musings conscious. Oft he writes,
> And blots, and writes again; and oft, by fits,
> Gazes intent with eyes of vacancy
> On thy bright face; and still at intervals,
> Dreading the critic's scorn, to thee commits,
> Sole confidant and safe, his fancies crude.[1]

---

[1] 'The First Fire', ll. 58–65, in *The Poems of Anna Laetitia Barbauld*, ed. William McCarthy and Elizabeth Kraft (Athens, Ga. and London: University of Georgia Press, 1994), 172. All references to Barbauld's poems are from this edn. unless otherwise stated.

This passage highlights and criticizes one of the major self-protective strategies adopted by poets in the late eighteenth and early nineteenth centuries—namely, their use of coterie audiences (Shaftesbury's 'mirror-writing') as sources of sympathy.[2] Barbauld suggests that there is something narcissistic in this deliberate choice of the private domestic sphere as one in which it is safe to be judged; and, moreover, she presents this choice as ultimately self-defeating. The poet saves himself from the critics only at the cost of his own creative efforts, which end by being consumed in the fire. His 'sole confidant' turns out to be no more supportive of his ambitions than the public.

Barbauld's critique has both a general relevance to a period when private acts of reception were used as dress rehearsals for emergence into the public sphere, and a specific application to Coleridge, who tended to subsume even the minimal element of otherness implied by a select audience into self-cloning constructions of the reader. In 'Frost at Midnight' (first published in the Quarto volume of 1798 entitled *Fears in Solitude*), Coleridge had taken Cowper's winter evening retreat as a starting-point for his own poetic musings; and some of Barbauld's readers would no doubt have heard an echo from his poem while simultaneously recognizing the Cowper source. Barbauld shows herself to be at once sympathetic towards and quizzically detached from the object of her satire. The bashfulness of the poet she describes is echoed in the hesitancy of a blank-verse idiom which precisely mimics Coleridge's meditative style, even down to an amusing repetition of his own repetition ('how oft, | How oft, at school, with most believing mind.')[3] Tonally, too, Barbauld positions herself with well-judged equivocation: words such as 'snug', 'vacancy', and 'crude' register just enough irony to be unsettling, but not enough to turn the poem into a fully-fledged parody. It is a lightly satirical portrait, and much of its good humour derives from the empathy and self-knowledge with which Barbauld considered the poet's plight. A woman writer in a literary climate still hostile to women, she was well placed to sympathize with the struggle to negotiate recognition (and had herself been initially reticent to publish). But the poem's special edge of irony derives from undercurrents of hostility between herself and Coleridge, dating back to what Henry Crabb Robinson described as Coleridge's 'ungenerous & unmanly attack' on her poetry

---

[2] See Ch. 1, above; and my discussion of Hazlitt's response to the practice of reading aloud, in Ch. 9, below.

[3] See 'Frost at Midnight', ll. 23–4.

in his 1812 lecture on Milton (*Lectures*, i. 407). The trajectory of her career had been antithetical to his, and ideological differences had shaped their poetics of reception to widely divergent ends. It is these differences which the 1815 poem brings sharply into focus.

Although Coleridge's upbringing was Anglican, he had begun his writing-career as a Dissenting radical, won notoriety lecturing in Bristol to revolutionary sympathizers, and shared with Barbauld during the 1790s a passionate commitment to parliamentary reform and the abolition of slavery. He moved for a while in the same circle as she did, among the London radicals (Godwin, Holcroft, Wollstonecraft) whose activities were centred around the publisher Joseph Johnson. But the middle years of Coleridge's career had marked a retreat into the privacy of imaginative contemplation, and by 1815 his Anglican allegiances were explicit and his political apostasy complete. He addressed his audience in an increasingly exclusive language designed to appeal mainly to highly educated members of the middle classes; his views were conservative; and he denied he had ever felt any sympathy with the Jacobin cause. Barbauld's career, by contrast, had followed a pattern of steadily widening and maturing political commitment. Educated at the Warrington Academy, where her father John Aikin DD was a celebrated tutor, she was surrounded in her early adult life by such distinguished intellectual radicals as William Enfield, Joseph Priestley, and Gilbert Wakefield. Her understanding of the public sphere was shaped at a time when the Test and Corporation Acts prohibited Dissenters from having a university education or holding public office. A spirit of fierce independence, and a determination to assert their political agency by alternative means, characterized the Nonconformists who gave Barbauld her upbringing. She left Warrington at the age of 31, when she married Rochemont Barbauld and moved to Suffolk. After an interlude of thirteen years running a boys' school and publishing educational tracts, the couple moved to Hampstead. This moment, as Anne Janowitz has argued, marked Barbauld's emergence into maturity as a political pamphleteer and poet, 'forging an autonomous public identity through the intellectual freedoms offered by Johnson's press'.[4]

A complicated interweaving of private with public concerns is common to Barbauld and Coleridge, but in very different ways. The latter's retreat from political activism coincided with an emphasis on the

---

[4] '"Free Familiar Conversation": Anna Barbauld in Warrington', in *Romantic Sociability*, ed. Claire Tuite and William Russell (Cambridge: Cambridge University Press, forthcoming).

importance of friendship and the domestic affections: these were celebrated in the 'conversation poems' of 1797–8 in which he found his
authentic voice as a poet, where they functioned as a means of redirect-
ing his early commitment to the ideals of fraternity and pantisocracy. By
contrast, Barbauld's objective of political intervention had been fostered
in early adult life by the unique atmosphere at Warrington, where no
evident distinction existed between familial and civic allegiances. Warrington offered more than an educational training for Nonconformists;
it was a family, a society of friends, an ideal community practising a
fraternalist ethic, a centre in which current political issues were enthu-
siastically debated, and a thoroughfare for the traffic of radical ideas and
publications. Fifteen years of life as a young woman in this environment
gave Barbauld a head start on Coleridge in the difficult task of forging a
public identity, and indeed in seeing how domestic life itself might be
lived as a form of political praxis. That she managed, with apparent
effortlessness, to appeal both to the coterie audience of Dissenting
intellectuals among whom her poems first circulated, and to the mass
audience by which she was subsequently acclaimed, may explain some of
Coleridge's motivation in conducting a 'sniping campaign' on her poetry.[5] But it also provides a context for understanding why Coleridge
figured on more than one occasion in her writing as an escapist. Like
Hazlitt, she saw Coleridge as a writer who had betrayed the republican
cause, ducked his responsibilities to the public sphere, and retreated into
a world of abstraction. By contrast, Barbauld's very sophisticated negotiation of the intermediate terrain between public and private was
apparent from her earliest publication to her last. It shaped a distinctive
poetics of reception, in many ways the obverse of Coleridge's, which is
the subject of this chapter.

I. BARBAULD'S MODES OF ADDRESS

'We congratulate the public on so great an accession to the literary
world, as the genius and talents of Miss Aikin'. This was the conclusion
delivered decisively in a review spanning two issues of the *Monthly
Review* of Barbauld's *Poems* (1773). The reviewer (William Woodfall)
began with a paragraph of mock-suspense, in which he described
himself brandishing his weapons ready for execution, while his

---

[5] See *Lectures* i. 407.

'trembling victims' awaited their doom.[6] Praised for 'a justness of thought and vigour of imagination inferior only to the works of Milton and Shakespeare' (p. 54), Barbauld is perceived to have a number of qualities—the 'strength of her imagination, the variety of her knowledge and the goodness of heart' (p. 137)—which make it possible for her to enter without impunity a traditionally masculine domain. Her education by John Aikin is held implicitly responsible for her lack of convention-ally feminine attributes (if her mother had played a greater part in her upbringing, Woodfall observed, her poetry would have merited praise for its 'feminine beauties' (p. 137), rather than its breadth of knowledge); and some criticism is levelled at her for the apparent mannishness of her poetic mode: 'We hoped the *Woman* was going to appear; and that while we admired the genius and learning of her graver compositions, we should be affected by the sensibility and passion of the softer pieces' (p. 133). But if it is as a woman trying to be a man that Barbauld is judged, she is at least judged favourably; and at this stage in her career the charge that she has 'trodden too much in the footsteps of men' is not extended to suggest that she has entered forbidden territory. This reviewer, among many others, excuses Barbauld's poetry for the masculine affili-ations which her education had conferred upon it, fully acknowledging that she achieves greatness in a man's own terms. It was only at a much later stage in Barbauld's reception that the castigation of unwomanliness would return to haunt her.

Barbauld had already established a reputation for poetry before its publication in 1773. At this date, she was nearly 30; but her work had circulated in manuscript for many years in the close-knit group of Dissenting intellectuals at Warrington to which she, her family, and her friends belonged. A number of the famous and influential figures who either taught or visited there—including the scientist and pamph-leteer Joseph Priestley, employed as tutor in languages—helped in the promotion of her poems, and were partly responsible for ensuring the instant success of her first volume, which went through four editions in twelve months, establishing Barbauld as a famous author.[7] But it was her

---

[6] *Monthly Review*, 48 (1773), 54–9, 113–7; 54 (page refs. will be given in the text); discussed by William McCarthy, ' "We hoped the *Woman* was going to appear": Repression, Desire and Gender in Anna Letitia Barbauld's Early Poems', in Paula Feldman and Theresa Kelley (eds.), *Romantic Women Writers: Voices and Counter-Voices* (Hanover, NH: University Press of New England, 1995), 113.

[7] See Betsy Rodgers, *Georgian Chronicle : Mrs Barbauld and her Family* (London: Methuen and Co., 1958), 57.

confidence and versatility, combined with an acute sensitivity to audience expectation, that guaranteed Barbauld's success in the longer term. An accomplished writer in an astonishing range of discursive media, Barbauld's poetic output included lyrics, songs, epitaphs, hymns, odes, eclogues, riddles, inscriptions, prologues, 'characters', mock-epic, blank verse, occasional verse, and satire; while her prose ranged from critical essays through allegories and fables to children's books and political pamphlets. Each of these media raised different kinds of expectation with respect to its readers or audience; and Barbauld's ability to enter them all, while adapting her mode of address accordingly, showed the extent to which she vividly imagined herself in dialogue with another.

Given that a marginalized, internally consensual circle of readers formed her first audience, it is unsurprising that much of her verse was written for friends, and in a language that was partly private. Her favoured medium was verse epistle of the lighter (more intimate and informal) variety, at first sight scarcely distinguishable from conventional album verse, of the kind written by men and women in educated circles throughout the eighteenth century. But Barbauld gave a distinctively Warringtonian slant to the conventional eighteenth-century language of sentiment. She formulated in her occasional lyrics what Janowitz has called 'a poetic of intellectual friendship, weaving together the values of sentiment and intellect'.[8] By far the majority of her poems are addressed to individuals whose names appeared in the poems' titles, linked either with a specific event—'To Dr Aikin, on his complaining that she neglected him, October 20th 1768', 'To Miss Rigby, on her Attendance upon her Mother at Brixton', 'Lines to Mr Wynch on his Forty-fifth Birthday'—or with an object that was concretely expressive of tenderness, intimacy, or respect. Ephemeral moments of gift-exchange are made emblematic and permanent by their very titles: 'To Mrs Priestley, with some drawings of Birds and Insects', 'Verses written in the leaves of an ivory pocket-book, presented to Master Turner', and 'To Mr Barbauld, with a Map of the Land of Matrimony'. This mode of address allows the reader to witness intimacy, much as one does in perusing letters that have been written for private consumption but with a view to their eventual publication. As William McCarthy points out,

The poems actually invite a biographical reading, even as they also slightly repel it by making the signs of the personal only partly intelligible [as in a poem

---

[8] ' "Free Familiar Conversation" ', forthcoming.

addressed to 'Mrs P——', not to Mrs Priestley']. The effect of half-disclosure is
to make the poems seem not really meant for the public eye; our relation to
them seems that of overhearers of private musings.[9]

A similar quality is evident, conversely, in Barbauld's private correspondence with John Aikin, which Betsy Rodgers claims was written with
the expectation that it would be read aloud to a circle of friends.[10]

Barbauld brought to stereotypically feminine topics a strong emphasis on sympathy. This is often expressed through the celebration
of what Wordsworth called 'those little, nameless unremembered acts |
Of kindnesss and of love', which made up the fabric of daily life in a
small community. Seemingly trivial moments of gift-exchange are recognized in her early poems for their power to bind members of that
community together, as in the tender domesticity of 'To Mrs.——, on
Returning a Fine Hyacinth Plant after the Bloom was over', or 'To a
Lady, with some painted Flowers'. Taken individually, such poems
convey no more than an ephemeral sentimentality. But their cumulative
effect is to create an ethic of interconnectedness which, by implication,
spreads out from the immediate network of family and friends into the
nation at large. Occasionally, poems stand out for the intensity of their
empathetic understanding. In 'To a little invisible Being who is expected
soon to become visible', Barbauld poignantly suspends her own condition of childlessness to enter into an unnamed mother's excited anticipation of her child's birth. The poem has two addressees, child and
mother, but the reader is almost convinced on first reading that the
poem is spoken by the latter, for it begins with maternal expressions of
endearment before standing back to observe the mother's own perspec-
tive: 'she only asks to lay her burden down, | That her glad arms that
burden may resume' (ll. 17–18). This shifting viewpoint draws the reader
into the subject's feelings, while also allowing Barbauld to explore as a
metaphorical paradox the process whereby every mother learns to love
'Part of herself, yet to herself unknown' (l. 22).

The peculiar combination of familial intimacy and intellectual endeavour which characterized the pedagogic structure at Warrington were
absorbed as features of Barbauld's steadily strengthening poetic. They
combined with a rationalist emphasis on the explicable, and a preference

---

[9] '"We hoped the *Woman* was going to appear"', 117.
[10] See *Georgian Chronicle*, 64. The hypothesis is particularly interesting in view of the close
association between 'reading aloud' and the Dissenting tradition of oratory which thrived at the
Warrington Academy (see Ch. 9, below).

for the local and the quotidian (as opposed to the elevated and the abstract) which were more widely characteristic of the culture and language of Dissent. Though her focus often shifted from immediate domestic topics to political issues, Barbauld conducted intellectual debate as though engaging in polite conversation. In this way, she put into practice a version of the discursive credo formulated by Priestley in his *Lectures on Oratory and Criticism*, which was later to prove a decisive factor in the shaping of Hazlitt's prose style.[11] Poems addressed to those unable to reciprocate are unusual in her oeuvre. Titles such as 'To a Great Nation', 'To the Poor', and 'To the New Year, 1823' stand out as surprising, in the same way as do her poems on abstract subjects ('Dejection' or 'Ode to Remorse'), the staple fare of mainstream Romantic writers. Even when her addressees were anonymous or generalized, Barbauld preferred to retain an ingredient of topicality, so that the addresser was connected to the sender at a specific time or place.

The easy familarity of speech, which Priestley advocated and which her poems aspired to, sometimes sits oddly alongside a more stilted register. This moving in and out of different idioms produces the stylistic incongruity—but also the versatility—which are typical of Barbauld's mature poetic voice. Through her exceptional alertness to audience, she was able to effect subtle displacements of generic expectation by a mixing and crossing of private and public modes of address. In this way, she successfully mediated between alternative spheres of reception, ensuring a safe passage from the domestic into the political. This poetic reflects the ethos of sociability Barbauld had experienced at Warrington, where familial and domestic friendships shaded subtly into a more publicly motivated form of fraternity. Occasional verse—a medium traditionally used to mark state occasions and grand public events—is subtly revised in 'On Mrs. Priestley's leaving Warrington', 'On the Birth of a Friend's eldest son', and 'On the Death of Mrs. Jennings', where events of local import acquire wider significance through the language of moral sentiment, carefully pitched between formal and informal registers. Conversely, in the poems written later in life—after she had reached maturity as a political writer—she crossed the 'occasional' genre with verse epistle to produce a generic hybrid. 'Lines to Samuel Rogers in Wales on the Eve of Bastille Day, 1791', for instance, or 'To Dr. Priestley. Dec. 29, 1792' focus on eminent figures who were also

[11] See Tom Paulin, *The Day-Star of Liberty: William Hazlitt's Radical Style* (London: Faber and Faber, 1998), 237–8.

acquaintances and friends. These poems incorporate events of moment-ous political import into the poetic of sociability which evolved out of Barbauld's daily conversation with radical figures.

Public occasional poems such as 'Corsica' (1769) and 'Epistle to William Wilberforce, Esq. on the Rejection of the Bill for abolishing the Slave Trade' (1791), addressed topical political events with the same urgency as did her 1790s prose tracts, *Address to the Opposers of the Repeal of the Corporation and Test Acts* (1790) and *Sins of the Government, Sins of The Nation* (1793). But her poetic voice is less overtly polemical, and its moral inflection allows generalizations to be drawn from specific events—as here in the last lines of her address to the Corsican people:

> There yet remains a freedom, nobler far
> Than king or senates can destroy or give;
> Beyond the proud oppressor's cruel grasp
> Seated secure; uninjur'd; undestroy'd;
> Worthy of Gods: The freedom of the mind.
>
> (ll. 197–201)

In the year 1769 Genoa ceded the island of Corsica to France, which prepared to conquer and invade it, and there was anti-government lobbying by radical pressure groups in favour of British intervention. Championing the Whig cause of disinterested liberty, Barbauld traces the history of Corsica—its emergence from poverty and oppression into an independent state—concluding with a lament for its vanquished heroes. Her final lines, though, move the concept of liberty onto a more abstract plane, anticipating Wordsworth's claims for the 'freedom of the individual mind'.[12]

Barbauld's political interventions were carefully modulated, at least in her poetry, to safeguard her from hostile reception while permitting her also to express views that would be unpopular outside her Dissenting audience. The diplomacy of her poetic was effected partly by shifts of register; but also by the ways in which, through her choice of subject-matter and focus, she acceptably softened her hard-hitting message. Just as, in her handling of the genre of inscription, Barbauld preferred interiors—'Verses written in an Alcove', 'Verses inscribed on a pair of screens', 'Lines placed over a Chimney-Piece'—to scenes from nature, so in her use of the genre of occasional poem, she shifted the centre of attention away from political events towards the thoughts and feelings

---

[12] See *Prelude (1805)*, x. 824–5; and 'To Toussaint L'Ouverture', ll. 9–14.

they provoked. As Marlon Ross has shown, some elements of tension and ambiguity were already inherent in the occasional genre itself, 'a form that during the period stood at the crossroads between overtly political satire (the province of political men) and apolitical sentiment (a province women were making increasingly their own)'. But Barbauld exploited these ambiguities to the full, both to camouflage and throw into relief her 'double dissension'.[13] The resulting poetic texture is too unresolved to be bland. In the 'Epistle to William Wilberforce', her voice of protest emerges all the more strongly for the late eighteenth-century pastoral idiom by which it is ironically framed:

> No milk-maid's song, or hum of village talk,
> Soothes the lone Poet in his evening walk:
> No willing arm the flail unweary'd plies,
> Where the mix'd sounds of cheerful labour rise.
>
> . . . .
>
> But shrieks and yells disturb the balmy air,
> Dumb sullen looks of woe announce despair,
> And angry eyes thro' dusky features glare.
>
> (ll. 73–6, 81–3)

William McCarthy has argued that Barbauld's subtle intermingling of private and public modes of address suggests an undermining of gender conventions which dictated that the private was the realm of the woman. Just as she 'smuggled' personal themes into public discourse, he says, so she gave private events a public dimension. Her poem addressed to her brother, 'To Dr. Aikin, on his complaining that she neglected him', can be read not only as an intimate letter of apology, but as a feminist poem of protest at the divergent paths to which their equal education is now leading them: Aikin to 'The nobler labours of a manly mind' and Barbauld herself to 'Less shining toils, and meaner praises'.[14] The coded nature of Barbauld's poems is for McCarthy accentuated by their mode of circulation, which emphasizes their character as messages even while it distances them from the sender:

Many were sent in letters to her intimate friend Elizabeth Belsham; others were deposited in places where they would be found later. The most famous ... is

---

[13] 'The Woman Writer and the Tradition of Dissent', in Carol Shiner Wilson and Joel Haefner (eds.), *Re-Visioning Romanticism: British Women Writers, 1776–1837* (Philadelphia: University of Pennsylvania Press, 1994), 95.
[14] 'To Dr Aikin on his Complaining that she neglected him, October 20th 1768', ll. 51, 53, in *Poems of Anna Letitia Barbauld*, 18.

'The Mouse's Petition', left in the cage of a mouse that Joseph Priestley had captured for use in an experiment.[15]

The mingling of directness and indirectness in her modes of address allowed Barbauld to camouflage personal or feminist agendas. It was the coded nature of her poems, McCarthy concludes, that lent them to 'duplicitous readings'.[16]

But Barbauld had inherited from the pre-Romantic poets of sensibility—Gray, Collins, and above all Cowper—a repertoire of poetic devices which already blurred the boundaries between 'feminine' and 'masculine', 'private' and 'public'. She extended and enriched a language which was already 'coded', and we should not underestimate the extent to which her readers were capable of seeing through these codes. When Hazlitt appeared to be damning Barbauld with faint phrase—'She is a very pretty poetess; and, to my fancy, strews the flowers of poetry most agreeably round the borders of religious controversy'[17]—a layer of irony may have complicated his apparent condescension. Hazlitt's comment highlights the combination of feminine and masculine characteristics in Barbauld's poetry which many readers in this century find limited and sentimental, but which enabled her to speak powerfully to her contemporary audience. Mary Scott, writing in *The Female Advocate* (1774) made Barbauld the apotheosis of a creation–reception aesthetic based on sympathetic identification: 'How fair, how beauteous to our gazing eyes | Thy vivid intellectual paintings rise! | We feel thy feelings, glow with all thy fires, | Adopt thy thought, and pant with thy desires'.[18] Acknowledged here is the synthesis of feeling and intellect which her poetry achieved, and which communicated itself to enthusiastic readers. She spoke to a Dissenting audience (of both sexes) attuned to the plain language of rational argumentation. But she also addressed a wider readership who were responsive to the claims of sensibility; and though not a novelist herself, she won the hearts of women who read *La Nouvelle Heloïse* with the same ardour as she had done. Male readers were equally impressed. When David Garrick, writing in the *Annual*

---

[15] ' "We hoped the *Woman* was going to appear" ', 125.

[16] Ibid., 122–3, 125.

[17] Howe v. 147; quoted in William Keach, 'A Regency Prophecy and the End of Anna Barbauld's Career', *Studies in Romanticism*, 33 (1994), 577.

[18] *The Female Advocate; A Poem. Occasioned by Reading Mr Duncombe's Feminead*, ll. 425–8 (London: Joseph Johnson, 1774), 35; quoted in McCarthy, ' "We hoped the woman was going to appear" ', 114. McCarthy also quotes 'Mira' in the *Gentleman's Magazine* (1774): 'Hail, charming Aikin, hail! thy name inspires | My glowing bosom with congenial fires'.

Register (1775), acknowledged Barbauld as the best poet of her generation, he did so by measuring her according to the straightforwardly competitive model which pertained among her male contemporaries. Paying her a compliment in chivalrous terms that recognized her femininity, he emphatically proclaimed her right to enter the lists and defeat all opposition: 'Who lately sang the sweetest lay? | A woman, woman, woman, still I say'.[19]

II. INTERVENTIONS AND TRESPASSES

Occasional verse was not the only medium in which Barbauld entered male territory, challenging preconceptions about gender and genre. Most of her poetry is dialogic, both in the general sense, that it engages with an implied or addressed reader (frequently a contemporary), and in the Bakhtinian sense, that it interrogates or parodies traditional poetic discourse. Some of her liveliest writing grew out of her acquaintance with Joseph Priestley, with whom she had a close and abiding friendship. The significance of Priestley's presence in her poetry may partly have derived from the role he played in starting Barbauld on her poetic career: 'Mrs Barbauld has told me that it was the perusal of some verses of mine that first induced her to write any thing in verse'.[20] But Priestley was also the father of a Dissenting oratorical tradition which claimed Barbauld's allegiance, and he had an important function in bringing the worlds of religion, science, poetry, and politics into conjunction. At a time when science and politics were beginning to claim priority over the arts, and the arts to defend themselves by asserting their own claims to progressiveness, Priestley stood for a spirit of humane and rational enlightenment in which scientific and literary experiment were seen as complementary.

Barbauld addressed a number of poems to Priestley, two of which show how her practical and theoretical interest in poetic identity intersected with her political concerns, stamping a strongly Warringtonian provenance on her writing. The first, composed in 1767, carries the lengthy title of 'Verses written on the Back of an old Visitation Copy of the Arms of Dr. Priestley's Family, with Proposals for a new Escutcheon'; and in it Barbauld gives playful expression to some serious revisionary arguments, in much the same spirit that Hannah More addressed her private audience in 'Bas Bleu'. The poem concerns

---

[19] *Annual Register*, 18 (1775); quoted in Rodgers, *Georgian Chronicle*, 61.
[20] See the editors' introd. to *Poems of Anna Letitia Barbauld*, p. xxix.

history, and it focuses on a family custom—the use of heraldic arms—
which was deeply questionable to a Dissenting thinker. The poem
indirectly defines Barbauld's own sense of the place of tradition in
poetry (and of her own place in tradition) as well as giving an insight
into her friendship. Opening with a challenge which is addressed specifically to Priestley as a radical and a scientist, Barbauld implicitly includes
a wider frame of reference in her attack on the use of heraldic arms—'—
Are these thy honours? Shall thy nobler name | From 'blazon'd arms and
'scutcheons borrow fame?' (ll. 1–2)—showing how this apparently
innocent icon carries a charge of ideological significance. Priestley is
accused not only of perpetuating warmongering values, but of being the
passive transmitter of a family tradition which he leaves unquestioned.
Barbauld projects a new design for his coat of arms along pacifist lines,
replacing Gothic towers and grinning uncouth monsters with '*harmless*
lightnings', the cap of liberty, and the pastoral hook. At the centre of this
escutcheon, she imagines the Palace of Fame, 'Where every bright
distinguish'd name appears | Through the long annals of three thousand
years' (ll. 29–30). Conventionally, the poem turns at this point into a
decorous tribute to Priestley, underrated now but to be included among
the famous when the final reckoning comes.[21] But less predictably, it
culminates with a self-reflexive allusion:

> Some hand—and let that hand be marked for mine,
> Shall sketch, with hasty strokes, the fair design.
> Then, touch'd by venial pride, even I might rise,
> And strut a straw breadth nearer to the skies.[22]

Using a standard eighteenth-century topos of modesty, Barbauld anticipates fame while suggesting that the hunger for it belongs to the
masculinist tradition she is critiquing. She thus negotiates a place for
herself within male discourse, but preserves a critical detachment from
its premisses.

---

[21] Twenty or so years later, Barbauld was again to return to the issue of fame, in 'To Dr.
Priestley. Dec. 29, 1792'. Written in the wake of the 'Church and King mob' riot in which
Priestley lost his house and property, the poem reassures him that he will be recompensed with
permanent acclaim. Interestingly, Barbauld uses the compensatory arguments which were
current among Romantic poets trying to convince themselves of their life in posterity. Note
esp. the Miltonic allusion, the trope of patience in adversity, and the projection beyond the
present into a comforting (here also a millennarian) futurity (ll. 11–21).

[22] ll. 39–42. For a comparable use of the modesty topos to frame an ambitious bid for
recognition, see the closing lines of William Collins's 'Ode on the Poetical Character', which
Barbauld may well have had in mind.

In a second poem addressed to her mentor, 'An Inventory of the Furniture in Dr. Priestley's Study' (1771), Barbauld investigates the 'premises' of masculine tradition both metaphorically and literally. Parodying Swift's irreverent style in poems such as 'The Lady's Dressing Room', she enters Dr Priestley's study as a female interloper in a masculine domain, but also as the affectionate surveyor of his accomplishments in the fields of science, letters, and politics. The inventory begins with a map of the world, then moves on to include his books, papers, and scientific paraphernalia. Opening abruptly, its register is colloquial, its pace rapid, and its style minimalist. No account is given of the observer's relation to her subject, nor of her mode of entry into his room; and indeed her presence and identity are elided, so as to suggest a similarity between her figural status as interpreter and the anonymous reader who construes her poem. Details are, however, used tellingly, to imply both her familiarity with the room itself, and her thorough knowledge of its occupant. Whereas 'The Lady's Dressing Room' lists intimate sartorial, cosmetic, and bodily details (some of them disgusting) in a manner that is scurrilously invasive, Barbauld's eye ranges more sympathetically over an assortment of objects connected with the scientist's intellectual life. She tells her audience, by these means, about his reading-habits, his consuming passion for experiments, and (by way of a treasonable innuendo) his republican politics.[23]

In her description of the high and low reading-matter which characterizes Priestley's library, and of the jumble of papers, pamphlets, and proof-sheets which lie scattered around among his jars and phials, Barbauld suggests the frenetic creativity of a mind that works equally well in the complementary realms of science and literature, and that experiments with every discursive medium available, 'from shilling touch to pompous folio' (l. 30). The freshness and speed of Priestley's creative activity, echoed in the racy tempo of Barbauld's writing, are a source of admiration in their own right and a means of defining her own dialogic medium. Contrasting the pomposity of stiff volumes ranged on the shelves with texts that have been 'stamped and coined' by Priestley himself, Barbauld expresses a distinct preference for the fluidity of living currency ('answer, remark, reply, rejoinder'), over what Paine called the 'manuscript assumed authority of the

---

[23] 'A group of all the British kings, | Fair emblem! on a packthread swings' (ll. 7–8), in *Poems of Anna Letitia Barbauld*, 38.

dead'.[24] The poem openly celebrates a language grounded in conversational immediacy. Priestley's role in shaping and applying that language to progressive ends is metaphorically encoded in the creative act which brings the poem to its climax.

Likening Priestley's creative output on the one hand to the products of procreation ('embryo schemes') and on the other to the materials of divine creation ('A mass of heterogeneous matter, | A chaos dark, nor land nor water', ll. 39–40), Barbauld draws two of the most powerful and abiding myths of creativity into an androgynous conflation. She then goes on to complicate this double metaphor with a further, protracted simile, in which incomplete books and fragments of argument are likened to infants—prematurely born, damaged, but nonetheless strong and destined for survival:

> New books, like new-born infants, stand,
> Waiting the printer's clothing hand;—
> Others, a motley ragged brood,
> Their limbs unfashioned all, and rude,
> Like Cadmus' half-formed men appear.[25]

By contrast with the earlier Priestley poem, there appears to be no disapproval here for spirited and masculine aggression: Barbauld acknowledges with affection the power of Priestley's controversial writing, and its defiance ('born with teeth, and sprung up fighting'), in ways that she could not approve his passive inheritance of a coat of arms, the conventional symbol of outdated and discredited values.

Barbauld celebrates Dissenting culture's strong allegiance to the spirit of progress and enlightenment associated with scientific experimentation, and shows how her identity as a poet and intellectual is bound up with the contribution made to knowledge by Warrington's most celebrated tutor. Her poem plays on the etymological links between 'inventory' and 'invention'. Her own creativity is implicitly drawn into the poem by way of analogies with female reproduction, suggesting a dialogue between the complementary worlds of science and poetry.

---

[24] 'I am contending for the rights of the *living*, and against their being willed away, and controlled and contracted for, by the manuscript assumed authority of the dead': *The Rights of Man* (1791–2), in *The Thomas Paine Reader*, ed. Michael Foot and Isaac Kramnick (Harmondsworth, Middlesex: Penguin, 1987), 204.

[25] ll. 41–5. The editors note that in Ovid's *Metamorphoses* 'Cadmus sows the teeth of a dragon; they then spring up, feet first, as armed men, who slay one another. The passage was often interpreted as an allegory of discord' (*Poems of Anna Letitia Barbauld*, 248.)

The overlapping of these two concerns becomes more apparent in the poem's abrupt, enigmatic conclusion:

> 'But what is this,' I hear you cry,
> 'Which saucily provokes my eye?'—
> A thing unknown, without a name,
> Born of the air and doomed to flame.

(ll. 55–8)

William McCarthy and Elizabeth Kraft have suggested that, because Priestley was 'accustomed to conduct experiments in the presence of friends', and because these lines 'seem to register a moment of discovery', the 'thing unknown, without a name' may be hydrogen, which was isolated before oxygen.[26] This explains the dramatic suddenness of Priestley's exclamation and Barbauld's presence as witness of his important (but unnamed) discovery. However, as well as being a laboratory poem in which scientific progress is witnessed, this is a poem about *self-discovery*—the emergence of Barbauld's poetic voice. Barbauld's playful handling of generic expectations helps to uncover this secondary thread of significance. It is usual in inventory poems for the spectator's viewing of a private room to take place in the absence of the room's occupant, and without his (more usually her) knowledge.[27] Accordingly, up till the line beginning 'But what is this', Barbauld has maintained the discreetly self-effacing position of spectator–reader, and Priestley himself has not been named (though his possessions have been enumerated in such a way as to make him vividly present to the reader's imagination). At this point, however, Barbauld introduces for the first time both the room's occupant and its observer, as though bringing them face to face. The sudden question which punctuates the poem's progress at line 55 might just as easily signal Priestley's surprise on entering his room to discover a female interloper, who 'saucily provokes [his] eye' by virtue of her gender and intrusion, as his discovery of hydrogen.

An amusing significance would be added to the line 'A thing unknown, without a name' if it were taken to identify Barbauld herself; but there would be an even richer ambiguity if what Barbauld intended here was to suggest a resemblance between her own status as (unknown)

---

[26] The editors quote from P. O'Brien, *Warrington Academy, 1757–1786: Its Predecessors and Successors* (Wigan, Lancs: Owl Books, 1989), 64: 'Perhaps hydrogen ("inflammmable air") which was isolated before oxygen'. See *Poems of Anna Letitia Barbauld*, 248.

[27] See Swift, 'The Lady's Dressing Room'.

female writer and an important but hitherto unrecognized chemical property. Insubstantiality is what links hydrogen ('born of the air and doomed to flame') with woman as she is traditionally perceived, but also with poetry, which Barbauld refers to elsewhere as a 'bubble'.[28] Women and poetry can be properly valued, Barbauld implies, just as the air itself may be deemed precious, by those equipped with enough understanding and appreciation to detect their hidden properties. Indeed, like hydrogen—or like Priestley himself, in the earlier poem—verse may eventually be doomed to *fame*. In her playful substitution of the conventional rhyme word that usually accompanies 'name', Barbauld positions herself somewhere between two alternative literary conventions, of ambitiously seeking fame and modestly bowing out of the public arena.

The analogy Barbauld makes between science and poetry in the context of fame has a striking topical relevance. Priestley's discoveries were undervalued and unrewarded during his lifetime; and the position he held as a marginalized Dissenter made him notoriously vulnerable to attack, eventually driving him into exile. In William Enfield's book on copyright, *Observations on Literary Property*, which was published in the same year as *The Speaker* (1774) Priestley was held up as an example of a great scientist neglected by the British public. Enfield quotes from a footnote in Priestley's *Experiments and Observations on Air*, in which the scientist had declared his determination not to publish his *History of Experimental Philosophy* because of the likelihood that he would not receive proper payment for his work:

This determination hath arisen, not from any dislike of the undertaking, but, in truth, because I see no prospect of being reasonably indemnified for so much labour and expence; notwithstanding the specimens I have already given of that work . . . have met with a much more favourable reception from the best judges, both at home and abroad, than I expected. Immortality, if I should have any view to it, is not the proper price of works such as these.[29]

Enfield uses the example of Priestley to argue that the state should be obliged to purchase new discoveries in the domain of mathematics, natural philosophy, and the arts. Inventors would thus be able to make their ideas generally available, while at the same time receiving their proper payment. Immortality and fame were the insubstantial rewards

---

[28] See the closing lines (85–6) of 'Washing-Day': 'Earth, air, and sky. and ocean, hath its bubbles, | And verse is one of them—this most of all'.

[29] *Observations on Literary Property* (London: Joseph Johnson, 1774), 49.

grudgingly allowed to poets and scientists by a society unwilling to remunerate them properly. In the context of this wider copyright debate, in which Priestley (and with him his Warrington Academy associates and disciples) was implicated, Barbauld's analogies between poetry, science, and womanhood take on a rich and complicated significance.

If Priestley's discovery of Barbauld as a poet is encoded in the reported question (' "But what is this?," I hear you cry'), might there also be a way of reading its ending as a riddle, one of Barbauld's favourite modes, in which the reader too is 'saucily provoked' by an inability to identify the 'thing unknown'? If poetry and fame, like women and air, are insubstantial, so too is identity; and Barbauld questions its ability to be defined even as she tantalizes her reader with the refusal to define it. Read in this way, the poem makes use of a strategy for redeeming what is undervalued that is closely comparable to Hannah More's description of female virtue: 'So pure its essence, 'twere destroyed | If known, and if commended void'.[30] Just as More's poem ('Bas Bleu') concludes with the surprise tactic of self-effacement, so Barbauld's inventory of Dr Priestley's furniture comes to an abrupt end the moment she is discovered, as though the writing-subject itself could be eclipsed by recognition. I shall be returning in Chapter 6 to the ways in which this strategy of recuperation through self-effacement contributed to a feminized poetics of reception.

III. ENIGMAS OF IDENTITY AND GENDER

The riddle, as Walter Ong reminds us, belongs in the oral world. 'To solve a riddle, canniness is needed: one draws on knowledge, often deeply unconscious, beyond the words themselves'. The possessive emphasis on the speaker's identity in utterance does not apply to riddles, whose dynamic—as it is anthropologically understood—has always been interactive. Riddles are not used 'simply to store knowledge but to engage others in verbal and intellectual combat: utterance of one proverb or riddle challenges hearers to top it with a more apposite or a contradictory one', as though in 'a polite duel, a contest of wits, an operation in oral agonistic'.[31] Most riddles follow a similar pattern to

---

[30] See Ch. 6, below, for the recurrent linkage between female writers and the position, figure, or trope of anonymity.

[31] *Orality and Literacy: The Technologizing of the Word* (London: Methuen and Co., 1982), 44, 68.

the poem just discussed, in that identity ceases to matter the moment it is recognized. The riddle presupposes a relationship of collaboration and complicity between author and reader, in which clues to an unsolved mystery are offered in good faith, and investigated according to the hermeneutic assumption that there is a single answer. For this reason the solving of riddles frequently involves the conjunction of pleasure and anticlimax, whereas unsolved riddles have the capacity to go on intriguing.

Barbauld's habitual recurrence to the riddle as a poetic form was one of the many ways in which she evinced her fascination with the elusiveness of identity. It is telling that so many of her riddles are genuinely enigmatic, and that at least one of them remains unsolved to this day.[32] The riddle was an ideal medium for her: lying somewhere between dramatic monologue and objective description, it allowed her the possibility of speaking from within the identity of another, while observing the other's characteristics from the outside. In this in-between world, Barbauld's own identity was camouflaged or teasingly withheld from the reader, as though momentarily borrowing the identity on which she rested. From this position, she was able to adumbrate a poetics of reception which resembled the discourse of 'negative capability' and 'anonymity' later defined by John Keats.

The subjects Barbauld chose to identify with in her riddles are revealing, because they so often reflect her concern with insubstantiality, fluidity, and metamorphosis. Sometimes these are given a paradoxical flavour: in one entitled 'Enigma', she focuses on the contradiction between the airy nothingness of words—'Unseen, unfelt, by night, by day'—and their capacity to 'wound like steel'; while in a more abstract description of the properties of Hope she uses the analogy of pursuer and pursued to suggest the elusiveness both of her subject and of the medium in which she writes:

> O'er hills and o'er valleys unwearied I fly,
> But should I o'ertake him, that instant I die;
> Yet I spring up again, and again I pursue,
> The object still distant, the passion still new.

---

[32] Riddle No III (in *Poems of Anna Letitia Barbauld*, 190): 'I never talk but in my sleep; | I never cry, but sometimes weep; | My doors are open day and night; Old age i help to better sight | I, like chamelion, feed on air | And dust to me is dainty fare'. Since writing this chapter, I have been informed by Jane Stabler that she and David Fairer have solved the riddle, whose answer is: 'the nose'.

> Now guess,—and to raise your astonishment most,
> While you see me you have me, when found I am lost.

> (ll. 17–22)

A similar sense of transformation, speed, and danger is conveyed in a riddle which resembles a spell, and whose solution is 'stars'—'We are spirits all in white, | On a field as black as night; | There we dance and sport and play, | Changing every changing day' (ll. 1–4)—where the conventional feminine attributes of fickleness and witchery are combined. It is not unusual for Barbauld's riddles to turn on the paradoxes and contradictions that are ascribed to women. More often, however, she uses the riddle's formal properties of ambiguity and equivocation to pose questions about the indistinct boundaries between gendered identities. Three of her wittiest riddles directly concern the question of gender: the first, addressing itself 'To the Ladies', is delivered in the persona of an umbrella, and contains an amusing combination of sexual innuendo (directed at male impotence) and irony (directed at the male custom of chivalry), which is designed to unsettle assumptions about who controls whom in the rituals surrounding fertility:

> Hard is my stem and dry, no root is found
> To draw nutritious juices from the ground;
> Yet of your ivory fingers' magic touch
> The quickening power and strange effect is such,
> My shrivelled trunk a sudden shade extends,
> And from rude storms your tender frame defends...

> (ll. 1–6)

The second, a logogriph on the word 'starch', is less gender-specific. It focuses on the uses to which starch is put by both women and men, for domestic and sartorial purposes:

> For man's support I came at first from earth,
> But man perverts the purpose of my birth;
> Beneath his plastic hand new forms I take,
> And either sex my services partake.

> (ll. 1–4)

Rebuking scientific progress for its exploitation of the natural world, her opening lines are addressed at men rather than women; but her real interest is in tracing the history of starch as it criss-crosses from one to the other gender. Through a subdued sexual innuendo, Barbauld suggests that the persona of the poem is itself androgynous—capable of assuming either sex, like Milton's angels, in the 'services' it performs. Pope, in *The Rape of the Lock*, had also made mischievous use of this Miltonic source: 'For Spirits, freed from mortal Laws, with ease | Assume what Sexes and what shapes they please'. (canto i, ll. 69–70)

Barbauld's poetry thrives on hazy ego-boundaries. In the same way that, in her riddles, she can describe herself as though she were anything from a natural entity such as a river or chameleon, or an abstract quality such as Hope, to a manufactured object such as an umbrella; so in her semi-parodic imitations she shows an ability to impersonate the voices of male poets while retaining a critical detachment from them. Her own 'identity' appears to consist of an ability to slide backwards and forwards across the writing–reading axis, occupying the position of both subject and object in the creative–critical process. In an unfinished poem addressed to Lord Byron, she walks on a fine line between imitation and critique. Advising the poet against his incursion into biblical subjects, she employs a diction and metre that are strongly reminiscent of his *Hebrew Melodies*—'Touch not the harp of Jesse's son, | Those strains may not by thee be won, | O Master of the lyre' ('To Lord Byron', ll. 1–3)— effecting a masterly impersonation which out-Byrons Byron for smoothness and ease, while simultaneously holding aloof from his poetic endeavours. Similarly, in a poem addressed 'To Mr. S. T. Coleridge' (1797), designed to warn Coleridge against the excesses of philosophic musing, Barbauld writes uncannily well in the idiom she subjects to critique. Adopting the meditative blank verse of the early 'conversation poems', she catches their tendency to excessive personification and vagueness in a sequence of metaphors which suggest that the 'filmy net' of such artificial diction has the power to 'arrest the foot | Of generous enterprize' (ll. 14–16). Coleridge's favourite Platonic metaphor for the indeterminate nature of reality figures in his ascent of the hill of science both as an allusion to his saturation in philosophy and as an appropriate metaphor for his hesitancies and confusions: these occur when, 'Athwart the mists, | Far into vacant space, huge shadows stretch | And seem realities; while things of life, | Obvious to sight and touch, all glowing round | Fade to the hue of shadows' (ll. 9–13). The sympathy she demonstrates towards Coleridge's poetic voice earns Barbauld the authority to speak firmly to him, in mischievously well-judged tones of concern and guardianship, of the 'sickly hesitation and blank fear' which 'palsy' his ambition (l. 18), and of his need to take a different poetic course: 'Youth belov'd | Of Science—of the Muse belov'd, not here, | Not in the maze of metaphysic lore | Build thou thy place of resting' (ll. 32–5). Coleridge is rebuked for his cowardly evasion of political commitment. While still dedicating himself to fighting 'the bloodless fight | Of Science, Freedom, and the Truth in Christ' ('Reflections on Leaving a Place of Retirement', ll. 61–2) he could claim to be championing a Dissenter's cause; but the moment he began sliding down the slippery slope into abstraction, he was lost. Barbauld's preference for a poetic of clarity and distinctness—her deep suspicion towards mystification—declare the strongly Warringtonian complexion of her allegiances.

Imitation was a mode which Barbauld made her own, and those who commented on her imitative powers appreciated them for their sympathy and susceptibility to others' feelings. In her essay 'On Romance: An Imitation' she caught the manner of Samuel Johnson's prose style so well that Johnson, despite observing in general that 'the imitations of my style have not hit it', made an exception in her case: 'Miss Aikin has done it the best; for she has imitated the sentiment as well as the diction'.[33] A similar observation was made by a reviewer comparing the works of Hannah More and Barbauld in the *Monthly Repository*: whereas More 'awakens and impresses', he argued, Barbauld 'meets our ideas, and seems to express what has passed through our own minds, much more forcibly than we could have done'. Following the principle of disinterested altruism which underpinned the Dissenting tradition, her powers of sympathetic identification reached out beyond stylistic echoes to an ability to empathize with those she addressed, so that her readers had 'a fellow-feeling with her' in all that she said. 'It is thus that we are carried away by her fervour of feeling', the reviewer observed.[34]

IV. SEXUAL POLITICS

Barbauld did not champion women's rights in the way that Wollstonecraft did, and her contribution to the politics of gender has frequently been overshadowed by comparison with her more forthright contemporary, whose reception history has followed an almost exactly opposite course to her own. In recent commentaries on Barbauld, some discomfiture with her attitudes to the role of women has arisen, especially in respect of her poem addressed to Wollstonecraft, 'The Rights of

---

[33] Quoted in Rodgers, *Georgian Chronicle*, 62.   [34] Quoted ibid. 66.

Woman' (of which more later), but also in relation to a biographical incident, around which important ideological issues have been focused. When Elizabeth Montagu asked Barbauld to set up an academy for young ladies, Barbauld declined with the observation that 'The best way for women to acquire knowledge is from conversation with a father, a brother, or friend, in the way of family intercourse and easy conversation, and by such a course of reading as they may recommend'. She went on to justify the apparent discrepancy between her own status (as a successful and highly educated woman) and her policy with respect to others in the following terms:

> Perhaps you may think, that having myself stepped out of the bounds of female reserve in becoming an author, it is with an ill grace I offer these sentiments: but though this circumstance may destroy the grace, it does not the justice of the remark; and I am full well convinced that to have a too great fondness for books is little favourable to the happiness of a woman, especially one not in affluent circumstances. My situation has been peculiar, and would be no rule for others.[35]

Compounded by the fact that Barbauld was a famous teacher of boys at her husband's school in Palgrave, this incident has aligned Barbauld with an extreme conservative position as regards women's education—more so even than More's, in the view of Marlon Ross.[36]

Her poetry tells a somewhat different story, in the sense that 'conversation with a father, a brother, or friend' provided the basis for a dialogic interaction with patriarchal culture of a kind that clearly articulated the difference of the sexes. Barbauld succeeded in demonstrating both her ability to be at home in the (predominantly male) literary tradition with which she engaged, while at the same time defining an aesthetic of sympathy which mediated between masculinity and femininity. Her interest in impersonating the voices of male writers was matched by her fascination with manufactured objects, especially recent inventions—the fridge, the folding umbrella, iron bridges, the first hot-air balloon—whose construction and inner workings she describes with intricate appreciation, as though from the perspective of a Martian. She

---

[35] *Works of Anna Laetitia Barbauld* (2 vols., London: Longman, 1825), vol. i, pp. xviii–xix; discussed by Carol Shiner Wilson, 'Lost Needles, Tangled Threads: Stitchery, Domesticity, and the Artistic Experience', in ead. and Haefner (eds.), *Re-Visioning Romanticism*, 182; and by Marlon Ross, *The Contours of Masculine Desire: Romanticism and the Rise of Poetry* (Oxford: Oxford University Press, 1989), 216.

[36] *Contours of Masculine Desire*, 216.

evinced a lively experimentation with contemporary male forms and
activities, entering a domain that was marked out as male (just as she
entered Dr Priestley's study) in a spirit of affectionate sympathy. But her
affection is far from betraying what Elizabeth Kowaleski-Wallace has
termed 'patriarchal complicity'. Indeed, her identity as a poet became
increasingly inseparable from her habits as a critical reader. Positioning
herself ambiguously in relation to gender-oppositions, Barbauld demands from her own readers a response that is similarly androgynous
and empathetic.

'Inscription for an Ice-House' (composed 1793; published 1825)
celebrates the primitive version of our modern refrigerator. The ice
house is used to symbolize the masculine terrain of science, about which
Barbauld felt excitement (but also some reservations); while as a place
designed to serve domestic purposes, it also symbolizes the world of
femininity as it is stereotypically understood—a world which Barbauld
celebrated in poems such as 'Washing Day' (1797), for its difference
from the masculine:

> The Muses are turned gossips; they have lost
> The buskin'd step, and clear high-sounding phrase,
> Language of gods. Come, then, domestic Muse,
> In slip-shod measure loosely prattling on...
>
> (ll. 1–4)

Just as the female activities which occur on 'the dreaded washing day' are
both dignified and belittled by Barbauld's mock-epic voice, so, in 'Inscription for an Ice-House' (which Isobel Armstrong has called 'one of
the earliest hymns to technology') the masculine terrain is brought into
conjunction with the feminine, in ways that subject both categories to
scrutiny.[37] The ice-house provides an amusing focus for Barbauld's
preoccupation with man-made constructs, but the poem is also concerned with scientific progress and its uses. Barbauld's reservations
about making nature serve humankind are made by way of an alignment
between science and Romantic aesthetics—both of them gendered as
male, associated with domination, and ironically naturalized by the use
of metaphor and personification.[38] Man becomes a 'great magician',

---

[37] See 'The Gush of the Feminine: How can we read Women's Poetry of the Romantic
Period?', in Feldman and Kelley (eds.), *Romantic Women Writers*, 14.

[38] Conversely, Isobel Armstrong argues that it is 'unusual to find a personified natural force
effectively... denatured and rendered a product of artifice—forced by violence into culture'
(ibid. 14–15).

controlling the elements and bending recalcitrant materials 'to do him service and perform his will'; while the ice-house (his invention) is personified as 'stern Winter', piling his 'treasured snows' into a 'rugged cave' which has earlier been likened to a locked and bolted cell, but which here takes on an added resemblance to a safe (ll. 8–11). Using the genre of blank-verse inscription as an appropriate medium in which to criticize Romantic aesthetics[39] Barbauld interrogates Burke's categories of the sublime and the beautiful, together with their explicit gender-alignments, by way of a suggested contrast between the rugged masculinity of the ice-house itself and the soft femininity of the 'melting peach' and 'nectarine smooth' which it contains. Just as man subdues nature to his own designs, so the ice is described as congealing, moulding, cooling, and darting frost into the fruits and ice cream which will eventually find their way onto the dinner table. And so, by implication, Burke's aesthetic theory involves the domination by masculine sublimity of the (beautiful) feminine.

Barbauld's critique does not remain content with echoing Burke's categories and exposing their hierarchical structure, but (by way of a biblical allusion, to 'fettered Sampson') revises the Burkean pattern of subjugation by suggesting that the ice-house itself is used to serve domestic purposes. In this way, she demonstrates that the sublime can be tamed by the beautiful—that it can be feminized and domesticated, just as the epic genre is made homely in 'Washing Day'. She teases her readers of both sexes with the possibility of an aesthetic which mediates between the masculine and the feminine (each needing the other for its completion) while at the same time offering a sharp and specific critique of the assumptions which underlie Romantic ideology.

Poems such as these show Barbauld's concern with gender-difference and the social construction of hierarchized gender-roles—a concern which she shared with Mary Wollstonecraft, who preceded her in deconstructing the Burkean sublime.[40] However, these two writers approached the question of gender-difference very differently, Barbauld seeking to move the category of the feminine from its subordinate position, Wollstonecraft attempting to abolish it altogether. In 'The

---

[39] See e.g. Wordsworth's 'Lines left upon a Seat in a Yew-Tree'; and 'Lines: Written with a Slate-Pencil'.

[40] See Mary Wollstonecraft, *A Vindication of the Rights of Woman*, ed. Carol H. Poston (New York: W. W. Norton and Co., 1975), ch. 2; and Ronald Paulson, *Representations of Revolution* (New Haven: Yale University Press, 1983), ch. 3.

Rights of Woman', a poem addressed to Wollstonecraft, Barbauld positions herself ambiguously in relation to the cause of female emancipation. Impersonating a voice of outraged indignation—'Yes, injured Woman! rise, assert thy right! | Woman! too long degraded, scorned, opprest' (ll. 1–2)—she disorients her readers sufficiently to make us uncertain whether or not there is irony in the commands which follow. If woman is to 'gird [her]self with grace', using 'Soft melting tones' as her 'cannon's roar', and blushes and fears as her artillery, does this free her, or subjugate her further? Is she rebuking her colleague for approaching the relation between the sexes as a struggle for power, or is she—as Carol Shiner Wilson argues—reinforcing the traditional claim that women exert power over men through their feminine grace, and that men submit to this power through chivalry?[41] If the former, then she is failing to engage with the central argument of the *Vindication*, which seeks to put women in command of themselves, not of men. If the latter, then it is difficult to make sense of the poem's warning that woman cannot hope to remain as the 'courted idol of mankind', on the 'proud eminence' constructed by male adulation, but must at length submit to loving and being loved. Much turns on whether the line 'Thou mayst command, but never canst be free' (l. 20) issues encouragement, or is causally linked to the preceding commands, and used as a warning against their consequences. Whichever way this question is answered, the poem is disconcerting for its avoidance of the more radical implications of Wollstonecraft's argument, where chivalry is dispensed with altogether.

But Barbauld was engaged here in a larger dispute, about the importance of the so-called 'feminine' attributes, which she believed were in danger of being underrated by the kind of feminism which makes women into surrogate men. Women, she claimed in a letter of 1774, are 'not only naturally inclined to love, but to all the soft and gentle affections, all the tender attentions and kind sympathies of nature': it is this that constitutes their distinctive ethical identity. Crucially, Barbauld differed from Wollstonecraft with respect to the politics of sensibility; as she put it in her essay, 'Thoughts on Devotional Taste': 'It is the character of the present age to allow little to sentiment, and all the warm and generous emotions are treated as romantic by the supercilious

---

[41] Wilson argues that Barbauld 'employs military tropes to reinforce the moral domain of the feminine ideal'. See 'Stitchery, Domesticity, and the Artistic Experience', 181.

brow of a cold-hearted philosophy'.[42] Taking it as read that women are creatures of feeling, who falsify their inner selves by adopting the characteristics of men, Barbauld argued that any attempt to replace sensibility with rationality, along the lines proposed in Wollstonecraft's *Vindication*, would be doomed to failure because it would be going against nature itself: only by acknowledging that 'separate rights are lost in mutual love' (l. 32) can progress be accomplished.

V. THE POLITICS OF SYMPATHY

If the limits and the possibilities of Barbauld's feminism were defined by her attitude to sensibility, so for the most part were both her poetry's contribution to broader political debate, and the ethical dimension of her critical essays. Barbauld shared with Wordsworth, Coleridge, and Wollstonecraft a mistrust for the excesses of sensibility encouraged in trashy novels. But nowhere in her literary criticism did she slip into the sententious tones adopted by these three writers, who dismissed the public's vulnerability to bad literature as though it revealed a fault in readers as much as in writers, and who condemned this susceptibility as the worst aspect of feminine and foreign taste. By contrast, Barbauld examined sensibility as an artistic medium which demanded sophisticated handling if it was to bring out the best in its readers, and which was as yet underdeveloped in British novelists. In an essay on 'Distress which Excites Agreeable Sensations'[43] she argues that the average novel-writer did not know how to render emotions affecting, other than through a sensationalist 'etiquette' of swoonings and death. A person experienced in this kind of reading became habituated to horror, turning over the pages 'with the utmost coolness and unconcern' (p. 220), and thus acquiring 'something of that apathy and indifference which the experience of real life would have given them, without its advantages' (p. 227). Sensibility does not increase with exercise, Barbauld concluded: rather, it is developed through its manifestation as virtuous action. Only the true artist of sensibility, capable of 'a thousand little touches of grief, which, though slight, are irresistible' (p. 220), could hope to have a palpable effect on ethics: the English were 'too gloomy a people' (p. 220) to manage such

---

[42] In *The Works of Anna Laetitia Barbauld* (2 vols.; London: Longman, Hurst, Rees, Orme, Brown, and Green, 1825), ii. 233.

[43] In Barbauld, *Works*, ii. Page refs. will be given in the text.

delicacy. Mischievously asserting that French novelists were better at this kind of writing, Barbauld risked the politically charged suggestion that superior Gallic tastes encourage superior Gallic morals. She thus unsettled the misogyny and insularity which underwrote Coleridge's and Wordsworth's caricatures of foreign literature, while at the same time redeeming sensibility from the charge brought against it by Wollstonecraft.

Wollstonecraft experimented with the novel because, as the feminine medium of sensibility which she most despised, it asked to be reformed from within, by a writer capable of subjecting it to intelligent critique. Her handling of the genre disclosed an explicitly political agenda. Barbauld by contrast avoided the novel, despite her greater sympathy for it, choosing instead to politicize and feminize sensibility in the medium of poetry. In her handling of poetic discourse, she demonstrated that the language of sensibility—'the thousand little touches of grief, which though slight are irresistible'—was better adapted to ethical purposes in poetry than it was in prose. Furthermore, as Marlon Ross has argued, her liberal political language was 'subtly transliterated into moralized sentiment and subtly transferred out of the sphere of topical satire and political factionalism'.[44] This allowed her to address a wider audience than Wollstonecraft, without risking the displeasure of women readers resistant to reform, or male readers who did not share her Dissenting background and political views.

In 'On the King's Illness', Barbauld spoke for the majority in voicing a deep sympathy for George III, well loved by the nation, whom she transformed into an embodiment of her own sympathetic ideals: 'For thou hadst human feelings, and hast liv'd | A man with men, and kindly charities, | Even such as warm the cottage hearth, were thine' (ll. 11–13). Her tribute to the sick and dying king becomes a tribute to sensibility itself, embodied in 'A Nation's pity and a Nation's love' (l. 23), which allows her to make an exception in this individual case to her republican politics: 'And therefore falls the tear from eyes not used | To gaze on kings with admiration fond' (ll. 14–15). However, in a pointed topical allusion, Barbauld deliberately introduces a note of qualification—'Yet, Oh that thou hadst closed the wounds of war! | That had been praise to suit a higher strain' (ll. 27–8)—so that, partly camouflaged by moral sentiment, her political perspective becomes discernible. Playfully

---

[44] 'The Woman Writer and the Tradition of Dissent', 99.

challenging her audience's generic expectations, she here implies that
the king's feeble state politics have cost him his entitlement to the
'higher strain' of poetry (the traditional, unsentimentalized, occasion
poem) he might otherwise have deserved. His conduct—unmanly in this
respect alone—invites to be treated in a lighter idiom.

A similar poem, deceptively titled 'On the Death of the Princess
Charlotte', approaches the demise of another hugely popular figure by
way of an unexpected focus on her father, the Prince Regent, whose
hard-hearted refusal to enter into the nation's mourning gives pause for
thought:

> Yet one there is
> Who midst this general burst of grief remains
> In strange tranquillity; whom not the stir
> And long drawn murmurs of the gathering crowd,
> That by his very windows trail the pomp
> Of hearse, and blazoned arms, and long array
> Of sad funereal rites, nor the loud groans
> And deep felt anguish of a husband's heart
> Can move to mingle with this flood one tear.
>
> (ll. 9–17)

Barbauld transforms the occasion of public mourning for Charlotte's
death into an occasion for privately mourning an absence of sensibility
in the nation's most unpopular public figure: 'Oh think of him, and set
apart one sigh, | From the full tide of sorrow spare one tear | For him
who does not weep' (ll. 34–6). Challengingly and disconcertingly, she
elicits from her readers a sympathy they presumably found it hard to
feel, thus disclosing their own hidden resemblance with the figure they
so despised. The poem is typical of her ability to question the consensus
view from within; and it demonstrates that Barbauld's subtle revisions of
generic expectation are inseparable from the politics (which includes the
gender-politics) of disinterested sympathy.

Her two most anthologized poems, 'The Mouse's Petition' and
'The Caterpillar', attempted to redeem sympathetic identification as a
powerful but underrated political tool. Using the genre of the sentimental occasional poem to throw into relief their political purpose,
they proceed from the assumption that, as Barbauld puts it in her
essay 'On Romances: An Imitation', 'few can reason, but all can
feel; and many who cannot enter into an argument, may yet listen to a

tale'.[45] 'The Mouse's Petition' was intended as a protest against oppression in general, its title referring to what Marlon Ross has called 'the most radical version of a political letter, which targets the heart of established power by directly addressing the monarch and parliament'.[46] But because of the strength with which it delineates the specific suffering of a mouse, the poem was widely interpreted as a criticism of the practice of vivisection, and used against Priestley. It is telling, for this reason, that in her later poem 'The Caterpillar', Barbauld addressed the problem of how specific cases of suffering measure against suffering in the abstract, and how a single poignant example can be more powerful than overwhelming numbers in stirring sympathy. Appropriately, in this poem, her method is to proceed from the minute particulars of a single specimen—'I have scanned thy form with curious eye, | Noted the silver line that streaks thy back, | The azure and the orange that divide | Thy velvet sides' (ll. 3–6)—to the general case, of 'tribes and embryo nations' of caterpillars, whom she treats as a pest (l. 16). Observing the discrepancy between her compassion in the individual case and her general indifference, she proceeds to a comparison with human warfare, where it is again apparent that 'capricious Pity, | Which would not stir for thousands, melts for one, | With sympathy spontaneous' (ll. 39–41). The poem concludes with a subtle paradox—''Tis not Virtue, | Yet 'tis the weakness of a virtuous mind' (ll. 41–2)—which is designed to answer not only the Godwinian plea for rational benevolence, but the feminist argument that sensibility, a female weakness, ought to be replaced by the masculine virtues of intellect and restraint.

Unusually for Barbauld, 'The Caterpillar' is addressed to its subject rather than delivered in its persona; but nonetheless, the poet conveys her customary strength of sympathetic identification in the delicate details of her description. The 'light pressure' of the caterpillar's hairy feet on her arm, and its movement 'with stretched out neck | Bending [its] head in airy vacancy' (ll. 10–11) suggest a bond of sympathy between human and insect that is worthy of Uncle Toby in *Tristram Shandy*.[47] Barbauld observes the caterpillar from the outside, while feeling for and with it, in the same way that she enters the imaginative

---

[45] See *Works*, ii. 172; the imitation is presumably of Johnson's 'On Modern Fiction', published in the *Rambler*, 31 Mar. 1750. For Johnson's appreciation of Barbauld's imitative skills, see Rodgers, *Georgian Chronicle*, 62.

[46] 'The Woman Writer and the Tradition of Dissent', 98.

[47] See esp. the famous episode in which Uncle Toby gently addresses a fly, reassuring it that he will bring it no harm (bk. 2, ch. 12).

world of the other in her riddles. Her poetic method succeeds in demonstrating precisely the response she hoped to elicit from her readers as the witnesses of human suffering: 'they who would ... reduce the sympathetic emotions of pity to a system of refined selfishness', she argued in her essay 'On Romance', 'have but ill attended to the genuine feelings of humanity'. Stories of suffering, she concluded, give us access to 'universally felt' emotion, teaching us 'to think, by inuring us to feel: they ventilate the mind by sudden gusts of passion; and prevent the stagnation of thought, by a fresh infusion of dissimilar ideas'.[48] Here as elsewhere, Barbauld defined an ethic and an aesthetic of sympathy which were central both to her poetic voice and to her distinctive brand of feminism.

VI. THE RECEPTION OF *EIGHTEEN HUNDRED AND ELEVEN*

It is an irony of Barbauld's long and successful publishing career—a career seemingly unruffled by anxieties about reception—that it was finally snuffed out by bad reviews, and that the poem responsible for this sudden denouement attracted more contemporary and posthumous attention than anything else she wrote. Having educated her public so pleasurably for forty-odd years, she chose in *Eighteen Hundred and Eleven* to deploy the medium of Juvenalian satire to explicitly political ends. Attacking the British government for its needless protraction of the war with France, she lamented the deplorable consequences for Britain's economy (which at the time of writing was near collapse), and for its status as a once-thriving international centre of science and culture, here elegiacally represented as on the decline. Through the forceful gravitas of her style—'And thinkst thou, Britain still to sit at ease, | An island Queen amidst thy subject seas?' (ll. 39–40)—Barbauld uncomfortably implicates the nation at large (not just those wielding ministerial power) for the complacency of its imperialism, adopting a tone to which one reviewer referred as 'in the most extraordinary degree unkindly and unpatriotic—we had almost said unfilial'.[49]

In its adaptation of the language of moral sentiment to topical events, the poem was in fact quite similar to Barbauld's other occasional verse, which attracted less notice. But its mode of address was more inclusive,

---

[48]   In Barbauld, *Works*, ii. 174, 175.
[49]   *Eclectic Review*, 8: 474; quoted in *Poems of Anna Letitia Barbauld*, 310.

its objects of criticism more likely to antagonize a wide range of readers, and its register and diction unusually lofty for a writer who tended to be at home (in both senses) in an intimate idiom, where her addressees were named and known. This elevated style was demanded of her by the genre of Juvenalian or 'tragical' satire, which traditionally laments the decay of human enterprise (the vanity of human wishes), from a detached and elegiac perspective. It was a style well suited to her theme, the passing of empire from east to west, and Barbauld maximized its elegiac potential to the full. Onto this traditional medium, she grafted a number of personally distinctive poetic topoi, the most important of which is her use of multiple narrative perspectives: these have the effect of introducing generic, stylistic, and tonal ambiguities, as well as the shifts of register with which she experimented elsewhere.

The poem's opening sequence is delivered in a judgmental voice, ranging panoramically over various consequences of the war in Europe at large, and lamenting in a language of abstraction and personification the reign of power, famine, and disease. The focus then narrows in on Regency Britain, addressed directly but formally, as 'thou', and accused in implicating and rebuking tones of deliberately prolonging war, with the inevitable effect of introducing 'Enfeebling Luxury and ghastly Want'. Britain is later addressed as a personified entity rather than as a nation state administered by a culpable government. Barbauld speaks proudly and patriotically of Britain's achievements in the arts and sciences, numbering amongst its famous thinkers, Locke and Paley, its poets, Milton and Thomson, and its dramatists, Shakespeare and Joanna Baillie. The ideology of empire is here upheld—'Wide spreads thy race from Ganges to the pole |, 'O'er half the western world thy accents roll: | Nations beyond the Apalachian hills | Thy hand has planted and thy spirit fills'(ll. 81–4)—in a way that flatly contradicts the charge made by Barbauld's reviewers of unpatriotic sentiments.

Barbauld's introduction of Fancy, through whose eyes the poem's central section is narrated, marks a further shift of subject-position and register. Fancy's prophetic powers are capable of imagining a time when Britain will be visited by the American descendants of exiles such as Priestley, nostalgically searching for their historical origins among the ruins of a vanished empire. Under the gaze of its New World tourists, London will be seen no longer as the thriving centre of commerce and international communication it once was, but as a deserted ruin, whose 'faded glories' take on a romantic aura:

> Pensive and thoughtful shall the wanderers greet
> Each splendid square, and still, untrodden street;
> Or of some crumbling turret, mined by time,
> The broken stairs with perilous step shall climb,
> Thence stretch their view the wide horizon round,
> By scattered hamlets trace its antient bound,
> And, choked no more with fleets, fair Thames survey
> Through reeds and sedge pursue his idle way.
>
> (ll. 169–76)

In this sudden and unexpected *mise en abîme*, we absorb the prospect of London in ruins as though it were a cameo in one of Gilpin's tourist guidebooks or a scene from Goldsmith's *Deserted Village*. Barbauld casts an affectionate backward gaze on the tradition of sensibility to which her own poetry belongs, pausing to lament its vanishment before she turns to embrace a progressive new age in the shape of America's promise.

As Julie Ellison has argued, the use of 'prospect' (the view from mental heights) 'furthers the female author's quest for a reading audience or for critical respect earned by taking on public matters'.[50] Barbauld's lofty position reaches Miltonic heights in the poem's final sequence. Invoking a nameless 'spirit', who has been variously understood as history, progress, liberty, knowledge, and civilization itself, Barbauld watches the advance of civilization (across the globe, and through the centuries) as it pursues first a northerly then a westerly direction. From this global perspective, England becomes a mere pinprick on the atlas, its rise and fall a short episode in world history. The poem glances briefly at Regency London once more, in order to press home its pointed charges of excess and complacency, before tracing the disappearance of civilization from Europe altogether. In a topical allusion which gives the poem its final biting edge, Barbauld implies that the independence movement among the Spanish colonies of South America represents, at the time of writing, humanity's finest achievement.

Among the many hostile contemporary reviews of this arresting and uncompromising poem, one in the Tory *Quarterly* (now attributed to John Wilson Croker) has become legendary for its misogynist abuse. Barbauld is found guilty of entering the political forum—'We had hoped ... that the empire might have been saved without the intervention of a lady-author'—and judged unworthy of a political voice, by

[50] 'Politics of Fancy in the Age of Sensibility', in Wilson and Haefner (eds.), *Re-Visioning Romanticism*, 230.

virtue of her pathetic and womanish naivety: 'an irresistible impulse of
public duty... [has] induced her to dash down her shagreen spectacles
and her knitting needles, and to sally forth... in the magnanimous
resolution of saving a sinking state'. Dismissing the remainder of her
poetry as 'something better than harmless', Croker warns her against
using the medium of satire, 'which indeed is satire on herself alone', and
entreats her not to 'put herself to the trouble of writing any more party
pamphlets in verse'.[51]

Allowing for the extremity of Croker's political bias, there could
scarcely be a stronger contrast with Barbauld's early reception than
this. The overwhelmingly negative response of Barbauld's reactionary
enemies was endorsed by others with political views much closer to her
own: Godwin, for instance, dismissed the poem as 'cowardly, time-
serving, Presbyterian',[52] presumably because it marked a decisive break
with the meliorist historical perspective of Dissenting ideology. Similarly, Henry Crabb Robinson wished she had not written the poem,
complaining that 'She does not content herself with expressing her fears
lest England should perish in the present struggle; she speaks with the
confidence of a prophet of the fall of the country as if she had seen in a
vision the very process of its ruin.'[53] So strong was the general disapprobation that even those who admired the poem felt unable to rise
publicly to Barbauld's defence: Maria Edgeworth claimed that 'a minute's reflection convinced [her] that silent contempt [was] the best
answer' to Croker's review, and that Barbauld's loyal public could be
trusted to have an altogether different reaction: 'The public, the *public*
will do you justice'.[54] But as it turned out, the reaction of enemies and
friends caused Barbauld to give up publishing her verse, even though
she continued to write. As William Keach succinctly puts it, 'A prolific
and influential literary career came to an end with Croker's croakings', in
a manner that recalls the mythology surrounding the death of Keats.[55]

If her lifelong success confirmed that she had the right to 'trespass' on
male territory, and to win renown on the same basis as men, the
reception of *Eighteen Hundred and Eleven* (of which Croker's review

---

[51] *Quarterly Review* (June 1811); quoted in *Poems of Anna Letitia Barbauld*, 310.

[52] *Henry Crabb Robinson on Books and Their Writers*, ed. Edith J. Morley (London: J. M. Dent
and sons, 1938), i. 63–4; cited in Keach, 'Regency Prophecy', 570.

[53] Ibid.

[54] Anna Letitia le Breton, *Memoir of Mrs Barbauld, Including Letters and Notices of her Family and
Friends* (London: George Bell, 1874), 155–6; quoted in Keach, 'Regency Prophecy', 571.

[55] 'Regency Prophecy', 571–2.

represented only the most extreme example) altogether removed Barbauld's trust in the reading-public. Condemned by Edgeworth as 'so ungentlemanlike, so unjust, so insolent',[56] Croker nonetheless voiced a consensus response from the public at large, implicitly defining a line beyond which women writers are not allowed to venture in their bid to achieve and contest authority. As Ellison puts it,

In order to oppose the dissenter, Croker excoriates the woman; in order to turn a poem into a 'pamphlet' he calls fancy 'satire', a masculine—or rather an unfeminine—literary type. Fancy is deflated so that Croker may claim that *Eighteen Hundred and Eleven* fails because of a mismatch of gender and genre.[57]

Within the hierarchical codes that were current at the time of publication, there was indeed a 'mismatch between gender and genre' in this poem; and that it caused Croker such discomfort confirms that this is one of the challenging aspects of Barbauld's most ambitious poetic achievement. If we attempt to restore to the poem its full political resonance we run the risk of moving it a little nearer to traditional norms of occasional verse satire which it subtly revises; but if we play down its satirical intent in the effort to preserve its debt to sentimentality, we lose the political edge which was so sharply felt by its contemporary readers. The poem puzzles because of its generic unclassifiability, a quality central to Barbauld's dialogic art. In its movement between registers and perspectives, its juxtaposition of the familiar and the unfamiliar through prospect and retrospect, its conflation of the elegiac and the satirical, the political and the sentimental, *Eighteen Hundred and Eleven* exhibits Barbauld's full discursive range, while at the same time reaching the new and 'manly' vantage point which an epic prospect affords. It is the sheer ambitiousness of her poetic project—the authority to which she lays claim, in entering and confidently mastering these various poetic realms—which most offended her contemporary readers.

That Barbauld's publishing career was finally silenced by the misogynist reception of this darkly dystopic poem was confirmation, not so much of the capriciousness of her audience, as of engrained prejudices in the reviewing-industry. The trajectory of her career suggests that, although she was vulnerable to anxieties of reception, Barbauld found a way of negotiating with her contemporary audience which was in many

---

[56] See Rodgers, *Georgian Chronicle*, 142.
[57] 'Politics of Fancy in the Age of Sensibility', 241.

respects more resourceful than Wordsworth's or Coleridge's; and that it was her well-judged choice of genre and mediation between discourses that ensured her almost lifelong success with the reading-public. This chapter has sought to understand her career—and specifically the construction, within it, of poetic identity—as a precarious balancing-act between sympathy and critique, in which she established herself as an amused but resisting reader of many aspects of contemporary culture, including the productions of male poets who were seeking to establish their permanent place in the canon. Barbauld's balancing-act is revealing, not only in respect of the high Romantic system of defence mechanisms with which it can be compared, but because it is an exemplary demonstration of what one might term a mixed hermeneutic, in which differentiation is complemented by sympathetic identification.

Part II

Crossings on the Creative–Critical Divide

CHAPTER 5

Competition and Collaboration in Periodical Culture

Those who do not read criticism, will not even merit to be criticized. Yet we have unreflecting students who inquire of the utility of criticism? Nothing may be of happier consequence than a habit of comparing his thoughts and style with the composition of the masters. If in the comparison, the silent voice of sentiment exclaims in his heart, 'I also am a painter' it is not improbable that the young artist may become a Coregio [*sic*].

Isaac D'Israeli, *The Literary Character*, 1846

I. THE QUESTION OF SECONDARINESS

In a retrospective essay of 1845, 'On Wordsworth's Poetry', De Quincey shows how that poet's claim to 'fitness for permanent life' is measured by the strength of his audience's initial resistance to him, which in time gives way to a juster estimate of his value. In making this claim, De Quincey follows Wordsworth's own defence strategies in the 'Essay Supplementary to the Preface' of 1815, which had prophesied lasting fame for its author.[1] His argument acts both as a homage to Wordsworth and as proof of his own status as sympathetic reader; but it does much more than that, as we see in an extraordinary passage of poetic prose, celebrating the power of genius to uncover profound truths. 'It is astonishing', De Quincey claims, 'how large a harvest of new truths

---

[1] De Quincey makes the point that Wordsworth's fame is deferred till his afterlife by a contrast with Young and Cowper, both of whom were well received in their time but lacked permanent depth value. The comparison is repeated from Wordsworth's 'Essay Supplementary to the Preface', as is the optimistic conclusion: 'Whatever is too original will be hated at the first. It must slowly mould a public for itself; and the resistance of the early thoughtless judgements must be overcome by a counter-resistance to itself in a better audience slowly mustering against the first.' ('On Wordsworth's Poetry', 1st pub. *Tait's Magazine* (Sept. 1845); repr. in Masson, xi. 321.)

would be reaped simply through the accident of a man's feeling, or being made to feel, more *deeply* than other men'. He illustrates this by introducing a parallel with astronomy, which works to unsettle the concept of originality in a scientific age:

In astronomy, to gain the rank of discoverer, it is not required that you should reveal a star absolutely new: find out with respect to an old star some new affection—as, for instance, that it has an ascertainable parallax—and immediately you bring it within the verge of a human interest; or, with respect to some old familiar planet, that its satellites suffer periodical eclipses, and immediately you bring it within the verge of terrestrial uses. Gleams of steadier vision that brighten into certainty appearances else doubtful, or that unfold relations else unsuspected, are not less discoveries of truth than the downright revelations of the telescope, or the absolute conquests of the diving-bell.[2]

The choice of astronomy as a metaphor for poetry, and the technical jargon introduced in the development of his scientific simile, are both appropriate to De Quincey's subject-matter. Not just because Wordsworth had claimed a place for poetry as the collaborator of science in his revised Preface to *Lyrical Ballads* (1802);[3] but because the semi-competitive relationship between science and poetry was a significant feature of nineteenth-century discussions about human progress, and about the utility of various kinds of knowledge.[4] Despite Wordsworth's early conviction that, if the time ever came when science was ready 'to put on a form of flesh and blood' he would 'lend his divine spirit to aid the transfiguration', and 'welcome the Being thus produced',[5] he showed signs of an anxiety that scientific knowledge might result in a deadening familiarity with mystery. As we saw in 'Star-Gazers', his fears centred on the commodification of literature and the indifference of an urban readership to poetry:[6] fears which are held at bay in the 'Essay Supple-

---

[2] Wordsworth, 'Essay Supplementary to the Preface', 315.

[3] Wordsworth inserted the long passage on poetry and science in his 1802 revisions to the Preface. See *Wordsworth Prose*, i. 141.

[4] The most well-known examples are Peacock's *The Four Ages of Poetry* and Hazlitt, 'Why the Arts are not Progressive'; but see also Robert Forsyth, *Principles of Moral Science*, discussed by Marilyn Butler in *Peacock Displayed: A Satirist in his Context* (London: Routledge and Kegan Paul, 1979), 286–90.

[5] *Wordsworth Prose*, i. 141. Wordsworth's references to poetry's collaboration with science have personal as well as general significance. As Maurice Hindle and John Birtwhistle argued in papers delivered at the 1998 conference 'Bristol: Romantic City', Wordsworth is acknowledging the importance of his friendship with Humphry Davy, and making an implicit parallel between their modes of experimentation. Both these scholars have noticed verbal echoes in the Preface (and its 1802 revisions) which can be traced to Davy.

[6] See Ch. 1, above.

mentary to the Preface' (1815) by the claim that great poetry is over-looked by its first readers, but has nonetheless a potential to endure.

Both telescope and stars reappear as symbols in De Quincey's essay, where they are used not just to confirm Wordsworth's self-protective claim for the power of poetry to go on creating wonder, but as proof that truly great poetry has the capacity to elicit new kinds of wonder with each successive viewing. De Quincey's point is that, in a culture whose emphasis falls on the commodity value of originality, the value of depth will frequently go unnoticed, as it has in the case of Wordsworth's short poems. But the overt analogy he is making, between poet and astronomer, becomes, as it develops, a simile for his own status as a deeply discerning critic. He it is who 'unfold[s] relations else unsuspected' between planets; who 'allows an old familiar planet to suffer periodical eclipses'; who witnesses the fall of Young and Cowper, the rise of Wordsworth, not just as examples of the capriciousness of the reading-public, but as proofs of the necessity for rigorous critical investigation (or what Coleridge called 'fixed canons of criticism').[7] Just as Wordsworth's genius does not consist in the novelty of invention (this is the domain of science, or 'the literature of knowledge'),[8] so De Quincey's selections and reconfigurations of the poetic galaxy give him a power like the poet's own. He too 'awakens into illuminated consciousness ancient lineaments of truth long slumbering in the mind, although too faint to have extorted attention'.[9]

This I take to be one of the founding moments of modernity, as the competitive ingredient within the critical act begins to find an acknowledged place for itself in critical rhetoric. What makes it, at the same time, peculiarly Romantic is that although the secondary here acquires some of the aura that surrounds the primary, the author loses none of his own mystique in the process. So carefully is De Quincey's own claim to the power of divination camouflaged by his homage to Wordsworth, that he succeeds in presenting their relationship as a collaborative enterprise involving the simultaneous defence of writing and reading

---

[7] See Coleridge's discussion of reviewing-standards in *BL*, ch. 3: 'till reviews are conducted on far other principles, and with far other motives; till in the place of arbitrary dictation and petulant sneers, the reviewers support their decisions by reference to fixed canons of criticism, previously established and deduced from the nature of man; reflecting minds will pronounce it arrogance in them thus to announce themselves to men of letters, as the guides of their taste and judgement' (*BL* i. 62).

[8] De Quincey, 'On the Poetry of Pope', in Masson, xi. 54.

[9] 'On Wordsworth's Poetry'; ibid. 315.

against a hostile and undiscerning public. The fear of repetition—of the multiplication of literature 'to an unmanageable excess'—begins to be allayed by the persuasion that selective critics and the passage of time will together ensure the survival of greatness.

It would have been less easy, as well as less advantageous, for De Quincey to have made this defence of Wordsworth's poetry thirty years earlier. At the time Wordsworth wrote his 'Essay Supplementary to the Preface', he was acutely anxious about his reception, and had no reason to suppose that hostility would give way to admiration (or even acceptance), either by the reviewers to whose approval he claimed indifference, or by the reading-public whose tastes he aimed to transform. Only in 1845 is De Quincey able to draw on the cultural capital of Wordsworth's achieved fame as though it were of the same substance as Milton's posthumous reputation, and to inscribe his own authority alongside Wordsworth's with advantage to himself. His tactics are a reminder that the anxiety of reception may be vicariously as well as directly experienced, and that it frequently manifests itself in an attachment to the past as assurance of continuing authority. But they also show how the apparently weak or secondary position of latecomer can be used for purposes of self-promotion.

The pragmatic motives which lie behind negotiations of this kind are frequently occluded; and in uncovering them there is some danger of turning the rise of criticism either into a story of marital strife, in which one partner seeks to assert mastery over the other; or into a variant of the host–parasite analogy (widely used in this context), which has one organism nestling into the other, with a palpable design on its life. Or, finally, into a drive to autonomy on the part of criticism that is unstoppably purposive and exploitative. The latter is essentially the tenor of George Steiner's rant against the 'prepotent, monumentalized station' occupied by the present-day critic, who exerts a 'narcissist terrorism' over literary works. Steiner claims that all criticism is 'adversative to' its object: 'Even where its programme is one of epiphany, of disclosure through placement and praise, even where it seems itself to be the devoted outrider and herald to the work of art, criticism stands not only "outside" and "after" its cause: it stands "against" it.'[10] Running counter to the critic's acknowledgement of the temporality of reading, and to some extent compensating for it, there is, Steiner insists, a

---

[10] 'Critic/Reader', in Philip Davis (ed.), *Real Voices on Reading* (Houndmills, Basingstoke: Macmillan Press, 1997), 18.

yearning in criticism to exist beyond its object: harbouring 'strong solicitations to autonomy', it exhibits a 'drive towards usurpation'. Reading, on the other hand, always provisional, enters a 'dialogue of encounter and vulnerability' with the other, opening itself to 'the autonomous being' of the text—to its 'iconic status'.[11] This suggestively gendered model of interpretation—resembling, as it does, the binary opposition between 'comparative' and 'divinatory' described in Schleiermacher's *Hermeneutics*—points to the deeply entrenched Romantic polarities which continue to inform critical discourse to this day.

In practice, the manifestations of criticism's drive towards autonomy are not always aggressive; and just as they are sometimes subtly disguised, so they are frequently subjected to a tact that derives from the more reverential model of reading implicitly advocated by Steiner. This is especially the case in Romantic criticism, where the notion of genius performs a strongly protective role in relation to the author's priority and autonomy. De Quincey's intervention in the process of canon-formation might be seen, in this light, as a kind of balancing-act between alternative hermeneutic models. Representative of the ways in which criticism succeeds in making a place for itself within Romantic tradition—thereby securing its own enduring status through a deferential but semi-rivalrous association with creative genius—it follows a pattern that is similar not only to literature's relation with science in the Romantic period, but to the equally complex interrelationships between poetry and prose, or between men's and women's writing at that time.

If, in the critical essays of this period, the 'secondary' begins to assert its kinship with the 'primary', it does so as much through sympathetic identification as through adversarial self-definition. And quite frequently there is a rhetorically discernible interplay between these two alternatives. In his 'Detached Thoughts on Books and Reading', Lamb uses Elia's reading-habits to define a sympathetic receptiveness to the ideas of others:

An ingenious acquaintance of my own ... has left off reading altogether, to the great improvement of his originality. At the hazard of losing some credit on this head, I must confess that I dedicate no inconsiderable portion of my life to other people's thoughts. I dream away my life in others' speculations. I love to lose myself in other men's minds. When I am not walking, I am reading; I cannot sit and think. Books think for me.[12]

---

[11] Ibid. 20–3.
[12] *Elia and the Last Essays of Elia*, ed. Jonathan Bate (Oxford: Oxford University Press, World's Classics, 1987), 195.

In describing the catholicity of Elia's tastes—his dreamy openness to the thoughts of other minds, his suspension of any voluntary will-to-power of his own in relation to the materials he reads—Lamb chooses to place a higher premium on what Steiner would call 'reading' (letting books 'think for him') than on 'criticism'. This is, however, a distinctly critical preference in an age which put a premium on originality, or 'self-possession'; and we should not underestimate the revisionary force of such innocent declarations. Explicitly contrasted with and preferred to the drive towards originality, Elia's version of 'negative capability' thus takes on an original force of its own.

The creative possibilities of intense sympathetic identification are recognized by Hazlitt as a distinctive feature of Lamb's poetics. In one of his most intriguing observations on the relation between imitation and originality, he comments on Lamb's use of an antiquated prose style, interested that Lamb can be at once so incontrovertibly himself and so absorbent of the identities of others:

Mr. Lamb is the only imitator of old English style I can read with pleasure; and he is so thoroughly imbued with the spirit of his authors, that the idea of imitation is almost done away.... The matter is completely his own, though the manner is assumed. Perhaps his ideas are altogether so marked and individual, as to require their point and pungency to be neutralized by the affectation of a singular but traditional form of conveyance. Tricked out in the prevailing costume, they would probably seem more startling and out of the way. The old English authors, Burton, Fuller, Coryate, Sir Thomas Brown [*sic*], are a kind of mediators between us and the more eccentric and whimsical modern, reconciling us to his peculiarities.[13]

Hazlitt compliments Lamb by discussing his essay style along lines that resemble the 'originality paradox' as it emerges in such geniuses as Milton and Shakespeare. Lamb is 'so thoroughly imbued' with the authors he admires that, instead of being a vehicle (or, as Keats would put it, a 'thoroughfare') for their voices, they provide a 'form of conveyance' for his. By a witty sleight of hand, Hazlitt's costume metaphor (which we might expect to apply to Lamb's antiquarianism) is used instead to connote contemporary language. Lamb would be artificial, Hazlitt insists, if he wrote 'like one of us': it is the depth of his familiarity with the past that makes his style 'familiar'. By way of his elective affinity with seventeenth-century writers, Lamb's audience is 'reconciled' to his

---

[13] 'On Familiar Style'; essay xxiv in *Table Talk* (Howe, viii. 245).

idiosyncracies, which make it uncertain to which century he really belongs. In the jumbled chronology of Hazlitt's sentence, a kind of composite identity, or doubling, is formed between past and present.

Paradoxes of this kind are typical of the rhetoric in which the relationship between creativity and criticism in the early nineteenth century is debated, and I want in this chapter to explore their implications for the power relations between rival discourses. Having considered the ways in which a creative–critical dialectic operates in the most distinguished Romantic poet-critics of the first generation, I shall concentrate here on its manifestations in the periodical culture on which second-generation Romanticism thrived, when criticism and poetry were apparently at war with each other, but when complex mergings between them were taking place. A number of key texts by (among others) Hunt, Peacock, Hazlitt, and Lamb—all of them characteristic of this more self-conscious phase in the rise of criticism—will provide a focus for discussion. These texts were written dialogically, as contributions to a much wider debate about the progress of civilization, in which the relative merits of the ancients and the moderns, poetry and prose, were hotly contested. They addressed an audience aware of the defensive status of poetry and of the incestuous infighting which was an acknowledged feature of periodical culture. They are satirical and ironic in intent, standing back from this culture with a 'nothing if not critical' eye; and they contain elements of parody which both complement and supplement their subjects, disclosing a mixed hermeneutic—one that oscillates between identification and differentiation—and deliberately teasing the reader with respect to the boundary separating writing- and reading-identities. Giving close attention to their formal, rhetorical, and allusive qualities, I shall read them here both as topical interventions in an ongoing debate and as commentaries on the sophisticated defences and counter-defences which make up the 'pathology' of high Romanticism.

II. HUNT'S DIALOGIC METHOD

Leigh Hunt's *The Feast of the Poets*, published originally in 1811 by the *Reflector* ('a magazine privately set up and not enjoying the usual means of continuance'),[14] was revised and enlarged, while Hunt was in prison for sedition, and reissued in 1814 with the addition of notes. In it, Hunt

---

[14] *The Feast of the Poets* (London: James Cawthorn, 1814), p. ix.

enters the debate over what constitutes a poet from an angle that is
irreverent towards avant-garde, elitist culture and sympathetic towards
popular, best-selling authors. This irreverence (which aligns it with
Bakhtin's 'dialogic' or 'carnivalesque' discourse) emerges in poetic
form in the first edition, and proves central to the lengthy notes which
accompanied the poem in 1814. The relation between poetic text and
prose notes has important (formal and generic, as well as historical)
implications.

Offering a playful satire on the contemporary poetical scene, Hunt
exploits the joint functions and prospects of poet and critic in *The Feast
of the Poets* to deliver summary judgement on his contemporaries and
immediate predecessors, as well as to engage in a more systematic
debunking of high Romanticism. Poetry since Dryden is seen (from
the neoclassical perspective of Apollo) to have steadily degenerated;[15]
but a select number of best-selling poets—Tom Moore, Walter Scott,
Robert Southey, and Thomas Campbell—are singled out for their
achievements, and allowed to constitute Apollo's poetic canon. The
formation of this canon is not without its ironies, however, since the
usefulness of poetry itself is brought playfully under question—both
through the central organizing metaphor of the feast (as the ambiguous
signifier of taste, indulgence, and luxury) and through the equivocal
representation of Apollo himself, as master of ceremonies. A visiting
rather than presiding genius, Apollo represents the spirit of the age,
falling in readily with the prevailing Regency values of leisure, pleasure,
and intoxication. Hunt disowns any resemblance between himself and
Apollo in a reference to his own absence from the feast;[16] but there are
significant parallels between their judgmental roles, later to be amplified
in the notes. Just as the poem parodies individual poets and their
respective idiolects (including a send-up of Wordsworth's bogus simplicity),[17] so it embodies in Apollo himself both a glorification of poetic
genius along classical lines, and a parodic critique of poetry's pretensions
to godlike status. Apollo was the Greek god with whom Shelley, Keats,

---

[15]   Hunt, *The Feast of the Poets*, 1–2.

[16]   Hunt's disclaimer comes comically late in the narrative: 'It can't be suppos'd I should
think of repeating | The fancies that flow'd at this laureat meeting; | I haven't the brains, and
besides, was not there' (ibid. 18).

[17]   'And t'other some lines he had made on a straw, | Shewing how he had made it, and what
it was for, | And how, when 'twas balanced, it stood like a spell!— | And how, when 'twas
balanc'd no longer, it fell!' (ibid. 12). Hunt claims in a note that he has been told 'on very good
authority' that his parody of Wordsworth's 'worst style of writing' has been 'taken for a serious
extract from him, and panegyrized accordingly' (ibid. 87).

and Byron all closely identified, and Hunt has him arriving in Regency London in a blaze of indeterminate glory, metamorphosed through poetic simile into a young soldier, a young traveller, a young poet on his wedding day, and even 'young Alfred' himself. (King Alfred is described in the notes as 'a Monarch, who with power to enslave, delighted to make free', and who—unlike other monarchs, closer to home—'could stop short of the love of conquest, and sheath his sword the moment it had done enough'.)[18] In this parody of sublime indeterminacy, the equivocal 'shape' finally assumed by Apollo—complete with obligatory reference to Milton's Death via Burke's sublime[19]—is the apotheosis of the classical virtues as embodied in contemporary art:

> Imagine however, if shape there must be,
> A figure sublim'd above mortal degree,
> His limbs the perfection of elegant strength,—
> A fine flowing roundness inclining to length,—
> A back dropping in,—an expansion of chest,
> (For the God, you'll observe, like his statues was drest)
> His throat like a pillar for smoothness and grace,
> His curls in a cluster—and then such a face.

(pp. 3–4)

In the shapely hands of Apollo rests the fate of contemporary poets, to be decided by who is invited and who excluded from his feast. Dethroning establishment figures by dismissing them—Crabbe is told to dine below with the servants, Hayley banished for his ingratiating hackwork,

---

[18] Ibid. 39. Page refs. will be given in the text. Implicitly, Hunt's homily on King Alfred is a critique of George III, who was held accountable (especially by those in radical circles) for the grave economic consequences of Britain's extended war with France. See my discussion of Barbauld's poems, 'On the King's Illness' and *Eighteen Hundred and Eleven* in Ch. 4, Sects. V and VI, above. Alfred was widely referred to as a national hero by libertarian thinkers. See e.g. the post-1811 entry in Charles Cowden Clarke's commonplace book, recently edited by John Barnard, in which 'Clarke says that Alfred the Great's fame needed no eulogist, only the evidence of his acts': 'Charles Cowden Clarke's "Cockney Commonplace Book"', in Nicholas Roe (ed.), *Keats and History* (Cambridge: Cambridge University Press, 1995), 76. See also *Examiner*, 2 Mar. 1817, in which Hunt refers to Alfred as an ancestor in the cause of English liberty.

[19] Burke, in his well-known chapter on 'Obscurity' in the 1759 *Philosophical Enquiry*, quotes from Milton's description of Death in *Paradise Lost*, and claims that in this description 'all is dark, uncertain and terrible to a degree'. See *A Philosophical Enquiry into the Origin of Our Ideas of the Sublime and the Beautiful*, ed. J. T. Boulton (Oxford: Oxford University Press, 1990), 59. The passage had wide critical currency: see my essay ' "Questionable Shape": The Aesthetics of Indeterminacy', in John Beer (ed.), *Questioning Romanticism* (Baltimore: Johns Hopkins University Press, 1995), 226–9.

Wordsworth and Coleridge sent packing—Apollo allows the four most successful poets of the age to remain behind; but even they are permitted to take their seats only after they have received a sharp rebuke. Scott, politely congratulated on his fashionable success, is advised as follows:

> . . . Well, Mr. Scott, you have manag'd the town;
> Now pray, copy less, —have a little temerity,—
> —Try if you can't also manage posterity.

> (p. 9)

Campbell is ticked off for a lack of 'invention', Tom Moore is welcomed with 'bland' accent because his poetry has of late shown improvement, and Southey escapes the fate of the other Lake Poets with a brisk 'warning', the content of which is not disclosed.

If Apollo's glamour and power remind one of Byronic 'strength',[20] epitomizing all that by this stage has come to be associated with the self-image of a Romantic poet, the god's self-arrogated right to dispense and confiscate poetic status suggests a caricature of the role played by reviewers and critics in deciding the fate of poetry. Holding court over his minions, who attempt to flatter their way to an invitation, Apollo becomes in their eyes the sine qua non of poetic success. They are represented as trembling and anxious in the presence of power ('For his host was a God,—what a very great thing! | And what was still greater in *his* eyes,—a King!', p. 9), he as brusque and arbitrary in his choice of favourites. The language of blushing, confusion and shame is used to gender their ingratiation as effeminate, by contrast with the rugged masculinity which characterizes his speech and actions. In this way, Hunt represents the contemporary literary scene as a courtly charade disguised as a meritocracy. The reputation of poets, like the honour of women, rests on the whims of a phantom; and their anxieties of reception are perpetuated by anachronistic models of patronage and monarchical power.

Using Apollo to amalgamate some of the attributes of poet and critic, Hunt discloses the affinities which bind creativity and criticism closely together. In the volume as a whole, the relation between poetic text and prose notes—as in *The Dunciad* or *The Wasteland*—allows a similar

---

[20] I refer to the Bloomian category reintroduced by Jerome Christensen in his recent study, *Lord Byron's Strength: Romantic Writing and Commercial Society* (Baltimore: Johns Hopkins University Press, 1993), discussed in Ch. 1, above.

dialectic to be played out on rhetorical and formal levels. The Preface draws attention to the fact that the poem has undergone two stages of composition, and addressed two different audiences: Hunt foregrounds his acts of poetic revision and critical expansion partly so as to excuse the length of his notes (which occupy 110 pages out of the volume's 158), but also because he wishes to be seen as fair in the critical enterprise on which his poem has embarked. Establishing the serious-ness of his credentials as a just and accurate critic, Hunt implicitly rebukes both the critical establishment for their habitual carelessness, and the poetical establishment for their assumption that all critics are slipshod. Having claimed authority and gravitas, he is then free to liberate his style as annotator from conventional constraints.

The 'inordinate' note (twenty-one pages long) which accompanies Hunt's six-line parody of Wordsworthian diction offers not only an important contemporary assessment of that poet's achievement, but a definition of the responsibilities which critics must fulfil towards poets (and vice versa). Significantly, however, this definition is offered in tones of gentle satirical mockery reminiscent of the poem itself, and designed to draw attention to Wordsworth's shortcomings:

He thinks us over-active, and would make us over-contemplative. . . . We are, he thinks, too much crowded together, and too subject, in consequence, to high-fevered tastes and worldly infections. Granted:—he, on the other hand, lives too much apart, and is subject, we think, to low-fevered tastes and solitary morbidities; —but as there is health in both of us, suppose both parties strike a bargain,—he to come among us a little more and get a true sense of our action,—we to go out of ourselves a little oftener and acquire a taste for his contemplation. We will make more holidays into nature with him; but he, in fairness, must earn them, as well as ourselves, by sharing our working-days.[21]

Using the two-faced rhetoric of compromise, Hunt gives with one hand what he takes away with another. Apparently mediating between the binary oppositions which underpin Wordsworth's poetics—activity–contemplation, city–country, disease–health,—he trumps all of these with the telling and implicating contrast between labour and leisure. Wordsworth is thus sarcastically reminded that the contract between a poet and his readers works both ways, and that poets cannot be allowed simply to exist like parasites on society.

---

[21] *Feast of the Poets*, 107–8 n. 20. Appropriately, Hunt's contrast between disease and health draws on and inverts the language used by Wordsworth in his 1800 Preface to *Lyrical Ballads*.

Hunt ostensibly distances his critical from his poetic persona; but if the poem is critical in its spirit, the notes are satirical in their content, and he achieves within the genre of commentary an acuity that both echoes and amplifies the poetic text. In the poem, for instance, Hayley's hesitant and anodyne sycophancy is briefly dramatized thus:

> And then, with a sort of a look of a blush,
> Came in Mr. Hayley, all polish'd confusion,
> And said, '*Will* Apollo excuse this intrusion?
> I might have kept back—but I thought 'twould look odd,—
> And friendship, you know,—pray how *is* my dear God?'
>
> (p. 6)

In the notes, Hunt observes that 'The worst part of Mr. Hayley is that smooth-tongued and overwrought complimentary style, in addressing and speaking of others, which, whether in conversation or writing, has always the ill-fortune, to say the least of it, of being suspected of sincerity' (p. 49). Hayley is relegated to fourth or fifth place as poet and human being, but Hunt uses the note to compliment him on his skills as a translator. Fairfax's Tasso is used to define good translation as 'closeness to the sense and sympathy with the spirit of the original', and an ability to 'go along with his author, and to be . . . of a piece with him'; but also as the capacity to add improvements, to give a turn 'unlike the original' (p. 52). In some instances, Hunt claims, 'Fairfax can contend with his author, even at his best' (p. 54). In this careful definition, two alternative hermeneutic models—of collaboration and competition— are kept in play, offering a meta-commentary on the relation between poetic and prose texts in Hunt's own volume, and of creativity and criticism in the culture Hunt satirizes.[22] Hayley, although a good translator, implicitly falls below the ideal embodied in Fairfax, because his hermeneutic is too faithful, too complimentary.

The continuity between notes and poetry in *The Feast of the Poets* demonstrates the difficulty of disentangling creative and critical functions, whose mutual dependency (posited on the likeness and difference between Apollo and Hunt) is the main source of irony in the volume as a

---

[22] See Wordsworth's use of translation as a metaphor for creative writing, in the Preface to *Lyrical Ballads*: 'it is proper that [the poet] should consider himself as in the situation of a translator, who does not scruple to substitute excellencies of another kind for those which are unattainable by him; and endeavors occasionally to surpass his original, in order to make some amends for the general inferiority to which he feels that he must submit' (*Wordsworth Prose*, i. 139).

whole. As Hunt puts it, in a note explaining why Southey is allowed to attend the feast and Wordsworth not,

Apollo, I am afraid, is not as easily to be defended as myself, for a want of foresight so unbecoming his prophetical character;—but this I leave to be settled by some future BURMAN or BIFFIUS, whenever he shall do me the honour to find out the learning of this egregious performance, and publish the Feast of the Poets in two volumes quarto. Apollo, like other vivacious spirits, chose to do without his foresight sometimes,—as the commentator will no doubt have the goodness to shew for me. (p. 82)

The difference in status between Apollo and Hunt is here replicated as a difference between Hunt himself and the learned annotator of his volume, who belongs to a future age and figures reading as both continuity and amplification (to the tune of two quartos). Crucially— and here Hunt's enterprise becomes Shandyan indeed—the notes are far longer, weightier, and more authoritative than the poem itself, a fact repeatedly emphasized in their apologies for digression, prolixity, and 'luxurious gossiping'. Each note—apparently included in order to gloss the appearance of a particular poet at the feast, and to explain the grounds for his summary dismissal—takes on the status of a critical essay in its own right, with an internal coherence, and a potential for detachment from its poetic context.

The first sentence, for instance, of Hunt's note on Scott—'of Mr. Walter Scott's innate and trusting reverence for thrones and domin- ations, the reader may find specimens abundantly nauseous in the edition of Dryden' (p. 62)—is perfectly balanced by its last, achieving an elegantly conclusive closure: 'Mr. Scott writes a very sprightly ballad, can sketch a good character from the life, and can hide himself to advantage in the costume of other times; but brought forward in his own unassisted person, and judged by a high standard of poetry, he wants originality and a language' (p. 68). The note which immediately follows this one, on Thomas Campbell, affords Hunt the opportunity to expand his concern with language into a poetic credo, which reflects backward onto Scott and forward onto Wordsworth: 'We demand,— not the copy of another's simplicity, but the simplicity of the speaker himself;—we want an unaffected, contemporaneous language, such as our ears and our hearts shall equally recognize, and such as our own feelings would utter, were they as eloquent as the poet's.' (pp. 70–1 n. 12) Woven together by such unifying threads, and considered as an integrated collection, these inordinately long notes (or concentratedly short essays) comprise Hunt's version of Hazlitt's 'Spirit of the Age': a coherent body of work, positioning its author both politically and aesthetically in relation to contemporary culture.

Formally, then, as well as thematically, it becomes difficult in reading this volume to determine which of two rhetorical modes is subordinate to the other—which is host, which parasite. Moving the critical from its inferior position in relation to the creative, Hunt allows the note, a form which is traditionally aligned with marginality, provisionality, and secondariness, to take centre stage. In doing so, he not only draws attention to the ways in which creativity and criticism work together, in a kind of collaborative and competitive dialogue; he also devises a method for crossing the creative–critical divide.

III. POETRY-PROSE DIALOGUE AND PARODY

The history of Romanticism might be interestingly written as an account of the dialogue between poetry and prose. This was a period of intense generic experimentation, in which the ancient hierarchical positioning of poetry over prose became unsettled, and writers seized on the precarious interplay between genres to make political claims. Joseph Priestley, in his *Lectures on Oratory* (which influenced a whole generation of Unitarians, among them the young Hazlitt) argued that prose style had its own poetics, and could be metrically analysed in the same way as verse. Blake, in *The Marriage of Heaven and Hell*, perceived the possibilities of a hybrid genre (prose-poetry). Wordsworth in 1798 showed that poetry written in the ordinary language of men was almost indistinguishable from prose. Shelley, in *The Defence of Poetry*, used an impassioned prose style which verged on the poetic. Hazlitt in his essay 'On the Prose Style of Poets' wondered about the appropriateness (or otherwise) of poets venturing into a different medium. It was to a readership that had become accustomed to subtle forms of generic dialogue that texts like Hunt's *The Feast of the Poets* made their appeal; and one of the most interesting sub-genres to emerge out of this dialogue was parody directed specifically at poems with inordinately long notes.

The topicality of this species of parody was at its height in the second decade of the nineteenth century. It coincided with the (largely unfavourable) reception of Wordsworth's volumes of poetry, infamous for their dependence on a heavily directive paraphernalia of advertisements, prefaces, and explanatory notes from the author. The hostility of readers to these authorial instructions pervaded periodical criticism. For instance, in the review of Percival Stockdale's *Lectures on the Truly Eminent English Poets* (1807) which appeared in the *Edinburgh* for April 1808, there appeared the following sentence:

> Whatever truth there may be in the assertion, that none but a poet should criticize a poet, we are nevertheless extremely happy to meet now and then with dissertations on poetry in sober prose; for most of our modern bards, as if they were afraid that posterity would not take the trouble to be their commentators, have enshrined themselves in their own annotations.[23]

To a contemporary reader, there can have been little doubt that the anonymous reviewer intended a sly dig at another publication which had appeared in print that year, Wordsworth's *Poems* (1807). A persistent and unsettling irony, directed at the supposed elevation of poetry over prose, could sometimes work as a way of poking fun at poets who fancied themselves critics. Even an apparently innocent observation such as this one from Francis Jeffrey may have an undercurrent of sarcasm when placed in the wider context of contemporary debate:

> We would rather see Mr. Campbell as a poet, than as a commentator on poetry:—because we would rather have a solid addition to the sum of our treasures, than the finest or most judicious account of their actual amount.[24]

Poets, this seems to imply, should stick to what they are good at, and increase the stock of primary goods, not make themselves secondary by turning commentators.

Reynolds's parody of 'Peter Bell' entered this debate. It set the tone for subsequent parodies by laughing at the disjunction between Wordsworth's poetic and prose styles—his assumption, in the prefaces and notes, of a diction only the educated could appreciate, alongside his adoption (in the poem itself) of a bogus simplicity that patronized the common reader. Reynolds brings the poet's use of critical apparatus to the foreground, exposing his hectoring, self-congratulatory rhetoric:

> It is now a period of one-and-twenty years since I first wrote some of the most perfect compositions (except certain pieces I have written in my later days) that ever dropped from poetical pen.[25]

---

[23] *Edinburgh Review*, 12/23, article iv (Apr. 1808), 62.
[24] Review of *Campbell's British Poets*, *Edinburgh Review*, 31 (Mar. 1819), 462.
[25] In Graeme Stones and John Strachan (eds.), *Parodies of the Romantic Age* (5 vols., London: Pickering and Chatto, 1999), ii. 185.

Wordsworth is used as the prime exemplar of the embattled relationship between poetry and prose which dominated periodical culture. Reynolds's parody includes a devastating critique of the various defences adopted by the poet to keep the reviewers and the reading-public at bay: his claiming of kinship with past genius ('I take this opportunity of telling the world I am a great man. Milton was also a great man. Ossian was a blind old fool'); his undignified promotion of his own publications ('Copies of my previous works may be had in any numbers, by application at my publisher'); his faith in his own posthumous reputation ('I commit my Ballad confidently to posterity'); and his competition with the most popular of contemporary writers, whose medium was prose ('N.B. The novel Rob Roy is not so good as my poem on the same subject'). At moments, his measured voice of authority gives way to almost hysterical defensiveness:

Accustomed to mountain solitudes, I can look with a calm and dis-passionate eye upon that fiend-like, vulture-souled, adder-fanged critic, whom I have not the patience to name, and of whose Review I loathe the title, and detest the contents. —Philosophy has taught me to forgive the misguided miscreant, and to speak of him only in terms of patience and pity.[26]

The parodist uses Wordsworth's prejudice against the novel as a cue for interrogating the traditional hierarchy of genres to which he subscribes. This generic hierarchy is seen as his main prop, in a climate where poetry was coming under threat; for the public, after all, was hungry for narrative. The poem itself is a long, loosely constructed, episodic narrative in which the abccb rhyme scheme of 'Peter Bell' provides the main method of propulsion from verse to verse. Most of the narrative is directionless padding. The parodist's target is Wordsworth's spurning of incident—a persistent feature of his poetic method, and implicitly a sign of his anxiety in relation to popular novelists like Scott. This translates, in Reynolds's critique, into a failure on the poet's part to provide his readers with an interesting story. (The hero of the poem, an old bespectacled man with no heroic attributes, is a skit on the ordinary and often elderly folk that feature in Wordsworth's poems of encounter.) The parodist also exposes the monotonous regularity with which Wordsworth's poems focus on the process of interpretation. Peter is figured as a reader, whose main activity in the poem is poring studiously over graves. The parodist here alludes to Wordsworth's morbid pre-

[26] Stones and John Strachan (eds.), *Parodies of the Romantic Age*, ii. 185.

occupation with death, epitaphs, and graveyards; but he also makes a mischievous judgement on his poetic personas, who spend their lives observing, speculating, and imagining. By means of a topical pun, Peter is linked to the educationalist Andrew Bell, whose name resonates with readerly associations. The Wordsworthian narrator congratulates him in patronizing tones for his childlike literacy:

> Peter Bell he readeth ably
> All his letters he can tell;
> Roman W, —Roman S,
> In a minute he can guess,
> Without the aid of Dr. Bell.[27]

Peter's solemn but somewhat inconsequential activity of grave-reading leads to his climactic encounter with the grave of Wordsworth himself, and to the lines, with their ironic use of Wordsworthian tautology: 'He reads—"Here lieth W.W.— | Who never more will trouble you, trouble you"'.[28] The poem thus turns on a symbolic scene of reading, in which the reader is shown to be heartened by the death of the author. The parodist, setting all civilities on one side, goes straight to the epicentre of Wordsworth's anxiety, confronting the fear of mortality which underpins all his defences. It is the prerogative of parody to cut through taboos in this way.

Another parody of 'Peter Bell' was to follow shortly and anonymously, in 1819, under the misleading title *Benjamin the Waggoner*. Wordsworth's poem had not yet been published, and the anonymous author wrote in ignorance of its content, much as Hazlitt did when he published his notorious 'review by anticipation' of Coleridge's *Lay Sermons* in 1816. The author has not been firmly identified, but readers have noticed a resemblance between this parody and the earlier one of 'Peter Bell', both of which make use of the tripartite structure of preface, poems, and notes. There is also a strong connection with Hunt's *Feast of the Poets*, for the anonymous parodist (like Hunt) has made the notes to his *Benjamin the Waggoner* far longer and weightier than the poem itself. This is a joke at the expense of Wordsworth's prosiness, but also a commentary on the competitive–collaborative relationship between poetry and prose more generally.

Like Reynolds, this parodist takes the dialogue of poetry and prose as his structural and thematic focus. The Preface (which is just as

[27] Ibid. 193.   [28] Ibid. 197.

important, if not more so, than the poem itself) parodies the practice of
introducing short poems with long, self-involved, narratives, not always
credible in their details.²⁹ It is written as an imitation in miniature of the
picaresque novel; and this choice of genre has an obvious relevance to
Wordsworth's concerns. It allows the parodist to explore the anxiety of
a poet who despised the novel as a form, and felt keenly the insult of
Scott's volumes being preferred to his own by the reading-public. The
first-person narrative centres on an encounter between the hero (a
young man whose literary ambitions become evident in due course)
and a gentleman who remains anonymous, but soon identifies himself as
Wordsworth. The encounter occurs in a stagecoach, much of its interest
deriving from the plot suspense that is carefully built up by the narrator
around the contents of two mysterious packages. The first, which is
handed to the gentleman when he gets into the carriage, contains a copy
of *Benjamin the Waggoner*—not as Wordsworth published it himself, but
as it appears in the parody that follows. The second, which is given to
him during breakfast at an inn (and which he thinks will contain a copy
of his latest volume, *Peter Bell*, fresh from Longman's) turns out instead
to contain Reynolds's parody of 'Peter Bell'. Wordsworth, mortified by
an insulting letter from the publishers (in which they make it clear that
they have confused the poet with his parodist) returns to the stagecoach
to collect the other, earlier, package. This he hurls on the fire before
disappearing in a huff. The narrator retrieves the book from the fire in
the nick of time, discovers its contents to be publishable, imagines
passing the volume off as his own, then decides virtuously against that
course of action. The poem that follows is of course the parody *Benjamin
the Waggoner*—the joke being that the parodist thereby 'passes off' as
Wordsworth's what is in fact his own.

    This rather involved plot, with its anonymous identities and ambi-
guities over literary property, serves as a mischievous commentary on
what Coleridge called 'the age of personality', when 'fame' and 'name'
were frequently rhymed, and there was a pressing concern with an
author's property rights before and after death. Wordsworth, who was
consistently preoccupied by originality and copyright, is mischievously
made the butt of his own jealousy: not only is he confused with his
parodist (an amusing skit on the Romantic cult of originality); he is also

---

²⁹ An almost exactly contemporary example was Coleridge's 'Kubla Khan', the Preface to
which was parodied by William Maginn in *Don Juan Unread* (1819). See Stones and Strachan
(eds.), *Parodies of the Romantic Age*, ii. 299.

exposed as the recycler of other people's wares. Throughout his exchanges with the young hero, he sits ready with a notebook, taking down his words and announcing that they will prove useful later. The title-page of his poem is a sequence of 'Elegant Extracts'—quotations taken from other authors, all of them on the theme of anxieties of authorship—and his extensive notes contain a tissue of further quotations stitched together. As John Strachan has observed, the parodist demonstrates that 'The poet who makes such claims to originality possesses a mind which resembles a scrap-book into which are pasted endless and seemingly unconnected clippings from other writers' work.'[30] Evidently, the main target of the parodist's satire is Wordsworth; but he is used to bring into focus a critique of the anxiety of reception that has further-reaching implications. Building on tropes that had become established by James Hogg and Reynolds, among others, the parodist focuses in on unmistakable signs of poetry's defensiveness in relation to critics and readers. Most of the journey recounted in the Preface involves a series of exchanges between the Wordsworth persona, anxious for reassurance, and the young hero, keen to establish his own literary credentials by parroting standard Wordsworthian and Coleridgean views. Their dialogue on the subject of reviewers is a typical example of the polarized positions into which contemporary debate had become concentrated: 'don't let them imagine that I suffer from their pertinacity' blusters the elderly gentleman, almost incoherent with indignation:

but it is the reverse, I know they like it—I know they desire it, and I can neither write too much, nor too often for them—I know well, Sir, what it is—those malignant, malevolent, malicious critics—yes, it is to them—but we have all run the gauntlet too often to regard, in the least, their flagellations[31]

To which the sycophantic hero replies, in standard high Romantic fashion,

Yes, Sir . . . critics with their *we*—their plural unit—their royal assumption—what are they, and who are they? Does not the whole information they have acquired, and all the knowledge they possess, of right belong to those very authors they traduce (p. 219)

Coleridge had complained in *Biographia Literaria* that reviewers 'are *anonymous* critics, and authorized as "synodical individuals" to speak of

---

[30] Stones and Strachan (eds.), *Parodies of the Romantic Age*, ii. 214.
[31] *Benjamin the Waggoner*, in Stones and Strachan (eds.), *Parodies of the Romantic Age*, 218–19. Page refs. will be given in the text.

themselves *plurali majestatico*' (*BL* i. 42), and the parodist here suggests a widespread hostility towards that practice among defensive writers.

The parodist uses against Wordsworth his own ironic exposure of those who exploit conversation as a mode of manipulation rather than of genuine exchange (see for instance 'Anecdote for Fathers', or 'We are Seven'). In revealing the poet's absolute dependence on obedient listeners, the satire is double-edged: directed partly at Wordsworth's 'palpable designs' on the reader, and partly at any reader who falls in with those designs. This message is ironically underlined at a later stage in the narrative, when the poet is observed poring over the latest issue of the *Edinburgh* (identifiable by its blue covers), and going into paroxysms of rage: 'what, Sir, would become of those same sage critics, if we, Sir, should cease to write? What would become of their barren pages?' (p. 221). His use of the royal 'we' (that 'plural unit') afforces a complicity between the poet and the reviewers he despises.

A more detailed analysis of Wordsworth's anxiety of reception appears in the notes. These are so extensive as entirely to overshadow the poem itself, and they are used to satirize a culture in which authors have become so preoccupied by their readers that they seek to pre-empt the act of reading. Among the unmistakable traits of Wordsworthian pathology which the poet singles out are the following: complacent self-congratulation (the poet-persona refers to the pleasure he has given his readers by his recitation of 'Peter Bell'); nervous ingratiation towards favourable reviewers (he thanks *Blackwood's* for their recent praise in a review of June 1819); sarcasm towards those who are his enemies ('I would recommend to you a quicker mode of despatch than the pincers, tomahawk, and scalping-knife; a guillotine, I think, would save a great deal of trouble to you'); and the adoption of an indulgently patronizing tone of voice when addressing the reading-public: 'O gentle reader! How I should injure you in your own estimation, if I was to suppose you so dull of apprehension, as not to give you the credit of seeing through this typical representation' (pp. 269–70). Most amusingly of all, the parodist includes among Wordsworth's defences the innocent use of quotations from inappropriate sources to support his views, as here on the topic of the difference between poetry and prose:

To quiet . . . the outcry of those who pretend to be judges of poetry, and protest that mine is no more than a new modification of prose, I beg leave to quote for their perusal an extract from Moliere's 'Bourgeois Gentilhomme' where it is clearly laid down by a Master of Philosophy, that all which is not poetry is prose, and all which is not prose is poetry. (pp. 243–4)

The joke is on Wordsworth for his lack of humour in wrenching the quotation from its original comedic context. The statement that 'all which is not poetry is prose, and all which is not prose is poetry' offers an exclusive and exhaustive separation of everything in the known universe into two categories, and is by definition nonsensical. Implicitly, the author is guilty of seeing everything through the filter of his own anxieties, which focus so concentratedly on the rivalry of poetry and prose as to exclude all other considerations, literary and otherwise.

At a time when generic mixtures were the norm, and some writers were experimenting with the possibility of an ideal synthesis between the poetic and the prosaic, Wordsworth's binarism seemed blinkered—all the more so, perhaps, since the *Lyrical Ballads* had been a progressive attempt to make poetry draw on the resources of prose. The parodist himself demonstrates the comedic possibilities of a dialogue between poetry and prose in the very form his parody takes; and he clinches his critique of Wordsworth's binary vision by making the narrative of his *Benjamin the Waggoner* once again reveal the poet's embattled preoccupations:

> At every world I touch, I ask
> If they have poets dwelling-there?
> They answer yes—and not a few,
> Poets of all sorts—critics too
> Enough of both, and some to spare—
>
> (p. 241)

Hunt, in *The Feast of the Poets*, had used the disproportionate size of prose commentary relative to poetic text as a means of elevating the status of prose writers and critics. The anonymous parodist of *Benjamin the Waggoner* goes one stage further, suggesting that poetry is crippled by its dependence on prose, and overshadowed by the importance of reviewers in an age of criticism. Wordsworth is shown to be so anxious about his reception that he is unable to leave his audience alone. Bullying the reading-public into the required response involves him in swapping the role of poet for that of commentator. In fashioning himself as the editor of his poems, Wordsworth becomes his own worst enemy: a sitting duck for reviewers, parodists, and all manner of resisting readers.

IV. PEACOCK: THE MOTIVES OF EQUIVOCATION

Peacock's position with respect to the relative roles of poetry and criticism is somewhat different from that of Hunt, Reynolds, or the anonymous parodist of *Benjamin the Waggoner*. His politics are less partisan, his mode of irony more unpredictable, and his role—best described in the words of David Bromwich—is that of an observer and commentator on struggles for power, not a participant:

> the unattached critic at this time—who wrote neither to pay off enemies of the government, nor to arrange a reception for his friends—lived in daily intimacy with a mood of self-irony which Hazlitt caught in a phrase: ' "We are nothing if not critical". Be it so: but then let us be critical, or we shall be nothing'.[32]

The mood of self-irony which pervades even Peacock's most serious writing is his modus vivendi in a literary climate riven by factionalism. Its purpose is not always as detached as it might seem; but its rhetoric of detachment gives it a special kind of authoritative purchase—paradoxically by emptying out and negating the struggle for authority. Peacock makes two important interventions on the subject of poetry's embattled relationship with the periodical culture by which it is received and the utilitarian society it seeks to transcend. The first, his 'Essay on Fashionable Literature' (1818), was neither completed nor published. The second, *The Four Ages of Poetry* (published in 1820) is well known—not least because it provoked Shelley into writing *The Defence of Poetry* (1821). The apparent opposition between these two essays—one attacking the reading-public and its reviewing-organs for philistinism, the other questioning the contribution made by poetry to human progress—has been the cause of much critical debate; and as we shall see, there are a number of important issues raised by Peacock's handling of the dialectic.

The 'Essay on Fashionable Literature' offers a searching critique of current reviewing-standards, seeking to undermine the authoritative status of reviewers as anonymous but powerful arbiters of public taste, and to defend Coleridge in particular against unfair vilification in the press. Peacock shares with Coleridge a wish to establish the grounds for a mode of criticism that is 'honestly and conscientiously conducted'; and he uses the *Edinburgh*'s recent review of the 'Christabel' volume as a detailed test case of all that is rascally in contemporary reviewing-

---

[32] 'Introductory Essay' to id. (ed.), *Romantic Critical Essays* (Cambridge: Cambridge University Press, 1987), 9.

standards. The review is exposed as 'a tissue of ignorance, folly, and fraud', in which Coleridge has been misquoted, subjected to predictable badinage, and accused of obscurity where his meaning is perfectly plain. The insults to which 'Christabel' has been subjected are shown to belong to an outworn critical repertoire, stretching back to the first reviews published in Pope's day, and repeated with remorseless tediousness ever since:

Reviews have been published in this country seventy years: eight hundred and forty months: and if we reckon only on an average four numbers to a month, we shall find that in that period three thousand three hundred and sixty numbers have been published: three thousand three hundred and sixty numbers, two hundred thousand pages, of sheer criticism, every page of which is now in existence. What a treasury of information! What a repertory of excellent jokes to be cracked on an unhappy author and his unfavored publications!... Yet on examination these excellent jokes reduce themselves to some half dozen, which have been repeated through every number of every review of the bulk of periodical criticism to the present day[33]

Voicing his horror both at the sheer numerical power and at the repetitive tendencies of this vast reproductive machinery of criticism, Peacock momentarily resembles De Quincey. But his is a species of mock-sublime, in which the subject triumphs over the fear of being overwhelmed by retaliatory and belittling sarcasm. The joke is finally on the reviewers themselves, not on the poets they ridicule, and Coleridge is no more a sacrificial victim than was Keats.

Peacock's remit in this essay is much wider than a single volume by Coleridge. His critique focuses on the *Edinburgh* and the *Quarterly*, whose extensive circulation is ascribed to their status as 'the organs and oracles of the two great political factions, the Whigs and Tories' (p. 267) and he moves associatively across the worlds of politics, medicine, religion, and jurisprudence in the search for a metaphor that will adequately describe the 'all-pervading quackery' of these two reviewing-authorities, whose only difference appears to lie in the fact that the *Quarterly*'s contributors are in the pay of the government. His underlying targets are the politicization of critical bodies and the professionalization of critical discourse—both of whose power derives from a mistaken belief on the part of '*country gentlemen*' that reviewers compose a centralized panel, akin

[33] 'Essay on Fashionable Literature', in *Peacock Works*, viii. 278–9. Page refs. will be given in the text. This edition produces two texts, and variants appear in square brackets where appropriate.

to a committee or a council, which delivers 'definitive judgement to the world' (p. 268). His analysis of the structure and abuse of critical power is in some respects unoriginal. It resembles Coleridge's accusation, that 'the multitudinous PUBLIC, shaped into personal unity by the magic of abstraction, sits nominal despot on the throne of criticism', as well as John Hamilton Reynolds's assertion that

In matters of literature and taste we were never inclined to pay a very humble deference to what is called *the judgement of the public*. The multiplication of nothings will not make a single unit, neither do the voices of weak men become oracular because the blockheads war in unison.[34]

But Peacock is less concerned with the reading-public than with its institutions. He moves beyond Coleridge's anger and Reynolds's more measured sarcasm into a systematic demystification of quack authorities by pointing to the widely scattered—indeed provincial—origin of these journals' contributors, whose 'only point of union ... is respect for the magic circle drawn by the compasses of faction and nationality' (p. 269). This image of the circle recurs later, in Peacock's deconstruction of the power politics which underpin the *Edinburgh* and the *Quarterly*—their 'little exclusive circles of favor and faction', in which one can trace 'half a dozen favored names circling in the preeminence of glory in that little circle, and scarcely named or known out of it' (p. 269).

In a dazzlingly playful sequence of elaborations, Peacock transforms a simile which had become common currency in political discourse to describe the progressive benevolence of the human species[35] into a graphic demonstration of the decentralized—and therefore, contrary to Coleridge's mythology—powerless behaviour of circles of influence in contemporary culture:

Glory, it is said, is like a circle in the water, that grows feebler and feebler as it recedes from the centre and expands with a wider circumference: but the glory of these little idols of little literary factions is like the many circles produced by the simultaneous splashing of a multitude of equal-sized pebbles, which each throws out for a few inches its own little series of concentric circles, limiting and limited by the small rings of brother pebbles, [while in the midst of all this petty

---

[34] Essay on 'Ben Jonson', *Champion*, 4 May 1817; repr. in *Reynolds Prose*, 108.

[35] See e.g. my discussion of John Thelwall in Ch. 9, below; and the famous passage in Lecture 3 of Coleridge's *Lectures on Revealed Religion*: 'Jesus knew our Nature—and that expands like the circles of a Lake—the Love of our Friends, parents and neighbours lead[s] us to the love of our Country to the Love of all Mankind' (*CC* i. 163). The editors cite Pope's *Essay on Man*, iv. 363–8 as the source of Coleridge's simile.

splashing in the pool of public favor Scott or Byron plunges a ponderous fragment in the centre and effaces them all with its eddy: but the disturbing power ceases: the splashings recommence, and the pebbles dance with joy in the rings of their self-created fame.] (pp. 269–70)

Peacock's use of this simile has a special appropriateness, in that it alludes to lines from Coleridge's poem 'The Picture' which had been quoted in his recently published Preface to 'Kubla Khan' (included in the 'Christabel' volume), and which describe an exactly opposite pattern of dispersal and reunification: 'all that phantom world so fair | Vanishes, and a thousand circlets spread, | And each mis-shape the other. . . . | And soon the fragments dim of lovely forms | Come trembling back, unite, and now once more | The pool becomes a mirror.'[36] Peacock's reversal of the tenor and direction of Coleridge's simile reinforces the point he is making about the disguised powerlessness of critical discourse: he offers his own version of Coleridge's simile, both as a comfort to Coleridge for the vilification of the 'Christabel' volume and as a corrective to what he sees as the other writer's naive adherence to the concept of unity. So long as Coleridge goes on thinking that he is at the mercy of a composite body of readers, rather than a diverse scattering of individual coteries, he will feel disempowered; and will vent his spleen in attacks on the reading-public of a kind that Peacock elsewhere satirizes so scathingly.[37]

The most appropriate response to the abuse of power exercised by reviewers is in Peacock's view a stance of robust cynicism—one which acknowledges that, at every level, literature has become a commodity that survives only because of networks of patronage, advocacy, and economic interest, following the more general pattern of influence ('widely diffused and mighty in its operation') as it is exercised in government and society at large:

The success of a new work is made to depend, in a great measure, not on the degree of its intrinsic merit, but on the degree of interest the publisher may have with the periodical press. . . . Personal or political alliance being the only passports to critical notice, the independence and high thinking, that keeps an individual aloof from all the petty subdivisions of faction, makes every several gang his foe: and of this the *late* Mr. Wordsworth is a striking example. (pp. 272–3)

---

[36] 'The Picture; or The Lover's Resolution', ll. 92–4.

[37] For an excellent discussion of Peacock's satires on Coleridge, and esp. his characterization of Mr Flosky, see Butler, *Peacock Displayed*, 114–17.

Giving with one hand what he takes away with another, Peacock here exploits one of the recurrent topoi in Romantic mythologies of reception (the poet's sacrificial victimization at the hands of the press) to suggest that the true Wordsworth, capable of 'independence and high thinking' has passed away under the pressure of bad reviews. In his place, there is merely a shadow-Wordsworth, whose recent improvement in fortunes exactly correlates with his proximity to the ministerial establishment. In a deft dismantling of Romantic mythologies of reception, Wordsworth is not so much 'snuffed out by an article' as made to die of complicity with the factionalism he had once repudiated.[38]

One of the strengths of the argument as Peacock conducts it in this essay is that any judgement he brings to bear—particularly on the *Edinburgh*'s reviewing methods—will not be seen as contaminated by party politics or motivated by the desire to 'puff' a friend. It is finally a plea neither for Coleridge nor for poetry, but for scrupulous reading; and its combination of painstaking analysis with general observation succeeds in extrapolating from the individual case a number of salient points, which are applied to the critical climate at large. This double action of defence and extrapolation tends to distract our attention from one of the essay's most interesting features—namely, its equivocation with respect to the function of poetry. In view of his satirical treatment of the Lake Poets elsewhere it is hard to believe that Peacock's defence of Coleridge in this essay is purely altruistic.[39] By claiming that the meaning of 'Kubla Khan' is as clear as daylight—'*simplex et unum* from first to last'—he succeeds in moving the requirements of poetry a little closer to the standards of utility, as they will be cynically espoused in *The Four Ages of Poetry*. There is no reason to think that Coleridge would have been grateful for such demystification, but this is hardly of concern to Peacock. The strategy of the essay as a whole is demystificatory, and Coleridge 'being a very visionary gentleman' (p. 290), is the most appropriate available focus for Peacock's critical agenda.

In his later, more polished essay, *The Four Ages of Poetry*, it is the poets, not the critics, who are subjected to ridicule. Adopting a utilitarian standpoint, Peacock here addresses the question of host–parasite relations between poetry and society. He offers an economic and anthro-

---

[38] Keats did not of course die until 1821; but the topos of death-by-neglect was well established by the time Peacock wrote this essay, largely because of the mythology surrounding Chatterton's suicide.

[39] See Butler, *Peacock Displayed*, 115.

pological analysis of poetry's place in history, asking it to justify its usefulness to the culture it is intended to serve, at a time when more evidently purposeful discourses (such as science and moral and political philosophy) are steadily advancing. Poets—and in particular the Lake School—are made to feel uncomfortable for attempting to preserve an aloofness from the question of utility, as from the economics of reception. They are accused of hypocritical complicity with the processes of commodification they seek to deny. This complicity has discernible origins, and can be traced through history.

The means by which Peacock drives home this accusation are cleverly adapted to the topical concerns of the moment, and especially to the debate about whether or not poetry is in decline. Peacock judges that there has been a devaluation in poetic standards which has taken place twice—once in the ancient world, and again in modernity. The impression thus conveyed is of cycles of degeneration and regeneration that repeat themselves. This cyclical vision is crucial to the charge Peacock brings against poetry in general, but against modern poets in particular. Poetry has always been a trade, he argues, and 'like all other trades, [it] takes its rise in the demand for the commodity, and flourishes in proportion to the extent of the market'.[40] At each stage in its development, it is to be judged by the uses it serves, rather than by any absolute standard of value. At a time when novelty has become the only criterion of success, the modern poet is accused of living as a 'semi-barbarian in a civilized community', establishing his claim to originality by a nostalgic recuperation of the past:

> While the historian and the philosopher are advancing in, and accelerating, the progress of knowledge, the poet is wallowing in the rubbish of departed ignorance, and raking up the ashes of dead savages to find gewgaws and rattles for the grown babies of the age. . . . He lives in the days that are past. His ideas, thoughts, feelings, associations, are all with barbarous manners, obsolete customs, and exploded superstitions. (pp. 19, 20)

All the force of Peacock's cumulative argument is brought to bear on the Lake Poets, whose recycling of outworn traditions demonstrates the poetic compulsion to repeat, but whose repetitions simply confirm that 'To read the promiscuous rubbish of the present time to the exclusion of the select treasures of the past, is to substitute the worse for the better variety of the same mode of enjoyment' (p. 22). Peacock here performs

---

[40] *The Four Ages of Poetry*, in *Peacock Works*, viii. 4. Page refs. will be given in the text.

his own balancing-act between the opposite values of originality and imitation, as they are precariously resolved in a high Romanticism. Coleridge, the very figure he had earlier sought to rescue from vilification, is accused of

a modern-antique compound of frippery and barbarism, in which the puling sentimentality of the present time is grafted on the misrepresented ruggedness of the past into a heterogeneous congeries of unamalgamating manners, sufficient to impose on the common readers of poetry, over whose understandings the poet of this class possesses that commanding advantage, which, in all circumstances and conditions of life, a man who knows something, however little, always possesses over one who knows nothing. (p. 20)

One explanation for the contradiction between Peacock's two essays has been outlined persuasively by Lorna Sage. In *The Four Ages of Poetry*, she argues, Peacock impersonates 'a bigoted Utilitarian...engaged in attacking the (equally bigoted) subjectivism and primitivism of contemporary Romantic poetry.... he uses one prestigious intellectual position as a satiric norm against which to measure another, without committing himself to either'.[41] But if this doubleness works with respect to one essay, it ought logically to work also with respect to both: we would then have to read the 'Essay on Fashionable Literature' as a mock-defence of Coleridge, in which the tones of indignation on his behalf are insincere. To do so seems counter-intuitive, especially given that more subtle similarities and equivocations take place between the two essays, read alongside each other.

Peacock is a consummate parodist. The seriousness of his allegations against the periodicals is never in doubt; but in his defence of Coleridge, equivocation and impartiality are closely allied, and the facetious vein in which he impersonates high Romanticism suggests further ambiguities. Take for instance his complaint, in the 'Essay on Fashionable Literature' about 'the reading of light and easy books which command attention without the labour of application, and amuse the idleness of fancy without disturbing the sleep of understanding' (p. 263). Distracted by this momentary resemblance to Coleridgean rhetoric, Peacock's readers might expect a further indictment of the reading-public's tastes and habits. Instead, the essay moves quickly on to its anatomization of periodical publications, whose claim to authoritative status is belittled by comparison with 'transitory literature'. Two pages into the essay,

---

[41] *Peacock: The Satirical Novels* (London: Macmillan, 1976), 14–15.

Peacock has successfully established that reading is a leisure activity indulged by those able to afford it, that the taste for light reading follows the same laws as the taste for any other fashionable commodity; and that periodicals are an ephemeral subspecies in 'The stream of new books [which] floats over the parlour window, the boudoir sofa, and the drawing-room table to furnish a ready answer to the question of Mr. Donothing as to what Mrs. Dolittle and her daughters are reading' (p. 264). His eagerness to exploit Romantic rhetoric for his own purposes is demonstrated in a metonymic association between women and frivolity, by way of a customary dismissal of fashionable women as the passive receptacles of 'light' reading.

The subtlety of Peacock's ventriloquism makes it difficult to be certain who is the target of his satire—the poets who dismiss a fashionable reading public, or the public itself—and the slipperiness of his irony is heightened by our awareness that he himself occupies multiple roles as novelist, poet, and critic. Thus, when he again impersonates Coleridge's derision for the reading-public in *The Four Ages*, he sounds momentarily as if he is conceding his position to high Romanticism. But he does so with a view to implicating the poet, as a figure who is both dependent on the public and complicit with it: 'there is always a multitude of listless idlers, yawning for amusement, and gaping for novelty: and the poet makes it his glory to be the foremost among their purveyors' (p. 12). Similarly, in expressing his revulsion at the repetition and excess of literature (which he shares with his Romantic contemporaries) he is even-handed in his condemnation of both reviews and poems, each of which constitute (in a phrase that vividly recalls Coleridge) 'the promiscuous rubbish of the present time'.

A more plausible explanation than Sage's for the relation between these two essays is that, considered dialectically, they offer a commentary on the competition between poetic and critical modes of discourse, each of which is shown establishing its authoritativeness at the expense of the other. Peacock seeks in both essays to strip authority of its privileges—whether these are embodied in the 'commanding advantage' of educated poets over uneducated readers, or in the collective anonymity of reviewing-bodies. And he seeks also to belittle the pretensions of both poetry and criticism, by comparison with what he calls 'valuable knowledge', which is alien to 'the degenerate fry of modern rhymesters, and their olympic judges, the magazine critics, who continue to debate and promulgate oracles about poetry, as if it were still what it was in the

Homeric age, the all-in-all of intellectual progression' (*Four Ages*, 24).
Peacock's stance is ultimately one of wry detachment, although in both
essays he takes up a position somewhere between advocacy and judgement—a position in itself ironic, with respect to the rhetorical procedures customary in contemporary periodical warfare.

V. HAZLITT AND THE DEFENCE OF CRITICISM

In an age when the ancients were derided by the reading-public in favour
of the moderns, and it was feared that true genius might be neglected,
the critic had a professional obligation to maintain artistic standards.
Critics were therefore, in Hazlitt's eyes, accountable to the public, as
both Coleridge and Peacock had insisted. But so too were journalists,
whom Hazlitt (unlike those writers) valued highly. It was with the
double intention of celebrating the rise of journalism/criticism and
bringing the journalist/critic to account that Hazlitt turned, in his essay
'On the Periodical Press', to a detailed account of the general diffusion of
the arts, and the place of the journalist within them. As the greatest
essayist of his generation, he saw the need to defend his profession from
attacks of the kind launched by Coleridge; and he did so from a position
that was outrightly antagonistic to the latter's conservatism. His argument in favour of critical and journalistic enterprise was underwritten by
a libertarian belief in the freedom of the press, and strengthened by the
admission of failings on the part of hack journalists (especially those in
the pay of the government).

'On the Periodical Press' appeared in the *Edinburgh Review* in May
1823, and it represented the summation of Hazlitt's thinking on genius
and fame, on popular and elitist literature, on the function of the critic,
and on the journalist's powers and responsibilities. Drawing on claims
he had made earlier with respect to the fine arts,[42] he here presents a
lengthy, reasoned, and provocative defence of professional criticism—
not the impartial criticism of someone claiming to be removed from
party politics, but criticism produced within and by the warring factions
of the press, whose task as he sees it is to stimulate and nourish as well as
to reflect a range of public opinions and tastes. He defends journalists
against their detractors on the grounds that they perform a crucial
function, both in disseminating the arts among an ever-widening audi-

---

[42] A wider ranging discussion of Hazlitt's views on these topics is offered in Ch. 7, below.

ence of readers, and in enhancing the public's enjoyment of the wealth
of literature daily produced. In thus foregrounding his liberal agenda, he
claims allegiance with the ideal of intellectual equality as it was symbolized by the spread of literacy throughout Europe in the early nineteenth
century: 'Knowledge is no longer confined to the few; the object therefore is, to make it accessible and attractive to the many' (Howe, xvi. 219–
20). The accessibility of knowledge is not, however, to be confused with
the progressive refinement of taste.

As an intervention in the ongoing debate as to whether or not
civilization is in decline—which embraces the related question, of the
relative contributions made by poetry and criticism to contemporary
culture—the essay is carefully designed to annoy (while appearing to
conciliate) supporters on both sides of the question; and it does so in a
sequence of brilliant rhetorical moves. 'Genius carries on an unequal
strife with Fame; nor will our bare word (if we presume to give it) make
the balance even' (Howe, xvi. 211). Adopting a stance consistent with
his previous *obiter dicta* on posthumous fame, Hazlitt begins by discon-
necting himself from the judgmental mode of criticism frequently
ascribed to the periodical press, and places himself in a position of
disarming reticence with respect to the unfolding destiny of his contemporaries: 'Time alone can show who are the authors of mortal or
immortal mould, and it is the height of wilful impertinence to anticipate
its award, and assume, because certain living authors are new, that they
never can become old' (Howe, xvi. 211). His stance of humility towards
posterity serves as a model to authors (popular and unpopular alike)
whose uncertain futures are embraced by his at first comforting but later
unsettling 'we'.

Celebrating criticism for its own sake, and not for its secondary status
in relation to literature, Hazlitt proceeds to discuss the question of
progress as though it were measurable in terms of critical discourse
alone. In doing so, he implicitly joins Peacock in parodying writers who
narrow the parameters of debate by considering poetry 'the all in all of
intellectual progression'. Answering the question with which he had
opened his essay ('We often hear it asked, *Whether Periodical Criticism is,
upon the whole, beneficial to the cause of literature?*') Hazlitt answers truculently,
but not without an irony that is self-implicating: '*periodical criticism is
favourable—to periodical criticism*' (Howe, xvi. 212).[43] He reworks the

---

[43] Bromwich, commenting on the sentence quoted, observes that 'with its splendid irony', it
is 'qualified and then refuted in an uncharacteristic way; a concession perhaps to the *Edinburgh*

concept of 'favour' so as to strip it of its connections with patronage, and thus to remove any obligation on the critic's part to be supportive to modern authors. Readers and critics have their own autonomy, and contemporary poets are reminded of their failure to appeal to the readership that reviewers are successfully claiming as their own. Criticism, Hazlitt argues, 'contributes to its own improvement—and its cultivation proves not only that it suits the spirit of the times, but advances it. It certainly never flourished more than at present. It never struck its roots so deep, nor spread its branches so widely and luxuriantly' (Howe, xvi. 212).

As we saw in the case of Coleridge, the horticultural term 'luxuriant' was used in political discourse to express a conservative revulsion against democratic leanings and promiscuous morals.[44] If Hazlitt has in mind Coleridge's offensive description of the reading-public as 'the misgrowth of our luxuriant activity', his readaptation of the term to signify a wholesale approval of the fecundity of professional criticism is doubly appropriate. '[L]et Reviews flourish', he later exclaims: '—let Magazines increase and multiply—let the Daily and Weekly Newspapers live for ever! We are optimists in literature, and hold, with certain limitations, that, in this respect, whatever is, is right!' (Howe, xvi. 220). Further extending the irony, Hazlitt reworks the standard demographic objections to excessive writing so that authors (not critics) are found guilty of overpopulating the world:

> Who is there that can boast of having read all the books that have been written, and that are worth reading? Who is there that can read all those with which the modern press teems, and which, did they not daily disappear and turn to dust, the world would not be able to contain them? (Howe, xvi. 213–14)

In a gentle parody of Malthusian discourse, the role of periodical critics is presented as a regulative check on the overproductiveness of authors, whose momentum for exponential growth is mirrored in the foregoing sequence of rhetorical questions. 'Are we to blame for despatching the most worthless of these from time to time' (Howe, xvi. 214) Hazlitt concludes, in a climax of De Quinceyan fervour, 'or for abridging process of getting at the marrow of others, and thus leaving the learned

---

Review banner under which, with his commission for the article, Hazlitt had consented gratefully to march'. See *Hazlitt: The Mind of a Critic* (New York: Oxford University Press, 1983), 122.

[44] See Ch. 2, above.

at leisure to contemplate the time-hallowed relics, as well as the ephemeral productions, of literature?'[45]

In response to those who claim that critics are cultural parasites, and that all literature is in danger of becoming, as Carlyle puts it, 'one boundless, self-devouring Review',[46] Hazlitt remains resolutely unapologetic. 'We complain that this is a Critical age' he asserts—again with disingenuous inclusiveness —'and that no great works of Genius appear, because so much is said and written about them; while we ought to reverse the argument, and say, that it is because so many works of genius *have appeared*, that they have left us little or nothing to do, but to think and talk about them' (Howe, xvi. 212). The age of criticism is an age of leisure. Readers have become sufficiently cultivated to enjoy what they have the time to consider, and it would be retrogressive to lament the natural course of history, which (as Hazlitt sees it) has brought art to its apogee at the very point where it has produced an audience ready and able to appreciate it: 'When art is a blank, then we want genius, enthusiasm, and industry to fill it up: when it is teeming with beauty and strength, then we want an eye to gaze at it, hands to point out its striking features, leisure to luxuriate in, and be enamoured of, its divine spirit' (Howe, xvi. 213).

Hazlitt's claim, in *The Spirit of the Age*, that 'the present is an age of talkers, not of doers, and the reason is, that the world is growing old', insinuates that retrospect is a complacent alternative to the spirit of intellectual progress: 'The accumulation of knowledge has been so great, that we are lost in wonder at the height it has reached, instead of attempting to climb or add to it; while the variety of objects distracts and dazzles the looker-on' (Howe, xi. 28–9). But Hazlitt is a dialectical writer; and his rhetoric, like Peacock's, is equivocal. The same assertion, turned the other way round, becomes a means of affirming the function of criticism.[47] Hazlitt's later emphasis on art as the giver of pleasure—its dependence on the eyes, hands, and hearts by which it is rendered important—announces an aesthetic whose focus is reception not creation. According to this aesthetic, the products of the past provide

---

[45] p. 214. See my discussion in Ch. 1, above, of the Malthusian language widely current in early 19th-cent. discussions of the explosion of literature.

[46] See Ch. 1 n. 80, above.

[47] Alert to the ways in which an observation Hazlitt makes in one context is contradicted or ironized by him elsewhere, Tom Paulin's recent book, *The Day-Star of Liberty: William Hazlitt's Radical Style* (London: Faber and Faber, 1998), gives the best available account of Hazlitt's dialectical style.

enough pleasure and stimulation for audiences to survive on; and there is no necessity that writers should go on producing, or striving to produce, literature of the kind that has been produced before:

we have writers in great numbers, respectable in their way, and suited to the mediocrity of the age we live in ... Instead of imitating the poets or prose writers of the age of Elizabeth, let us admire them at a distance. Let us remember, that there is a great gulf between them and us—the gulf of ever-rolling years.—Let them be something sacred, and venerable to the imagination: but let us be contented to serve as priests at the shrine of ancient genius, and not attempt to mount the pedestal ourselves, or disturb the sanctuary with our unwarranted pretensions. (Howe, xvi. 218)

Hazlitt began his essay by suggesting that criticism had no right to claim a privileged position of power over literature. His continued use of the royal 'we' afforces an uneasy alliance between these two rival discourses up till the point where contemporary writers are dismissed as 'respectable in their way, and suited to the mediocrity of the age we live in'. Here the underlying motivations behind his camaraderie show through. He is determined that both authors and critics should see all possibilities of future progress in terms of enhanced faculties of appreciation, rather than improvements in the creative faculty itself. 'Half the cant of criticism', he argues, 'is envy of the moderns, rather than admiration of the ancients'. 'It is not that we really wish our contemporaries to rival their predecessors in grandeur, in force and depth; but that we wish them to fall short of themselves in elegance, in taste, in ingenuity, and facility' (Howe, xvi. 218–19). Measuring contemporary writing against the past as though it could compete is thus a way of blinding writers to the potentialities (and the sibling rivalries) of their own age. Since 'there is a change in the world, and we must conform to it', the only authentic course of action is to cultivate 'sound principles of taste and criticism'. Combining denegration with encouragement, Hazlitt claims that the early nineteenth century has 'taken [a] decided turn in a critical channel' and passed from the creators of art to its receivers. The task of all writers is to entertain, while at the same time allowing genius to be something appreciated from a distance.

But what of the damaging effects produced by critics who fail to recognize genius when they see it? And what of the ideological motivations which determine how genius is defined? Hazlitt's emphasis on the crucial role played by the critic carries with it a burden of accountability, which the last section of the essay 'On the Periodical Press' addresses seriously and at considerable length. Hazlitt shares some of the same concerns as Peacock, or even Coleridge, about the pressures exerted by party politics on publishing conditions. But he gives them a sharply divergent inflection. Coleridge features briefly in his discussion of 'that base system of mean and malignant defamation by which our Periodical Press has recently been polluted and disgraced' (Howe, xvi. 239); and having himself been the victim of public scandal, Hazlitt does not pass by the opportunity to pour scorn on the unprincipled fashion for malice. Instructively, though, his strongest reservations about the press do not concern the invasion of privacy and the spreading of gossip—to both of which it must plead guilty—but rather the *illiberality* of certain influential journals (what he calls in *The Spirit of the Age* 'Government-critics, the authorized censors of the press')[48] who use the mask of anonymity to disguise their true identities in the same way that they use aesthetic criteria to conceal their political prejudices. Significantly, the contemporary on whom Hazlitt focuses his sympathetic concern is not Coleridge, but 'poor Keats', whose politics are more palatable than Coleridge's, and whose iconic status as a victim allows Hazlitt to underscore his ethical and political message so that it will appeal to the popular imagination:

[Keats's] fine fancy and powerful invention were too obvious to be treated with mere neglect; and as he had not been ushered into the world with the court stamp upon him, he was to be crushed as a warning to genius how it keeps company with honesty, and as a sure means of inoculating the ingenuous spirit and talent of the country with timely and systematic servility! (Howe, xvi. 237)

Hazlitt's sustained conviction that ethical standards must apply equally, to all kinds of writing, combined with his constitutional opposition to all forms of 'cant', had led in 1819 to a vitriolic denunciation of the 'hired malignity' of Gifford, editor of the *Quarterly Review*, whose mauling of Keats had been motivated by purely political considerations:

When you say that an author cannot write common sense or English, you mean that he does not believe in the doctrine of *divine right*. . . . The dingy cover that wraps the pages of the Quarterly Review does not contain a concentrated

---

[48] 'Mr Coleridge' (Howe, xi. 37). The phrase 'government critic' is used again by Hazlitt in an article published in the *Examiner* (14 June 1818) on 'The Editor of the Quarterly Review': 'He is a *Government Critic*, a character nicely differing from that of a government spy—the invisible link, that connects literature with the police' (Howe, xix. 210).

essence of taste and knowledge, but is a receptacle for the scum and sediment of all the prejudice, bigotry, ill-will, ignorance, and rancour afloat in the kingdom. (Howe, ix. 14)

The same accusation (delivered in a less aggressive manner) underpins his argument in the 1823 essay that Jacobins, Republicans, and Dissenters are effectively marginalized by the cowardly practice of public bullying on the part of '*literary police*', to whom the reading-public ('timid, indolent, and easily influenced by a little swaggering and an air of authority' (Howe, xvi. 238)) offers no resistance. 'The continuance of this nuisance', he concludes, 'rests not with the writers, but with the public; it is they that pamper it into the monster it is' (Howe, xvi. 233). Hazlitt's concluding plea is that journalists should review their own practices, and that the reading-public should become more self-conscious, more reflective, and more responsible in its habits of reception. The essay as a whole thus follows a pattern widely used in progressive discourse, gradually expanding its circle of implicated readers to include the nation at large. The fact that, in the course of the argument, Hazlitt reaches conclusions with respect to public taste not far different from Coleridge's is an irony that can have escaped neither the author of *The Statesman's Manual* nor readers of the *Edinburgh Review*.

VI. LAMB'S DEFENCE OF READING

Lamb's 'Detached Thoughts on Books and Reading', first published in the *London Magazine* and later collected in *The Last Essays of Elia* (1833), represents a self-conscious attempt to separate the preferences of a casual and amateur reader from those of a professional critic: 'I can read almost any thing. I bless my stars for a taste so catholic, so unexcluding'.[49] In this unpartisan assertion, Lamb pokes fun not only at those avatars of high culture who condemned all forms of popular reading-matter for the undiscriminating tastes they fostered, but at the doctrinaire concept of taste in general. Far from signalling neutrality, his 'detachment' in this essay amounts to a personal credo, every sentence expressing a strongly held opinion with respect to the prejudices and pieties of the day. But Lamb's stance is neither predictable nor consistent. His readers are successfully compelled, by the idiosyncrasy of his Elian persona, to identify with a bundle of assorted beliefs that are

---

[49] In *Elia and the Last Essays of Elia*, ed. Bate, 196. Page refs. will be given in the text.

presented anecdotally, as the whimsical thoughts of an individual rather than as the considered opinions of a particular party line. By means of this identification, Lamb unsettles the orthodox dichotomies of early nineteenth-century debate, disclosing a more subtle agenda in the practice of reading which his essay style fosters.

The special quality of Lamb's irony derives from the changing direction of its reference and the lightness of touch with which it moves from one target to the next. No sooner has he established the catholicity of Elia's reading habits than he draws his persona up, with mock indignation, to protest against the invasion of real literature by foreign interlopers: Elia hates, he says, to see *'things in books' clothing* perched upon shelves, like false saints, usurpers of true shrines, intruders into the sanctuary, thrusting out the legitimate occupants' (p. 196). We might be forgiven if, taken in for a moment by the defensively elevated tone and diction, we expect it to be followed by a Coleridgean diatribe against the popularity of contemporary novels, or—a twin threat—against the rise of criticism as embodied in magazines and periodical literature. But in the next sentence, Elia's invective alights instead on more serious reading-matter of the day: Malthus on population, and Adam Smith. Lamb thus deflects attention away from the customary rivalry between poets and their critics, onto the battle between the 'literature of knowledge' and the 'literature of power'. Elia's 'catalogue of *books which are no books—biblia a-biblia'* (p. 195) includes (alongside court calendars, directories, and pocketbooks) the works of Hume, Gibbon, and Paley. The false gods of contemporary culture exposed in this essay are not the upstart reviewers of Coleridgean demonology, but the purveyors of what Peacock calls 'valuable knowledge': political philosophy, history, science, and utilitarianism. By comparison with unimaginative literature of this kind, Lamb implies, critics and journalists (such as himself) are on the side of the angels.

In this sense, Lamb discloses a high Romantic allegiance which remains undeconstructed by his otherwise inclusive irony: there is nothing in this essay to suggest why one form of knowledge is considered more valuable than another at any given historical moment, or why Romantic efforts to elevate literature over economics might be considered sheer hypocrisy. But Lamb does acknowledge the economic contingencies underlying the formation of canons of taste, and in his discussion of the relative value accorded to different kinds of literature by their bindings, he provides a wry commentary on the generic preferences which motivate Romantic discourse. 'How beautiful, to a genuine lover of reading', Elia claims, issuing a tongue-in-cheek challenge to the establishment, 'are the sullied leaves, and worn out appearance, nay the very odour . . . of an old "Circulating Library" Tom Jones, or Vicar of Wakefield!'

How they speak of the thousand thumbs, that have turned over their pages with delight!—of the lone sempstress, whom they may have cheered . . . after her long day's needle-toil . . . Who would have them a whit less soiled? What better condition could we desire to see them in? (pp. 196–7)

Even though his examples of popular culture are not 'the handy and popular duodecimos' by women writers which rapidly 'became the symbol of all that was objectionable in reading',[10] but the honorary classics of a steadily strengthening male vernacular tradition, the political resonance of Lamb's prose is hard to miss. In a semi-parodic rhapsody of enthusiasm, he turns high Romanticism on its head, relishing all those signs of popularity—the worn-down appearance of novels, their appeal to female readers and members of the working class, their function as entertainment—which for decades had been the butt of jibes against the circulating-library, its contents, and its pernicious effects.

In a similarly irreverent inversion, Shakespeare and Milton (the traditional Romantic icons of poetic genius) are removed from their pedestals and placed in the same category as modern novelists. '[I]t were mere foppery to trick [them] out in gay apparel', Elia asserts, since 'The possession of them confers no distinction. The exterior of them (the things themselves being so common), strange to say, raises no sweet emotions, no tickling sense of property in the owner' (p. 196). Ironizing an antiquarian interest in rare books as investments or curiosities, and disclosing in the process a sharp awareness of books both as material possessions with a market value and as symbolic objects attracting fetishization, Lamb goes on to suggest that the better a volume is the less it demands from its binding; and that only those books which 'have not endenizened themselves (nor possibly ever will) in the national heart, so as to become stock books' are worth possessing 'in durable and costly covers' (p. 197). Elia does not want to own a First Folio of Shakespeare, because the rarity value of the volume is far outstripped by the intrinsic value of the plays themselves. Since the extent and durability of that

---

[10]   See John Tinnon Taylor, *Early Opposition to the English Novel: The Popular Reaction from 1760–1830* (1943; New York: King's Crown Press, 1970), 40.

value is measured in terms of the bard's absorption into the popular imagination, it does not matter if the volume in which his works are read is battered and worn; nor (Lamb would seem to imply) if the edition is pirated or faulty: 'I have a community of feeling with my countrymen about his Plays', Elia explains, 'and I like those editions of him best, which have been oftenest tumbled about and handled' (p. 197.)

Making an intervention, in this way, into discussions about the status—if any—of literary 'property', the essay draws on recognizable components from both sides of the originality debate as it had been conducted throughout the eighteenth century with respect to perpetual copyright. The ingenuity of Lamb's argument is that he appears to be upholding a Romantic aesthetic based on the belief that the true worth of books is individual, intrinsic, and lasting while simultaneously making the more unsettling suggestion that popularity is the only determinant of a book's value, and that the likes of Shakespeare and Milton are significant precisely in so far as they have become the 'common property' of the people. Lamb plays on the paradoxical model of Romantic genius—its appeal both to individualist notions of self-possession and communitarian ideals of self-diffusion—to press home the point that readers, not authors, determine what will be valued in a hundred years time. The perishability of cheaply produced eighteenth-century novels, far from signalling that they are doomed to oblivion, is an index of their likely survival, whereas the durable binding of an expensively produced book of memoirs (the *Life of the Duke of Newcastle by his Duchess*) reflects back on the fragility of both its contents and its author:

Fielding, Smollet [*sic*], Sterne, and all that class of perpetually self-reproductive volumes—Great Natures's Stereotypes—we see them individually perish with less regret, because we know the copies of them to be 'eterne.' But where a book is at once both good and rare—where the individual is almost the species . . . no casket is rich enough, no casing sufficiently durable, to honour and keep safe such a jewel. (p. 197)

Touching on all the elements which motivate Romantic anxieties of reception—the fear of literature as a 'perpetually self-reproductive' machine; the fear that some literature will perish altogether; the fear that precious and rare literature may be an endangered species—Lamb's words are carefully chosen to suggest that quality is not synonymous with rarity, while leaving open the possibility that an expensively bound book might also happen to be good. His slightly asymmetric inversion of the equation between quality and rarity serves gently and indirectly to undercut the defensiveness of Romantic writers such as Wordsworth, who based their claims to immortality on the hope that, where reception is concerned, fitness and fewness exist in inverse proportion one to the other.

'Detached Thoughts on Books and Reading' is thus carefully designed to appeal to Lamb's own audience—the middle-class readers of periodical literature, who preferred novels to poetry—rather than to the posterity in whom Wordsworth places his trust. Its displacement of poetry from centre stage is chiefly accomplished by reassuring readers that their tastes matter, and that the 'public' is not as far from representing 'the people' as Wordsworth would wish to believe.[51] This reassurance is effected not so much by the art of persuasion as through the tones of confiding intimacy with which Elia talks about the reading-habits of personal acquaintances: 'Poor Tobin', for instance, 'who latterly fell blind', is said to be happy to manage without *Paradise Lost* and *Comus*, but to be missing 'the pleasure of skimming over with his own eye a magazine, or a light pamphlet' (p. 199). The readiness with which he is prepared to share his reading-pleasures with others is matched by the familiarity with which Elia assumes his reading-pleasures to be shared:

Coming in to an inn at night—having ordered your supper—what can be more delightful than to find lying in the window-seat...two or three numbers of the old Town and Country Magazine, with its *tete a tete* pictures...and such like antiquated scandal? Would you exchange it—at that time, and in that place—for a better book? (p. 199)

Equally, the embarassments, potential and actual, of reading the 'wrong' things at the wrong times and places suggest Elia's credentials as a closet reader of popular and anti-establishment materials: 'I should not care to be caught in the serious avenues of some cathedral alone, and reading *Candide*' (p. 199), he observes conspiratorially. Such anecdotes have the virtue of allowing Lamb to widen the parameters of his readership by moving his own acts of reading into unexpected places. Just as the bindings on books play a role that is part-literal part-symbolic in his anatomization of the mismatch between perceived and intrinsic value, so the contexts in which reading takes place are given minute attention for the various unorthodoxies they disclose.

---

[51] For Wordsworth's distinction between the 'public' and the 'people', see above, Ch. 3.

Lamb takes to its logical extreme a theory of reading that is based in sympathetic identification by implying that the bindings of books, the places in which they are read, even the positions adopted while reading them, should reflect the creative spirit of the author by whom they are written. This ideal of the reader's openness to the author—his 'negative capability' in the act of reception—extends, in the case of the essayist himself, to a willingness to take on the characteristics of another writer's style. Thus, in sentimental/confessional vein, Elia recalls the 'whimsical surprise' of 'having been once detected—by a familiar damsel—reclined at my ease upon the grass, on Primrose Hill, reading—*Pamela*' (p. 199). Wittily turning the discomfort of this encounter to his advantage, Lamb uses it to seduce his female readership into a complicity of pleasure, whose object is partly the book's contents, partly Elia's embarrassment, and partly the illicit sexual encounter that is taking place between the lines of a deftly euphemistic narrative that mirrors its object:

There was nothing in the book to make a man seriously ashamed at the exposure; but as she seated herself down by me, and seemed determined to read in company, I could have wished it had been—any other book. We read on very sociably for a few pages; and, not finding the author much to her taste, she got up, and—went away. Gentle casuist, I leave it to thee to conjecture, whether the blush (for there was one between us) was the property of the nymph or the swain in this dilemma. From me you shall never get the secret. (pp. 199–200)

The prose conducts an impersonation of Sterne within a parody of Richardson, teasing the reader with periphrasis, hesitation, and bathos. The joke is on Elia for being caught reading a sentimental novel; and he is appropriately feminized (like the true Man of Feeling he is) by a blush. Just as the pleasure of the joke is one he willingly shares with his reader, so the blush that passes between gentleman and lady is the companionable 'property' of them both. Lamb gives us a model of the reading-process, here, and one that is tactfully adapted to appeal to contemporary novel-readers of both sexes, whose intimacy with Richardson and Sterne will enable them to perceive the extent of sympathetic identification in Lamb's prose style. In-jokes are the staple fare of this kind of writing, and in an interpretative community where the reader's kinship with the essayist is taken on trust, they thrive on minute—to a modern eye almost imperceptible—breeches of decorum. As Lamb puts it, in 'Newspapers Thirty Five Years Ago':

What an occasion to a truly chaste writer, like ourself, of touching that nice brink, and yet never tumbling over it, of a seemingly ever approximating something 'not quite proper;' while, like a skilful posture-master, balancing betwixt decorums and their opposites, he keeps the line, from which a hair's breadth deviation is destruction; hovering in the confines of light and darkness, or where 'both seem either;' a hazy uncertain delicacy.[52]

Alongside a carefully judged appeal to the collective self-respect of his readership—based in the trust that he shares their tastes and proclivities—Lamb simultaneously effects a more personal realignment of generic preferences, which has the effect of undercutting the construction of a centralized national poetic identity. David Bromwich has rightly observed that 'The conscious or institutional making of a canon was on the whole foreign to the interests' of Romantic essayists.[53] Instead, moving the focus of interest from creation to reception, they asserted the importance of a plurality and catholicity of individual tastes. Elia's selection of the Elizabethan writers with whom he feels an elective affinity is an expression of the idiosyncrasies which make him credible as a model reader:

Shall I be thought fantastical, if I confess, that the names of some of our poets sound sweeter, and have a finer relish to the ear—to mine, at least—than that of Milton or Shakespeare? It may be, that the latter are more staled and rung upon in common discourse. The sweetest names, and which carry a perfume in the mention, are, Kit Marlowe, Drayton, Drummond of Hawthornden, and Cowley. (p. 198)

At the same time, this selection represents an ideologically motivated attempt to direct his actual readers away from normative standards of taste as they were embodied in multi-volume anthologies of established poets, and reinforced by contemporaries eager to fit the canon round themselves. Lamb's oblique and subtle revisionary strategies are thus directed at the very mechanisms, so instrumental in contemporary canon-formation, which give expression to Romantic anxieties of reception. It can be no accident that the reading-scene with which he closes his essay occurs in a poem by a 'quaint poetess of our day' who in 'two very touching but homely stanzas' describes a poverty-stricken boy, furtively reading a book he cannot afford while standing outside a London bookstall (p. 200). Lamb shares Elia's affection for this 'class

---

[52]   In *Elia And The Last Essays of Elia*, 251.
[53]   Bromwich (ed.), *Romantic Critical Essays*, 17.

of street-readers', often on the margins of society, whose enthusiasm for reading overcomes all obstacles. But he gives the last word to another marginalized figure, Mary Lamb, with whose touching homeliness he is even more familiar.[54]

VII. ENVY, IRONY, AND THE RIVALRY OF GENRES

In a remarkable recent essay, Martin Aske has examined the pervasive presence of what he calls an 'aesthetics of *ressentiment*' in early nineteenth-century writings on literature, criticism, and the fine arts. He shows how the discourse of envy is used by poets and artists to describe the aspirations of critics, and he demonstrates that there is a persistent connection between the ideas of envy and malignity.[55] Aske's focus is primarily a political one: he is interested in Hunt's construction of Gifford as a 'sour little gentleman' whose reactionary stance 'exemplifies a whole state's nervous response to the possible actions of a "restless and revolutionary spirit" in Britain'; and he emphasizes a crucial contrast between Coleridge's efforts to suppress the political animus of *ressentiment*, and Hazlitt's recuperation of its creative possibilities. In the course of his argument, he uncovers a paradox which is germane to the concerns of this chapter. When a writing-subject constructs the other as envious, this produces in the writing-subject itself a form of envious doubling, or mimicry. An episode recounted by Hunt, in which he catches Gifford staring at him, represents for Aske a primal scene, in which the mutual gaze of these two men locks them in a prolonged moment of silent, deadly hatred. Similarly, Northcote's observation that 'criticism is the child that devours its own parent' produces from Aske the following moment of distilled extrapolation: 'The envy of the young in collision with the envy of the old, each position constituting the other within the "autoreferential" structure of *ressentiment*: this is one way of representing the spirit of change in an age of revolution'.[56] Aske's poetic parallel for these scenes of specular doubling is drawn from *The Four Zoas*, where Los and Urizen 'reflect each other's mutual resentment' in frozen hatred; and in the same vein one might examine the mirror/echo

---

[54] Appropriately, Lamb's essay ends (as it starts) by quoting the words of another, and thus enacting the sociable poetics of reception it celebrates. The stanzas quoted are by Mary Lamb, and they were published in *Poetry for Children* (1809).

[55] 'Critical Disfigurings: The "Jealous Leer Malign" in Romantic Criticism', in Beer (ed.), *Questioning Romanticism*, 49–70.

[56] Ibid. 68.

structure which binds Prometheus to Jupiter in Shelley's *Prometheus Unbound*, or the moment when Christabel's features, resigned to the 'sole image' of Geraldine, exactly replicate the malignant gaze of her experienced other.[57]

The Coleridgean analogy is especially suggestive, and my point in returning to it is to bring into focus an important element in the doublings, mirrorings, and crossings that take place in Romantic rhetoric: namely, the 'forced unconscious sympathy' connecting poets and their critics. In an age when each constructed the other as dominant, seeing themselves by comparison as marginalized and underrated, the ' "autoreferential structure" of *ressentiment*' is everywhere apparent. What emerges with extraordinary persistence is the bond of sympathy which traverses and complicates the rivalry between genres. Isaac D'Israeli put his finger on the potential for this bond when he observed in the 1846 edition of *Literary Character of Men of Genius* that 'the writer toils, and repeatedly toils, to throw into our minds that sympathy with which we hang over the illusion of his pages, and become himself'.[58]

Hazlitt, whose aesthetics were grounded in Shaftesburyan and Hutchesonian ethics, placed sympathy at the centre of his definition of taste:

taste . . . is strictly the power of being properly affected by works of genius. It is the proportioning admiration to power, pleasure to beauty: it is entire sympathy with the finest impulses of the imagination, not antipathy, not indifference to them. (Howe, xvii. 57)

The critic is a man of disinterested taste, and therefore a man of intense sympathy. A person's pretensions to taste can be measured by the degree of their 'sensibility to the highest and most various excellence' (Howe, xvii. 61), not by the strength of their dislikes:

I would rather be a man of disinterested taste and liberal feeling, to see and acknowledge truth and beauty wherever I found it, than a man of greater and more original genius, to hate, envy, and deny all excellence but my own. (Howe, viii. 225)

Sympathy accounts not only for the extensive use of quotation and paraphrase in early nineteenth-century reviewing-practices, but for the predominance of a mimetic ingredient in literary criticism. Thus Hunt, describing Hazlitt's highest qualities as a drama critic, draws attention to

---

[57] See my discussion of this passage in Ch. 2, above.
[58] *Literary Character* (London: Frederick Wark and Co., 1846), 80.

'the very striking susceptibility with which he changes his own humour
and manner according to the nature of the play he comes upon; like a
spectator in a theatre, who accompanies the turns of the actor's face
with his own'.[59] This mimetic art is something Hazlitt repeatedly turns
to advantage: in his review of Coleridge's 'Lay Sermon', he confesses
that 'It is impossible, in short . . . to describe this strange rhapsody
without falling a little into the style of it,—and, to do it complete justice,
we must use its very words';[60] and in *The Spirit of the Age* his dazzling
mimicry of Coleridge's immethodical rhapsodizing is sustained for three
long pages of breathless prose.[61] In the subtlety with which he handles
the art of sympathy, Hazlitt shows how the critic's stance of obedience
to the author's voice can be both complimentary and parodic.

The doubleness of this mimetic art has important implications for the
power relations between author and critic, as for the hierarchy of genres.
Each of the writers examined in this chapter has their own idiolect and
personal preoccupations, but a common thread uniting their works is
the acknowledgement of an underlying affinity between the rival sides of
contemporary debate, and a subtle deployment of the paradoxes to
which this gives rise. Parody is a medium ideally adapted to the explor-
ation of this affinity, for the parodist by definition enters into his subject
with a combination of sympathy and critical detachment: he is at one
and the same time a writing-subject rhetorically manipulating his readers
and a reading-subject resistant to those manipulations. Irony involves a
less obvious element of sympathetic identification. Just as the expan-
siveness of the notes to *The Feast of the Poets* speaks symbolically of the
rise of criticism from its marginal status, so Hunt's affiliation with poetry
(and his own claims as a poet) are mounted in the text itself, where his
parodic idiom bespeaks the depth and strength of his poetic sympathies.
The play between prose and poetry allows him to explore his own
equivocal status as poet-critic, but also to dramatize and ironize the
rivalry between genres. In a similar way, Peacock's sympathy for
Coleridge as the victim of abuse shows him standing back from the
unethical practices of contemporary criticism, while his countermand-
ing sympathy with the utilitarians puts the pretensions of poetry—its

---

[59] Reviewing Hazlitt's 'On the Characters of Shakespeare's Plays', 26 Oct. 1817, in *Leigh Hunt's Dramatic Criticism, 1808–1831*, ed. Lawrence Huston Houtchens and Carolyn Washburn Houtchens (London: Geoffrey Cumberledge; Oxford University Press, 1950), 169.
[60] Published in *Edinburgh Review* (Dec. 1816); repr. in Howe, xvi. 100.
[61] Howe, xi. 32–4. See Ch. 9 for the symbolic significance of Coleridge the Talker.

self-mystifying drive towards autonomy and transcendence—in a wider perspective. The point, for Peacock, is not to take sides (except in so far as ventriloquism allows this) but to define the only kind of critical intelligence it is worth having. Hazlitt's use of paradox, by contrast, goes beyond what Hunt called his 'fair play' or 'great impartiality of assault'.[62] In his sympathy with genius he disparages the present in relation to the past, thus establishing the grounds for claiming that his own age is an age of criticism. His persistent use of the second-person plural works to afforce amongst contemporary poets and artists a humility that is the uneasy, envious shadow of his own.

Pushing the affinity between true criticism and past genius as far as he can, Hazlitt empowers the critic in relation to the poet, much as De Quincey elevates the 'secondary' in the passage with which this chapter began. In this respect, he draws attention to the underlying presence of envy in his critical discourse. If Bromwich is right in thinking that Hazlitt's attack on programmes for the invigoration of the arts 'eased his own renunciation' of an artistic career, helping him 'to make peace with his ambitions',[63] much the same might be said of his antagonistic relationship with the great poets of his age, whose pretensions he systematically cut down to size. 'He was sharing the bad tidings', Bromwich concludes; 'and he did not tire of repeating them. The aim after all was to teach others a habit of suspicion he had learned for himself'.[64] One at least among his contemporaries was quick to perceive how his 'habit of suspicion' might be construed: 'A diligent reader of Mr. Hazlitt may easily discover what it is that our man of letters, while he professes to be *totus in illis*, condescends to be envious of', Hunt writes in his 'Remarks on the *Plain Speaker*', 'and why he bestows so many alternate cuffs and plaisters on heads that are his hearty admirers'.[65] A little later, in a rather acid observation about Hazlitt's 'Whether Genius is conscious of its powers', Hunt picks up the topic again:

Mr Hazlitt, at all events, can hardly be said to be unconscious of his. He is only anxious that we should not suppose him capable of equalling himself with the great names of past times; and he adds a caution to others to practice a like

---

[62] Hunt uses this phrase in a letter to Hazlitt (unpublished); quoted by Bromwich, *Hazlitt: The Mind of a Critic*, 109.

[63] *Hazlitt: The Mind of a Critic*, 120.

[64] Ibid.

[65] 'Remarks Suggested by the Perusal of Mr Hazlitt's *Plain Speaker: Opinions on Books, Men and Things* (12 Mar. 1828), 251–2; repr. in *Leigh Hunt's Literary Criticism*, 251–2.

modesty. We apprehend there are very few who will misbehave themselves in this particular; but we would caution them, for our parts, how they said much about it.[66]

Hunt's observation not only draws attention to the keenly competitive ingredient in Hazlitt's critical enterprise, but to the topos of modesty by means of which it is expressed. In doing so, he highlights a vital ingredient of the periodical culture in which his own aspirations thrived.

The politics of envy doubtless illuminate not only the rivalries between different genres in this period, but internal competition among their advocates. The crucial point is that in speaking from a self-consciously marginalized position, the essayist is able to observe and ironize his own 'sympathy with power'. Hunt, for instance, frequently demonstrates that humility—in the context of periodical criticism—has ironic possibilities. It is this that invests even the smallest of his observations with their polemical edge—as when, in the closing paragraph of his essay on 'Old Books and Bookshops' he writes:

It appears to us, magazinically speaking (that is, modestly; for a magazine is absolutely lost, if it does not practise this kind of bashfulness) that we have hit a point of novelty in thus making an article out of a *bit* of an author. But a relish is a relish, far better than 'your loads of meat'; and we hope to welcome the reader often to this sort of dainty of old English literature, ever fresh as the junkets of the fairies.[67]

The tone in which he disparages his own essay is used, not just to satirize a culture which condemns journalists as inferior, the essay form as fragmentary, and readers as the consumers of titbits, but to comment on the journalist himself, as one who willingly underwrites that culture with his diplomacy. '[H]ow many pleasant modes are there of getting rid of a periodical essay?', he asks, with characteristic impishness, in his 'On Periodical Essays':

It may assist your meditation by lighting your pipe . . . it may curl the tresses of your daughter or your sister, or lastly, if you are not rich enough to possess an urn or a cloth-holder, it may save you a world of opodeldoc by wrapping the handle of your tea-kettle. These are advantages.[68]

Falling in with the utilitarians, Hunt's persona here undercuts the pretensions of poetry by enumerating the practical 'advantages' of

---

[66] Ibid. 253.   [67] 'Old Books and Bookshops', in *Leigh Hunt's Literary Criticism*, 478.
[68] 'On Period Essays', in *Leigh Hunt's Literary Criticism*, 77.

periodical essays. His irony, semi-detached from the terms of the debate, pokes fun at the rivalry of genres, while his political sympathies declare themselves openly on the side of informal, underrated, transient, disposable prose.

This same topos, as used by the Elian persona of his 'Men and Books' (1833) succeeds in elevating bookishness, even as it puts the cat among the pigeons with respect to the relative merits of poets and prose writers, ancients and moderns:

> so passionately attached am I to everything connected with reading, that next to the authors who would have been poets under any circumstances, and to the best romancers and novelists, I like those who are poets only because others were...poets by the grace of books. I think them a delightful race, and prefer them before any prose-writers, though I may not always give them so great a share of my admiration. Certainly the greatest poets have reason to love them, as being the readers that do them the most honour.[69]

Hunt's rhetoric elevates reading in relation to writing, first by suggesting an implicit analogy between the dependent status of reader–critics and reader–authors (both of whom take their materials from the past), and secondly by declaring that in each case the position of latecomer has its advantages: 'Next to the book-poets, give me (for love, though not always for knowledge) the book prose-men', Hunt writes: 'I mean such as write books *about* books, or upon authors, or out of them, or are made up of scholarship and anecdote, or who in any way, great or small, provided it be delightful, would not have been authors, but for authors before them.'[70]

The single most outstanding feature of Elian rhetoric is its emphasis on the overlooked importance of the 'secondary'—an emphasis which can be seen pervading critical essays in the period when Lamb's influence reached its height. Isaac D'Israeli, having dedicated most of his early career to redeeming the undervalued status of authors, turned his attention later in life to marginalized or unrecognized forms: miscellanies, anecdotes, prefaces, indices, familiar letters. An Elian persona is distinctly visible in the tone and method of his essays, which gently ironize Romantic ideology by affirming a catholicity of tastes. Miscellanists, D'Israeli asserts mischievously, are 'the most popular writers among every people; for it is they who form a communication between the learned and the unlearned, and, as it were, throw a bridge between

---

[69] 'Men and Books', in *Leigh Hunt's Literary Criticism*, 409.   [70] Ibid. 410.

those two great divisions of the public'.[71] He continues with a restitution of this widely appreciated (but nonetheless underrated) genre, making an implied allusion to the treatise on anecdotes for which he had become famous:

miscellanists are conformable to all our humours. We dart along their airy and concise page; and their lively anecdote or their profound observation are so many interstitial pleasures in our listless hours. (p. 285)

D'Israeli puts himself on the same level as his middle-class readers, promoting a model of the writer–reader relationship which is comfortable because it is egalitarian: he praises composition 'which seems above all others to identify the reader with the writer' and which are 'in a fugitive state, but to which their authors were prompted by the fine impulses of genius' (p. 283). The 'scattered notices' which the miscellany offers are preferable to the continuous narrative thread of biography because they are truer to the fragmentariness of life. The 'self-characters' which authors give in their prefaces are similarly endearing because of their humanness: 'I declare myself infinitely delighted by a preface', D'Israeli declares in his most whimsical tones; 'There is no lie to which a prefacer is not tempted' (pp. 286, 287).

In all this one hears a distinct echo of Lamb's preference for the 'fragments and scattered pieces of Truth', for the 'hints and glimpses, germs and crude essays at a system' ('Imperfect Sympathies') as distinct from grander, more unified forms; and of his sustained vindication of prose rather than poetry. It is significant that this goes alongside an emphasis on the reading side of the writing–reading axis. D'Israeli's essay 'On Reading' is one of the clearest articulations of the politics of reception for periodical essayists at this time, when hermeneutic and generic preferences often worked interchangeably, as codes for each other. 'Writing is justly denominated an art; I think that reading claims the same distinction' (p. 298), D'Israeli proclaims:

readers must not imagine that all the pleasures of composition depend on the author, for there is something which a reader himself must bring to the book that the book may please.... like the game of shuttlecock, where if the reader do not quickly rebound the feathered cock to the author, the game is destroyed, and the whole spirit of the work falls extinct.[72]

---

[71] 'Literary Miscellanies' in *Literary Character* (1846), 281. Page refs. will be given in the text.
[72] 'On Reading', in *Literary Character*, 300–1.

Because it appears alongside and in the same binding as his essays on marginalized genres, this elevation of reading in relation to writing has the effect of redeeming the author's own status as prose writer in relation to high Romanticism. The complex interweaving of these two modes of restitution had been discernible from the earliest appearance of *The Literary Character* onward. In the 1795 edition, D'Israeli had identified more obviously with researchers and scholars (the admirers of genius) than with authors themselves: 'These students are . . . useful members in the republic of letters', he declared, 'and may be compared to those subterranean streams, which flow into spacious lakes, and which, though they flow invisibly, enlarge the waters which attract the public eye'.[73] In a later text (published in the 1881 edition of his works), he again identified with the man of letters, as distinct from the author, characterizing him as somewhere between the two poles of authorship and reception:

Men of letters occupy an intermediate station between authors and readers . . . An author's works form his solitary pride, and his secret power; while half his life wears away in the slow maturity of composition, and still the ambition of authorship torments its victim. . . . But soothing is the solitude of the MAN OF LETTERS.[74]

D'Israeli's early (and failed) attempt to become a poet had given him a special insight into the downtrodden status of critics, scholars, and amateur writers with no established credentials. He never turned his attention (as he might well have done, given his sustained interest in various kinds of literary subculture) to the women writers of his generation. But some of the ingredients of his rhetoric—the emphasis, for instance, on the 'invisibility' of men of letters, their displacement from the centre stage of literary competition—suggest that he would have done so sympathetically.

Used for purposes of parody and self-definition, the discourse of *ressentiment* in nineteenth-century periodical essays suggests an intelligent opportunism, always alert to the ways in which hierarchies can be reversed or differently construed. In this sense, it discloses an affinity with strategies used by women writers to feminize the poetics of reception: an affinity which is sometimes highlighted by self-conscious generic choices or gender alignments. In analysing the rhetorical complexity

---

[73] *An Essay on the Manners and Genius of the Literary Character* (London: T. Cadell and W. Davies, 1795), 20.
[74] *Literary Character* (1881), 227.

of writers such as Hunt, Peacock, Hazlitt, Lamb, and D'Israeli, we see how Romantic irony succeeds in both supporting and unsettling the terms of high Romanticism, thus assuring its own place within the Romantic canon. This mode of irony reaches its apotheosis in Lamb's 'Detached Thoughts on Books and Reading', where creativity's wariness towards criticism is defused by simultaneously emphasizing the secondariness (temporal and hierarchical) of the essayist, and accentuating the 'sympathetic' or 'divinatory' side of the hermeneutic spectrum. If this double movement has the effect of reinforcing the chameleon rhetoric of Romanticism, it also ensures the survival of a collaborative/competitive model for the relationship between poets and their critics.

CHAPTER 6

Feminizing the Poetics of Reception

> The author, who dismisses to the public the darling object of her solitary cares, must be prepared to consider, with some degree of indifference, the various receptions it may then meet.
>
> Mary Tighe, Preface to *Psyche; or The Legend of Love*, 1805

I. WOMEN WRITERS AND THE ANXIETY OF AUTHORSHIP

In women's writing, across the full discursive range in the late eighteenth and early nineteenth centuries, it is difficult to distinguish between a genuine 'anxiety of reception' and a culturally induced rhetoric of self-deprecation. Mary Poovey has drawn attention to the ways in which the ideology of the 'Proper Lady' shaped women writers' representations of themselves as modest and retiring (despite the strength and efficacy of their public interventions) in such a way as to lead to a divided self, and to the deployment of an ambivalent rhetoric:

the legacy of this period is a repertoire of the strategies that enabled women either to conceive of themselves in two apparently incompatible ways or to express themselves in a code capable of being read in two ways: as acquiescence to the norm and as departure from it.[1]

When Frances Sheridan, in her Prologue to *The Discovery*, figured poetry as an authoritative discourse—almost wholly the province of men—in which the woman writer anticipated castigation as an interloper, one suspects that she is teasingly provoking her audience with respect to conventions that were already becoming anachronistic:

[1] *The Proper Lady and the Woman Writer, Ideology as Style in the Works of Mary Wollstonecraft, Mary Shelley, and Jane Austen* (Chicago: Chicago University Press, 1984), 41. Poovey's description of the split self or 'double consciousness' of women bears some resemblance to the Laingian model of the 'divided self' whose implications for the poetics of reception I discussed in my Preface.

A Female culprit at your bar appears,
Not destitute of hope, nor free from fears.
Her utmost crime she's ready to confess,
A simple trespass—neither more nor less;
For, truant-like, she rambled out of bounds,
And dar'd to venture on poetic grounds.[2]

Her rhetoric is nicely judged to ironize a culture in which prejudices against women writers still survived ('For women, like state criminals, [men] think | Should be debarr'd the use of pen and ink'). She addresses herself to a female readership in the Prologue, on the grounds that women will be fairer judges than men, but her vigorous criticism of male prejudice includes an implied audience of the opposite sex:

> *Our author, who disclaims such partial laws,*
> *To her own sex appeals to judge her cause.*
> *She pleads old magna charta on her side,*
> *That British subjects by their peers be try'd.*

As the century advanced, women poets (as well as novelists and writers of political prose) became steadily more visible on the cultural map. By 1832, when John Hamilton Reynolds cast a retrospective glance over several decades of women's poetry, it was clear that, in terms of volumes published, successes achieved, and reputations formed, 'The ladies' had been 'dealing largely and profitably at the hands of the Muses':

Apollo is beginning to discharge his retinue of sprawling men-servants, and to have handmaids about his immortal person, to dust his rays and polish his bow and fire-irons. If the great He-creatures intend to get into place again, they must take Mrs. Bramble's advice, and 'have an eye to the maids.'[3]

---

[2] *The Discovery. A Comedy. As it is Performed At the Theatre-Royal, In Drury Lane*. Written by the Editor of Miss Sidney Bidulph (London: T. Davies, R. & J. Dodsley, G. Kearsley, J. Coote, and J. Walker, 1763), Prologue unpaginated. The passage is discussed by Catherine Burroughs, 'English Romantic Women Writers and Theatre Theory', Carol Shiner Wilson and Joel Haefner (eds.), in *Re-Visioning Romanticism: British Women Writers, 1776–1837* (Philadelphia: University of Pennsylvania Press, 1994), 277. Frances Sheridan (née Chamberlaine) is an interesting figure in this context. Her father, a Dublin rector, 'held eccentric views on women's education, disapproving of teaching them to read or write for fear of encouraging 'the multiplication of love letters when they grew up'; but she was taught in secret by her brothers and produced her first novel when only 15. Her marriage to Thomas Sheridan followed a courtship which she herself initiated by sending him an anonymous letter. She played an active and vocal role among the actors, dramatists, and intellectuals in whose circle she moved. See Linda Kelly, *Richard Brinsley Sheridan: A Life* (London: Sinclair-Stevenson, 1997), 9, 16.

[3] *Reynolds Prose*, 422.

The rhetoric of modesty continued, nonetheless, to pervade women's representations of themselves as writers, becoming increasingly difficult to decode as the reading public adjusted to their pervasive presence, and to the likelihood that self-deprecation camouflaged ambition. If in many instances (as Catherine Burroughs has argued), it was out of politic convention that women tended to portray themselves as 'anxious' and 'trembling' at the fear of public representation, we cannot be sure that this was always the case.[4] For less well-known women writers of the period, the ambition to be recognized by a public readership was seldom acknowledged, and when acknowledged was hedged around with a rhetoric that recalls Sheridan's 'culprit', but in which the familiar topos of modesty reflected genuinely low self-esteem. Schooled by her stepmother to condemn 'the evil of a scribbling turn in young ladies', Fanny Burney feared the 'utter discredit of being known as a female writer of novels and romances'. Having made a bonfire of her compositions at the age of 15, she struggled to give up writing altogether; but when this proved impossible, *Evelina* was published anonymously in 1778. Burney attempted to preserve the shield of anonymity—even in respect of family members—for some time after her authorship had become publicly known. 'I was so much agitated by the certainty of being known as a scribbler, that I was really ill all night, and could not sleep', she wrote in her journal.[5]

Anxiety was accentuated (as in this case) when a woman who lived in close proximity with a male role model began to experiment with writing, thus entering a terrain that was seen, both professionally and privately, as his own. This was especially so when the role model happened also to be a father, husband, or brother. Here is Fanny Burney's account of entering her father's study to learn what he thought of her first novel:

I was almost *afraid—& quite* ashamed to be alone with him—but he soon sent for me to his little gallery cabinet—& then with a significant smile that told me what was coming, & made me glow to my forehead with anxious expectation, he said, 'I have read your Book, Fanny—but you need not blush at it—it is full of merit—it is really extraordinary.' I fell upon his neck with heart-beating emotion, and he folded me in his arms so tenderly that I sobbed upon his shoulder—so delighted was I with his precious approbation.[6]

    [4] Burroughs, 'English Romantic Women Writers', 277.
    [5] Quoted in John Tinnon Taylor, *Early Opposition to the English Novel: The Popular Reaction from 1760–1830* (1943; New York: King's Crown Press, 1970), 83.
    [6] From a MS of *Memoirs of Dr Burney* quoted by Elizabeth Kowaleski-Wallace, *Their Fathers' Daughters: Hannah More, Maria Edgeworth and Patriarchal Complicity* (New York: Oxford University Press, 1991), 10–11.

Observing the innuendoes of this passage—'the embarrassment at exposure to her father's "gaze", the revealing blush, the climax involving increased pulse rate followed by tender caresses'—Elizabeth Kowaleski-Wallace makes the case that Burney wrote the novel metaphorically to 'seduce' her father, and that she succeeded.[7] The journal entry reflects not only the way in which the act of writing barely sublimated erotic desire, but the fact that sympathetic reading, the fulfilment of that desire, was for Burney inescapably connected with the law of the father. There are, however, ingredients in the anecdote that redeem it from 'patriarchal complicity'. As an account of initiation, cast in distinctly novelistic terms, it makes Burney into the sentimental heroine of her own life-story, and her father into the lover she desires and wins. Burney enters into the innermost sanctum of her father's room—its 'little gallery cabinet'—but the novelistic discourse in which she speaks is entirely her own.

Mary Shelley, who wrote prolifically both before and after her husband's death, strove 'to consider [her]self a faint continuation of [Shelley's] being, and, as far as possible, the revelation to the earth of what he was';[8] but she appears to have suffered intense anxieties about being considered as a professional author in her own right. According to her friend Eliza Rennie, she was 'almost morbidly averse to the least allusion to herself as an authoress', and sought to conceal her profession as though it were a guilty secret:

To call on her and find her table covered with all the accessories and unmistakeable traces of *book-making*, such as copy, proofs for correction, etc., made her nearly as nervous and unself-possessed as if she had been detected in the commission of some offence against the conventionalities of society, or the code of morality.[9]

In her Preface to *Frankenstein* (1831) Mary described herself as 'very averse to bringing herself forward in print'; and she disowned her personal ambitions by implying that she wrote under pressure from Percy: 'My husband...was from the first, very anxious that I should prove myself worthy of my parentage, and enrol myself on the page of fame. He was ever inciting me to obtain literary reputation.'[10] This reluctance to achieve fame intensified after Shelley's death into a dislike

[7] Ibid. 11.   [8] Quoted in Poovey, *The Proper Lady and the Woman Writer*, 147.
[9] Eliza Rennie, *Traits of Character* (2 vols., London, 1860), i. 113; quoted ibid. 171.
[10] Quoted ibid. 121.

of personal exposure, which is recorded with particular vividness in a letter to Edward Trelawney of April 1829:

There is nothing I shrink from more fearfully than publicity ... I will tell you what I am—a silly goose—who far from wishing to stand forward to assert myself in any way, now that I am alone in the world, have but the desire to wrap night and the obscurity of insignificance about me. This is weakness—but I cannot help it—to be in print—the subject of *men's* observations—of the bitter hard world's commentaries, to be attacked or defended!—this ill becomes one who knows how little she possesses worthy to attract attention—and whose merit—if it be one—is a love of that privacy which no woman can emerge from without regret ... I only seek to be forgotten.[11]

To read confessions such as this one is to become conscious of the deep level at which the ideology of the 'Proper Lady' was absorbed, even by a writer as intelligently alert to the workings of ideology as Mary Shelley. Disavowing the importance of fame may have allowed her, indirectly, to criticize the 'bitter hard world' of publication and authorship which she pointedly gendered as masculine; but her critique is undermined by its acceptance of cultural stereotypes.

If Mary Shelley's self-presentation as a shrinking and fearful woman, whose only desire was 'to be forgotten', sat oddly alongside her professional accomplishment in the public domain, the case of Dorothy Wordsworth, who never published her journals, and who suffered from being considered as the provider of source material for her brother's poetry, is at first sight more evidently disempowered. In a letter to Catherine Clarkson, explaining why she did not wish to publish her narrative of George and Sarah Green, Dorothy declared: 'I should detest the idea of setting myself up as an Author': in Susan Levin's words she 'constantly denigrates herself and her talent in a manner that goes far beyond common protestations of modesty'.[12] Adopting an intensely self-deprecatory stance when put under pressure to produce poems herself, she wrote to Lady Beaumont in 1806:

And you would persuade *me* that I am capable of writing poems that might give pleasure to others besides my own particular friends!! indeed, indeed you do not know me thoroughly; you think far better of me than I deserve. ... Believe me, since I received your letter I have made several attempts ... and have been obliged to give it up in despair; looking into my mind I find nothing there, even

---

[11]   Quoted Rennie, *Traits of Character*, i. 159.

[12]   *Dorothy Wordsworth and Romanticism* (New Brunswick: Rutgers University Press, 1987), 3; letter to Clarkson quoted ibid. 67.

if I had the gift of language and numbers, that I could have the vanity to suppose could be of any use beyond our own fireside, or to please, as in your case, a few partial friends. (*MY* i. 24–5)

The image of the fireside, which recurred consistently in the Grasmere Journals as the centrepiece for various writing–reading tableaux—William reading his own poems aloud to Dorothy; William writing while Dorothy reads to herself; Dorothy reading aloud (from Chaucer or Milton) to William—suggests the genial warmth that is needed to nurture a private creative self, but which is insufficient to ensure the safe passage of writing into a hostile public environment.

This passage from the private to the public sphere was of course one that must be negotiated by men as well as women. But there is evidence to suggest that women writers found such negotiations more difficult, especially when family members chose to reinforce the conventional expectation that publishing (or—worse—writing for money) was vulgar and unwomanly. Dorothy chose to withdraw her *Recollections of a Tour made in Scotland* because Wordsworth 'reinforced her anxieties by suggesting that the strain of authorship and publicity would be too much for her';[13] and when three of her poems were included in his 1815 collected edition, he assured his readers that they had been unwillingly 'extorted' from their authoress.[14] Similarly, when his daughter Dora published her *Journal of a Few Months' Residence in Portugal* (albeit anonymously), he insisted that she had been 'induced' to do so at the request of Moxon (*LY* iv. 836). According to Sara Coleridge, this vicarious modesty was shared by Mary Wordsworth, who 'all her life wished her daughter to be above both marriage and authorship'. Explaining this curious yoking of activities under a single disapproval, Michael Baron has claimed that both marriage and authorship provoked in Mary a 'fear of a kind of exhibitionism':

Either way, women should be reticent in addressing men whether in person or in print: they should not solicit publication, or, failing that, not put their name to the work. On this view, publication *is* like marriage: a woman loses her name.[15]

From their greater familarity with resistant or hostile reception, women writers held in suspicion any reception aesthetic basing its expectation of

---

[13] Ibid. 66.

[14] Preface (1815) in *Wordsworth's Poetical Works*, ed. E. De Selincourt (5 vols., Oxford: Clarendon Press, 1949), ii. 444; cited in Michael Baron, *Language and Relationship in Wordsworth's Writing* (London: Longman, 1995), 178.

[15] *Language and Relationship in Wordsworth's Writing*, 178.

approval entirely on the sympathy of friends. 'An author', observed
Mary Wollstonecraft in a letter of advice to Mary Hays in 1792, 'especially a woman, should be cautious lest she too hastily swallows the
crude praises which partial friend and polite acquaintance bestow
thoughtlessly when the supplicating eye looks for them'.[16] As Coleridge
learnt to his cost, approval from friends might be merely a form of
patronization, and in no way indicative of how a work would be more
generally received. And as Lamb mischievously reminded Wordsworth,
in a letter referring to the three poems by Dorothy he had included with
his own, there was no guarantee that a woman's writing would receive
acclaim simply by virtue of her connections:

> We were glad to see the poems by a female friend [Dorothy]...Being only
> three, you might perhaps have clapt a *D*. at the corner and let it have past as a
> print[e]rs mark to the uninitiated, as a delightful hint to the better-instructed. As
> it is, *Expect a formal criticism of the Poems of your female friend* and she must expect
> it—(Marrs, iii. 141)

Like Wollstonecraft, Dorothy showed herself to be acutely conscious of
the role played by 'partial friends' and family members in the construction of literary identity. This put her in a position to be critical with her
sympathy when it came to observing the self-protective strategies of
those who had public careers. Writing again to Lady Beaumont later in
1806 she lamented the fact that Coleridge chose the ephemeral medium
of talking rather than the permanent one of writing, as a means of
bringing his listeners closer:

> I would fain see him address the whole powers of his soul to some great work
> in prose or verse, of which the effect would be permanent, and not personal and
> transitory. I do not mean to say that much permanent good may not be
> produced by communicating knowledge by means of lectures, but a man is
> perpetually tempted to lower himself to his hearers to bring them into sympathy
> with him, and no one would be more likely to yield to such temptation than
> Coleridge. (*MY* i. 83)

We have already seen how accurately Dorothy prophesied Coleridge's
humiliating habits of ingratiation as a lecturer. Here, we may simply
observe the two poles between which female anxieties of reception
oscillated during the Romantic period. On the one hand, the hearth

---

[16] *The Collected Letters of Mary Wollstonecraft*, ed. Ralph M. Wardle (Ithaca, NY: Cornell
University Press, 1979) (12 Nov. 1792), 219; quoted in Poovey, *The Proper Lady and the Woman
Writer*, 69.

guaranteed a safe but collusive sympathy; while on the other the public threatened either indifference or hostility. Somewhere, transcending both, there was envisaged the possibility of a writer's permanent influence over his or her audience. But significantly, it was a permanence which Dorothy imagined for others like Coleridge or Wordsworth, not for herself.

If Dorothy's own position with respect to the public sphere gave her a degree of sympathy, insight, and critical purchase so far as the vicarious anxiety of reception was concerned, she did not herself find the private sphere much more consoling. Evidence that she suffered from an anxiety of both influence and reception in relation to her brother is disclosed in the painful sense of inferiority with which she described her own attempts at poetry:

I have no command of language, no power of expressing my ideas, and no one was ever more inapt at molding [*sic*] words into regular metre. I have often tried when I have been walking alone (muttering to myself as is my Brother's custom) to express my feelings in verse; feelings, and *ideas* such as they were, I have never wanted at those times; but prose and rhyme and blank verse were jumbled together and nothing came of it. (*MY* i. 25)

For Dorothy, poetry both embodied an authoritative discourse to which she aspired and a medium in which she avowedly felt uncomfortable. She betrays the extent to which she lived in her brother's shadow by alluding to her involuntary mimicry of his habits of composition. An uncanny frisson is conveyed by her imitative 'muttering', partly because it suggests a strength of sympathetic identification that comes near to impersonation and partly because it is so uncomfortably fuelled by envy. These suggestions are later confirmed when Dorothy alludes more overtly to her sense of inferiority: comparing her own poems with William's, she explains the pleasure that they have evidently given to Lady Beaumont, not in terms of her own skill in writing, but in terms of 'the spirit which William gave them in the reading' (*MY* i. 25). Her account of these poems makes them composite twice over: muttered by herself impersonating Wordsworth at the moment of composition, and rendered interesting by Wordsworth's voice at the moment of reception.

And yet, the writer who so determinedly denied her own voice in this letter, complaining bitterly that her efforts at poetry come out as 'prose and rhyme and blank verse...jumbled together', also found that the terrain between poetry and prose was her ideal medium in the Grasmere

Journals, and later arranged extended prose passages in verse form, experimenting with 'what in the hands of writers like Baudelaire and Rimbaud would become the sophisticated form of the prose poem'.[17] In Margaret Homans's influential reading, Dorothy's tendency to omit a central or prominent self in her writing is sharply distinguished from 'William's habitual concentration on the self', and this allowed her to achieve a uniquely individuated form of poetic notation. Responding to 'the overwhelming demand that she remain an amanuensis', she did not 'seek the position of the subject in literary discourse'. Instead, she was willing to write descriptions that seemed 'genuinely not to impose a literary vision on nature', composing 'from the position of the silenced female object'.[18] A similar erasure of the 'I' allowed for a distinctive reworking of the concept of poetic identity: in poems such as 'Floating Island', the dissolving self is figured in the island, but 'the island's operation as a figure is also submerged': 'The "I" in the poem casts loose, like the island, and becomes similarly diffuse, though it is unclear which causes the other to dissolve, because by the end they have collapsed into each other.'[19] Perhaps it was an awareness of poetic devices such as these that enabled Dorothy to claim (with a touch of triumph, directed at William?), that she was 'more than half a poet'.[20] It was frequently the case in this period that creative identities were constructed from positions of apparent weakness—or rather, that identity was itself reconfigured, so as to make apparent weaknesses into strengths. Women writers were intensely alive to the ways in which they might turn their own subordinate status to creative use; and they frequently collapsed the division between writing- and reading-subjects as a mode of self-empowerment.

II. ATTENDING, LISTENING, SYMPATHIZING, IDENTIFYING, AND ECHOING

A focus on identity might be defined as the hallmark of a (male) Romantic poetics of reception. But as we have seen in the case of

[17] Levin, *Dorothy Wordsworth and Romanticism*, 109.

[18] *Bearing the Word: Language and Female Experience in Nineteenth Century Women's Writing* (Chicago: Chicago University Press, 1986), 41, 67.

[19] Ead., *Women Writers and Poetic Identity: Dorothy Wordsworth, Emily Bronte, and Emily Dickinson* (Princeton: Princeton University Press, 1980), 83.

[20] See her journal entry for Thursday 18 Mar. 1802; *Journals of Dorothy Wordsworth*, ed. E. De Selincourt (2 vols., London: Macmillan and Co., 1941), i. 127.

Dorothy Wordsworth, this may not apply equally—or in the same way—to women writers. In the past two decades, attempts have been made to understand the role played by gender in the formation of identity. According to Jean Baker Miller, Nancy Chodorow, and Carol Gilligan, male identity is understood to evolve negatively, through a steady process of differentiation (and separation) from the mother; whereas female identity emerges positively, in two separate stages: first through identification, and later through symbiotic re-creation. As a result of these different patterns of maturation, men are thought to 'define themselves through individuation and separation from others, while women have more flexible ego boundaries and define and experience themselves in terms of their affiliations and relationships with others'.[21] Where biological | psychological models of identity-formation have been mapped onto critical theories of writing and reading, it has frequently been in order to demonstrate that major areas of difference occur across the gender-divide. For Judith Kegan Gardiner, the fact that 'female identity is a process, and primary identity for women is more flexible and relational than for men' explains why, in women's writing, there is 'a continual crossing of self and other', as well as a blurring of the distinction between public and private discourse.[22] Cognitive research into gender and reading has tended to confirm these binary oppositions, as in the work undertaken by David Bleich, who concludes that 'men draw boundaries much more decisively [than women]'; that 'novels [are] more self-consciously *appropriated* by the men than by the women, who tended more to "enter" the tale'; that 'women [are] less likely to offer a judgement of individual figures and more likely to describe differential allegiances to various figures and situations', and that 'otherness, or objectivity, for women is a much more provisional mental act'.[23]

Major differences, of the kind outlined above, are both plausible and verifiable. But we must avoid making essentialist generalizations; and we should be wary of allowing theoretical constructions to interfere with an awareness of the practices of individual writers and readers. As Virginia

---

[21] This is Patrocinio Schweickart's summary of the theories of reading offered by Miller, Chodorow, and Gilligan. See 'Reading Ourselves: Towards a Feminist Theory of Reading', in Andrew Bennett (ed.), *Readers and Reading* (London: Longman, 1995), 86.

[22] 'On Female Identity and Writing by Women', *Critical Inquiry* 8 (1981), 347– 61: 354, 355.

[23] 'Gender Interests in Reading and Language', in Elizabeth Flynn and Patrocinio Schweickart (eds.), *Gender and Reading: Essays on Readers, Texts, and Contexts* (Baltimore: Johns Hopkins University Press, 1986), 265.

Woolf once said, 'We may stress the value of sympathy; we may try to sink our identity as we read. But we know that we cannot sympathise wholly or immerse ourselves wholly'.[24] No one person reads in a certain way simply by virtue of their gender, and no reading-practice can be straightforwardly labelled according to a binary opposition between detachment and sympathetic identification. Furthermore, it has been just as important, historically speaking, for women to argue on behalf of their capacity to 'partition' identity as it has been to argue that they merge their identity with others. The evolution of feminist reader-response theory over the last twenty years has borne out the significance of these two complementary approaches, which have their origins in Romantic hermeneutics. Thus, the language used in the 1970s by Anglo-American feminists to describe the process of reading was not significantly different from the terminology of strength and struggle used by Harold Bloom to characterize the poetics of misreading: 'My book is for me more than an academic matter, more than an act of literary criticism', Judith Fetterley argues in *The Resisting Reader*:

> ... it is an act of survival. It is based on the premise that we read and that what we read affects us—drenches us, to use Rich's language, in its assumptions, and that to avoid drowning in this drench of assumptions we must learn to re-read. Thus, I see my book as a self-defense survival manual for the woman reader lost in 'the masculine wilderness of the American novel'.[25]

Fetterley's description of the ways in which women are progressively 'immasculated' by the materials they read draws attention to features of the anxiety of reception that are distinctly feminist, but which may nonetheless be considered as conducive to a 'divided self'. The metaphor of drowning that Fetterley uses to describe the threat posed by alien identities is one that Laing also uses in describing the self's fear of 'engulfment'. Similarly, Fetterley draws implicitly on Laingian terminology in describing what it is to be an 'immasculated reader', who experiences

not simply the powerlessness which derives from not seeing one's experience articulated, clarified, and legitimised in art, but more significantly the powerlessness which results from the endless division of self against self, the con-

---

[24] 'How should one read a book?', in *The Common Reader, Second Series* (London: Hogarth Press, 1932), 268; quoted by Jean Kennard, 'A Theory for Lesbian Readers' in Flynn and Schweickart (eds.), *Gender and Reading*, 71.
[25] *The Resisting Reader: A Feminist Approach to American Fiction* (Bloomington, Ind.: Indiana Press, 1978), p. viii.

sequence of the invocation to identify as male while being reminded that to be male—to be universal, to be American—is to be *not female*.[26]

In Fetterley's view, women readers and writers are forever in danger of succumbing to an 'alien sub-identity' or 'false consciousness' in the shape of the culture that surrounds them; and their response to the patriarchal assumptions they negotiate is frequently bifurcated. Unless they use a negative hermeneutic in their reading and writing practices, they risk passivity and acquiescence with respect to patriarchal culture. As Adrienne Rich puts it, in a passage that is crucial to Fetterley's own act of self-definition, 'the drive to self-knowledge, for a woman, is more than a search for identity: it is part of her refusal of the self-destructiveness of male-dominated society'.[27] More recently, Fetterley's notion of reading as survival has been resuscitated by the recognition of a lesbian agenda in the reading process. Jean Kennard, outlining 'A Theory for Lesbian Readers', echoes Laingian terminology when she re-poses Fetterley's question: 'How can we read alien texts and avoid the schizophrenia (often more severe for a lesbian than for a heterosexual woman) that so many feminists have described as a result of their education in the male tradition?'[28] Kennard's essay not only reminds us of the circumstances under which a woman might choose to become a resisting reader, but draws attention to the fact that a hermeneutic of differentiation can be just as crucial to a woman's reading-identity as it is to a man's.

The danger of essentialist generalizations with respect to gender has recently been illustrated by Joel Haefner in a study more immediately pertinent to the period with which we are concerned. Discussing scenes of creation in early nineteenth-century poetry, Haefner lists the following as the distinguishing characteristics of a female poetics:

an emphasis on spontaneity . . . an aesthetics that is obviously expressive but is also clearly audience-centred; a sense of the poet speaking for her audience, becoming almost a collective speaker, like a Greek chorus; an emphasis on the emotional and sympathetic dimension of discourse; and a belief in the importance of conversation and dialogue in the creative process.[29]

[26] Ibid., p. xiii.
[27] Quoted ibid.
[28] 'Theory for Lesbian Readers', 67.
[29] 'The Romantic Scene(s) of Writing', in Wilson and Haefner (eds.), *Re-Visioning Romanticism*, 269.

Most of these ingredients were also present in male writers of the Romantic period: indeed, spontaneity, expressivity, and sympathy have long been recognized as essential components of mainstream Romanticism. That they have acquired a significantly heightened emphasis in women's poetry is due to the political significance they receive in the eyes of their readers by virtue of their writers' gender. Just as consciousness of gender influences the ways in which every poetic utterance— every attempt to enter or negotiate the evolving literary canon—is interpreted by its readers, so the marginalized or subordinate position from which a woman is understood by her readers to speak has a radical effect on how her accounts of creation and reception are viewed. But the question as to what is 'masculine' or 'feminine' in the poetics of reception becomes ambiguous at a time when conventional gender-alignments are being redrawn. And when are they not?

In the remainder of this chapter, I shall trace the recurrence in women's poetry of a number of traditionally 'feminine' activities such as conversing, attending, listening, sympathizing, identifying, and echoing. My intention is to show how these apparently secondary positions are reconfigured by women poets—made to work on behalf of an emergent feminism—even while they appear to be endorsing patriarchal ideology. Overturning the active–passive dichotomy which is sometimes played out in terms of gender-alignments, women ensure that new relations between subject and object begin to occur across and between a range of binary oppositions: creation–reception, voice–echo, writing–reading, male–female, masculine–feminine. The point, then, is not that women poets challenge Romantic assumptions by adopting a more open, flexible, and sympathetic model of communication, but rather that they make equivocal use of their traditional role as sympathizers to unsettle hierarchies of gender and genre.

Because my survey is necessarily brief, I am obliged to traverse a large area rather rapidly. Beginning with a lengthy poem by Hannah More (designed to appeal to the relatively comfortable world of London literati just before anxieties about audience reached their pitch at the turn of the eighteenth century), I shall consider the emergence of a feminized poetics of reception as a complex and partly ironic negotiation of the conduct-book ideology to which More herself contributed, where the role of the female writer–reader was carefully prescribed. If women writers experienced the anxiety of reception primarily as an anxiety about being denied their own agency—made into objects in the receiving process—then through a reorganization of power relations between writer and reader, they were able to redress this imbalance at its discursive root. More's 'Bas Bleu', I shall argue, speaks implicitly for the experience of those who lived in the shadow of male writers (and whose subordinate power was understood in terms of their capacity to listen to or echo their master's voice); but it does so in ways that were carefully camouflaged by the conservative ideology out of which it grew. My argument then proceeds by way of comparison with a selection of poems composed in the early decades of the nineteenth century: by writers such as Ann Radcliffe, Anna Barbauld, and Mary Robinson, contemporaries of the first generation of Romantics whom they engaged in dialogue; and subsequently by Felicia Hemans, Letitia Landon, and Maria Jane Jewsbury, who belonged to the more securely established second generation of Romantic women poets. Against the shifting ideological parameters of this historical period, a number of significant poetic strategies will be seen to emerge, for which More's 'Bas Bleu' is—if not the prototype—the exemplary expression. While not quite proving that self-effacement was a poetic trope for self-empowerment, we shall see, from More onwards, how closely interwoven were the gestures of complicity and resistance in the construction of a feminized poetic identity.

III. HANNAH MORE AND THE EFFICACY OF CONVERSATION

'Bas Bleu: or, Conversation' was the 'signature poem' of the circle of Bluestockings. As Marlon Ross has observed, this group of writers met under conditions that closely resembled those of the Augustan coffee house.[30] Writing in the first place for members of their own coterie, they aimed to set standards of taste and conduct for society at large. By placing the accent on conversation as a means of influencing conduct, the Bluestockings played a crucial role in revising and updating the ideology of 'the proper lady', whose aloofness from the world of commercial publishing signified moral rectitude. As Ross puts it, 'Their freedom to scribble is seen as part of the larger freedom to converse. ...They do not so much desire to change literary discourse, its themes and forms, as to alter the practice of that discourse by making women

[30] *The Contours of Masculine Desire: Romanticism and the Rise of Poetry* (Oxford: Oxford University Press, 1989), 192.

active participants within it.'[31] In this sense, the Bluestockings instigated a new and important phase in the professionalization of women's writing, serving the interests of a generation who wrote 'but published reluctantly and with trepidation', helping younger women 'to develop more professional attitudes', and stimulating them 'to be more ambitious, and to write and publish for money'.[32]

Composed in 1787 and never intended for publication, 'Bas Bleu' passed from hand to hand in manuscript and 'enraptured London society'. Johnson claimed that 'there was no name in poetry that might not be glad to own it', and its fame reached the ears of King George, at whose request Hannah More sat up one night in April 1784 to make a copy.[33] The poem was, however, underestimated by More herself, perhaps because of the light vein in which it raised issues that were later to become of profound concern to her in *Strictures on the Modern System of Female Education* (1799). Addressed to Mrs Vesey— writer, Bluestocking, and society hostess—it was provoked by a topical event. Vesey had recently and successfully introduced a new arrangement into her social gatherings, whereby small groups of guests addressed each other informally: this replaced the earlier custom of conversing in a vast semicircle, which (in the words of Fanny Burney) 'retained throughout the whole evening its unbroken form with the precision of a Brobdingnagian compass'.[34] Making this new arrangement the occasion for a celebration of intimate gatherings over impersonal (constraining and intimidating) ones, More's poem is at every stage concerned with conversation both as a mode of social interaction and as a model for poetic discourse. The poem's elegantly informal couplets offer an appropriate medium for this subject-matter, their imagery wittily combining the masculine Enlightenment domain of mathematics with the feminine Romantic domain of witchery, to transform Vesey into an androgynous magician, presiding over interactions between alternative kinds of knowledge, as well as between speakers and listeners.

---

[31] Ibid. 270.

[32] Sylvia Myers, *The Bluestocking Circle: Women, Friendship and the Life of the Mind in Eighteenth-Century England* (Oxford: Clarendon Press, 1990), 270. See also Mary Poovey's claim that the Bluestockings 'preserved their unimpeachable reputations *and* published for profit and public esteem. Thus they helped to elevate what had been a genteel amateurism into an acceptable professional career': *The Proper Lady and the Woman Writer*, 37.

[33] See M. G. Jones, *Hannah More* (Cambridge: Cambridge University Press, 1952), 47–8, 51.

[34] Quoted ibid. 52.

Despite the very different milieux for which they wrote, More's preoccupations were at first sight not far different from those of other writers at the end of the eighteenth century, for whom coterie audiences represented a reassuring alternative to the threat of a rapidly expanding readership, and to whom conversation offered an ideal for the mutual interchange of writer and reader. We have seen already how Coleridge used conversation, not only as a metaphor for this kind of intimate and immediate bond, but, in his blank-verse meditative poems from 1797 onwards, for the inauguration of a new poetic genre. By the same token, Wordsworth in *Lyrical Ballads* developed what Michael Baron has called

the use of oral locutions, stylistic features that reproduce or imitate oral narration, often in front of an imagined audience that can be called on to agree or disagree, to acknowledge comprehension or incomprehension, to be, at all events, a community of readers in sympathy with the writer.[35]

By comparison with Coleridge and Wordsworth, however, the conversational model of poetry advocated in 'Bas Bleu' was more evidently cultivated, holding out the possibility for a meaningful exchange of ideas in a drawing-room context (somewhere between private and public spheres) that could be occupied equally by women and men. At a time when the utility of poetry was under question, conversation was a medium whose function was defined in terms of praxis. As Joel Haefner puts it, 'Conversation "kindles" knowledge; amalgamates art, science, and ethics; catalyzes morality; secures the stability of society; and is preeminently practical, useful'.[36]

Hester Chapone, in her chapter 'On Conversation' in *Miscellanies in Prose and Verse* (1775), described its democratizing function in ways that are particularly suggestive for women writers:

When we are considering what are the means of doing good entrusted to us, perhaps the sphere of conversation is seldom thought of; yet surely it gives ample scope for the exertion of that active principle of beneficence in which true virtue consists; and it is a sphere of action, from which no station or circumstances can exclude us: there is not a man who drinks his pot of porter at the ale-house, but has somebody who looks up to his opinion, and whose manners and conduct may be influenced by his sentiments.[37]

---

[35] *Language and Relationship in Wordsworth's Writing*, 77.

[36] 'Romantic Scene(s) of Writing', 263.

[37] *Miscellanies in Prose and Verse* (London: E. and C. Dilly, 1775), 38.

More herself was quick to seize on the accessibility of conversation, both as an educational tool that would bring her writing to the masses, and as a medium particularly suitable for encouraging the moral improvement of women. She used a directive mode of dialogue, in her immensely success-ful pamphlet, *Village Politics* (1792) as counter-revolutionary propaganda for chastening the lower classes; and in her pastoral poem, *A Search After Happiness*, dialogue is the means whereby a group of women are morally instructed, both by sharing each other's experience and by learning from the example of their superior, Urania. In *Hints Towards Forming the Char-acter of a Young Princess*, More stressed the educational importance of conversation as a morally and socially improving complement to book-learning: 'Books alone will never form the character.... It is *conversation* which must develope what is obscure, raise what is low, correct what is defective, qualify what is exaggerated, and gently and almost insensibly raise the understanding, form the heart, and fix the taste.'[38]

'Bas Bleu' not only celebrates conversation for its socially cohesive function, but presents it as a means of exhibiting knowledge of all varieties, which would become available to both sexes on an equal basis if educational standards were to be improved:

> O'er books, the mind inactive lies,
> Books, the mind's food, not exercise
> Her vigorous wings she scarcely feels,
> 'Till use the latent strength reveals;
> Her slumbering energies call'd forth,
> She rises, conscious of her worth;
> And, at her new-found powers elated,
> Thinks them not rous'd, but new-created.[39]

It is no accident that 'mind' is firmly gendered as female in this context; or that the image More uses, of a bird preparing for flight, suggests female aspiration. Notoriously sceptical of the female tendency towards excessive sympathy when she writes about novels and their readers in her polemic and educational tracts, in 'Bas Bleu' it is through 'kindling sympathies' that speaker and listener become bonded in a 'Communion' that passes 'from heart to heart' (ll. 279–81). Conversation is at its best, More suggests, not in a virtuoso display of wit, which frequently in-

---

[38] *The Complete Works* (2 vols., New York: Harper and Brothers, 1835), ii. 10; quoted in Ross, *Contours of Masculine Desire*, 211.

[39] *Selected Writings of Hannah More*, ed. Robert Hole (London: William Pickering, 1996), 33; ll. 268–75.

volves the mischievous humiliation or exclusion of others, but rather in a generous capacity to elicit from others their own best qualities. Addressing a male audience, she corrects their adversarial conversational tactics with her own: 'Your conquests were to gain a name, | This conquest triumphs over Fame' (ll. 314–15). Then, widening out her implied audience to include the 'letter'd and the fair' as well as the witty of both sexes, she warns those who suffer from anxieties of reception that without the 'gracious power' of attention, all their scientific knowledge, their fancy, their inventiveness and classical learning will count for nothing: 'In vain shall listening crowds approve, | They'll praise you, but they will not love' (ll. 333–4).

As well as being a light-hearted occasional piece, More's poem is a complex and serious consideration of writer–reader relations—its shifting register, its movement in and out of alternative discourses, the sliding direction of its reference to females and males (and finally both together) giving it a power to implicate and disconcert in all quarters. Its most intriguing ingredient of all, however, is the identification of 'attention' as the highest conversational attribute. Attention is one of the features of female manners encouraged by conduct-books in the latter half of the eighteenth century, of which Dr Gregory's *A Father's Legacy to His Daughters* (1774) is a typical example:

Modesty will naturally dispose you to be rather silent in company . . . [But] one may take a share in conversation without uttering a syllable. The expression in the countenance shews it, and never escapes an observing eye.[40]

The extent to which this patriarchal injunction was internalized by highly educated women, and perpetuated in their own programmes of conduct and education, can be gauged by Hester Chapone's *Letters on the Improvement of Mind* (1775), the most widely read book of the first generation of Bluestockings, which went through at least fifteen editions between 1800 and 1829, many of them used in schools.[41] Women readers are here reminded that 'a real desire of obliging, and a respectful attention will in a great measure supply the want of knowledge'; and that

When you are silent, your looks should shew your attention and presence to the company: a respectful and earnest attention is the most delicate kind of praise, and never fails to gratify and please.[42]

---

[40] Quoted in Poovey, *The Proper Lady and the Woman Writer*, 24.
[41] Myers, *Bluestocking Circle*, 231.
[42] *Letters on the Improvement of Mind* (2 vols., London: H. Hughs, 1775), ii. 103–4.

Attentiveness to others, the clearest sign of good breeding, allows women to set their companions 'in the most advantageous point of light, by giving each the opportunity of displaying their most agreeable talents, and by carefully avoiding all occasions of exposing their defects'.[43] For both Chapone and More, it was essentially an uncompetitive rhetorical mode, which nonetheless accrued certain advantages to those who practised it. As More later puts it, in her *Strictures on Female Education*, 'An inviolable and marked attention may shew, that a woman is pleased with a subject, and an illuminated countenance may prove that she understands it, almost as unequivocally as language itself'.[44] In some senses, More's promotion of attention can be read as entirely predictable within the species of conservative ideology that she and Chapone (alongside Gregory, Knox, Burton, and others) were responsible for promoting: attention was a faculty associated with careful listening and careful reading, both of which it was the aim of More's educational writings to encourage in female readers whom she notoriously saw as inattentive, lazy, and mindless. In 'Bas Bleu', however, she enters into a much more generous engagement with her audience, signalling the possibility that women could indeed be superior to their male counterparts in a sympathetic faculty which builds the listener into the act of communication. She allows, furthermore, for a collapsing of the boundaries between reading- and writing-models in a way that endorses rather than contradicts her educational ideals. In this respect, the rise of attentiveness from a position of womanly inferiority to conversational centrality may be seen, in 'Bas Bleu', not only as a bid for the importance of women's writing, but as a corrective to any theory of reading or writing which subordinates the receiver as a passive entity.

IV. IRONIC FIGURES OF MODESTY, SELF-EFFACEMENT, ANONYMITY, AND INVISIBILITY

Just as strategies of modesty, self-effacement, and self-denial can be read both as an expression of and as a disguised resistance to conduct-book ideology, so there are procedures in a female poetics of reception that work both for and against the bid for public recognition. In foregrounding 'attention' as a specifically feminine attribute, More implicitly defines

---

[43] Chapone, *Letters on the Improvement of Mind*, 98–9.

[44] *Strictures on the Modern System of Female Education With a view on the principles and conduct prevalent among women of rank and fortune* (2 vols., London: Cadell and Davies, 1799), ii. 66–7.

a poetics which holds aloof from the urge for fame and posterity, resembling nothing so much as a Richardsonian definition of virtue: 'So pure its essence, 'twere destroy'd | If known, and if commended, void' ('Bas Bleu', ll. 316–17). However, as the rhetorical complexity of her text suggests, attention was an ambiguous signifier, which could be used both straightforwardly and ironically. Belonging as comfortably to the playful register of 'Bas Bleu' as to the solemnity of an educational treatise, its mobility rendered it useful as a political tool: More was thus able to dignify the apparently 'secondary' status of women, while simultaneously drawing on cultural capital to underwrite her own authority.

Similarly, the 'Introductory Address' to her pastoral poem, *A Search After Happiness* can be read both as a repudiation of masculine culture in the age of criticism and as the mock-apology of a woman writer whose urge to self-publicity was healthily robust:

> With trembling diffidence, with modest fear,
> Before this gentle audience we appear.
> Ladies! survey us with a tender eye,
> Put on good-nature, and lay judgment by.
> No deep-laid plot adorns our humble page,
> But scenes adapted to our sex and age
>
> . . . .
>
> Simplicity is all our author's aim,
> *She* does not write, nor do *we* speak for *fame*.[45]

Poking fun at traditional gender-alignments while simultaneously upholding them, More divides the politics of reception into two separate camps: male = public and critical; female = private and sympathetic, thus appealing simultaneously to women readers (with whom she claimed solidarity) and to male readers, flattered by the apparent submissiveness of her feminine persona:

> She claims no merit but her love of truth,
> No plea to favor, but her *sex* and *youth*:
> With thee alone to boast, she sends me here,
> To beg your kind, indulgent, partial ear.
> Of critic *man* she could not stand the test,
> But you with softer, gentler hearts are bless'd:
> With *him* she dares not rest her feeble cause,

[45] *A Search After Happiness: A Pastoral in Three Dialogues.* By a Young Lady (London: S. Farley, 1783), 'Introductory Address', ll. 1–6, 9–10.

> Too low a mark for satire, or applause.
> Ladies, protect her—do not be satyric,
> Spare censure, she expects not panegyric.
>
> (ll. 13–20)

The moral of More's *A Search After Happiness* can be summarized in the words of Urania, who advises Florissa, Pastorella, and Laurinda with respect to the conventional female virtues of domestic tranquillity: 'woman, born to dignify retreat, | Unknown to flourish, and unseen be great: |...Fearful of fame, unwilling to be known, | Should seek but Heav'ns applauses and her own'.[46] The key terms here—unknown, unseen, fearful, unwilling to be known—function as signifiers of traditional femininity, which More sought to recuperate on behalf of her peculiar brand of evangelical feminism. In wider poetic currency, as we shall see, the same terms carried an ironic resonance that was more pronounced.

Ann Radcliffe's 'Song of a Spirit' (1791)—a poem quite different in kind from More's in that it apparently floats free of historical or political determinants—evinces a similar preoccupation with the hidden and unacknowledged resources of women. The speaker's identity remains concealed throughout, but her anonymity and invisibility go hand in hand with a sympathetic omnipresence, expressed in figures of mobility, speed, and flux: 'In the sightless air I dwell, | On the sloping sun-beams play'; 'Oft I mount with rapid force | Above the wide earth's shadowy zone'.[47] In the course of this extended lyric, some of the actions of the speaker are what might be called passive or secondary—listening, watching, and hearing. But they accrue a significant degree of power through the repeated and forceful immediacy of the present tense, attached to the insistent personal pronoun ('I dwell', 'I mount', 'I watch', 'I sit at ease', 'I watch', 'I hear them now'). And in the final stanza, the paradoxical play of identity and its dispersal reaches its climax:

> Unseen, I move—unknown am feared!
> Fancy's wildest dreams I weave;
> And oft by bards my voice is heard
> To die along the gales of eve.
>
> (ll. 45–8)

---

[46] More, *A Search After Happiness*, 27.

[47] 'Song of a Spirit', ll. 1–2, 9–10; text in Andrew Ashfield (ed.), *Romantic Women Poets 1770–1838. An Anthology* (2 vols., Manchester: Manchester University Press, 1995), i. 138–40.

In this ambiguous poem, the song Radcliffe gives her spirit is one of occluded defiance. The poet discloses a yearning to be 'unseen' and 'unknown' alongside the aspiration to be *heard by bards*—to have a voice that is given recognition, and whose prolonged dying assimilates it into nature.

Read out of its original context, Radcliffe's lyric is an exemplary expression of her own ambivalence towards authorship—an ambivalence which showed itself in her reluctance to enter competitively into the public arena: 'The very thought of appearing in person as the author of her romances shocked the delicacy of her mind', an early biographer records. As Roger Lonsdale puts it, 'She could not "publish herself" or sink "the gentlewoman in the novelist"'.[48] But by restoring its original context, as an inset in *The Romance of the Forest,* the poem can also be read as the confessional utterance of a poet who was diffident with respect to her poetic powers. Having established her success on the basis of novel-writing, Radcliffe went on in later life to become a poet; but her gifts in this genre were under-acknowledged, both during and after her lifetime. When she included poems in her novels, she sometimes drew attention to this fact on the title-page, thus foregrounding the hybrid generic nature of her creative achievement;[49] but she also distanced the poems from herself by assigning their authorship to her heroines, or by suggesting that their author was unknown. The doubleness of this gesture is suggestive of the ways in which Radcliffe questioned (while appearing to accept) the conventional expectation that women write novels, while men have access to the higher poetic domain. And in the same way, 'Song of a Spirit' thematizes Radcliffe's own anxieties: we can read the speaker's reluctance–desire to be 'heard by bards' as symptomatic of her awareness that a hierarchy of genres existed, but also as indicative of her wish to undermine that hierarchy from within. Her acknowledged and acceptable public persona as female novelist was complicated by poetic ambition, which she half-concealed and half-disclosed.

A similar ambivalence can frequently be detected in the way that women poets used conversation as an upwardly mobile figure for poetic

---

[48] See *Eighteenth-Century Women Poets: An Oxford Anthology* (Oxford: Oxford University Press, 1989), 449.

[49] Paula Feldman notes the importance of two titles in particular, both of which show Radcliffe asserting her claim to be considered as a poet-novelist: *The Romance of the Forest: Interspersed with Some Pieces of Poetry* (1791) and *The Mysteries of Udolpho, A Romance; Interspersed with Some Pieces of Poetry* (1794). See Feldman (ed.), *British Women Poets of the Romantic Era: An Anthology* (Baltimore: Johns Hopkins University Press, 1997), 559.

discourse. Polite conversation (as distinct from the democratic speech-act championed in Dissenting traditions of oratory) was conventionally gendered as female, by virtue of its immediacy, its ephemerality, and its inferiority to the written word. Along with gossip, anecdote, and repetition, it was considered, in the words of Michael Baron, as a 'devalued verbal practice' or as 'language not authorised for serious debate', and, when used by a man—as in Wordsworth's *Lyrical Ballads*—it could be dismissed as feeble or puerile.[50] In conduct-book ideology it was frequently represented as superficial: 'Your sex, it must be confessed, are fond of ornamental accomplishments', wrote Burton, in his *Lectures on Female Education* (1793): 'And can there be one more ornamental, than the art of pleasing in conversation?'[51] But it could be redeemed from this position of devaluation by strategies of the kind deployed by Hester Chapone, when she declared that 'it is a sphere of action, from which no station or cicumstances can exclude us',[52] or by Hannah More, when she demonstrated that through conversation women can become 'conscious of her worth'. As Joel Haefner puts it, because conversation 'successfully negotiates the perils of gender and genius', there were some strategic advantages to be derived from stressing the achievement of women within its realm. Inevitably though, if 'woman's art based on woman's skills . . . will slip by cultural censors/critics', it ran the danger of accepting generic limitations, and so of underwriting patriarchal ideology.[53] A path between diplomacy and irony had to be carefully steered if resistance within this gendered domain was to be rhetorically effective.

In the opening lines of 'Washing Day' (1797), Anna Barbauld departs from the rules of mock-epic by announcing, not the subject of her poem, but its register, its position in a hierarchical system of discursive values: 'The Muses are turned gossips; they have lost | The buskin'd step, and clear high-sounding phrase, | Language of gods'.[54] Mock-epic is here feminized in such a way as to suggest an analogy between the place of women and the place of a second-order poetry, whose function is largely mischievous, like gossip itself. Implicit in Barbauld's chosen genre is a double movement, of dignification and belittlement, which

---

[50] *Language and Relationship in Wordsworth's Writing*, 80.

[51] *Lectures on Female Education and Manners* (New York: Samuel Campbell, 1794), 125.

[52] *Miscellanies in Prose and Verse*, 38.

[53] 'Romantic Scene(s) of Writing', 268.

[54] ll. 1–3, in *The Poems of Anna Laetitia Barbauld*, ed. William McCarthy and Elizabeth Kraft (Athens, Ga.: University of Georgia Press, 1994), 133.

works both for and against a claim for the equality of women with men. Her poem ends by suggesting a similarity between soap-bubbles, Mongolfier's air-balloon, and poetry: 'Earth, air, and sky, and ocean, hath its bubbles, | And verse is one of them—this most of all' (ll. 85–6). Claims to permanent value are shown to be similarly empty in the domains of feminine domesticity, masculine science, and poetry. This levelling inclusiveness alerts us to the implicit motivation behind Barbauld's mock-epic voice, which effectively ironizes a conventional hierarchy of genres, even as it appears to uphold it.

In Elizabeth Hands's 'A Poem on the Supposition of an Advertisement Appearing in the Morning Paper, of the Publication of a Volume of Poems, by a Servant-Maid' (1789), female conversation is both celebrated and satirized. The lively jauntiness of this poem, written in an idiomatic register and including direct speech in rhyming dialogue, establishes drawing-room conversation as both the poem's subject-matter and its rhetorical mode. Hands brings poetry off its pedestal by making gossip into poetic material; but she also pokes fun at the women's anti-poetic topic of conversation. Mrs Consequence, Madam Du Bloom, and Miss Coquetilla all condemn the publication of a volume of poems by a maidservant (the alter ego for Hands herself, who came from a working-class background). These women are ironized for their middle-class prejudice, their readiness to dismiss the aspirations of a servant to poetic status:

> 'A servant write verses!' says Madam Du Bloom:
> 'Pray what is the subject—a mop, or a broom?'
> 'He, he, he', says Miss Flounce: 'I suppose we shall see
> An ode on a dishclout—what else can it be?'[55]

They are thus drawn into complicity with men, who hold similarly prejudiced views with respect to women (as the gendered exclamation 'He, he, he' fortuitously suggests). Hands makes this complicity clear in a companion-poem, 'On the Supposition of the Book having been Published and Read', where the same topic is addressed again, this time by a mixed company. Her satire is directed equally at women and men (who are shown to use the medium of conversation to similar ends) in much the same way that Barbauld's mock-epic voice levels the generic distinctions that are used to underwrite gender dichotomies.

---

[55] ll. 11–14, in Jennifer Breen (ed.), *Women Romantic Poets, 1785–1832* (London: J. M. Dent and Sons, 1994), 26.

As (in their different ways) the poems by Radcliffe, Barbauld, and Hands demonstrate, a woman writer's identification with a particular discursive mode could involve an ironic take on how that genre was conventionally gendered, and therefore a mobility in relation to contemporary hierarchies. Conversation was a significant model of poetic discourse in this respect, not simply by virtue of its temporal and gender associations, but because its interactive structure implicitly invoked the listener or receiver, and therefore the place of the secondary in relation to the primary. For this reason, its occurrence could be read as a figure for reception.

V. READING ECHO: BARBAULD AND JONES

Conversation was not the only medium closely identified with women in this period. According to contemporary gender-stereotypes (as typically defined, for instance by the *Ladies Magazine* for 1828) the role of women in relation to men was that of sympathetic listeners:

The world is dead to sympathy. Man is too much occupied in the pursuit of wealth or fame, to lend a willing ear, or a consoling voice ... But there is an ear, which is open to the sorrows of man; there is a voice, whose sweetest accents are the accents of comfort and consolation.[56]

In the households of Romantic poets, an echoic function was performed by women, who were seen as the upholders and preservers of creative spirit: 'An Author', wrote Mary Shelley, 'requires sympathy, a world to listen, and the echoes of assent'.[57] But in women's poetry the figure of echo (like the figure of conversation) recurred frequently and ambiguously as a site of encounter between the rival claims of writing and reading, speaking and listening. This recurrence may be explained partly in mythological terms, since Echo (like the nightingale) is a traditional symbol of female suffering and oppression. (In Ovid's *Metamorphoses* she is a woman deprived of normal speech as a punishment for chattering too much.) But it also reflects the fact that she has an indeterminate status as a mythological but also a rhetorical entity, and as such is open to reconstruction.

---

[56] 'Female Character', *Ladies Magazine*, 1/5 (1828), 197; quoted in Poovey, *The Proper Lady and the Woman Writer*, 10.

[57] In Shelley's 'Life of Alfieri'; quoted in Stephen Behrendt, 'Mary Shelley, Frankenstein, and the Woman-Writer's Fate', in Paula Feldman and Theresa Kelley (eds.), *Romantic Women Writers: Voices and Counter-Voices* (Hanover, NH: University Press of New England, 1995), 84.

Whereas Echo played a subordinate role in male poetic discourse by virtue of her temporal distance from the originating word, she had, in women's poetry, a power of her own; and nowhere is this more apparent than in a poem by Anna Barbauld, entitled simply 'A Riddle':

> If the poet sublime
> Address me in rime,
> In rime I support conversation;
> To the lover's fond moan
> I return groan for groan.
> And by sympathy give consolation.
>
> Though I'm apt, 't is averr'd
> To love the last word,
> Nor can I pretend 't is a fiction;
> I shall ne'er be so rude
> On your talk to intrude
> With anything like contradiction.
>
> The fair damsels of old
> By their mothers were told,
> That maids should be seen and not heard;
> The reverse is my case,
> For you'll ne'er see my face.
> To my voice all my charms are transferr'd.[58]

As a poetic figure, Echo was traditionally favoured by poets for her feminine receptivity; and Romantic poets in particular used echo to confirm their own creative power. Coleridge, for instance, in 'Frost at Midnight', sought in the fluttering stranger an 'echo or mirror' of his own solipsistic musings: interpreting everything 'by his own moods', he found thereby a 'companionable form' who held 'dim sympathies' with his state of mind. Echo was also used by Romantic writers to establish the depth of their attachment to the past, or the future's attachment to them. In his 'Ad Vilmum Axiologum', Coleridge imagined the afterlife of Wordsworth's poetry as a chorus of voices refracted from one single creative source: 'List! the Hearts of the Pure, like caves in the ancient mountains | Deep, deep *in* the Bosom and *from* the Bosom resound it' (ll. 3–4). But in Barbauld's rehandling of this ancient figure, hidden structures of power are playfully uncovered. Echo becomes a woman who refuses to behave as a figure; who resists the pressure to be decorative

---

[58] 'A Riddle' ('An Unfortunate Maid'), ll. 13–30, in *Poems of Anna Letitia Barbauld*, 193.

(seen and not heard); and whose habit of obedient response is transformed into a species of 'answering back', of loving 'the last word'.

Barbauld's reversal of poetic convention is simultaneously an act of political intervention. Using a rhyme scheme and metrical arrangement appropriate to her subject-matter, she suggests the delayed and unsettling difference of echo from voice. Pairs of short lines suggestive of Echo's immediate and chiming accord (sublime/rime, moan/groan), are counterpointed with longer lines in which the rhyme words are ironically chosen both for their feminine associations and for their feminine endings (conversation/consolation, fiction/contradiction). In this way, Barbauld succeeds in showing how it is that even a supportive and echoic model of reading may contain its own critical and creative motivations. Playing back to her contemporaries a version of their anxiety of reception, which focuses on the dangerous collapse of subject into object, writing into reading, she confirms that sympathetic identification may indeed shade into usurpation. But her touch is so light as to defuse all hostilities; and her mischievous combination of competition with collaboration is brilliantly parodic of the cultural defences of her time.

A similar resistance is enacted in a sonnet by Anna Maria Jones (1793) where Echo's intermediate status as rhetorical figure and legendary woman is played out through a sequence of vivid, almost violent alternations between sight and sound, voice and silence, shadowy half-absence and tangible presence:

> I saw her in the fleeting Wind,
> I heard Her on the sounding Shore;
> The fairy Nymph of shadowy Kind,
> That oft derides the Winter's Roar:
> I heard her lash from Rock to Rock,
> With shrill repeating solemn Shock;
> I met her in the twilight's Shade
> As flitting o'er my pensive Glade;
> O'er yonder tepid Lake she flew,
> Her Mantle gemmed with silver Dew;
> The bursting Note swept through the Sky
> As the young Valleys passed the Sigh:
> In Accents varied as the Passions change,
> The Nymph, wild Echo, sweeps the hallow Range.[59]

---

[59] In Ashfield (ed.), *Romantic Women Poets*, i. 108.

Jones, like Barbauld, stresses the refusal of figure to remain purely figurative; but whereas Barbauld does this by a denial of Echo's decorative status ('You'll ne'er see my face | To my voice all my charms are transferr'd'), Jones plays on Echo's power to be seen and encountered, as well as heard. The speaker in this poem is not the originator of Echo's voice—indeed, no originator is ever identified—but she is in some senses Echo's double; and Echo's power to haunt her is apparent, both in the insistent repetitions of their meeting and in the increasing actuality which her presence acquires as the poem progresses ('I saw her', 'I heard her', 'I heard her', 'I met her', 'she flew'). By the closing lines of the sonnet, the transience and secondariness of Echo have been discountenanced: the past tense changes to the present, in a recuperative gesture which allows Echo her own immediate and unmediated poetic voice.

V. ECHOIC READING AND POETIC IDENTITY: WILLIAMS, ROBINSON, JEWSBURY, HEMANS, AND LANDON

In a sophisticated recent attempt to understand the exclusion of women poets from the Romantic canon, Andrew Bennett has contrasted the masculine cult of 'Romantic posterity' with a number of alternative trajectories for women's poetry, among which are included

contemporary fame and posthumous neglect; contemporary *and* posthumous neglect; the poet's concern with contemporary fame but unconcern toward her posthumous reputation; the poet's 'domestic' neglect of fame both present and future, the poet's active *rejection* of fame both contemporary *and* posthumous and her expression of a desire for oblivion[60]

Although dealing with only one side of our temporal model of the writing–reading subject, Bennett's proposition helps us to approach the question of how women's poetry might be situated in relation to high Romanticism. In Bennett's argument, the difference between male and female figurations of temporality is used to explain why the canon is a largely masculine construct: Romantic ideology is shown to be performative, successfully relinquishing the desire for immediate acclaim in favour of posterity; while women's poetry, standing outside that ideology, chooses to write itself out of the canon. Bennett also

---

[60] *Romantic Poets and the Culture of Posterity* (Cambridge: Cambridge University Press, 1999), 66.

helps us to understand that contemporaneity, ephemerality, and the quotidian might be seen as appropriate figures for women's discursive practices, rather than as appropriately 'feminine' preoccupations and themes.

However, as we have already seen, the allegiance of women writers to a particular temporal or discursive model may be a way of consolidating identity and negotiating existing power structures, rather than of bowing out of the struggle for survival. Just as the apparently subordinate positions of listening, attending, and echoing were recuperated by women poets, thus revising conventional gender-assumptions, so the figures of obscurity, anonymity, and retirement could function as ironic signifiers of the need for recognition. Complicating Bennett's model, to accommodate the various ambivalences I have so far examined, one might argue as follows: if high Romanticism evolved through a system of defences designed to fend off the threat of modernity, it did so through a double movement of denial, rooting identity and authority in the past, while simultaneously deferring reception (the dispersal of identity) to the future. Women's poetry, by contrast, embraced the present. In disclosing this temporal allegiance, however, women poets did not so much relinquish the quest for posterity as seek to maintain identity in a culture where they were constructed as temporary rather than permanent, sympathetically receptive rather than creative. And often their apparent complicity with these constructions can be read as a coded resistance to them.

The revisionary transformations we have seen at work in the figure of Echo are carried through in the practice of echoic reading as it was defined by women poets throughout the Romantic period. Again, however, we have to look carefully at the way that the revisionary makes itself felt, because it sometimes takes occluded and camouflaged forms. The strategies whereby male poets engaged with tradition, challenging and displacing their precursors, are less visible in women's writing than are their complex and often ambivalent relationships with contemporaries. The relative unimportance for women of a diachronic model of intertextual relations has tended to obscure the role of 'the resisting reader'[61] in women's poetry, and may have played its part in suggesting an overly schematic contrast between collaborative and competitive models of reception across the gender-divide.

---

[61] See Fetterley, *Resisting Reader. A Feminist Approach to American Fiction.*

If it was the case that women poets tended to adopt more egalitarian and collaborative models of reading than men, and to be less defensively concerned with the preservation of authority, this was not because they were by nature less competitive; nor was it self-evidently because of their concern with the primacy of the family and the ethics of care.[62] Rather, it was because (by virtue of their position as relative latecomers to the literary scene) their anxieties were more closely focused on the present—where they had the opportunity actively to contest literary authority—than on the past, from which they were always already excluded. 'Revision', or the exercise of a 'negative hermeneutic' was nonetheless just as important to women as to men; and poetic identity could be negotiated by women in such a way that the position of latecomer was redeemed. In the poems analysed below, women poets can be seen apparently accepting their subordination to male forebears and contemporaries, while reconfiguring secondariness itself as a mode of self-empowerment.

A text such as Helen Maria Williams's 'An Address to Poetry' (1790) is a relatively rare phenomenon, both in its explicit negotiation of the canon and its underwriting of values we have so far identified as belonging to the male tradition—namely, a belief in the sanctity of the past, and a hope that poetic genius would be perpetuated by sympathetic readers in posterity. However, a number of ingredients in Williams's model of creation–reception allow us to read this text as an exemplary rather than an anomalous expression of female poetic desire. Williams addresses the spirit of poetry by invoking a sequence of writers—Shakespeare, Milton, Pope, Thomson, Gray—all of whom might be expected to figure prominently in a Romantic roll-call of major precursors at a time when what Greg Kucich has described as 'the promulgation of an exclusively masculine official recurrent history, outlined and reaffirmed throughout the span of thousands of volumes of British classics' regularly included their names. If Kucich is right, that 'the presentation of long swaths of major works by male authors ... reinforced a growing impression of miscellanies, and their female-authored "poetical beauties", as fragmentary and insubstantial',[63] Williams makes no overt attempt to unsettle that impression or to disrupt official literary

---

[62] Here I differ from Anne K. Mellor, *Romanticism and Gender* (New York: Routledge, 1993), 84.

[63] 'Gendering the Canons of Romanticism: Past and Present', *Wordsworth Circle* 27/2 (Spring 1996) 100.

history. In summoning these male poets, she does not identify them as
models for her own poetic utterance, but instead assigns them the more
ambiguous role of inspirational voices, with whom she communes as a
reader. Tacitly remaining content with this secondary or echoic position,
she nonetheless uses it to transform these traditional voices, in ways that
are suggestive of a feminized literary tradition. Shakespeare is invoked
via his strongest female heroines—the weird sisters in *Macbeth*, Cordelia,
Desdemona, and Ophelia—Pope is praised for his portrait of Eloïse,
Thomson for his sympathy with nature, and Gray for his preoccupation
with mournfulness and death. In tracing a continuity between these
disparate poetic identities, Williams figures the literary past as a preparation for the poetry of sensibility, a genre to which her own text belongs.
She also suggests that these poets—and indeed the spirit of poetry in
general—are subject to Nature, who gradually comes to occupy the
position of addressee in a poem nominally addressed to poetry itself. In
this way, Williams effects a subtle displacement of male poetic identity:
through her reconfiguration of the triad Nature/Poetry/Genius, Nature
is portrayed both as the spirit of continuity into which male poets are
continually absorbed, and as a composite source of poetic genius with
which she can herself identify: 'Oh Nature! thou whose works divine |
Such rapture in this breast inspire, | As makes me dream one spark is
mine | Of Poesy's celestial fire.'[64]

If Williams's poem can be read as a manifesto for echoic reading,
in which the subordinate role of the female reader is used to sustain
but also to revise romantic ideology, Mary Robinson's 'To the Poet
Coleridge' (1800) represents a more daring intervention. The poem
announces itself as a collaborative utterance—one in which the
speaker, as listener to Coleridge's 'Kubla Khan', responds eagerly to
his tacit invitation to become a 'fellow-labourer' in the construction
of poetic meaning. Entering Coleridge's domain alongside him, she
redescribes his paradisal landscape in exclamatory ejaculations that
echo and amplify his own, making her poem both tribute and tributary
to his:

> Rapt in the visionary theme!
>   Spirit Divine! with thee I'll wander!
> Where the blue, wavy, lucid stream,
>   'Mid forest glooms shall slow meander!

[64] 'An Address to Poetry', in Ashfield (ed.), *Romantic Women Poets*, i. 71.

> With thee I'll trace the circling bounds
> Of thy New Paradise, extended;
> And listen to the varying sounds
> Of winds, and foamy torrents blended![65]

The speaker's repetitions of companionship—'with thee I'll wander...
With thee I'll trace'—are ambiguous signifiers of poetic aspiration,
suggesting both her willingness to be 'led' or 'guided' by the poet and
her wish to be included on equal terms in his act of creation. The poem's
refrain, repeated four times in all, figures reading as the carefully secondary activity of 'tracing' (or copying) what exists already in Coleridge's
poetic text and as the act of 'extending' a paradise he has created. This
slippage from an imitative to a supplementary model of reading–writing
is suggested also in the use of the ambiguous verb 'mark', as well as in
the transition between actions performed in the poet's company and
actions that are performed by the speaker alone ('I'll listen', 'Then will I
climb', 'I'll pause', 'I'll gather', 'I'll raptured trace...and listen').
The latter occur with increasing frequency as the poem progresses,
performatively underlining the speaker's steady acquisition of poetic
autonomy.

Whereas Coleridge, using the conditional tense, had figured his
retrieval of dream vision as a suspended or deferred possibility, open
to himself alone ('Could I revive within me...To such a deep delight
t'would win me', ll. 42–3), Robinson uses the future tense to suggest a
collaborative act of reception which she both performs and intends to
repeat: 'Spirit divine! with thee I'll trace, | Imagination's boundless
space!' Switching from the future-continuous to the present tense in
her final stanza, she figures herself both as a reader who will go on
revisiting 'Kubla Khan' and as a writer who has immediate and unconditional access to paradisal vision in the here and now. Poised between
obedience and transgression, her poem succeeds in bypassing the anxieties of imagination which are implicit in Coleridge's text. Having
ignored the tones of prohibition and warning with which his vision
had closed ('Beware, beware, his flashing eyes, his floating hair'), Robinson tacitly refuses to accept that Milton's paradisal territory is off-
limits, and outlines instead a poetics of reception which is fearless in its
entry to a previously inhabited poetic domain. Further trespassing on
Coleridge's territory, she imagines herself wandering through a vaster

---

[65] 'To the Poet Coleridge', in Ashfield (ed.), *Romantic Women Poets*, i. 131.

and more varied landscape than his, in which the categories of sublimity and beauty are significantly jumbled and merged. Her revisionary handling of poetic space implies a resistance to traditional aesthetic hierarchies, in the same way that her reconfiguration of Coleridgean temporality suggests a redistribution of imaginative power. The opening up of poetic terrain which her poem celebrates suggests that she prefers the sociably diffusive side of a Romantic poetics of reception to its proprietorial alternative.

Robinson's adjustments to the temporal and geographical layout of 'Kubla Khan' demonstrate the close alliance between competition and collaboration which can occur in the practice of echoic reading, and they also confirm that women writers with their own poetic agendas were able to camouflage ambition by paying homage to the poets against and through whom they defined themselves. In this way, revisionary strategies of self-definition which were remarkably similar to those adopted by male writers appeared under the guise of appreciative attention— precisely the attribute which was expected of female readers in conduct-book ideology, and of the female entourage as it was habitually predicated by a high Romantic poetics of reception. Acts of difference could thus be construed as acts of deference, even while the seemless continuity between poet and reader, voice and echo, was called into question.

Although an understanding of the revisionary content of women's poetry can help us to understand the doubleness of its rhetoric, this does not always allay the unease which modern readers experience in relation to its unresolved residue of patriarchal ideology. Poems such as Williams's 'An Address to Poetry' or Robinson's 'To the Poet Coleridge' rescue themselves from the charge of parasitism by the 'negative hermeneutic' which they display in their practices of reading. But they also hover extremely close to impersonation, giving us a frisson reminiscent of the moment when Dorothy Wordsworth confesses to imitating her brother's methods of composition, and indicative of the indeterminate boundaries separating patriarchal complicity from its opposite, within a poetic language that is predicated on the marginalization of women.

The difficulties we face in understanding this kind of double rhetoric are nowhere more evident than in a highly self-conscious ode by Maria Jane Jewsbury, 'The Glory of the Heights' (1829), which features briefly in Andrew Bennett's discussion of the contrast between a male Romantic 'cult of posterity' and a female Romantic poetics of self-effacement. Where Robinson achieved female autonomy within the discourse of attentive reading prescribed by Hannah More, Jewsbury worried more uneasily about whether the Romantic poetic identity to which she aspired might be purchased at too great a cost to female athenticity. In this subtle and complex text, she explores her divided allegiances to two alternative forms of poetic discourse, which are given both gender- and temporal-alignments by way of sustained allusions to Burke's treatise on the sublime. She longs on the one hand for permanent poetic power as it is embodied in the 'masculine' mountains; and on the other hand for the peace and tranquillity—the domestic happiness—which are to be found in the beautiful and changeful ('feminine') vale. Her poem opens with a lament that these opposites cannot be synthesized—'O mockery to dream of genius wed | To quiet happiness!'—a lament which is reiterated throughout the poem, only to be resolved at the end by the invocation of eternal religious values. The poem's third and fourth stanzas contain the kernel of Jewsbury's poetics of reception, which is itself an attempt to perform some kind of mediation:

> Yet have the mountains glory;—not repose
> The bright monotony of cloudless days,
> Living and dying in a sunny haze,—
> Their glory is the storm;—the storm that throws
>   Its kindling power around,
>   Till passive things rebound,
> And weaker elements arise, and share
> The lofty strife, that else they might not dare.
>
> Yet have the mountains glory;—they remain
> The earth's eternal tenants; while the vale
> Changing and changing like tradition's tale,
> May scarcely one old lineament retain,—
>   They from their solitude
>   Oft see the world renewed,
> The history of each age—power—pomp—decay—
> And then oblivion:—not so their sway.[66]

Positioning herself ambiguously in relation to high Romanticism, Jewsbury uses the rhetoric of consolation to suggest both the advantages and the drawbacks of a commitment to permanence at the expense of the

---

[66] 'The Glory of the Heights', in Ashfield (ed.), *Romantic Women Poets*, i. 200.

quotidian. She seeks to reconcile the grandeur of historical overview with the repetitions of local tradition. Furthermore, she suggests that, within the category of the sublime itself, there is room for manoeuvre. If, in response to sublimity, 'passive things' are enabled to 'rebound' and 'weaker elements' to 'arise', this suggests that the point of intersection between hierarchical and temporal models of difference could be successfully negotiated by women, in such a way as to allow them access to the sublime. Tacitly, her claim was that women readers, in their response to sublimity, could themselves 'share | The lofty strife, that else they might not dare'.

If Jewsbury plays on various ambiguities in order to deconstruct the binary oppositions which underwrite gender hierarchies, she does so without dislodging Romantic ideology; and for this reason it is difficult to draw the line between her subtle critique of the Burkean sublime and her willingness to become 'immasculated' or 'patriarchally complicit'. In an intertextual reading of the poem, one might pursue further the complex ramifications of this ambivalence, mindful of Jewsbury's strong identification with Wordsworth (who is echoed in the opening stanza), of the ways in which her poetry has been associated with masculinity, and of the fact that, elsewhere in her writing, there is an evident preference for the ideals of permanence and stillness, as opposed to fashion and change. In a passage, for instance, from *Phantasmagoria*, showing how deeply she has imbibed Wordsworthian quietism, she complains that

The strength of modern intellect is given to the flitting fancies and evanescent interests, which alternately rise and fall on the surface of the present moment, while the silent depths of human nature, those principles, and powers, and passions, which neither change nor pass away, are left comparatively unfathomed and unsearched.[67]

With this preference in mind, a close analysis of Wordsworthian reverberations in 'The Glory of the Heights' would I think yield as equivocal an intertextual relationship as Robinson's with Coleridge, but one in which Jewsbury is less comfortable with her divided allegiances. If she

[67] *Phantasmagoria; or Sketches of Life and Literature* (London: Hurst, Robinson and Co., 1825), 8. Jewsbury's debt to Wordsworth is formally acknowledged on the title-page of *Phantasmagoria*, which bears the following dedication: 'To William Wordsworth, Esquire, These volumes are most respectfully inscribed; as a testimony of grateful feeling, for the high delight, and essential benefit, which the author has derived from the study of his poems'. Jewsbury's poem, 'A simple solitary Flower', which appears on the following page, is an intricately intertextual tribute to Wordsworthian simplicity, of the kind celebrated in his lyric poetry of 1802.

was concerned to qualify Romantic ideology, her stronger instinct was to uphold and reverence its manliness, and this confusion is played out in the indeterminacy of her rhetoric.

The potentially collusive part played by Echo in the poetics of reception becomes particularly apparent wherever the afterlife of poetry is either literally or figuratively considered by women writers. In the final stanza of Jewsbury's poem, a consoling poetic synthesis is deferred onward and upward to a heavenly plane in a movement which mimes the male Romantic yearning for an ideal reception, beyond the fickle constraints of fashion. In Robinson's poem, Coleridge is given an 'extended' existence during his own lifetime through his admiring female reader, in obedience to the reception aesthetic encoded and elicited by that poem's complex framing-devices. And in a poem by Felicia Hemans addressed 'To Wordsworth' (1823), death is prefigured, only to be triumphed over by the fulfilment of a Wordsworthian ideal of natural absorption:

> There is a strain to read among the hills,
> The old and full of voices—by the source
> Of some free stream, whose gladdening presence fills
> The solitude with sound; for in its course
> Even such is thy deep song, that seems a part
> Of those high scenes, a fountain from the heart.[68]

In this allegory of the reception process, Wordsworth becomes merged with the landscape that is the stuff of his poetry. His readers hear his language as though his spirit were at one with the mountain brooks and fountains he describes. He inhabits or haunts the various scenes in which his poetry is read—'the sunny garden bowers', the 'hearth where happy faces meet', the burial ground where 'shadows of dark solemn yews | Brood silently' (ll. 9, 13, 19–20)—and this absorption of his humanity into nature is accompanied by the revivification of his poetic powers in those of others, who 'sleep' awhile unseen, until they are touched into life by his writing.

A tribute such as this, to the enduring potency of Wordsworth's poetry, is written from deep within the ideology it upholds, its diction and cadences uncannily mirroring Wordsworth's own. At the same time, however, Hemans effects a subtle process of displacement in her figuration of a posterity which precedes death itself, and which ineluctibly

---

[68] ll. 1–6 in Breen (ed.), *Women Romantic Poets*, 147.

assimilates Wordsworth's poetic identity into his 'second selves'. Wordsworth becomes the type of a poetic genius so empathetic and protean that it vanishes into the forms it animates—so attenuated among its anonymous survivors that it relinquishes all resemblance to conventional 'fame'. In this feminized reconfiguration of genius, the terms of Worsdworth's longing for posterity are not so much obediently followed as quietly transliterated into the domestic ideology which underpins Hemans's poetic art. His poetry is given new meaning by the 'gentle [female] voice' in which it is read aloud—'sweet | As antique music, linked with household words' (l. 16)—and by the family values it serves to cherish: 'While in pleased murmurs woman's lip might move, | And the raised eye of childhood shine in love' (ll. 17–18). In this sentimentalized version of 'natural piety', we see the apotheosis of the Victorian Wordsworth, inspiring in his readers the 'glow of hope and courage high, | And steadfast faith's victorious constancy' (ll. 23–4).

Mourning the death of Felicia Hemans in 1838, Letitia Landon considered her afterlife as an instance in which the identities of writer and readers appeared to merge. Blurring the distinction between creation and reception, as in 'Sappho', she suggests that Hemans's readers became echoic extensions of her spirit both during her life and after her death: in this sense, she might be said to amplify the figure of Echo so that it describes both an immediate and an unmediated transference of power from writer to reader. Hemans is endowed with a capacity for procreative and omnipresent sympathy of the kind that she had figured in Wordsworth; and in this model of genius (comparable in some respects to Keats's definitions of 'negative capability' and 'the chameleon poet'), creative identity is both lost and found, dispersed and refracted:

> Thou hast been round us, like a viewless spirit,
> Known only by the music on the air;
> The leaf or flowers which thou hast named inherit
> A beauty known but from thy breathing there:
> For thou didst on them fling thy strong emotion,
> The likeness from itself the fond heart gave;
> As planets from afar look down on ocean,
> And give their own sweet image to the wave.[69]

---

[69] In Ashfield (ed.), *Romantic Women Poets*, i. 220.

Landon assures Hemans of immortality, not by explicitly invoking the
concept of authority—a chain of historical connections, linking the poet
backwards and forwards through time—but through the assertion that a
'genius' of poetry inhabits widely separated geographical and temporal
locations: 'A general bond of union is the poet, | By its immortal verse is
language known, | And for the sake of song do others know it— | One
glorious poet makes the world his own.' The unexpected gendering of
the poet as masculine in this context is underwritten by a distinct echo of
Shakespeare ('One touch of nature makes the whole world kin')[70]
drawing attention to the egalitarian model of poetic community which
Landon figures as her ideal, and for which Shakespeare himself is the
traditional example. Hemans—by analogy with Shakespeare, and on an
equal basis with him—is thought to have found her true reception a long
way from contemporary England, in which women are 'unkindly
treated— | By careless tongues and by ungenerous words'.

Landon's revisionary relationship with a high Romantic poetics of
reception is thus expressed, not by a straightforward reversal of its
temporal model, but by a careful adaptation of its rhetoric to her own
political agenda:

> And thou—how far thy gentle sway extended!
> The heart's sweet empire over land and sea;
> Many a stranger and far flower was blended
> In the soft wreath that glory bound for thee.
> The echoes of the Susquehanna's waters
> Paused in the pine-woods words of thine to hear;
> And to the wide Atlantic's younger daughters
> Thy name was lovely, and thy song was dear.[71]

In this distinctly feminized model of reception, the transhistorical
fraternity of readers figured by mainstream Romanticism is replaced
by a sisterhood of young American women, closely bonded to Hemans
through their shared allegiance to the ideology of empire. Distinct

[70] See Ulysses' speech in *Troilus and Cressida* III. iii. 175–9: 'One touch of nature makes the
whole world kin— | That all with one consent praise new-born gauds, | Though they are made
and moulded of things past, | And give to dust that is a little gilt | More laud than gilt
o'erdusted'. The echo is a strong one, and the discussion of value which it invokes is highly
pertinent to the issues surrounding the politics of reception in the early 19th cent. Landon's
tacit agreement with a high Romantic poetics of reception can be appreciated by placing
Ulysses' scornful rejection of novelty alongside that of Wordsworth, Coleridge, or Hazlitt: see
Ch. 7, below.
[71] In Ashfield (ed.), *Romantic Women Poets*, i. 220.

Romantic echoes can be heard in a rhetoric which associates the dispersal of poetic genius with the education and raising to consciousness of Americans; but Landon inflects this Romantic model of primitivism to include Susquehanna's waters and pinewoods, as well as its people, in an imperialist celebration of Hemans's communicative power.

This chapter has shown how women poets in the Romantic period contributed to an important shift in power relations, which operated not only across the writing–reading axis, but with respect to the relative importance of tradition and contemporaneity in poetic discourse. In women's writing generally at this time, a synchronic model of intertextual relations unsettled the mostly diachronic patterns which predominated in the male canonical tradition (and which provided the strongest defence of Romantic writers against the anxiety of reception). But in poetry especially, women entered into a vigorous critical dialogue with what Mikhael Bakhtin has seen as the dominant authoritative discourse, established by long tradition as poetic and male.[72] In examining a spectrum of political inflections and nuances in women's relationship with patriarchal ideology, we have seen how that ideology could be transformed and resisted, without necessarily being transcended. Poems such as 'The Glory of the Heights', 'To Wordsworth', and 'Felicia Hemans' serve as a reminder of the tenacious adaptability of Romantic ideology to readers of various political persuasions, including women readers who were far from servile in their theories and practices of echoic reading.

---

[72] See *The Dialogic Imagination*, ed. Michael Holquist, trans. Caryl Emerson and Michael Holquist (Austin, Tex.: University of Texas Press, 1981).

CHAPTER 7

'One Power with a Double Aspect': The Formation of a System of Defences

If there be any antidote to that restless craving for the wonders of the day, which in conjunction with the appetite for publicity is spreading like an efflorescence on the surface of our national character... that antidote must be sought for in the collation of the present with the past, in the habit of thoughtfully assimilating the events of our own age to those of the time before us.

Coleridge, *The Statesman's Manual,* 1816

Damn the age; I will write for Antiquity!

Charles Lamb, Letter, January 1829

I. THE PAST, POSTERITY, AND ORIGINAL GENIUS

'We shall often find that not only the best, but the most individual parts of [a writer's] work, may be those in which the dead poets, his ancestors, assert their immortality most vigorously'.[1] So T. S. Eliot claimed, forty years before *The Anxiety of Influence*, in a startling anticipation of Bloom's 'apophrades'—the sixth revisionary ratio, which ensures the return of the dead.[2] Eliot's doctrine of the writer's impersonality seems a strange place for the idea of individuality to surface, as it does once again, when Eliot claims that the 'continual self-sacrifice', the

---

[1] 'Tradition and the Individual Talent', in *Selected Essays* (London: Faber and Faber, 1932), 14. For a parallel in Geoffrey Hartman's writing, consider the following sentence: 'The presence of greatness is what matters, a beforeness which makes readers, like poets, see for a moment nothing but one master-spirit'; 'War in Heaven: A Review of Harold Bloom's *The Anxiety of Influence: A Theory of Poetry*', in *The Fate of Reading* (Chicago: University of Chicago Press, 1975), 51.

[2] See *The Anxiety of Influence: A Theory of Poetry* (London: Oxford University Press, 1973), 15–16.

'continual extinction of personality' which writing involves is recuperated in the larger collective identity of tradition. The 'historical
sense', Eliot argues (sounding for all the world like Wordsworth or
Shelley), 'involves a perception, not only of the pastness of the past,
but of its presence; [it] compels a man to write not merely with his own
generation in his bones, but with a feeling that the whole of the literature
of Europe from Homer and within it the whole of the literature of his
own country has a simultaneous existence and composes a simultaneous
order.'[3] In this invocation of a canon that is both diachronic and
synchronic, temporality itself seems suspended. The possibility of a
life in posterity is both realized and perpetuated in Eliot's tribute to
past authors.

The notion of an identity which discovers itself in binding the present
to the past, and which can be confirmed in writing, goes back a long way
further than Eliot, into the Romantic tradition he claimed to disown.
Towards the end of the eighteenth century it played an important part in
reconciling two quite different systems of aesthetic value. While there
still survived the neoclassical assumption that authority is tradition, this
was contested, from the mid-eighteenth century onward, by a new and
urgent pressure to be innovative—to produce what Edward Young
called 'original composition'. 'The man possessed of original genius
[has] sole property of [his works]' wrote Young in 1759; 'which Property alone can confer the noble title of an *Author*; that is, of one who
thinks and *composes*; while other invaders of the Press, how voluminous,
and learned soever . . . only *read* and *write*.'[4] To claim the credentials of
original genius—and thereby to distinguish themselves from scribblers—authors must enter into a spirit of competition with their contemporaries and precursors: 'What glory to come near, what glory to
reach, what glory (presumptuous thought!) to surpass, our Predecessors!'[5] So influential was Young's essay (and so accurately did he reflect
the spirit of the age, blending what Mark Rose has called 'the liberal
theory of property' with 'the eighteenth-century discourse of original
genius')[6] that in 1770, when he published his 'Life of Milton', Johnson
could assert 'The highest praise of genius is original invention' without

---

[3] 'Tradition and the Individual Talent', 17, 14.

[4] *Conjectures on Original Composition in a Letter to the Author of Sir Charles Grandison* (London: A.
Millar and R. and R. Dodsley, 1759), 54.

[5] Ibid. 23.

[6] *Authors and Owners: The Invention of Copyright* (Cambridge, Mass.: Harvard University Press,
1993), 6.

any thought of being challenged.[7] At the turn of the century—by which time the cult of originality had gathered yet further momentum— 'invention' was widely regarded as a prerequisite for artistic success: 'An artist should enter into a competition with his original', wrote Joshua Reynolds in the sixth of his Discourses, 'and endeavour to improve what he is appropriating to his own work'.[8] Moreover, since no less was at stake than the author's claim to ownership of his own ideas, originality had acquired commercial value in a capitalist culture. This fact was humorously exposed by Blake, in one of his annotations to Reynolds's *Works*:

When a Man talks of Acquiring Invention, & of learning how to produce Original Conception, he must be expected to be call'd a Fool by Men of Understanding; but such a Hired Knave cares not for the Few. His Eye is on the Many, or, rather, on the Money.[9]

'Originality' and 'invention' had always been terms more readily applicable to advances in science than in the arts, however. This meant that with the burgeoning of scientific entrepreneurialism and utility during the industrial revolution, promoters of the arts began to come under attack as parasites—repetitious purveyors, as Peacock whimsically put it, of 'disjointed relics of tradition and fragments of second-hand observation'; 'wasters of [their] own time and [robbers] of that of others'.[10] As Schiller lamented, in his *Aesthetic Letters*, 'Utility is the great idol of our age, to which all powers are in thrall and to which all talent must pay homage. Weighed in this crude balance, the insubstantial merits of art scarce tip the scale, and, bereft of all encouragement, she shuns the noisy market-place of our century'.[11] Sharing a similar sense of beleaguered resistance to the cultural and economic climate of their day, English Romantic writers found themselves in an ambivalent relation towards the asset called 'originality', on which they depended for their livelihood, self-esteem, and lasting reputation, but which appeared complicit with the commodification of reading and writing they resented. In these

---

[7] *Johnson's Lives of the Most Eminent Poets*, ed. George Birkbeck Hill (3 vols.: New York: Octagon, 1967), i. 194; cited in Rose, *Authors and Owners*, 6.

[8] *Discourses on Art*, ed. Robert R. Wark (San Marino, Calif.: The Huntington Library, 1959), 107.

[9] Annotations to vol. i of Joshua Reynolds's *Works*, in *The Complete Writings of William Blake*, ed. Geoffrey Keynes (London: Oxford University Press, 1966), 469.

[10] Peacock *Works*, viii. 20, 22.

[11] *Aesthetic Letters*, ii. 6–7; cited in Martha Woodmansee, *The Author, Art, and the Market: Rereading the History of Aesthetics* (New York: Columbia University Press, 1994), 85–6.

circumstances, the best defence of the arts was not by way of similarity with science (a route adopted by Wordsworth, somewhat defiantly, in his revisions to the *Lyrical Ballads*, 1802), but by way of difference, as Hazlitt found when he explained 'Why the Arts are not Progressive' in 1814, and as De Quincey rediscovered in his much later essay contrasting the 'Literature of Knowledge' with the 'Literature of Power'. '[I]t is the grandeur of all truth which *can* occupy a very high place in human interests', De Quincey claimed, 'that it is never absolutely novel to the meanest of minds: it exists eternally by way of germ or latent principle in the lowest as in the highest, needing to be developed, but never to be planted.'[12]

The spiritualization of authorship as 'genius' (accompanied by the separation between literary originality and other forms of invention in the domains of science and manufacture) became a central feature of the Romantic movement. It ensured that, although writers were under pressure to be considered merely as commodity producers, they also acquired the status of what Mark Rose has called 'mystified figure[s] of special authority'—the 'aristocrats of productive society'.[13] This conception of genius was implicitly invoked by Wordsworth when he claimed that its 'only infallible sign' in the fine arts was 'the widening the sphere of human sensibility, for the delight, honour, and benefit of human nature':

Genius is the introduction of a new element into the intellectual universe: or, if that be not allowed, it is the application of powers to objects on which they had not before been exercised, or the employment of them in such a manner as to produce effects hitherto unknown.[14]

The wavering in his sentence ('or if that be not allowed') suggests the difficulty of defining an anti-utilitarian model of genius, and thus distinguishing what is original because it is of lasting significance and benefit from what is merely new. Rescinding his earlier claims for the compatibility between science and the arts, Wordsworth asserted in 1838 that 'the analogy, which has been elsewhere much dwelt upon, between literary property and mechanical inventions and chemical discoveries . . . is, as might be shown in a few words, altogether fallacious.'[15]

[12]   'The Poetry of Pope', in Masson, xi. 55.   [13] *Authors and Owners*, 74.
[14]   'Essay Supplementary to the Preface', in *Wordsworth Prose*, iii. 82.
[15]   '*To the Editor of the Kendal Mercury*' (12 Apr. 1838), in *Wordsworth Prose*, iii. 312.

'Surely in an age when the smallest contribution to science is duly estimated, and useful knowledge not only held in honour but diffused, poetry ought not to be despised?'[16] These are the words with which John Wilson, as late as 1831, challenged utilitarian culture. The tones of aggrieved indignation are characteristic of a certain kind of rhetoric which arose in the 1770s and survived to the 1850s, or even longer. Isaac D'Israeli's *Essay on the Manners and Genius of the Literary Character* (first published in 1795, and enlarged in subsequent editions, the last being in 1881) provides an insight into the changing conditions under which the concept of genius came to play its crucial role in the formation of this distinctively Romantic rhetoric. In the first edition of the essay, his protest against society's treatment of authors is directed at no one in particular. The low esteem in which authors were held was the inevitable consequence, as he saw it, of the diffusion of knowledge, which placed the knowledgeable in a less and less revered position: 'Since, with incessant industry, volumes have multiplied, and their prices rendered them accessible to the lowest artisans, the literary character has gradually fallen into disrepute', he lamented;

Men of letters, in our country resemble 'Houseless wanderers,' scattered and solitary, disunited and languid; whose talents are frequently unknown to their companions, and by the inertness of an unhappy situation, often unperceived by themselves.[17]

By the 1846 edition, D'Israeli had a much more clearly defined target of attack in the spirit of utilitarianism: 'A new race of jargonists', he wrote, 'the barbarous metaphysicians of political economy, have struck at the essential existence of the productions of genius in literature and art; for, appreciating them by their own standard, they have miserably degraded the professors.'[18] The revisions to this book spanned the period associated with the Romantic movement, and demonstrate the steadily strengthening ideology which gave it the power to survive.

D'Israeli's ambition was to redeem the status of men of letters, and rescue them from oblivion. He saw authors as, potentially, the agents of public transformation, whose originality was to be measured by their effects on those who read them. Adapting his message to the spirit of the

---

[16] 'An Hour's Talk about Poetry', in *Recreations of Christopher North* (3 vols., Edinburgh and London: William Blackwood), i. 321.

[17] *An Essay on the Manners and Genius of the Literary Character* (London: T. Cadell and W. Davies, 1795), 2.

[18] *Literary Character of Men of Genius* (London: Frederick Wark and Co., 1846), 15.

age, he defined an author's contribution to society in terms of its usefulness:

An author sometimes appears, who gives a new direction to the national character. In mechanics, no impulsion, from a single hand, can communicate to a body the force of eternal movement. In morals it is different; for there an individual power can for ever endow with action the TRUTH it impels. These are the few authors who form revolutions, not, perhaps in the sublime sciences, which are reserved for the contemplation of a few, but in that happier knowledge which is of daily use, and addressed to those who most want instruction.[19]

The author's influence was greater—more valuable because more spiritual—than that of the scientist or inventor. In redefining utility in terms of moral enlightenment, D'Israeli's defence of the man of letters as hero anticipated Shelley's belief in poets as the 'unackowledged legislators' of humankind: 'What has been long meditated in the silence of the study', he prophesied, 'will one day resound in the aweful voice of public opinion' (p. 176). Crucially, however, he did not identify this transformative influence as the property of poets alone. Among the great figures of his age he included the critics and journalists who were his own role models:

These authors are not a Newton and a Locke; but an Addison and a Fontanelle ... The Spectators introduced literature and morals in the nation; the young, the gay, and the fair, who flew from the terrific form of a folio, were attracted by the light graces of a fugitive page. Since that happy moment the diffusion of taste, and the curiosity of knowledge, have produced readers who are now enabled to discern the shades of elegance; to appreciate compositions of genius; and to adjust the merits of ingenious competitors by the scale of philosophical taste. We have become a reading, and of course a critical nation. (p. 167)

When this essay first appeared, the rivalry between poetry and prose had not yet become the focus for heated debate, as it was to do in the second decade of the nineteenth century. D'Israeli's claims for the prose writer represented one of the earliest attempts to redeem the critic's downtrodden status alongside that of the poet, and to envisage a republic of letters in which the gentleman scholar might play an important role. His association of 'genius' and 'originality' with figures such as Addison was a significant blow against utilitarian culture, and one which critics such

---

[19] *Essay on the Manners and Genius of the Literary Character*, 166–7. Page refs. will be given in the text.

as Hazlitt would later amplify when making their own claims for the public role of writers and intellectuals.

D'Israeli attempted to give the ideal of a republic of letters a practical shape by envisaging a literary academy. Its function (modelled on that of the French Academy) would be to foster the diffusion of taste and learning. '[T]he taste of every associate would become more brilliant', D'Israeli urged, 'because it would continually receive the attrition and contact...of the finest understandings in the nation....In this hive of literary bees, no indolent member should remain a member; all must be animation, all must be labour' (pp. 205–6, 207). A national institution to support authors and promote their influence was never, in practice, implemented in D'Israeli's lifetime. But it persisted as an ideal towards which many Romantic writers aspired; and in some ways their habits of intertextuality and canon-formation came to perform its function.

II. COPYRIGHT AND THE PARADOX OF ROMANTIC AUTHORSHIP

If genius was the linchpin of a Romantic system of defences designed to give authors a special and mysterious importance, copyright was the mechanism which secured genius against plagiarism and piracy. Mark Rose, tracing 'the simultaneous emergence in legal discourse of the proprietary author and the literary work' has rightly claimed that 'like the twin suns of a binary star locked in orbit' these concepts 'define the center of the modern literary system'.[20] They answered the growing need of writers to establish ownership of the products of their labour, but the discourse surrounding them was characterized by a repugnance with the consumer society: 'there has always appeared to me, something monstrous in the existing relation between Author & Bookseller or Publisher, as regards remuneration' wrote one of Wordsworth's friends, in support of the poet's campaign for the extension of copyright: '...a positive reversing of the natural order of things, as we find it obtains in all matters else—a subservience (pro tanto) of the spiritual to the material'.[21] Copyright, 'the practice of securing marketable rights in texts that are treated as commodities'[22] bore witness to the reluctant determination with which writers negotiated their own value in a society

---

[20] *Authors and Owners*, 91.   [21] *Wordsworth Prose*, iii. 317.
[22] Rose, *Authors and Owners*, 3.

by which they were alienated, and at every level its rhetoric was riddled with paradox and ambivalence.

The plea that authors had a right, as Thomas Noon Talfourd puts it, to derive 'solid benefits from that which springs solely from within'[23] encountered resistance not only from those who placed a higher premium on utility than on culture, but from those attached to a more traditional understanding of the author's function. Samuel Johnson, espousing a communitarian ideal, had argued that 'For the general good of the world...whatever valuable work has once been created by an authour, and issued out by him, should be understood as no longer in his power, but as belonging to the publick'. According to what was essentially an economy of gift-exchange, the writer handed over the ownership of his ideas the moment he expressed them, and with them all right to intervene in the advancement of learning which was brought about by their diffusion: 'no book, however useful could be universally diffused amongst mankind, should the proprietor take it into his head to restrain its circulation'.[24] This argument provided the basis for Lord Camden's claim that 'Science and Learning are in their Nature *publici Juris*, and they ought to be as free and general as Air or Water'. Authors and inventors were 'those sublime Spirits, who share the Ray of Divinity which we call Genius' and must not keep to themselves 'that Instruction which Heaven meant for universal Benefit'.[25]

Any attempt to plead the writer's cause on the strength of his genius ran the danger of playing into the hands of those who exalted writers 'so high in the Regions of Speculation, that they should be above all other worldly inducements'[26] while at the same time fuelling a growing material grievance with respect to their undervaluation. By the same token, once the notion of genius had been invoked, the difficulty of arguing that ideas were a species of property was that they 'have no bounds, or marks whatever, nothing that is capable of a visible possession, nothing that can sustain any one of the qualities or incidents of property. Their whole existence is in the mind alone...safe and invulnerable, from their own immateriality.'[27] It was to resolve a perceived contradiction

---

[23] *Speech of Sergeant Talfourd on Literary Property* (18 May 1837) (London: Sherwood and Co., 1837), 3.

[24] Boswell reports that Johnson said this in 1773. See Rose, *Authors and Owners*, 85.

[25] Quoted in Rose, *Authors and Owners*, 104.

[26] James Ralph, *The Case of Authors by Profession or Trade. Stated with regard to Booksellers, the Stage, and the Public, No Matter by Whom* (London: R. Griffiths, 1758), 59–60.

[27] Quoted in Rose, *Authors and Owners*, 86–7.

between the immateriality of genius and its status as a commodity that metaphors of landed property, of inheritance, and of paternity proved invaluable. Copyright up till the reign of Queen Anne had been the subject of family settlements, and it was with the intention of restoring this ancient (and only recently suspended) tradition that a number of writers argued—along strongly Burkean lines—that copyright should pass from father to son. Such metaphors survived in the Romantic discourse of genius and originality as reminders of the historical origins of the modern idea of authorship. In a cultural climate where the author expressed disdain for the commodification of literature, they performed the important function of moving his claim to value away from the market place and back into the private domain of the family.

Wordsworth's argument for perpetual copyright, which began to formulate itself as early as 1808, grew out of an indignation with the marginalized and undervalued status of the author. But it was marked by an equally strong concern to distinguish works of genius from commodities by establishing their importance for posterity:

The law as it now stands merely consults the interest of the useful drudges in Literature, or of flimsy and shallow writers, whose works are upon a level with the taste and knowledge of the age; while men of real power, who go before their age, are deprived of all hope of their families being benefited by their exertions.[28]

Paradoxically, the author's removal from temporality demonstrated his detachment from economic concerns; but the posthumous recognition of his value was nonetheless measured in terms of whether or not his family benefited financially from his success. Laying claim to what Milton called the 'human right, which commands that every author should have the property of his own work reserved to him after death, as well as the living',[29] Wordsworth's 1838 letter *To the Editor of the Kendal Mercury* argued that the denial of perpetual copyright violated this fundamental right, 'by leaving that species of property which has the highest claim to protection, with the least share of it'.[30]

---

[28] Wordsworth to Richard Sharp, 27 Sept. 1808 (*MY* i. 266). Wordsworth here anticipates the argument later used in his 'Essay Supplementary to the Preface' (1815) to imply that his own fame, like Milton's, will arrive in posterity. He points to Hartley's *Observations on Man* and Milton's minor poems as examples of works that slept for a long time 'in almost entire oblivion'.

[29] *John Milton: Complete Poems and Major Prose* (Indianapolis: Odyssey, 1957), 794; quoted by Rose, *Authors and Owners*, 30.

[30] The Law of Copyright. Mr Wordsworth to Sergeant Talfourd, M.P. (18 Apr. 1838). In *Wordsworth Prose*, iii. 312.

Despite detecting the underlying irony of a culture that promulgated spiritual rather than material rewards for literary achievement (thus justifying its neglect of writers in terms of higher ideals), Wordsworth used the Romantic concept of genius to argue that the very immateriality of ideas was what entitled them to protection. According to this argument, genius did not in any respect diminish the author's 'right in perpetuity' which 'descends to his heirs, and is transferable to those to whom he or they may assign it'.[31] Indeed, the beauty of invoking genius in this context was that it allowed a refutation of the Johnsonian argument that 'by giving his thoughts to the world, an author abandons all right to consider the vehicle as private property'.[32] On the contrary, by virtue of the author's discursive potential—his status as the originator of ideas that might eventually, in Johnson's words, be 'universally diffused amongst mankind'—his works were due the highest possible estimation.

III. THE TRANSCENDENCE OF POPULARITY

In the context of defensiveness—of the necessity to find a place for the arts that was unthreatened by utilitarianism—an aesthetic emerged which transcended economics, claiming for the 'literature of power' a status which was enduring while it was not yet recognized. 'It seems the fate of all originality of thinking to be immediately opposed', D'Israeli complained: 'a contemporary is not prepared for its comprehension, and too often cautiously avoids it, from the prudential motive which turns away from a new and solitary path.... Men of genius produce their usefulness in privacy, but it may not be of immediate application, and is often undervalued by their own generation'.[33] 'We think it is clear that Genius has essentially nothing to do with what is called popularity', wrote John Hamilton Reynolds, in his essay 'On Popular Poetry' (1816)—'no more than gold in its native bed has to do with a Bank note in a clerk's bill-book'. And he went on to draw an ironic analogy between gold bullion and genius, both of them undergoing devaluation at a time when paper currency circulated in excess:

---

[31] The Law of Copyright. Mr Wordsworth to Sergeant Talfourd, M.P. (18 Apr. 1839), in *Wordsworth Prose*, iii. 313.

[32] Ibid.

[33] *Literary Character* (1846), 74.

Paper and Gold, as we have found, in our time, cannot circulate together; that is to say, if the first fixes the standard of value in the public estimation. The same may be affirmed of Popularity and Genius:—the latter must be either withdrawn or debased, when it is not allowed to pass but according to the current *par* of the former.[34]

Making a clear equation between vulgarity, popular taste, and mass-reading audiences, Reynolds advocated a traditionalist valuation of past literature, repudiating anything that smacked of 'nouveau riche' literary taste. In his view, intrinsic worth was everywhere sacrificed—either to utility or to fashion—when the wider distribution of literature became the sole criterion of its success:

The Paper system has been productive of facilities and distributions: it has given importance to the mass: it has put means in the hands of the many:—it has spread country-houses and shooting-boxes over the face of the country, and filled roads with curricles and gigs. But in the mean time, moated castles and coaches and six have vanished. So Magazines have pushed Epics from their stools and shelves.[35]

Sarcastic interventions from critics such as Francis Jeffrey, pinpointing the essentially defensive nature of an unworldly Romantic aesthetic, sought to reassert the economic groundedness of literature, its collusion with the laws of supply and demand. 'Now, the fame of a poet is popular, or nothing', he announced tersely, in the review of Campbell's *British Poets* which appeared in the March 1819 issue of the *Edinburgh Review.*

Present popularity, whatever disappointed writers may say, is, after all, the only safe presage of future glory;—and it is really as unlikely that good poetry should be produced in any quantity where it is not relished, as that cloth should be manufactured and thrust into the market, of a pattern and fashion for which there is no demand.[36]

Jeffrey thus lent both his own authority, and that of the *Edinburgh*, to a theory of art that, as Martha Woodmansee puts it, 'affirms art's complete integration into an economy in which the value of an object is a function of its utility to consumers who cannot be wrong—except by consuming

---

[34] *Reynolds Prose*, 71.

[35] Ibid.

[36] Jeffrey, reviewing Campbell's *Specimens of the British Poets*, is here taking the opportunity to refute Wordsworth's argument in the 'Essay Supplementary to the Preface' of 1815. See *Edinburgh Review* (31 Mar. 1819), 470, 466–7.

too little'.[37] In much the same way, Peacock argued that the prevailing tastes of readers determine the market for authors:

Milton would be forthcoming if he were wanted; but in our time Milton was not wanted, and Walter Scott was. We do not agree with the doctrine implied in Wordsworth's sonnet ['Milton! thou shouldst be living at this hour']. England would have been the better for him, if England would have attended to him, but England would not have attended to him if she had had him'.[38]

The Lake Poets' avant-garde construction of genius met with a similarly sceptical response from John Wilson. He insisted on the importance of popular writers, whose greatness was recognized by the age in which they lived. 'An Hour's Talk about Poetry' celebrated the extraordinary achievement of contemporary writers such as Scott, Burns, Moore, and Bloomfield. But it was Thomson, a poet belonging to the immediately pre-Romantic era, whom Wilson saw as transcending time altogether by his universal appeal:

to what era, pray, did Thomson belong? To none. Thomson had no precursor—and till Cowper no follower. He effulged all at once sunlike—like Scotland's storm-loving, mist enamoured sun.[39]

Wordsworth had slighted Thomson in his 'Essay Supplementary to the Preface' of 1815, so Wilson may be seen as throwing down the gauntlet, here, to the envious elitism which characterized the Lake School. Even D'Israeli, the period's most tenacious adherent to the concept of the genius as misunderstood, insisted that being misunderstood was not the only qualification for genius. Granted, 'The literary work which requires the greatest skill and difficulty, and the longest labour, is not commercially valued with that hasty, spurious novelty, for which the public taste is craving', so that popular works might be said to lose value, while those of 'nobler design' rose in 'value and rarity'.[40] But there were nonetheless writers who managed to combine popularity and commercial success with greatness: economic and aesthetic values were not mutually exclusive. On the prose side was Walter Scott, 'the finest genius of our times' and also 'the most delightful man'. And on the poetic side was Lord Byron, the figure D'Israeli looked up to throughout the latter part of his career, and identified as 'the great poetical genius of our times'.[41]

---

[37] *The Author, Art, and the Market*, 136.   [38] 'The Epicier', in *Peacock Works*, ix. 294.
[39] 'An Hour's Talk about Poetry', in *Recreations of Christopher North*, i. 327.
[40] *Literary Character* (1846), 195.   [41] Ibid. 100, 88.

The challenge posed by claims of this kind served only to increase the recalcitrance with which Romantic writers repudiated their place in the market economy. The power of literary works to endure became linked, for many English Romantics, not just with the refusal to be new, but with the failure to be popular; and past literary models were frequently used to support this transparently self-protective equation. Blake's truculent dismissal of the 'hired knave' who courts the many rather than the few, or Wordsworth's somewhat tortured defence of his hostile reception in the 'Essay Supplementary' of 1815, both involved a deference to Milton, who chose to address a 'fit audience, though few', and whose lasting fame was thought to have followed as a consequence.

When Reynolds (fresh from a reading of the 'Essay Supplementary') looked back in 1815 on the history of Wordsworth's reception, he repeated the tenor of Wordsworth's defensive self-justification. Lamenting the impercipience of those who had dismissed the *Lyrical Ballads* on its first appearance, he used an implicit parallel between Wordsworth and Milton to argue in favour of measuring poetry's value by criteria other than its immediate popularity:

'the million' saw nothing beyond the surface,—they could not reach where the calm philosophy rested;—these Poems, therefore, were violently opposed, and, as it would seem, overpowered. But they remained alive in the hearts and the minds of a few, and have been quietly gaining strength up to the present hour.[42]

With its traditional and topical resonances, the word 'few' acted as poetic shorthand for a complex teleological argument. The poet was hailed as a prophet by virtue of his audience's inability to comprehend him, and the delay in recognizing his greatness became a retrospective guarantee of his lasting importance. A complex variant of this argument appeared implicitly in one of Keats's poems. Keats did not wholly identify with high Romantic ideology, but held to his own version of the Miltonic belief that a select audience was preferable to a large one. In the fragmentary 'Ode to May', he wistfully claims an affinity with 'Bards who died content in pleasant sward, | Leaving great verse unto a little clan', and goes on to address them as role models:

> Oh, give me their old vigour, and unheard,
> Save of the quiet primrose and the span
> Of Heaven and few ears,

---

[42] Reynolds's essay, 'Mr Wordsworth's Poetry' was published in the *Champion* (9 Dec. 1815); rept. in *Reynolds Prose*, 25–7.

> Rounded by thee, my song should die away
>   Content as theirs,
> Rich in the simple worship of a day.[43]

On the surface, Keats appears to be repudiating the Romantic cult of posterity, in favour of the brief, ephemeral fame which belonged to ancient bards. But the word 'few' supplies a Miltonic intertext of longing for the permanent fame which is achieved by those who seek it least. Milton was frequently invoked, in this way, as the exemplar of an indifference to immediate fame which was rewarded by success in posterity. Meshing neatly with his own self-construction, this Miltonic trope became a stock feature in contemporary mythologies of reception, including those that found their way into pamphlets discussing the issue of copyright. It is clearly discernible for instance in the heroic rhetoric of Wordsworth's 1838 petition, addressed through Thomas Noon Talfourd to the House of Commons, which marked the culmination of his long campaign to have the duration of copyright extended. Living poets, Wordsworth argued, who had 'persevered in literary labour, less with the expectation of producing immediate or speedy effect, than with a view to interest and benefit society, though remotely, yet permanently' had a right to feel grievance at being denied their inalienable rights.[44]

In a deliberate flouting of popularity, Blake quoted the predictable passage from Milton in the advertisement to his 1809 exhibition. His habitual repudiation of commercial success—'Where any view of Money exists Art cannot be carried on'[45]—was founded on the perception that a culture dominated by material considerations adversely affected the quality of artistic production (*'he is Counted the Greatest Genius who can sell a Good for Nothing Commodity for a Great Price'*)[46] and that mediocrity replaced individuality when art was made to obey the laws of supply and demand: 'Commerce Cannot endure Individual Merit its insatiable Maw must be fed by What all can do Equally well at least it is so in England as I have found to my Cost these Forty years.'[47] Kurt Heinzelman has argued that, for Blake, 'the imagination cannot be

---

[43] 'Ode to May', ll. 9–14, in *Keats: The Complete Poems*, ed. Miriam Allott (London: Longman, 1970), 354.

[44] *Wordsworth Prose*, iii. 318.

[45] From Blake's engraving, *The Laocoon*, in *The Poetry and Prose of William Blake*, ed. David Erdman (4th edn. rev; New York: Doubleday, 1965), 272.

[46] 'Public Address', in *Notebook* (*Poetry and Prose*, ed. Erdman, 565).

[47] Ibid. 562.

priced by other measures than itself', and that he confronted 'economic reality and its myths' in order to demonstrate 'the imaginative fallacy of economic value'. True art, he believed, 'must be liberated from the money curse'.[48] Blake's radical agenda was paradoxically combined with an exclusive mode of address and production, such that it 'almost assures [his] alienation from the audience at large'.[49] Unlike Coleridge and Wordsworth, however, his disdain was not for the reading-public itself, but for systems of connoisseurship which diminished the faith of readers in their own imaginations, making them unable to distinguish between orginality and novelty. Blake refused to compromise vision in order to accommodate difficulties in comprehension: 'You say that I want somebody to Elucidate my Ideas', he wrote to Dr Trusler in 1799, 'But you ought to know that What is Grand is necessarily obscure to Weak men. That which can be made Explicit to the Idiot is not worth my care.'[50] Although the immediate effect of such disdain was to exclude the uncomprehending, Blake trusted in the longer view that his own poetry would become as widely received as the Bible itself. The Old Testament prophets were accordingly used in his poetry as examples of 'how to have an audience without being subjugated to it',[51] and of how to sacrifice immediate personal recognition for the sake of an enlightenment yet to come. Blake's 'Address to the Public' in *Jerusalem* alludes to Isaiah's dictum 'I cared not for consequences but wrote' in order to claim allegiance with the prophet's defiance; and his ideal model for the artist's relation to his readership was Jesus Christ himself, whose words 'Ye have not chosen me, but I have chosen you' summarized an elective construction of audience which this poet shared with Milton.[52]

Just as Christ, the Bible, and Milton (and Blake) were believed to have an ideal reception that was necessarily delayed until long after their deaths, so the prophetic stance of patience in adversity was used to transcend the desire for immediate success. This stance was adopted by writers of widely divergent political and religious perspectives, reminding us that ideological allegiances can sometimes cross over and merge

---

[48] *The Economics of the Imagination* (Amherst, Mass.: University of Massachusetts Press, 1980), 113, 121, 122.

[49] Morris Eaves, 'Romantic Expressive Theory and Blake's Idea of the Audience', *PMLA* 95/5 (1980), 784–801: 790.

[50] In *Poetry and Prose*, ed. Erdman, 676.

[51] Eaves, 'Romantic Expressive Theory', 793.

[52] See ibid. 792–4.

where 'the posthumous life of writing' is concerned.[53] Although Blake's radical Christianity was quite distinct from Byron's aristocratic bravado, the two extremes met in their anger with respect to contemporary culture. Both refused to suffer fools gladly, or to make concessions to a readership they perceived as unready to understand them; and both 'selected' their readers through the literary models and traditions to which they defensively turned. Byron's usual role model was Pope; but in the proud and moving address to his audience which concludes *The Prophecy of Dante*, he adopts both a prophetic stance and a Miltonic language of allusion to suggest his exile from a culture he himself disowned:

> I may not overleap the eternal bar
> Built up between us, and will die alone,
> Beholding, with the dark eye of a seer,
> The evil days to gifted souls foreshown,
> Foretelling them to those who will not hear,
> As in the old time, till the hour to come
> When Truth shall strike their eyes through many a tear,
> And make them own the Prophet in his tomb.[54]

D'Israeli, who saw Byron as the quintessential genius of the Romantic age, noticed how important the stance of exile was to his identity: 'the great poetical genius of our own times has openly alienated himself from the land of his brothers. He becomes immortal in the language of a people whom he would contemn'.[55] Figuring himself as bravely resigned to be misunderstood until posterity was ready to claim him, Byron's posturing was histrionic in a way that only Byron could be. But his strategies for self-recuperation alert us to a complex displacement of temporality which was more generally typical of Romantic aesthetics.

'At present we resist what is strange to us, as something that is inferior to us', wrote Reynolds, in an attempt to explain the time lag between an author's contemporary reception and his posthumous fame: 'we question it,—not ourselves. We like best what tries us least;—and he who comes prepared to address what we are, is sure to be received more favourably than he who would render us something we

---

[53] The phrase is Andrew Bennett's. See *Keats, Narrative and Audience: The Posthumous Life of Writing* (Cambridge: Cambridge University Press, 1994), 11.

[54] In Lord Byron, *The Complete Poetical Works*, ed. Jerome J. McGann (7 vols., 1980–93; Oxford: Clarendon Press, 1986), iv. 238–9.

[55] *Literary Character*, 88.

are not'.[56] Implicit in this claim is a Wordsworthian assumption that genius is unassimilable at the time it is produced, but that it can succeed in creating the conditions for its proper recognition at some future date. Through a kind of elective affinity, past writers were seen to have found their ideal audience in Blake, Wordsworth, Coleridge, Byron, Shelley, Keats, Hazlitt, Lamb, and De Quincey rather than among their contemporary readers. Temporality itself became displaced, in this model of reading, by a kind of prophetic hindsight which slipped backward and forward across the writing–reading axis. Chaucer, Shakespeare, and Milton were brought forward in time, to where they could be properly understood by their Romantic readers, just as the true understanding of Romantic writers was deferred to an undefined future. But they were also *held back* in the past, because only from that position could they anticipate their power to endure.

Milton 'could not read [*Paradise Lost*] as we do' claimed Hazlitt, 'with the weight of impression that a hundred years of admiration have added to it . . . with the sense of the number of editions it has passed through with still increasing reputation, with the tone of solidity, time-proof, which it has received from the breath of cold, envious maligners, with the sound which the voice of Fame has lent to every line of it!' (Howe, xii. 117). Turning back to earlier models of greatness performed the double function for Romantic writers of attesting to the worth of what was traditional and claiming kinship with what had endured. In thus laying claim to past authority as a constitutive ingredient in their own 'literature of power', these writers made a double bid for the importance of tradition. Their practices of allusion, which combined reading-as-collaboration with reading-as-competition, demonstrated at a practical level that the materials of great poetry were not original because they were new, but because they were lasting. And in the same way, their practices of rereading the great literature of the past (implicitly, of consolidating the canon, as though it were analogous to the Scriptures) resisted what Coleridge calls the 'frivolous craving for novelty', establishing that 'whatever is within us must be as old as the first dawn of human reason'.[57] Age-old procedures of literary echo and quotation

---

[56] *Reynolds Prose*, 75.

[57] *SM*, 25. Coleridge's primary intention was to revivify the Scriptures as evidence of the living power of the Logos. For a more ironic appeal to the reforming power of ancient ideas—made from the other side of the political spectrum, but with the same distaste for fashionable modernity—see Hazlitt's review of Owen's *A New View of Society*, published in the *Examiner* on 4 Aug. 1816 (Howe, vii. 99).

gained a new emphasis in the light of an emerging and steadily strength-ening Romantic aesthetic, which defended itself from the charge of repeating the past by claiming that an echoic affinity with past writers revealed the endurance of deep truths. Thus, 'To find no contradiction in the union of the old and new, to contemplate the ANCIENT OF DAYS, his words and works, with a feeling as fresh as if they were now first springing forth at his fiat—this characterizes the minds that feel the riddle of the world and may help to unravel it!' (*SM* 25).

IV. POSTHUMOUS FAME AND THE PLACE OF CRITICISM

If 'the old time' and 'the hour to come' were seen as twinned and mutually reflective images—what Coleridge called 'one power with a double aspect'—they invoked a poetic realm into which contemporan-eity could not enter, and where anxieties of reception were comfortingly resolved. As Hazlitt put it, in his lecture 'On the Living Poets' (1818),

Those minds . . . which are the most entitled to expect it, can best put up with the postponement of their claims to lasting fame. They can afford to wait. They are not afraid that truth and nature will ever wear out; will lose their gloss with novelty, or their effect with fashion. . . . They know that no applause, however loud and violent, can anticipate or over-rule the judgement of posterity; that the opinion of no one individual, nor of any one generation, can have the weight, the authority (to say nothing of the force of sympathy and prejudice), which must belong to that of successive generations. (Howe, v. 145)

Hazlitt placed an emphasis on the crucial role of taste in protecting and promoting genius; but despite his progressive politics, he consistently denied the possibility that taste might be either universal or capable of improvement. In 'Why the Arts are not Progressive', he took the sceptical view that 'The principle of universal suffrage . . . is by no means applicable to matters of taste, which can only be decided upon by the most refined understandings'. Since 'The diffusion of taste is not the same thing as the improvement of taste', public taste was no more capable of 'gradual improvement' than the arts themselves. This left the question of art's proper reception with critics, whose job was to cultivate standards on which the public could rely:

It may be objected, that the public taste is capable of gradual improvement, because, in the end, the public do justice to works of the greatest merit. This is a mistake. The reputation ultimately, and often slowly affixed to works of genius is stamped upon them by authority, not by popular consent or the common sense of the world. (Howe, iv. 164)

The primary function of the critic, in Hazlitt's view, was to recognize genius and to assist in making it accessible to the many. Neither the critic nor the author could determine its reception, however, since this was in the hands of time, and time—as 'On a Sun-Dial' reminds us—has its own ineluctible momentum: it 'moves on the same, whatever disparity there may be in our mode of keeping count of it, like true fame in spite of the cavils and contradictions of the critics' (Howe, xvii. 241).

Hazlitt's formulations of posterity, scattered over the whole range of his output, consistently levelled the functions of creativity and criticism by reminding artists, writers, critics, and journalists alike that popularity had little to do with lasting recognition: 'the multitude will agree with us, if we agree with them', he argued in his essay 'On Different Sorts of Fame' (1817). But their taste is notoriously unreliable:

accident, the caprice of fashion, the prejudice of the moment, may give a fleeting reputation; our only certain appeal, therefore, is to posterity; the voice of fame is alone the voice of truth. (Howe, iv. 94)

The words 'novelty', 'fashion', and 'popularity' were usually negative in Hazlitt's lexicon; and even though he had a more favourable view of the reading-public than some of his contemporaries, he had little faith in the public's powers of judgement. A 'new book', he complained, 'is the property, the prey of ephemeral criticism, which it darts triumphantly upon; there is a raw thin air of ignorance or uncertainty about it, not filled up by any recorded opinion; and curiosity, impertinence, and vanity rush eagerly into the vacuum' (Howe, xvii. 201–2).

For Hazlitt, 'No man is truly great, who is great only in his life-time'. Greatness is 'great power, producing great effects', as he put it in 'The Indian Jugglers' (1821); and since it is in the nature of greatness 'to propagate an idea of itself, as wave impels wave, circle without circle' (Howe, viii. 84, 86), subsequent generations alone are in a position to measure the extent and value of that generative power. If 'Popularity is neither fame nor greatness', and if 'The test of greatness is the page of history' (Howe, viii. 84), then just as the achievements of the past could only be truly valued by the present, so posterity must be the judge of modernity. This was why no real genius was able to be conscious of its powers:

Every man, in judging of himself, is his own contemporary. He may feel the gale of popularity, but he cannot know how long it will last. His opinion of himself wants distance, wants time, wants numbers, to set it off and confirm it. (Howe, ix. 117–18)

A contemporary audience is not without standards of taste whereby to measure its own works of art, however, because good criticism consists precisely in a deference to what Arnold called 'touchstones'. Here Hazlitt became evangelical. Taste, for him, was deeply and reverentially retrospective, and in this it revealed its affinity with genius:

Those who are to come after us and push us from the stage seem like upstarts and pretenders, that may be said to exist *in vacuo*, we know not upon what, except as they are blown up with vain and self conceit by their patrons among the moderns. But the ancients are true and *bona-fide* people, to whom we are bound by aggregate knowledge and filial ties, and in whom seen by the mellow light of history we feel our own existence doubled and our pride consoled, as we ruminate on the vestiges of the past. ('On a Sun-Dial', in Howe, xvii. 242)

The critic could valuably contribute to the present and future recognition of genius only by giving the past its due. In this sense, criticism fell in with the temporal logic which underpinned Romantic ideology. As Hazlitt put it, in the (thinly disguised) self-portrait of those who possess 'Good-Nature': 'They love excellence, and bow to fame, which is the shadow of it. Above all, they are anxious to see justice done to the dead, as the best encouragement to the living, and the lasting inheritance of future generations' (Howe, iv. 102).

In his two essays 'On the Catalogue Raisonné of the British Institution' (1817), envy and opposition to established fame are exposed as 'peculiar to the race of modern Artists', whose training in taste has taught them to set a higher premium on novelty than on genius: 'A picture is with them like the frame it is in, *as good as new*; and the best picture, that which was last painted' (Howe iv. 146). Hazlitt angrily repudiated the British Institution's envy-driven attempt to coerce the public into recognizing the superiority of modern British artists over Dutch and Flemish masters: 'do not the Academicians know, that it is a contradiction in terms, that a man should enjoy the advantages of posthumous fame in his lifetime?'

Most men cease to be of any consequence at all when they are dead; but it is the privilege of the man of genius to survive himself. But he cannot in the nature of things anticipate this privilege—because in all that appeals to the general intellect of mankind, this appeal is strengthened, as it spreads wider and is acknowledged. (Howe iv. 148)

Any attempt on the part of patronage to intervene in the reception of the fine arts was, in Hazlitt's view, doomed to failure. Deserved fame, of the kind posthumously 'enjoyed' by Rembrandt, could come only with the diffusion of taste for which the great works of the past were responsible. An author's place in the republic of letters was not foreseeable, 'because a man cannot unite in himself personally the suffrages of distant ages and nations; because popularity, a newspaper puff, cannot have the certainty of lasting fame; because it does not carry the same weight of sympathy with it; because it cannot have the same interest, the same refinement or grandeur' (Howe, iv. 148).

'It is only by a liberal education', Hazlitt declared, 'that we learn to feel respect for the past, or to take an interest in the future' (Howe, iv. 147). What this 'liberal education' taught was that art was not to be judged by its improvement on the past, but by its own intrinsic merit. To argue that the arts are 'progressive' was to put art on a par with mechanical or utilitarian products; just as to argue that art was a national resource (and therefore the focus of patriotic pride) was to demean its true worth:

Patriotism and the Fine Arts have nothing to do with one another—because patriotism relates to exclusive advantages, and the advantages of the Fine Arts are not exclusive, but communicable. . . . We do not consume the works of Art as articles of food, or clothing, or fuel; but we brood over their *idea*, which is accessible to all, and may be multiplied without end, 'with riches fineless.' (Howe, iv. 144)

In giving the arts a status that transcended economics, Hazlitt moved them closer to the elitist construction of poetry associated with Wordsworth or Coleridge than to the materialist reconfiguration offered by Peacock. But the democratic impulse underpinning his theory of art became clear at the point where he used the distinction between consumption and reception to promote the idea of art's incalculably diffusive effects:

Art subsists by communication, not by exclusion. The light of art, like that light of nature, shines on all alike; and its benefit, like that of the sun, is in being seen and felt. The spirit of art is not the spirit of trade: it is not a question between the grower or consumer of some perishable and personal commodity: but it is a question between human genius and human taste, how much the one can produce for the benefit of mankind, and how much the other can enjoy. It is 'the link of peaceful commerce 'twixt dividable shores.' To take from it this character is to take from it its best privilege, its humanity. (Howe, iv. 144)

Reviving the Johnsonian argument (which had been used against perpetual copyright) that genius is the 'property' of no one, Hazlitt shifted the focus of attention away from how art is possessed and protected to how it is diffused and appreciated, thus idealizing it as the harmonizing agent in a multinational community. 'How much mankind can enjoy' was thus given an equivalent weight to 'how much mankind can produce'; and both were valued in terms of the lasting benefit they were able to provide.

V. LITERARY CONSTITUTIONS: ANALOGUES FOR THE IMITATION–ORIGINALITY DEBATE IN POLITICAL DISCOURSE

That writers with such divergent political perspectives as Blake, D'Israeli, Wordsworth, Reynolds, Byron, De Quincey, and Hazlitt should have coincided in their need to distinguish between the depth value of 'genius' and the commodity value of novelty is a reminder that what Eagleton calls the 'ideology of the aesthetic' is a belief system which contains assorted elements, and may appear jumbled according to both contemporary and current judgements of what is or is not conservative. This becomes even more apparent if we look to contextualize the relationship between individual talent and tradition in the political terms most appropriate to English Romantic writers. Expanding individualism put the status of past authority under question at no time more urgently than in the immediate aftermath of the French Revolution, when Edmund Burke sought to defend the British monarchical system according to a patrilineal model of inherited wealth, backed up by organic notions of continuity:

the people of England well know, that the idea of inheritance furnishes a sure principle of conservation, and a sure principle of transmission;...Whatever advantages are obtained by a state proceeding on these maxims, are locked fast as in a sort of family settlement; grasped as in a kind of mortmain for ever. By a constitutional policy, working after the pattern of nature, we receive, we hold, we transmit our government and our privileges, in the same manner in which we enjoy and transmit our property and our lives.[58]

---

[58] *Reflections on the Revolution in France*, ed. with introd. Connor Cruise O'Brien (Harmondsworth, Middlesex: Penguin, 1968), 119–20.

Paine, however, in *The Rights of Man*, dismissed monarchy as no more than a 'silly thing', and the doctrine of precedents as a device on the part of reactionary government to prevent revolution. 'Governments now act as if they were afraid to awaken a single reflection in man', he asserted: 'They are softly leading him to the sepulchre of precedents, to deaden his faculties and call his attention from the scene of revolutions. They feel that he is arriving at knowledge faster than they wish, and their policy of precedents is the barometer of their fears.'[59]

This debate is suggestive of two alternative models of canon-formation, which have their reverberations both in Romantic writing, and in current critical positions. Poetic authority has frequently been seen along roughly Burkean lines as something to be 'received, retained, and prolonged in the same way that "We receive, we hold, we transmit ... our property and our lives" '[60] and even now, when the canon is being vigorously challenged and reconfigured, the cognate models of survival, legacy, and continuity occasionally recur. The tenacity of such models has not been ideologically straightforward, however. While a close connection between political and literary constitutions exists, in the political arena ideological factions are clearly demarcated, whereas in the domain of poetics it has always been harder to distinguish democratic from elitist ideals.

We can see this in the unexpected affiliations which sometimes occur between writers of opposite political persuasions. Hazlitt, for instance (whose unwavering support of the French Revolution lasted a lifetime) could occasionally sound like Burke, whose style he revered but whose post-1789 politics he found repugnant. In his essay 'On Reading New Books', he wrote:

About the time of the French Revolution, it was agreed that the world had hitherto been in its dotage, or its infancy; and that Mr. Godwin, Condorcet, and others were to begin a new race of men—a new epoch in society. ... The past was barren of interest—had neither thought nor object worthy to arrest our attention; and the future would be equally a senseless void, except as we projected ourselves and our theories into it. There is nothing I hate more than I do this exclusive, upstart spirit. ... By despising all that has preceded us, we teach others to despise ourselves. Where there is no established scale nor

---

[59] *The Thomas Paine Reader*, ed. Michael Foot and Isaac Kramnick (Harmondsworth, Middlesex: Penguin, 1987), 295.

[60] See David Bromwich's discussion in *A Choice of Inheritance: Self and Community from Edmund Burke to Robert Frost* (Cambridge, Mass.: Harvard University Press, 1989), ch. 3.

rooted faith in excellence, all superiority—our own as well as that of others—soon comes to the ground. (Howe, xvii. 209–10)

Coleridge, on the other hand, whom we might expect to have held a position similar to Burke's with respect to the value of inheritance in literary tradition, gave on one occcasion a quite opposite impression:

The first rule I have observed in notes on Milton and others is to take for granted that no man ever had a thought originate in his own mind; in consequence of which, if there is anything in a book like it before, it was certainly taken from that. And you may g⸂ on, particularly by their likenesses, to the time of the deluge, and at last it amounts to this: that no man had a thought but someone found it, and it has gone down as an heirloom which one is lucky enough to get and then another.[61]

Coleridge's choice of the word 'heirloom' carries a distinctly anti-Burkean resonance, as does the whole tenor of this passage if one reads it in the light of the Revolution debate, which still went on resonating as late as 1819. 'Those who lived a hundred or a thousand years ago', Paine had reasoned, 'were then moderns, as we are now':

They had *their* ancients, and those ancients had others, and we also shall be ancients in our turn. If the mere name of antiquity is to govern in the affairs of life, the people who are to live an hundred or thousand years hence, may as well take us for a precedent, as we make a precedent of those who lived an hundred or a thousand years ago. The fact is, that portions of antiquity, by proving everything, establish nothing. It is authority against authority all the way.[62]

Paine's repugnance for the view of history as endlessly reiterative found its echo in Coleridge's rejection of the 'heirloom' theory of tradition, which saw the individual writer as no more than the passive recipient of inherited wealth, denied the agency to transform or to renew. Underlying both passages there was a fear of repetition, which in Coleridge's case was combined with the need to justify literary activity—his own in particular—against the charge of plagiarism. This momentary affinity between Paine and Coleridge is a surprising but not unique example of extremes meeting. It does not of course move Coleridge onto the Paineite side of the political spectrum, but it reminds us that his own understanding of how the individual engages with tradition (like

---

[61] 'Philosophical Lectures at the Crown and Anchor', lecture 10 (1 Mar. 1819), as cited by J. A. Wittreich Jr (ed.), in *The Romantics on Milton: Formal Essays and Critical Asides* (Cleveland, Ohio, 1970), 238–9.

[62] *Thomas Paine Reader*, 215.

Hazlitt's and De Quincey's) must include agency and transformation alongside continuity. This might be described as a mediating position (rather than a position of neutrality), in which different political allegiances are borrowed for rhetorical purposes. Coleridge was particularly adept at such mediations.

The case of Godwin, on the other hand, offers a rather more striking example of political affiliations being cancelled out. Godwin's republicanism, his distaste for arbitrary authority, and his repudiation of all forms of hereditary property, put him firmly in Paine's camp so far as political sympathies were concerned. Predictably, too, in the majority of his public statements about the respective roles of reading and writing, he espoused a progressive view of literary history, in which the tyranny of tradition was overthrown, and a revisionary theory of reading, in which interpretation was seen as active and transformative. In his essay 'On Learning', for instance, he argued along lines that Milton had used in *Areopagitica* for a promiscuous programme of reading, on the grounds that good reading is never passive: 'if the systems we read, were always to remain in masses upon the mind, unconcocted and unaltered, undoubtedly in that case they would only deform it. But, if we read in a just spirit, perhaps we cannot read too much'.[63] Reading in a 'just spirit' is defined more closely when Godwin observes that 'A judicious reader will have a greater number of ideas that are his own passing through his mind, than of ideas presented to him by his author'—a claim which takes him very close to the hermeneutic first theorized on the Continent by Schleiermacher, which has recently been described by Tilottama Rajan as the 'supplement of reading'.

Unsurprisingly, this theory of supplementarity supports (and is supported by) a revisionary theory of history; and here the anti-Burkean resonances in Godwin's argument become more apparent. In his essay 'On English Style', he points to the constraining influence of past writers when observing 'how much the best authors are apt to be misled, by proposing to themselves injudicious models, and seeking rather to go back to what we were, than to go forward to higher and nobler improvements'.[64] He was more pointedly political, however, when it came to analysing a similar reliance on past authority in a historical context. In a sophisticated study of the relation between history and

---

[63] Essay XI in the *Enquirer*, repr. in *Godwin Works*, v. *Educational and Literary Writings*, ed. Pamela Clemit, 237.

[64] Essay XII in the *Enquirer*, repr. in *Godwin Works*, v. 286.

romance, Godwin argues that since all stories are inevitably biased, good historians must return to primary sources to make their own stories, rather than passively accept the biased stories that are relayed to them by previous historians. Godwin's accent falls on the independence of each person's reading of the past, as a refusal of inherited narratives; and the logical end point of this account of history is a narrative that cannot be passed down like Burkean property, but is unique to individual readers: 'each man', Godwin claims, 'instead of resting in the inventions of another, may invent his history for himself, and possess his creed as he possesses his property, single and incommunicable.'[65]

One very notable exception to these revisionary arguments arises, however, in Godwin's highly idiosyncratic 'Essay on Sepulchres' (1809), where tradition and memory are reconsidered as a means of preserving important values. Godwin, who had earlier argued in *Political Justice* that mankind would eventually progress so far as to surmount mortality altogether, here confronts the absolute certainty of death as an affront to human dignity. Lamenting 'how much of good perishes, when a great and excellent man dies', he complains about the capriciousness of 'the muse of monumental fame':

> we cut ourselves off from the inheritance of our ancestors; we seem to conspire from time to time to cancel old scores, and begin the affairs of the human species afresh.... ordinary tombstones are removed much after the manner, that the farmer removes the stubble of this year's crop that he may make room for the seed of the next.[66]

He then argues for a properly reverential attitude towards the dead, to be monitored by the systematic upkeep of plain and uncostly memorials, so that future generations will be able to commune directly with the spirit of the dead on the physical spot where their remains are to be found:

> while pyramids, and aqueducts, roads of the most substantial structure, and vast cities, shall perish, these simple land-marks, which any child might overthrow, shall be regarded as sacred, and remain undisturbed witnesses of the most extraordinary revolutions. (p. 26)

It is a deeply Burkean essay—saturated with the terror of futurity that gives Burke's *Reflections* their almost hysterical feel—but tempered by a

---

[65] 'On History and Romance', in *Godwin Works*, v. 300.

[66] 'Essay on Sepulchres: or, a proposal for erecting some memorial of the illustrious dead in all ages on the spot where their remains have been interred', in *Godwin Works*, vi. *Essays*, ed. Mark Philp, researcher Austin Gee, 8, 14.

Wordsworthian sense of the value of rootedness, and by an equally Wordsworthian sensitivity to the sacred properties of a particular spot of ground. 'Do not fear to remember too much'; Godwin pleads, 'only be on your guard not to forget any thing that is worthy to be remembered' (p. 28).

VI. CANON-FORMATION, CONNECTIVENESS, AND RECUPERATION

Godwin's proposal that 'by a simple and perhaps infallible means, we should paralyse the hand of Oblivion' (p. 22) reminds us that where death the leveller is concerned, strategies of self-preservation tended to cut across ideological commitments, uniting writers in the wish to find recuperative models of reading. A similar blurring of political boundaries was apparent in Romantic writing, wherever the acquisition and transmission of poetic power were figured as connectiveness. But these figures are different from the cases we have previously examined, in that they are historically *un*specific, and can be politicized with equal validity in both reactionary and progressive terms. Coleridge believed that 'The truly great | Have all one age, and from one visible space | Shed influence'. The products of genius were valued not just for themselves, but because they made audible 'a linkéd lay of Truth, | Of Truth profound a sweet continuous lay'.[67] Wordsworth, likewise, envisaged a line of poets, 'each with each | Connected in a mighty scheme of truth' (*Prelude (1805)*, xii. 301–2). And Shelley described 'that great poem, which all poets, like the co-operating thought of one great mind, have built up since the beginning of the world'.[68] Godwin, as we have seen, wrote about his need to commune not 'only with the generation of men that now happens to subsist', but with 'the Illustrious Dead of All Ages',[69] as though they were simultaneously present and alive; while John Hamilton Reynolds expressed a distinct preference for dead over living poets because 'The dead have become blended with, and spiritualized in, their poetry;—and they are no longer mortal men. They have passed into fame, and we can only hear their names echoing about the air-clad world, day after day,

---

[67] 'To William Wordsworth', ll. 51–2, 58–9.

[68] 'A Defence of Poetry', in *Shelley's Poetry and Prose*, selected and ed. Donald H. Reiman and Sharon B. Powers (New York: Norton, 1977), 493.

[69] 'Essay on Sepulchres', 22.

and for ever'.[70] Despite their very different political perspectives, these writers appear to have shared a notion of authority as both continuous and synchronic. Their overriding concern was with the preservation of poetic spirit—with defeating the curse of time.

When Coleridge paid homage to Wordsworth in his 'Hexameters', he did so by imagining a reverberating chain of echoes, which would prolong the poet's voice beyond his life:

> This be the meed, that thy song creates a thousand-fold echo!
> . . . .
> Each with a different tone, complete or in musical fragments—
> All have welcomed thy Voice, and receive and retain and prolong it![71]

The act of prolonging voice performed a cohesive function—in bridging past and present, and in assembling a fraternity of readers whose corporate ethos depended on prior authority. These readers, belonging to no specified time or place, could be imagined either as the family coterie that Wordsworth assembled around him, who read his poems in manuscript and responded intimately; or they could be envisaged as a hostile reading-public, grown suddenly receptive; or they could be projected into a deferred future, when the poet's fame would be safely assured. The advantage of voice, as a figure for this act of reception, was its materiality: preserving an illusion of connectiveness between poet and listener, it restored what De Certeau calls the 'murmur of vocal articulation' to the act of reading.

Something comparable in its defiant bodilyness occurs in Keats's extraordinary fragment poem, 'This Living Hand', which offers what Andrew Bennett describes as 'an exemplary expression of the posthumous life of writing'.[72] These lines do not imply a communitarian model of reading, but the figure of (apolitical) fraternity is once again strongly realized:

> This living hand, now warm and capable
> Of earnest grasping, would, if it were cold
> And in the icy silence of the tomb,
> So haunt thy days and chill thy dreaming nights
> That thou would wish thine own heart dry of blood
> So in my veins red life might stream again,

---

[70] *Reynolds Prose*, 232.   [71] 'Ad Vilmum Axiologum', ll. 1, 5–6.
[72] *Keats, Narrative and Audience*, 11.

> And thou be conscience-calmed. See here it is—
> I hold it towards you.[73]

Bennett draws attention, not only to the vivid and tactile immediacy of Keats's 'earnest grasp', but to the teasing paradox of the poet's survival beyond the 'icy silence of the tomb'. His resuscitation depends on the reader (and curiously, on the reader's conscience, his or her implicatedness in the poet's welfare); but it seems also to entail the reader's death, since a transfusion of blood into the body of the text must be taking place—as if literally, in the act of reading—to enable the poet to gesture thus with his 'living hand'. This act of recuperation, unlike Coleridge's, does not involve a continuity of voice—indeed it takes place in a deathly silence all its own; but it substitutes touch for voice as a more literalizing figure for the writer's 'hold' over his reader; and it makes the most arresting bid for intimacy imaginable in its metaphor of blood transfusion.

A less eerily private figure of connectiveness is to be found in 'Ode to a Nightingale', where Keats describes the immortality of the bird's song by way of a metaphor that moves in an opposite direction—backward, through a layered history of listeners, rather than forward, to a single implicated reader:

> No hungry generations tread thee down;
> The voice I hear this passing night was heard
> In ancient days by emperor and clown:
> Perhaps the self-same song that found a path
> Through the sad heart of Ruth, when, sick for home,
> She stood in tears amid the alien corn[74]

Marlon Ross, comparing Keats with Wordsworth, describes how the poet's desire at this point became 'not a uniquely self-addressing voice in the midst of an internalized nature, but a choir whose common desire enforces a sympathetic bond across generations and geography and social class'.[75] In Ruth, Keats constructed an eternalized figure of readerly sympathy: a figure whose sad receptiveness echoed his own, through centuries of history.

[73] The fragment was probably composed in Nov. 1819, and appears on a sheet containing stanza 51 of *The Cap and Bells*. Miriam Allott hypothesizes that it was intended for use in a possible future poem or play; and she compares it to a line from *The Fall of Hyperion*: 'When this warm scribe my hand is in the grave' (i. 18). See *Keats: Poems*, ed. Allott, 700–1.
[74] 'Ode to a Nightingale', ll. 62–7, in *Keats: Poems*, ed. Allott, 530.
[75] *The Contours of Masculine Desire: Romanticism and the Rise of Poetry* (Oxford: Oxford University Press, 1989), 174.

If the ideal of a sympathetic bond between author and reader was central to Romantic models of reception, so too was the concept of a corporate national identity; and these two different notions of connectiveness converged in ideas of canon-formation (and the practices of reading they encouraged) from the mid-eighteenth century onwards. As Greg Kucich has shown, the emergence of poetic miscellanies provided 'the earliest significant form of a national poetic canon',[76] but it was not until the 1770s, when the first multi-volume collections of British poetry appeared, that the reading-public were invited (by the structure and layout of volumes) to think about possible continuities between dead and living poets, or consciously to celebrate the traditions that the living upheld. Perhaps predictably, since the impulse behind these early anthologies was an antiquarian one, many of them failed to include the living alongside the dead. Francis Jeffrey, reviewing Campbell's *British Poets* for the *Edinburgh* in 1819, lamented that the anthologist's accent had fallen so much on the past. He could see the endearing piety of 'thus gathering up the ashes of reknown that has passed away', and of 'calling back the departed life for a transitory glow', but it seemed more pointful to concentrate on what was in danger of current neglect. Since Campbell's antiquarian endeavour was itself proof that 'the genius of a living Poet' could 'shed a fresh grace over the fading glories of so many of his departed brothers', was it not time to turn to the living?

We wish somebody would continue the work, by furnishing us with Specimens of our Living Poets. It would be more difficult, to be sure, and more dangerous; but, in some respects, it would also be more useful.... In point of courage and candour, we do not know anybody who would do it better than ourselves.... we should like nothing better than to suspend these periodical lucubrations, and furnish out a gallery of living bards, to match this exhibition of the departed.[77]

Jeffrey's ambition on behalf of the *Edinburgh* was never realized in the form of an anthology, although it bore fruit in the journal's critical remit, which was shared by journals with a similar political agenda. But as Annette Cafarelli has shown, the Johnsonian model of collective biography was widely used in the Romantic period.[78] John Scott's *Living Authors* series for the *London Magazine* and Leigh Hunt's *Sketches of the Living Poets* (1821) for the *Examiner* performed the same function with

---

[76] 'Gendering the Canons of Romanticism: Past and Present', *Wordsworth Circle*, 27/2 (Spring 1996), 96.

[77] *Edinburgh Review* (Mar. 1819), 496–7.

[78] See *Prose in the Age of Poets*, esp. 103, 129.

respect to living authors that was performed for the dead in Hazlitt's three narrative cycles on the progress of the arts: *The English Poets*, the *Comic Writers*, and *The Age of Elizabeth*. Group biographies, like anthologies, allowed national resemblances between authors to be configured unobtrusively, as well as openly celebrated.

Anthologies, though—unlike biographies—had the great virtue of allowing an author's voice to speak directly to the reader; and for this reason they played a crucial role, not just in constructing the canon as we know it, but in understanding the past as something that could be reconfigured in the present. Jeffrey likened the structure of Campbell's miscellany to a gallery, and the reader to a spectator viewing each successive component of the overall spectacle as part of a developing sequence:

the juxtaposition and arrangement of the pieces not only gives room for endless comparison and contrasts,—but displays, as it were in miniature, the whole of its wonderful progress, and sets before us, as in a great gallery of pictures, the whole course and history of the art, from its first rude and infant beginnings, to its maturity, and perhaps its decline.[79]

The gallery metaphor allowed Jeffrey to present literary history as something constructed by the act of reading, which took place either synchronically (through comparison or contrast) or diachronically (as part of an understanding of the progression–decline of civilization). This choice became a crucial one in the numerous discussions of canon-formation which occurred in the periodical press, many of them as responses to the publication of anthologies like Campbell's.

J. H. Reynolds, repudiating the idea of popular poetry in 1816, was able, because of the dissemination of such anthologies, to appeal to a widely shared ideal of national culture as a means of upholding normative standards of taste. Constructing a model of composite survival, he figured the great authors of the past as a continuous spirit that amalgamated with successive generations of readers:

The value of opinion as to the past is, that the taste has been created for all, or is professed by all as a matter of pride,—not on the frail and blind judgement of the multitude, but according to the dogmas of superior spirits who survive after the multitude has perished, and thus collectively joining their different eras, form a cloud of witnesses instructing us as to what has gone before us. [Past writers] fashion out their epochs, giving them their form and pressure,—and

[79] *Edinburgh Review* (Mar. 1819), 468.

the periods exist in our imaginations modelled according to the greatest minds they produced.[80]

The 'superior spirits who survive after the multitude has perished' were not only poets themselves, who by a process of natural selection found their way into anthologies (and thereby durable national canons); but also the readers who proved themselves fit to be their proper audience after a sufficient lapse of time. In a sequence of metaphorical slippages, Reynolds elided the difference between writers and their readers, as between the successive historical periods which produce them, his language becoming vague and idealistic in its evocation of 'a cloud of witnesses' whose function was to 'collectively join' the different eras over which they preside.

In Godwin's 'Of Choice in Reading'—where the ideal of a national canon is used to make extravagant claims on behalf of the permanent civilizing influence exerted by genius—the communicative potency of Britain's greatest poets is figured as a kind of intellectual contagion, 'passing from man to man', much as enthusiasm does in the radical discourse of the 1790s:

I cannot tell what I should have been, if Shakespear [*sic*] or Milton had not written. The poorest peasant in the remotest corner of England, is probably a different man from what he would have been but for these authors. Every man who is changed from what he was by the perusal of their works, communicates a portion of the inspiration all around him. It passes from man to man, till it influences the whole mass. I cannot tell that the wisest mandarin now living in China, is not indebted for part of his energy and sagacity to the writings of Milton and Shakespear, even though it should happen that he never heard of their names.[81]

In this fraternalist model of reception, genius is not so much the 'property' of an individual person or nation, as a diffusive spirit, available to all on an equal basis—even those unable to read. The proof of its permanence lies not in its attachment to a name or fame, but in its power to modify consciousness: 'Milton' and 'Shakespear' survive, then, by virtue of a discursive potential so extensive it passes into anonymity.

It seems to be the general tendency of Romantic rhetoric to move outward, from national, multinational, and international claims for the canon's significance to a vaguer, atemporal configuration of its power.

---

[80] 'Popular Poetry', in *Reynolds Prose*, 74.   [81] *Godwin Works*, v. 141.

The opening pages of D'Israeli's 1846 edition of *The Literary Character* triumphantly announced that the ideal of a 'republic of letters' had been realized in the spread of taste and enlightenment performed by authors of genius:

Diffused over enlightened Europe, an order of men has arisen, who, uninfluenced by the interests or the passions which give an impulse to the other classes of society, are connected by the secret links of congenial pursuits, and, insensibly to themselves, are combining in the same common labours, and participating in the same divided glory.... Such is the wide and the perpetual influence of this living intercourse of literary minds.[82]

As the essay develops, this European model is gradually displaced by a more ambitious construction of genius, in which the greatness of men of letters is imagined as a kind of family resemblance that transcends geographical/temporal location. Evoking the 'consanguinity of men of genius' whose 'genealogy may be traced among their own races', D'Israeli figures the canon as a family, spread to the four corners of the earth, and passing its genes down through the generations:

Men of genius in their different classes, living at distinct periods, or in remote countries, seem to reappear under another name; and in this manner there exists in the literary character an eternal transmigration. In the great march of the human intellect the same individual spirit seems still occupying the same place, and is still carrying on, with the same powers, his great work through a line of centuries.[83]

D'Israeli's earlier ideal of the republic of letters as a multinational community of collaborative equals is here replaced by an apolitical and transhistorical model of the canon, as a family of the elect. 'A father-spirit has many sons; and several of the great revolutions of man have been carried on by the secret creations of minds visibly operating on human affairs'.[84]

Similarly, the magnificent peroration with which Thomas Noon Talfourd concluded his case for copyright in 1837 envisaged the spread of intellectual power over the globe. Strongly resonating with echoes of both Burke and Godwin, his prose bespeaks its saturation in the rhetoric which, for half a century, had characterized the discourse of genius:

The great minds of our times have now an audience to impress far vaster than it entered into the minds of their predecessors to hope for—an audience increas-

---

[82] *Literary Character*, 11.   [83] Ibid. 276.   [84] Ibid. 277.

ing as population thickens in the cities of America, and spreads itself out through its long untrodden wilds—who speak our language, and who look at our old poets as their own immortal ancestry. And if thus our literature shall be theirs ... if the deeper woods which shall encircle the still-extending states of civilization shall be haunted with visions of beauty which our poets have created, let those who thus are softening the ruggedness of young society have some personal interest about which affection may gather; and at least let them be protected from those who would exhibit them mangled or corrupted to the new world of their admiring disciples.[85]

Talfourd's power to persuade his listeners was evidenced in the Act of Parliament which in 1837 extended copyright from twenty-eight to sixty years. Its persuasive force consisted in the ability to sustain alongside each other two contradictory claims to immortality on the poet's behalf. The curse of time was defeated on the one hand by realizing the value of poetry as a species of property that can be 'locked as in a family settlement, grasped in a kind of mortmain for ever'; and on the other hand by celebrating the immeasurable power it exerted over its audience.

This chapter has argued that the defence strategies that constitute Romantic ideology are visible both in the practices of individual writers, and in larger cultural and ideological trends. Just as the habit of reading aloud returned reception to its earlier manifestations (affirming a cohesive bond between performer and listener by appealing to oral customs that are deeply embedded in communal life); so the concepts of genius, originality, posterity, and canonicity functioned for Romantic writers as comforting symbols of transhistorical connectiveness with their ideal readers. The 'communion of shared echo, of participatory reflex' which Steiner sees as 'pertinent to the notion of canon' is absolutely central to high Romanticism and the work it has gone on performing.[86]

In Romantic models of influence, intertextuality, and canon-formation (as in the concept of genius which underwrites them), the curse of time is defeated by a habit of reading which looks for the underlying similarities between different epochs, discerning the spirit of continuity that unites them, and celebrating the amalgamation of individual authorial identities in a larger connective whole. The anthropological function of

---

[85] *Speech of Sergeant Talfourd on Literary Property*, 15–16.
[86] 'Critic/Reader', in Philip Davis (ed.), *Real Voices on Reading* (Houndmills, Basingstoke: Macmillan Press, 1997), 26.

these models is essentially totemic, in that they ward off the fear of death. Thus the notion of a corporate writing–reading identity provides reassurance that survival in some form or other will occur beyond the grave, in the same way that analogies of paternity and inheritance used in copyright discourse secure the author's 'property' through generations. If the defensiveness of these ideas consists, not in their straightforward allegiance to one or other of two opposed economic or political models, but in their appeal simultaneously to both, might this ingredient also account for the strength, resilience, and adaptability of 'Romantic Ideology'? What better way to find reassurance that authority will not be eroded by the encroaching power of the reader than by establishing each author in an authoritative chain, either stretching across nations and back through history, or gathered together in one place and time? And how better to ensure one's own survival among future communities of readers? It begins to become apparent, not only why a Romantic poetics of reception is so difficult to dislodge (if that is what we feel, as emancipated readers, we must do), but why any attempt to do so appears to be already anticipated in the chameleon rhetoric of Romanticism.

CHAPTER 8

The Terror of Futurity: Repetition, Identification, and Doubling

I. THE TEMPORALITY OF READING

In the opening of *The Prelude*, Book V, which ponders the transience of civilization in the face of overwhelming natural disasters, Wordsworth asks a question which had pressing relevance for the status of writing in an age of revolutions. If the authority of the past was brought under question—indeed, if time itself was reconfigured so as to cancel the past, as it had been by Jacobin propagandists when they invented the revolutionary calendar—then how could the printed book, as the cherished repository of human wisdom, hope to survive? 'Oh, why hath not the Mind | Some element to stamp her image on | In nature somewhat nearer to her own? | Why, gifted with such powers to send abroad | Her spirit, must it lodge in shrines so frail?' (*Prelude (1805)*, v. 44–8). In a nightmare vision of futurity, Wordsworth imagines 'the fleet waters of the drowning world' in pursuit of a figure who carries a stone and a shell—the first an emblem of mathematics, the other of poetry—twinned here as evidence of civilization's potential for progress, but also of the frailty of spiritual and intellectual achievements.[1] In this disturbing and disruptive dream sequence, we see something akin to what David Bromwich has described, with respect to Edmund Burke, as 'A horror of the thoughtless iconoclasm of revolution—the obliteration of all records, all monuments, all art without a plain use'.[2]

---

[1] See J. Hillis Miller, 'The Stone and the Shell: The Problem of Poetic Form in Wordsworth's Dream of the Arab', *Mouvements premiers: Études offertes a Georges Poulet* (Paris, 1972); and Jonathan Wordsworth, *William Wordsworth: The Borders of Vision* (Oxford: Clarendon Press, 1982), ch. 7.

[2] *A Choice of Inheritance: Self and Community from Edmund Burke to Robert Frost* (Cambridge, Mass.: Harvard University Press, 1989), 53.

De Quincey may have been attempting to answer a question similar to Wordsworth's when he wrote the densely allusive and technical passage in *Suspiria de Profundis* describing the historical circumstances under which 'palimpsests' came into being in the Middle Ages. Citing a contemporary paleographic authority, he hypothesizes that a long-continued shortage of vellum and parchment meant that materials carrying the records of ancient Greek civilization gradually rose so far in value as to be deemed more precious than the history they recorded. Chemicals were therefore (of necessity) invented to enable the ancient handwriting to be cleared away, and successive layers of superscription to take its place. Because of subsequent scientific discoveries, however, it became possible to counteract the effect of these chemicals, and to unravel each successive layer of superscription, back to the original. Our medieval ancestors obscured the past, De Quincey observes, 'but not so radically as to prevent us, their posterity, from *un*doing it. They expelled the handwriting sufficiently to leave a field for the new manuscript, and yet not sufficiently to make the traces of the elder manuscript irrecoverable for us.'[3]

The primary function performed by the palimpsest, in the developing narrative of *Suspiria*, is as a simile of the human mind, which is seen by analogy to accumulate apparently fleeting and accidental impressions, storing them as the indelible marks of its passage through life. In this sense, like the palimpsest, it may be deemed incapable of forgetting: 'What else than a natural and mighty palimpsest is the human brain?', De Quincey asks, after a typically elaborate digression: 'Such a palimpsest is my brain; such a palimpsest, O reader! is yours' (p. 144). This application of the figure of the palimpsest might be said to reassure Wordsworth, in Wordsworthian terms, that just as the printed book is paradoxically less 'valuable' than vellum or parchment (in that it records the finality of an author's thoughts, not their successive development), so the human mind has a permanent value which allows it to transcend the need for records and monuments. The palimpsest embodies the 'somewhat nearer to [our] own' which Wordsworth seeks, but not so nearly that it challenges the supremacy of mind itself. Human memory, not written records, is the guarantee of humanity's survival.

De Quincey is dealing, though, not just with the function of memory within individual consciousness, but with the collective memory of

---

[3] *Confessions of an English Opium Eater and Other Writings*, ed. with introd. Grevel Lindop (Oxford: Oxford University Press, 1989), 141. Page refs. will be given in the text.

tradition, as it is realized through successive generations. In this sense, he might be said to bring into conjunction one of the questions central to Romantic hermeneutics—namely, how the past can properly be read and understood from outside itself—with a question which proved central to a Romantic poetics of reception, namely, what value can be ascribed to works of art, under the changing conditions of successive generations of readers. Romantic hermeneutics, as formulated by Schleiermacher and his followers, placed a new emphasis on historicism—the necessity of understanding the past in its own terms, without projection or anachronism, through an awareness of the past's otherness or difference from the present.[4] The poetics of reception I outlined in Chapter 7, following a parallel but complicating trajectory, sought to transcend its dissatisfaction with contemporary culture by claiming that only after a lapse of time could works come to be properly valued. On both these fronts, Romanticism revealed its underlying preoccupation with the temporality of reading. For the rigorous hermeneuticist, temporality is both inevitable and necessary, in the sense that being in time is precisely what grounds one's own difference from predecessors, allowing readers to maintain a historical purchase on earlier writing. For a Romantic poetics of reception, however, there was a more discomforting possibility implicit in this relativistic model of history. What if the past was misunderstood and mis-valued by the present? Or, more worryingly still, what if posterity, instead of being a dependable haven, in which the writer's message was thankfully received, should itself prove indifferent both to the writing's intrinsic significance and to its lasting value?

In attempting to protect the fragility and contingency of writing from a time continuum that is forever effacing the past, De Quincey considers many of the preoccupations with which my previous chapter was concerned, redeploying some of the defence mechanisms we have so far considered. Indeed, a number of significant features in the complex

    [4] For a historical account of the context out of which Schleiermacher's hermeneutic project arose, see the introd. to *Hermeneutics: The Handwritten Manuscripts*, ed. Heinz Kimmerle, trans. James Duke and Jack Forstman (Missoula, Mont.: Scholars Press, 1977), esp. 2–14. For a more detailed discussion of the relation between biblical exegesis, philological methodology, and the science of linguistic understanding see Richard E. Palmer, *Hermeneutics: Interpretation Theory in Schleiermacher, Dilthey, Heidegger, and Gadamer* (Evanston, Ill.: 1969), 20–40. For the significance of the hermeneutic project to Romanticism, see Tilottama Rajan, *The Supplement of Reading: Figures of Understanding in Romantic Theory and Practice* (Ithaca, NY: Cornell University Press, 1990), esp. 41–61; and for a recent account of the role played by hermeneutics in the evolution of historicism, see Paul Hamilton, *Historicism* (London: Routledge, 1996).

and extended development of his simile allow us to read it as an allegory of Romantic anxieties of reception, in which Wordsworth's terror of futurity keeps resurfacing above the very defences meant to keep it down. The economic analysis which De Quincey brings to bear on the devaluation of writing over the passage of time offers an ironic perspective, both on contemporary debates about the utility of poetry, and on the tendency of Romantic poets to consider literature as rising above the fluctuating demands of the market place:

Once it had been the impress of a human mind which stamped its value upon the vellum; the vellum, though costly, had contributed but a secondary element of value to the total result. At length, however, this relation between the vehicle and its freight has gradually been undermined. The vellum, from having been the setting of the jewel, has risen at length to be the jewel itself; and the burden of thought, from having given the chief value to the vellum, has now become the chief obstacle to its value; nay, has totally extinguished its value, unless it can be dissociated from the connexion. Yet, if this unlinking *can* be effected, then—fast as the inscription upon the membrane is sinking into rubbish—the membrane is reviving in its separate importance; and from bearing a ministerial value, the vellum has come at last to absorb the whole value. (p. 140)

In this analysis, the sacred authority of tradition is seen to be overthrown in the Middle Ages, just as literature is seen to undergo commodification during the nineteenth century. The hierarchy of spirit over matter (tenor over vehicle) which is customarily used to underwrite authority, becomes reversed under the pressures of economic exigency—offering an arresting analogy for what De Quincey saw as the devaluation of literature in a climate which valued utility rather than culture, the literature of knowledge over the literature of power.

De Quincey focuses here on the question of how human progress is to be measured, given that the concerns of one generation are not those of the next 'under changes of opinion or of taste'. In the context of nineteenth-century discussions about the relative merits of science and literature in contributing to human progress, his analysis of the role of science—first as the obscurer and subsequently as the archaeologist of the past—takes on a distinctly equivocal significance:

Had *they* been better chemists, had *we* been worse—the mixed result, viz. that, dying for *them*, the flower should revive for *us*, could not have been effected: They did the thing proposed to them: they did it effectually; for they founded upon it all that was wanted; and yet ineffectually, since we unravelled their work;

effacing all above which they had superscribed; restoring all below which they had effaced. (p. 141)

Technology allows a magical resurrection of the past, just as it performs its burial; and although the difference between old and new chemistry represents progress of a sort, it is a strangely cyclical progress that takes us back to our distant ancestors. De Quincey is careful to emphasize that the cost of resurrecting the past is an 'effacing of all that [the Middle Ages] had superscribed'; so that ironically the present simply repeats the mistakes of the past, even as it seeks to undo them. In this relativistic vision of history, the possibility of scientific or literary progress seems to be brought under question. All that can be promised is a cycle of successive obliterations and resuscitations, in a pattern which frighteningly plays out to infinity De Quincey's underlying fear of repetition.

The most important feature of all in this passage is its relevance for models of reader-response and reception, both of which are implicitly invoked by De Quincey at the point where he stands back from his own simile, and asks the reader—significantly gendered, here, as female—to make her own application:

What would you think, fair reader, of a problem such as this—to write a book which should be sense for your own generation, nonsense for the next, should revive into sense for the next after that, but again become nonsense for the fourth; and so on by alternate successions, sinking into night or blazing into day... through a long vista of alternations? Such a problem, you say, is impossible. But really it is a problem not harder apparently than—to bid a generation kill, but so that a subsequent generation may call back into life; bury, but so that posterity may command to rise again. (p. 141)

In a culture which depended heavily on the possibility of posthumous fame (as recompense for contemporary rejection) this passage is hardly reassuring: it imagines literature, not as a permanent entity of increasing worth, but as a fashionable commodity (hence the condescending address to a 'fair reader') whose market value will fluctuate from generation to generation, depending entirely on the whims and prejudices of its readers. The recovery of the past is not here associated with hermeneutic responsibility, but rather with appropriation or projection—a valuation of the past in the present's own terms. Posterity is not the bearer of permanent value in this model of reading, as it is in Wordsworth's 'Essay Supplementary to the Preface', but simply another of the repetitious and contingent layerings which characterize the reception of any author or text.

De Quincey clinches this central point by a comparison between the compulsion of readers to destroy then reanimate, and the oscillation between war and peace in the history of civilization. In this respect, his simile may be compared with Coleridge's female Janus, 'one power with a double aspect', whose alternation between friendship and hostility provides a compelling analogy for writer–reader relations. Just as Coleridge attempted to mediate between creation and reception by using a time model which was simultaneously linear and circular—'having modified the present by the past, he at the same time weds the past in the present to some prepared and corresponsive future'—so De Quincey seeks to make a theodicy from the cycles of burial and resurrection which he sees as endemic to history. Neither of these models of time successfully allays the fear of repetition, and both imply the writing-subject's difficulty in directly experiencing the present. This difficulty, reflected in the compulsive turning back to the past and deferral to the future which characterized high Romanticism, is perhaps a response to the reconfiguration of time which occurred with the French Revolution. If, as Godwin puts it, 'we cut ourselves off from the inheritance of our ancestors, [and] conspire from time to time to cancel old scores, and begin the affairs of the human species afresh',[5] then the present becomes little more than a limbo—'a living place where we in waiting lie',[6] preoccupied, above all, with mortality.

II. THE DOUBLE BIND OF TEMPORALITY: READERS AS SECOND SELVES

As De Quincey's allegory reminds us, the endurance of writers is not simply a matter of how they construct their own authority in relation to contemporary and future readers, but of how reading-models are themselves constructed. To understand how the Romantics might have explained this two-way dependency, we can do no better than to reflect on a single sentence written by Edmund Burke—'people will not look forward to posterity, who never look back to their ancestors'—in the

---

[5] 'Essay on Sepulchres', discussed in Ch. 7, sect. V, above.
[6] Wordsworth, 'Ode: Intimations of Immortality', l. 123; text in Jared Curtis, *Wordsworth's Experiments with Tradition: The Lyric Poems of 1802* (Ithaca, NY: Cornell University Press, 1971), 164–70.

way that David Bromwich, in an exemplary reading of Burke, has elaborated it:

the idea of oneself in the present, as recalled by someone in the future, is already an imaginative idea of a past. In the same gesture by which we honor people and things that have survived in memory, we make a possible place for the survival of something of ourselves.[7]

The concern with a heritable identity, looking before and after, provided a conceptual method of bridging the duality of the writing-reading subect, while at the same time reconnecting selfhood and community. Romantic writers thus pre-empted the threat of extinction, by imagining readers as their 'second selves'.

When Wordsworth uses the phrase 'second self' in 'Michael', it is with the hope that, after his death, future poets will inherit his mantle, ensure the continuity of his voice, carry his name forward through the centuries. He constructs a model of reading–writing which is analogous to a father–son relationship, in which repetition is the guarantee of survival:

> Therefore, although it be a history
> Homely and rude, I will relate the same
> For the delight of a few natural hearts,
> And with yet fonder feeling, for the sake
> Of youthful Poets, who among these Hills
> Will be my second self when I am gone.
>
> (ll. 34–9)

But to imagine the reader as a 'second self' has its own dangers, hinted at (ironically and involuntarily) by the occurrence of these lines in a narrative concerning a father–son relationship that proves tragically flawed. Just as the inexplicably sudden rupture of filial love mourned in this poem reflects Michael's (and the poet-persona's) need for compensating memorials—for a 'second self' in posterity—so one may see that the concept of poetic filiation is a fragile defence against obscurity after death. As Susan Eilenberg puts it, 'when we multiply what we fear to lose, our copies remind us of our fear'.[8]

According to the logic of the writing–reading dialectic, every defence against the anxiety of reception involves a double bind; and the twinned

---

[7] *Choice of Inheritance*, 52.

[8] *Strange Power of Speech: Wordsworth, Coleridge and Literary Possession* (Oxford: Oxford University Press, 1992), 207.

ideas of posterity and repetition prove no exception to this rule. Repetition is both sought after, because the idea of a double offers hope of survival in perpetuity, and feared, because the irreducible identity—the 'genius' or 'originality'—of writers consists in their differentiation from others, past, present, and future. To be a writing–reading subject is always and necessarily to be conscious that what applies in the case of the present's relation to the past will apply also to the future's relation to the present. For Hazlitt, that is one of the inevitable effects of the passage of time:

The brightest living reputation cannot be equally imposing to the imagination, with that which is covered and rendered venerable with the hoar of innumerable ages. No modern production can have the same atmosphere of sentiment around it, as the remains of classical antiquity. But then our moderns may console themselves with the reflection, that they will be old in their turn, and will either be remembered with still increasing honours, or quite forgotten![9]

Just as Romantic writers are original by virtue of their revisionary reading of past writers, so they in turn may be eclipsed, outdone, neglected, overwritten, obscured. This is the danger that De Quincey touches on when he asks his 'fair reader' what she would think 'of a problem such as this—to write a book which should be of sense for [her] own generation, nonsense for the next, should revive into sense the next after that . . . and so on by alternate successions'? In this sense, wherever the reader is required to function as the writer's double, the paradox of the Freudian 'uncanny' is revealed: the double originally acted as an insurance against the destruction of the ego, but 'when this stage has been surmounted, the "double" reverses its aspect. From having been an assurance of immortality, it becomes the uncanny harbinger of death'.[10]

Much the same ambiguity is implied by the role of sympathetic identification in the process of interpretation. The idea of a receptivity so highly developed as to dissolve the boundaries between writing and reading (across and despite the temporality which intervenes) proved central to Romantic criticism, to Romantic hermeneutics, and to reader-response as it was gendered (and understood in relation to genre) during the Romantic period. But it too was the source of a number of difficulties and anxieties. At the hermeneutic level, it involved a supension of

---

[9] Howe, v. 145. The first half of this paragraph from Hazlitt's Lecture 'On the Living Poets' is quoted in Ch. 7, Sect. IV above.

[10] Quoted by Eilenberg, *Strange Power of Speech*, 208–9.

the belief that reading was historically conditioned, and that any attempt to read the past must respect the past's difference from the present. At the level of psychology (or identity-formation) it involved the possibility of a reading-function which threatened the writing-function, by virtue of an uncanny mimicry. Georges Poulet uses the phrase 'second self' to describe the reader's relationship to the writer: 'When I am absorbed in reading, a second self takes over ... Withdrawn in some recess of myself, do I then silently witness this dispossession?'[11] But as we have already seen in Maurice Blanchot, there is an equivalent 'take-over', which occurs the other way round.[12]

As a brief example of how these anxieties (with respect to repetition, doubling, and the erasure of difference between identities) translate into Romantic literary criticism, let us consider two apparently polarized definitions of the reading-process: one from Godwin, who is describing what it feels like to read Milton; the other from Hazlitt, who is defining the nature of Milton's creative genius by describing his own habits of reading and imitation. Godwin says, 'when I read Milton, I become Milton. I find myself a sort of intellectual camelion, assuming the colour of the substances on which I rest'.[13] Hazlitt describes something rather different: 'In reading his works, we feel ourselves under the influence of a mighty intellect, that the nearer it approaches to others, becomes more distinct from them.'[14] I shall be returning later to the implications of these two models of reading (crudely identified as identification and differentiation) which recur in different guises elsewhere in Romantic criticism; but first let me tease out their significance as complementary polarities. Godwin's description (like Charles Lamb's 'I dream away my life in others' speculations. I love to lose myself in other men's minds')[15] closely resembles Keats's idea of the chameleon poet, as one who 'has no identity'—one who relinquishes identity through a kind of receptive sympathy to those around him.[16] It is a model of writing, as much as of

[11] 'Phenomenology of Reading'; *New Literary History*, I (1969), 57.

[12] See my Preface.

[13] Essay v, 'Of an Early Taste for Reading', in the *Enquirer*, repr. in *Godwin Works*, v. 96.

[14] 'On Shakspeare [*sic*] and Milton', *Lectures on the English Poets* (Howe, v. 58).

[15] See Lamb's essay 'Detached Thoughts on Books and Reading', in *Elia and the Last Essays of Elia*, ed. Jonathan Bate (Oxford: Oxford University Press, World's Classics, 1987), 195.

[16] 'As to the poetical Character itself, (I mean that sort of which, if I am any thing, I am a Member; that sort distinguished from the wordsworthian or egotistical sublime; which is a thing per se and stands alone) it is not itself—it has no self—it is every thing and nothing'. Keats to Richard Woodhouse, 27 Oct. 1818, in *Letters of John Keats, 1814–1821*, ed. H. E. Rollins (2 vols., Cambridge, Mass.: Harvard University Press, 1958), i. 386–7.

reading, and it revels opportunistically in the possibility of assuming the shape of others, to whose creativity it aspires. In Hazlitt's description, on the other hand, the power to identify and to sympathize is balanced alongside the capacity to remain distinct, to preserve separateness; and this balancing-act occurs because, by implication, there is a danger of self-loss involved in the idea of a resemblance which comes too close.

In reading Hazlitt's sentence, a curious suspension of temporality and subject–object relations occurs: the 'others' whom Milton is said to approach and hold himself aloof from are not just the past writers he imitates, but future readers and writers by whom he will in turn be approached. The all-inclusive 'we' keeps his readers aloof from Milton, just as it keeps him aloof from the precursors he most resembles. At the same time, the logic grants readers the possibility that they might share some of Milton's ability to approach without losing their own identity. In this way, what appears to be a description of authorial consciousness moves over to become a description of reading. The difference-within-similarity that pertains in the creative act applies also to the relation between Milton and Hazlitt, past and present, writers and their readers.

The polarization of Godwin's and Hazlitt's reading-models suggests two alternative possibilities for the internally divided writing–reading subject: in Godwin's case the ideal of assimilation is envisaged as a creative opportunity for the reader, who willingly exchanges his own identity for another, but still at the risk of losing himself. In Hazlitt's case, the fears of usurpation and dispossession (which both readers and writers share) are allayed by an ideal of differentiation. Roughly speaking, these alternatives correspond to the contrasting models of interpretation outlined by the continental philologist Schleiermacher, in his *Hermeneutics*. Schleiermacher divided understanding into two faculties: the 'divinatory' and the 'comparative'. The first understands individual authors through mimetic sympathy, 'leading the reader to transform himself into the author so as to gain an immediate comprehension of the author as an individual'. The second proceeds 'by assuming the author under a general type'—understanding the author, that is, in terms of his historical typicality, and thus preserving a distance from his identity. Interestingly, for our purposes, these two hermeneutic practices were explicitly gendered by Schleiermacher:

Divinatory knowledge is the feminine strength in knowing people; comparative knowledge, the masculine... The divinatory is based on the assumption that each person is not only a unique individual in his own right, but that he has a receptivity to the uniqueness of every other person.[17]

Sympathy and differentiation are held together, in an implicitly hierarchical structure of mutual dependency, along lines similar to Locke's wit and judgement or Burke's categories of the sublime and the beautiful: 'Divination becomes certain only when it is corroborated by comparisons', Schleiermacher claimed; 'Without this confirmation, it always tends to be fanatical'.[18] This hierarchy suggests that for Schleiermacher (as for his English contemporaries) the act of sympathetic identification on the reader's part contained threatening possibilities for the author, and that the function of masculine comparison was to restore to both reader and writer their separate identities.

The English variants of Schleiermacher's complementary polarities ran alongside each other in Romantic criticism with so persistent an oscillation that the occurrence of one tended to call the other to mind. And, although they were available as alternative possibilities for the reader, it is crucial to observe that their function as reading-models was inseparable from their value as methods for preserving the sovereignty of writing. They were, in other words, models of a creative authority which could slip either way across the writing–reading axis, and in this sense they performed a historical role similar to that ascribed by Tillottama Rajan to hermeneutics, namely as the conservers of 'a continued though problematical logocentric impulse in romanticism'.[19]

III. THE SHAKESPEARE–MILTON DUALITY[20]

If Romantic models of creative authority and Romantic models of reading were frequently interchangeable, and if this fact in itself registered an ambivalence towards the emerging power of the reader, nowhere does this become more apparent than in the construction of Shakespeare and Milton as a duality. Romantic criticism anticipated the findings of twentieth-century semioticians such as Umberto Eco, by outlining two models of creativity—the open and the closed, the

---

[17] *Hermeneutics*, 150.

[18] Ibid. 151.

[19] *Supplement of Reading*, 29.

[20] This section of Ch. 8 is a revised version of section V from my essay '"Questionable Shape": The Aesthetics of Indeterminacy', in John Beer (ed.), *Questioning Romanticism* (Baltimore: Johns Hopkins University Press, 1995), 109–33.

dialogic and the monologic, the suggestive and the didactic, the anonymous and the personal, the neutral and the political, in its contrasting caricatures of these two writers. Shakespeare was associated with pathos and tenderness; Milton with the sublime; Shakespeare could enter fully into frailties, Milton stood aloof from them; Shakespeare was all relativism and humanness, while Milton was a synecdoche for the Judaeo-Christian God. Most important of all, for our purposes, Shakespeare's protean imagination held out the possibility of a delightful ethical irresponsibility in acts of creation or identification, whereas Milton firmly implicated writing and reading in ideology, morality, and religion.

This polarization of authorial imaginations codified an uncertainty about the direction in which Romanticism wished to move its theories of authority and interpretation. An alignment with Milton would suggest that interpretation must have theological ramifications, since here the reader submitted to the author in the same way that the subject was humbled by inscrutable divinity. But Shakespeare held out a heuristic alternative—in which the reader gained independence from the author, just as the dramatic medium discovered freedom in its refusal of closure. (Thus, for Hazlitt, Shakespeare 'was the least of an egoist that it was possible to be. He was nothing in himself; but he was all that others were, or that they could become.')[21] The evolution of aesthetics towards the Shakespearian model was an inevitable by-product of secularization. During the Romantic period, a choice between them was much more than a matter of taste and personal allegiance: the whole future of subjectivity hung in the balance.

I say that this polarization anticipated semiotics. And yet Romantic criticism was clearly not a scientific endeavour to understand writing as a system of signs, involving author and reader in a collaborative enterprise. Rather, it offered value judgements about different kinds of creative genius, resting on contrasting models of poetic authority. It explored the tensions between closure and indeterminacy, authorial restrictions and interpretative rights, but it did so as though these were purely a matter of artistic characteristics, kinds of consciousness. Its observations began and ended with the author—and this remained the case, whichever kind of prejudice a given writer brought to bear on the question. Coleridge, for instance, strongly supportive of hermeneutic

---

[21] 'On Shakspeare and Milton', *Lectures on the English Poets* (Howe, v. 47): 'The striking peculiarity of Shakspeare's mind was its generic quality, its power of communication with all other minds'.

practices, was intent on mystifying Shakespeare and Milton equally, by aligning their two kinds of imagination with immanent versus transcendent models of divinity: 'Shakspeare [*sic*] is the Spinozistic Deity, an omnipresent creativeness', he claims, 'Milton is Prescience; he stands ab extra'.[22] Keats, approaching the problem from a purely secular angle, ascribed to Shakespeare, not himself as reader, the capacity to remain 'in uncertainties, Mysteries, doubts, without any irritable reaching after fact & reason', while he saw in Milton a denial and authoritarianism he found stifling: 'I have but lately stood on my guard against Milton. Life to him would be death to me'.[23] Wordsworth, somewhere in between these two positions, claimed the works of Milton as one of the 'grand store-houses of enthusiastic and meditative Imagination', while Shakespeare, the epitome of 'human and dramatic Imagination' was equally valued as a role model.[24]

So strongly did the preoccupation with authority maintain a stranglehold on Romantic criticism that it blinded writers to their own readingpractices. For it is a striking fact about the reception of Milton and Shakespeare that, when one comes to look closely at Romantic poetry, the division between kinds of imagination collapses entirely. Even while exposing the closure of Milton's imagination in their critical observations, the Romantics were involved in revealing a quite different Milton—open-ended, ambiguous, negatively capable—when it came to rewriting his poems. This reception paradox offers an extreme example of the way in which Romantic criticism subjected interpretative activity to authorial control. There ought to be no contradiction between critical and poetic endeavours, since each has an equally strong investment in affirming the power of the subject to transform the material on which it works. The paradox arises because criticism during this period suffered from a sense of secondariness in relation to great canonical writers, whose creativity it rarely sought to match, and whose authority it left unquestioned: Romantic critics seldom moved, therefore, beyond deferential obeisance towards such geniuses as Shakespeare and Milton. Romantic poets, on the other hand, were concerned to establish their own primariness, their own originality, by revisionary readings of these same precursors, each of whom lent themselves equally well to creative transformation. That Romantic theory should go so much against the

---

[22] *Table Talk*, ed. Carl Woodring, *CC* xiv/1: 125.
[23] *Letters of Keats*, i. 193; ii. 212.   [24] *Wordsworth Prose*, iii. 34, 35.

grain of its own reading-practices is a measure of the extent to which writers, confused or threatened by the latent power of the reader, sought to defend the writing side of the writing–reading axis through an ideology of genius which attached specifically to authors. This in turn reflects the more imponderable problem Romanticism faced in attempting to negotiate a stable place for the subject in relation to authority— especially the authority of the past.

IV. THE DEFENCE AGAINST REPETITION: APPLICATIONS OF A MIXED HERMENEUTIC

As defences against the anxiety of reception, Romantic pairings such as Milton–Shakespeare performed a dialectical function: taken singly, they allowed for a choice between a 'positive' (feminine) and a 'negative' (masculine) hermeneutic; but taken as twin halves of an integrated system, they held out the promise of a mixed hermeneutic, in which sympathy and differentiation were resolved. Thus, for Coleridge, the proposition that 'All things and modes of action shape themselves anew in the being of *Milton*; while *Shakespeare* becomes all things, yet for ever remaining himself' (*BL* ii. 28) worked as a claim for the equal significance of identification and differentiation in the hold that genius exerts over its admirers. In keeping with the mediatory function of a Romantic poetics of reception, that is, it allowed readers to be both like and unlike the authors they read, defining reading itself as a process which honoured the spirit of the past without repeating it. Self-possession and self-diffusion were thus reconciled.

A version of this paradox has already been seen, in the discourse surrounding claims for perpetual copyright. Both Wordsworth and Talfourd invoked the concept of the author as an individual finite entity, whose works were considered as a species of heritable property, and whose survival consisted in 'self-possession', even after death. But the language in which they made this appeal shows their saturation in a less proprietorial idea of authorship—one in which an author was valued precisely in so far as his ideas had the potential to influence others and bring about change. Genius, in this context, was seen as so influential that its source could no longer be detected, so copious that it spilled over into its receptors: 'Because genius of necessity comunicates so much, we cannot conceive it as retaining any thing for its possessor', Talfourd argued:

because [poets'] thoughts become our thoughts, and their phrases uncon-
sciously enrich our daily language—because their works, harmonious in themselves, suggest to us the rules of composition by which their imitators should be
guided . . . we cannot fancy them apart from ourselves, or admit that they have
any property except in our praise.[25]

Appropriately enough, the poet whom Talfourd used to demonstrate
the diffusive potential of genius was Coleridge—a notorious plagiar-
izer—who 'scattered abroad the seeds of beauty and of wisdom, to take
root in congenial minds, and was content to witness their fruits in the
productions of those who received them'.[26] His habit of disregarding
the boundaries that separate one literary property from another is made
an essential ingredient in the mythology of a genius 'dispossessed' by its
own generosity. Talfourd saw Coleridge as no different in this respect
from Milton or Wordsworth: all are invoked as influential authors,
neglected in their time but subsequently 'pervading every part of the
national literature', and 'invariably quoted by our most popular writers'.
Their spirits, abstracted from individual identities, are believed to mingle
with the 'intellectual atmosphere'.[27]

The defensive structure of Romantic literary theory becomes discernible in the binary oppositions which it negotiated and sought to resolve
through the deployment of a 'mixed hermeneutic'. The paradox of
genius—that it is at one and the same time a possession unique to a
single individual, and a discursive potential valued for its influence on
and absorption into other discourses—was mirrored by an equally
paradoxical theory of reading, in which no amount of openness to the
ideas of others could threaten the integrity of self. Taken to their
extreme, Romantic applications of this hermeneutic led to the formation
of what one might see as a complex of defences, a kind of interpersonal
'pathology'.

Coleridge's cyclical theory of history, as it is described in *The Friend*,
provides an exemplary demonstration of the ways in which a 'mixed
hermeneutic' operates. 'The events and characters of one age, like the
strains of music, recal [*sic*] those of another', Coleridge claims; 'and the
variety by which each is individualized, not only gives a charm and
poignancy to the resemblance, but likewise renders the whole more

---

[25] *Speech of Sergeant Talfourd on Literary Property* (18 May 1837) (London: Sherwood and Co.,
1837), 11.
[26] Ibid. 10.
[27] Ibid. 13, 14.

intelligible'. He goes on, with tenacious ingenuity, to trace the secret parallels that pertain between Erasmus, Luther, and Munster on the one hand, and Voltaire, Rousseau, and Robespierre on the other. Deriving 'the deepest interest, from the comparison of men, whose characters at the first view appear widely dissimilar', he seeks to establish a 'real resemblance in the radical character' which depends neither on 'identity of opinions' nor on 'similarity of events and outward actions', but on the expression of analogous powers. Thus, the quality of influence which Erasmus and Voltaire exerted over their age is seen as drawing them together in an ahistorical alliance—'the *effects* remain parallel, the *circumstances* analogous, and the *instruments* the same'—even while the men themselves are *'essentially* different'. Coleridge's argument sustains a 'mixed hermeneutic' for five pages of densely illustrated prose (*Friend*, i. 129–34). At one point (acknowledging that his theorizing hovers on the verge of the uncanny) he refers to his own procedures as 'this our ... new dance of death, or rather of the shadows which we have brought forth—two by two—from the historic ark'. As if to dispel the impression of absolute repetition or mimicry conveyed by the idea of the double, he qualifies similarity by recapitulating difference, thus establishing that although history might be said to 'repeat itself', it also discloses the properties of uniqueness and individuality that pertain to human beings.

In a *Notebook* definition of what Thomas McFarland has termed the 'originality paradox'[28] the Shakespearian symbol is given a less idiosyncratic application:

That Proteus Essence that could assume the very form, but yet known & felt not to be the Thing by that difference of the Substance which made every atom of the Form another thing |—that likeness not identity—an exact web, every line of direction miraculously the same, but the one worsted, the other silk (*Notebooks*, ii. 2274).

The distinction between 'likeness' and 'identity' was crucial to Coleridge, who thereby introduced an important qualification into his Protean analogy by suggesting that endless modifications of identity were not incompatible with an underlying stability of self. In much the same way, his desynonymization of 'imitation' and 'copy' was a method for keeping at bay the danger of an excessive convergence between two distinct identities: as he put it, in his essay 'On Aesthetic Problems', 'The fine

---

[28] *Originality and Imagination* (Baltimore: Johns Hopkins University Press, 1985), 1–30.

Arts are works of Imitation—mimetic—how in Imitation as contra-dist, from Copy. Difference is as *essential* as Likeness.'[29] Just as his repeated emphasis on the untranslatability of words maintained their inviolable individuality, so his careful mediation between a positive and a negative hermeneutic allowed both the author's and the reader's identity to be preserved from the dangerous coalescence of mimicry. His ideal model of literary influence was, as Raimonda Modiano has shrewdly put it,

a relationship in which difference is not attained at the expense of sameness, nor likeness at the expense of distinctness. This relationship is conspicuously free of Oedipal tensions or rivalry and remains for that matter a pure abstraction, almost religious in nature.[30]

In Coleridge's prose, two opposite meanings of the word 'identity' are played off against each other. Identity is both the convergence into one of two separate entities, and the preservation against convergence of entity itself. Romantic definitions of genius—which is neither imitation nor originality, but both at once—returned again and again to this paradox. Hazlitt claimed that Milton is a poet who 'has borrowed more than any other writer, and exhausted every source of imitation, sacred and profane; yet... is perfectly distinct from every other writer': he is 'a writer of centos, yet in originality scarcely inferior to Homer' (Howe, v. 58). Wordsworth seemed to Coleridge to stand 'nearest of all modern writers to Shakespeare and Milton; and yet in a kind perfectly unborrowed and his own' (*BL* ii. 151), while to De Quincey he provided living proof that

The author who wins notice the most is not he that perplexes men by truths drawn from fountains of absolute novelty,—truths as yet unsunned, and from that cause obscure,—but he that awakens into illuminated consciousness ancient lineaments of truth long slumbering in the mind.[31]

All three writers implied that the past can be recovered without repetition: by suggesting that the 'ancient lineaments of truth' were given new life in and by the 'illuminated consciousness' which awoke them; and by offering genius as something which retained its own identity, no matter how closely it appeared to resemble others. Human works of beauty, De Quincey argued,

[29] 'On Aesthetic Problems', *Shorter Works and Fragments, CC* xi/1. 348.
[30] 'The Ethics of Gift Exchange and Literary Ownership: Coleridge and Wordsworth', *Wordsworth Circle*, 22 (Spring 1989), 113–20: 120.
[31] 'On Wordsworth's Poetry', 1st pub. *Tait's Magazine* (Sept. 1845); repr. in Masson, xi. 315.

never absolutely repeat each other, never approach so near as not to differ...they differ by undecipherable and incommunicable differences, that cannot be taught by mimicries, that cannot be reflected in the mirror of copies, that cannot become ponderable in the scales of vulgar comparison.[32]

This belief in the paradoxical nature of genius or originality was not confined to the practitioners of high Romanticism, but was a widespread and recurrent feature of nineteenth-century critical discourse. For the Scottish critic John Wilson, it was Burns rather than Milton who provided archetypal proof that originality had little to do with novelty—indeed, that its deepest affinity was with the vanishing past. The distinctive nature of Burns's genius, Wilson argued, lay precisely in his openness to centuries of oral tradition, for which his own poetry became the thoroughfare:

Burns never saw or heard a jewel or a tune of a thought or a feeling, but he immediately made it his own—that is, stole it. He was too honest a man to refrain from such thefts. The thoughts and feelings—to whom by divine right did they belong? To Nature. But Burns beheld them 'waif and stray,' and in peril of being lost for ever. He seized then on those 'snatches of old songs,' wavering away into the same oblivion that lies on the graves of the nameless bards who first gave them being; and now, spiritually interfused with his own lays, they are secured against decay—and like them immortal. [33]

Wilson plays wittily on his readers' prejudice against imitation, using the property metaphors that are a commonplace in contemporary discussions of copyright to define a species of literary 'theft' which is no theft at all. Burns's 'sources' are to be found in the Scottish culture whose anonymous songs he inherited and rescued from oblivion, not in a canon of identifiable authors. Like the English self-taught poets Bloomfield and Clare, with whom Wilson compares him, he 'plagiarized' from Nature; and like theirs, his own claim to originality lay in his fidelity to natural resources. In the complex nationalist argument Wilson is mounting, England is reminded that she should be proud of Bloomfield and Clare (in the same way that Scotland was proud of Burns) for their representativeness or typicality, not for their distinctiveness. So long as

[32] 'On the Poetry of Pope', in Masson xi. 58. 'Genius became a Romantic obsession', Jonathan Bate argues, 'because it was a conception that seemed to guarantee individuality. It is, in Thomas McFarland's words 'an analogue of the unduplicatability, always hoped for even if only precariously real, of the individual'. See 'Shakespeare and Original Genius', in Penelope Murray (ed.), *Genius: The History of an Idea* (Oxford: Basil Blackwell, 1989), 94.
[33] 'An Hour's Talk about Poetry' in *Recreations of Christopher North* (3 vols., Edinburgh and London: William Blackwood, 1842), i. 306.

Bloomfield (here representative of poets more generally) was true to his origins, he would be original:

The soil in which the native virtues of the English character grow, is unexhausted and inexhaustible; let him break it up on any spot he chooses, and poetry will spring to light like clover from lime. Nor need he fear being an imitator. His mind is an original one, his most indifferent verses prove it; for though he must have read much poetry since his earlier day...he retains his own style, which, though it be not marked by any very strong characteristics, is yet sufficiently peculiar to show that it belongs to himself, and is a natural gift.[34]

Shelley, arguing from a less nationalist perspective, rests his case for the eternal verity of poetry on its essentially mimetic properties. The poet's status as the spokesman of universal human feeling derives from his fidelity to nature, just as it does in Wilson's celebration of the poet as one who affirms and upholds the nation's continuing identity. Shelley formulates the relation between originality and imitation in terms that deliberately marginalize novelty, while at the same time comforting poets that they cannot simply repeat or straightforwardly reflect:

As to imitation; Poetry is a mimetic art. It creates, but it creates by combination and representation. Poetical abstractions are beautiful and new, not because the portions of which they are composed had no previous existence in the mind of man or in nature, but because the whole produced by their combination has some intelligible and beautiful analogy with those sources of emotion and thought, and with the contemporary condition of them.[35]

This being the case, Shelley claims, poets need not strain anxiously to differentiate themselves from others who precede or surround them, but can trust that the modifying power of their own consciousness will distinguish what they have to say, and more importantly, will communicate its truth to the reader.

A Poet, is the combined product of such internal powers as modify the nature of others, and of such external influences as excite and sustain these powers; he is not one, but both. Every man's mind is in this respect modified by all the objects of nature and art, by every word and every suggestion which he ever admitted to act upon his consciousness; it is the mirror upon which all forms are reflected, and in which they compose one form.[36]

---

[34] Wilson, *Recreations of Christopher North*, 319.
[35] 'Preface' to *Prometheus Unbound*, in *Shelley's Poetry and Prose*, selected and ed. Donald Reiman and Sharon B. Powers (New York: Norton, 1977), 134.
[36] Ibid. 135.

In Shelley's hermeneutic ideal, influence, reception, and creation follow the same laws, and are subject to the same mimetic structure in which difference modifies similarity to produce infinite variables on shared or repeated perceptions. His model of the corporate influences to which a poet is subject becomes, in its turn, a model for the reader's willingness to be open to the poet's influence without fear of self-loss. His claim that the poet is the product of 'internal powers' and 'external influences', reassures—and is designed to reassure—both poet and reader, not one but both.

V. WOMEN READERS AND THE DANGERS OF SYMPATHETIC IDENTIFICATION

We have seen that the rise of criticism in the Romantic era provoked a hermeneutic anxiety, especially among poets who were also critics, and whose allegiances were consequently divided between the claims of readers and writers. We have also seen how, in high Romantic writers, the anxiety of reception manifested itself as a double attachment to the past and to genius, both of which were protected from readerly appropriations and transformations. I want in the remainder of this chapter to contextualize and politicize anxieties about reading by focusing on the question of how writers dealt with the threat posed by modernity, as it was embodied in a specific genre. What are the implications of Mary Wollstonecraft's complaint that 'from reading to writing novels the transition is very easy',[37] where sympathetic identification is gendered as female, associated with a usurpatory potential in the reading process, and identified with the novel? What does the association of these ideas—sympathy, woman, novel, and reader—tell us about the place of contemporary culture in Romantic anxieties of reception? And in what sense might there be a parallel, here, for the fears of doubling and repetition with which Romantic poets and critics were so concerned?

During the latter part of the eighteenth century, sympathy became the locus for a number of ethical and political ambiguities—especially with respect to gender alignments, as Claudia Johnson has shown in her study of women's writing, *Equivocal Beings*.[38] Subsequently, in the counter-revolutionary rhetoric of the 1790s (which Wollstonecraft borrowed in

---

[37] See Ch. 1, above.

[38] *Equivocal Beings: Politics, Gender, and Sentimentality in the 1790's: Wollstonecraft, Radcliffe, Burney, Austen* (Chicago: University of Chicago Press, 1995), esp. introd. and chs. 1–2.

her description of the novel), sympathy carried a distinctly subversive charge of meaning. This derived in part from its affiliations with the sentimental tradition, but more especially from its association with the French Revolution. In Laetitia Hawkins's *Letters on the Female Mind* (1793), intended as a conservative response to Helen Maria Williams's *Letters Written in France* (1790), sympathy was allied to sentiment, and condemned as a species of enthusiasm capable of endangering the entire fabric of society:

> The dominion allowed to the passions under the specious name of sentiment, has, to the grief of all serious persons, dreadfully shaken the foundation of all moral virtue: the more noisy but equally insidious clamour for universal liberty, will be the fatal blow to this lovely fabric.[39]

The repeated association between sympathy, commotion, and violence which characterized counter-revolutionary discourse found its way into representations of popular culture—especially French novels and German dramas of sensibility, against which Romantics on both sides of the Channel sought to make their aesthetic claims. In the reaction of audiences to such dramatists as Kotzebue, high Romantic writers saw a species of sympathetic identification which they considered to be amoral; and poets such as Burger were castigated for pandering to the same taste for over-stimulation. Of the latter, Schiller makes the characteristic complaint that 'the poet's enthusiasm not infrequently borders on madness, that his fire often becomes fury, that for just this reason the emotional state in which one lays down the poem is not the beneficent, harmonious state in which we want to see the poet put us.'[40] Martha Woodmansee has shown that Schiller defined himself in opposition to 'the instrumentalist aesthetic . . . in which a work's excellence is measured by its capacity to affect an audience'. Claiming on one occasion that 'the first, essential condition for the perfection of a poem is that it possess an absolute intrinsic value that is entirely independent of the powers of comprehension of its reader'[41] he found Burger's writing antipathetic because 'far from preventing readers from recognizing

---

[39] *Letters on the Female Mind, Its Powers and Pursuits. Addressed to Miss H.M. Williams with Particular Reference to her Letters from France* (2 vols., London: Hookham and Carpenter, 1793), i. 105; quoted in Mary Poovey, *The Proper Lady and the Woman Writer: Ideology and Style in the Works of Mary Wollstonecraft, Mary Shelley, and Jane Austen* (Chicago: Chicago University Press, 1984), 32.

[40] Quoted by Martha Woodmansee, *The Author, Art, and The Market: Rereading the History of Aesthetics* (New York: Columbia University Press, 1994), 76.

[41] Ibid. 78.

themselves in the poet's representations', Burger caused readers 'to recognize themselves all too readily, to respond, that is, all too power-fully and immediately'.[42] His revulsion against emotive writing bore witness to his suspicion with respect to the loss of *individuality* that could occur in an overly empathetic reader-response. Ironically enough, how-ever, Schiller was himself seen as vulnerable to this very species of reception. Commenting on the first performance of *The Robbers* in 1782, one contemporary eyewitness recorded the audience's responsive-ness in a vocabulary that anticipates Wordsworth's castigations of sensationalism in the Preface to *Lyrical Ballads*:

The theatre was like a madhouse—rolling eyes, clenched fists, hoarse cries in the auditorium. Strangers fell sobbing into each other's arms, women on the point of fainting staggered towards the exit. There was a universal commotion as in chaos, out of the mists of which a new creation bursts forth.[43]

Just as an implied connection between sympathy and radical enthusiasm is suggested, here, in a prophetic reference to the new dawn of revolu-tion, so the feminine language of sentiment traditionally associated with heroines in novels—sobbing and fainting—is taken to its extreme, suggesting a species of sympathy so contagious that it reduces rational human beings to insanity.

In the field of English educational writing, sympathy had an even more overtly gendered inflection, and began to be subjected to critique because of its association with the unreflective habits of women readers, as they were encouraged by sentimental novels. Pastorella, one of the benighted women seeking enlightenment in Hannah More's *A Search After Happiness: A Pastoral*, recalls her introduction to novel-reading as though it involved a personal 'fall' from rationality:

Left to myself to cultivate my mind
Pernicious *novels* their soft entrance find:
Their pois'nous influence led my mind astray...
Folly within my heart her empire found,
My passions floating and my judgement drown'd.[44]

This was the standard view of English educationalists throughout the latter part of the eighteenth century, especially those who addressed a

[42] Ibid. 77.
[43] Quoted by Lesley Sharpe, *Friedrich Schiller: Drama, Thought and Politics* (Cambridge: Cam-bridge University Press, 1991), 29.
[44] *A Search After Happiness*... (London: S. Farley, 1783), 15–16.

specifically female audience. In Hester Chapone's *Letters on the Improvement of Mind* (1775) novel-reading is seen as influencing the passions of youth in such a way as 'to vitiate ... stile' and 'to mislead [the] heart and understanding'.[45] Mostly it was the sympathy between readers and heroines that was of concern, because here, it was believed, there was the danger that women's morals might become tainted by escapist fantasies in which conventional codes of morality were suspended. As the conservative Squire Worthy puts it, discussing the damaging effects of novels on women in More's 'Mr Bragwell and his Two Daughters',

Parental authority is set at nought. Nay plots and contrivances against parents and guardians, fill half the volumes. They make love as the great business of human life, and even teach that it is impossible to be regulated or restrained, and to the indulgence of this passion, every duty is therefore sacrificed. [46]

Excessive readerly sympathy not only results in a raising of false expectations on the part of susceptible females—Bragwell complains that his daughters 'always seem to be on the look-out for something', and 'will not keep company with their equals'—but also in the overturning of traditional hierarchies, as women seek to marry above themselves, and servants to become princesses: 'this corrupt reading is now got down even among some of the lowest class', Worthy laments, 'And it is an evil which is spreading every day.'[47]

The identification between female reader and heroine was understood by conservative and progressive educationalists alike in terms of a dangerously collusive passivity—'had she thought while she read, her mind would have been contaminated', Wollstonecraft writes of the silly Eliza in her first novel, *Mary: A Fiction*.[48] This led to the conclusion that reading must be strictly regulated, especially during the early years of a woman's life, so as to protect her from bad influences. In her *Thoughts on the Education of Daughters* (1787), Wollstonecraft argued that 'productions which give a wrong account of the human passions ... ought not to be read before the judgement is formed'. Such accounts were 'one great cause of the affectation of young women. Sensibility is described and praised, and the effects of it represented in a way so different from

[45] *Letters on the Improvement of Mind* (2 vols., London: H. Hughs, 1775), ii. 144–5.
[46] *Selected Writings of Hannah More*, ed. Robert Hole (London: William Pickering, 1995), 86.
[47] Ibid. 81.
[48] *Mary, a Fiction and The Wrongs of Woman*, ed. with introd., Gary Kelly (London: Oxford University Press, 1976), 3.

nature, that those who imitate it must make themselves very ridiculous'.[49]

The anxiety that reading might bring about a 'ruinous discontent' in women, affecting manners and standards of conduct, often boiled down, as John Tinnon Taylor has suggested, to 'the much-quoted fear that a copy would produce an original':

in the opinion of those who constantly dreaded the new, two of the greatest contributions of the eighteenth century, woman's freedom and the novel, were assisting each other along the road to corruption. The 'reading Miss' was led step by step toward becoming the original of the heroines whose scandalous conduct forced booksellers to replace with new copies the worn and dog-eared duodecimos.[50]

But alongside the theory that an 'identifying propensity' caused life and art to swop places, there was the much more threatening matter of an over-identification between reader and author. It was this latter collusion, with its actively aspiring implications, that had repercussions for an anxiety of reception. Wollstonecraft's complaint that the transition between reading and writing is very easy suggests a sense in which the novel became the site for a dangerous convergence between writing- and reading-identities in the period. 'Such is the frightful facility of this species of composition', wrote Hannah More, this time in her *Strictures on Female Education*:

that every raw girl, while she reads, is tempted to fancy that she can also write. And as Alexander, on perusing the Iliad, found by congenial sympathy the image of Achilles in his own ardent soul, and felt himself the hero he was studying; and as Corregio, on first beholding a picture which exhibited the perfection of the Graphic art, prophetically felt all his own future greatness, and cried out in rapture, 'And I too am a painter!' so a thorough-paced novel-reading Miss, at the close of every tissue of hackney'd adventures, feels within herself the stirring impulse of corresponding genius, and triumphantly exclaims, 'And I too am an author!'[51]

The suggestion here is that too easy a habit of sympathetic identification will result in the usurpation of the author's function by readers who have no credentials whatsoever for writing: a suggestion that is echoed, in a

[49] In *Wollstonecraft Works*, iv. 20.
[50] *Early Opposition to the English Novel: The Popular Reaction from 1760–1830* (1943; New York: King's Crown Press, 1970), 79.
[51] *Strictures on the Modern System of Female Education* ... (2 vols., London: Cadell and Davies, 1799), i. 184–5.

later article in the *Miniature* (1804), by a reviewer's dismissive reference to 'the fairer sex, who not content with being readers, must become writers; who distracted with the nonsensical emotions they feel in their own breasts, must needs disseminate the publication of their infectious vagaries through all the female world'.[52] Excessive sympathy becomes responsible, in these two independant critiques, both for the prolific reproduction of literature, and for an impoverishment in literary standards.

VI. GENDER AND THE HIERARCHY OF GENRES

In Romantic literary theory, as we saw earlier, a hermeneutic of differentiation (masculine, logocentric, univocal) was counterpointed by a hermeneutic of identification (feminine, secular, protean). The co-presence of these complementary polarities in Romantic theories and practices of reading provided a defence, I argued, against anxieties with respect to the rise of the reader. In the light of high Romantic repudiations of the novel, we can now approach the implicitly hierarchical structure which subordinates sympathetic identification to differentiation with a more informed sense of why it was that the 'masculine' was used by Romantic writers to discipline and police its feminine other. The specific conjunction of ideas—woman, novel, and reader, or 'the woman novel-reader'—was, for Romantic writers, an organizing figure for the threat posed by modernity to the authority of the writing-subject, gendered by tradition as poetic and male. Eminent past poets were preferred to novels because, as Hannah More put it, they 'throw the generality of readers at such an unapproachable distance as to check presumption, instead of exciting it'.[53] The unapproachability of such geniuses as Shakespeare and Milton was both an inevitable product of their mysterious otherness, and an insurance policy against the creative aspirations of reading.

At a time when the question 'What is a poet?' was asked more frequently than ever before or since, the figure of the poet was closely bound up with the formation of a system of Romantic defences; and whatever the practices of poets in this period may have been, it was usually the case that when a defence of poetry as a genre was launched, it

[52] *Miniature*, 11 (30 Apr., 1804), 15–16; quoted in Taylor, *Early Opposition to the English Novel*, 81.

[53] *Strictures on Female Education*, 184.

reflected the need to protect authority—and patriarchal authority at that—against the encroaching power of readers. Commenting on the significance of this tendency, and the generic stratifications by which it was underpinned during the early nineteenth century, Marlon Ross has claimed that 'Even while equivocating between self-annihilation (negative capability) and self-aggrandizement (the egotistical sublime) the romantic poet recognizes that the only match for an overwhelming mass [of readers] is a poetics of mythic self-possession'.[54] This consoling myth arose because poetry was under threat, both from the utilitarian culture it attempted to win over (while also transcending) and from women writers who began to make it their own terrain. 'Poetry motivated and shaped by the desire for self-possession, determined by the poet's aggressive relation to his fellows and the world, is not *intrinsically* masculine, but it is *sociohistorically masculine*', Ross concludes. Metaphors of power used in the defence of poetry allowed poets to reassert the importance of a vocation that was 'on the verge of losing whatever influence it had'[55] and thus to maintain a hold on both their professional self-esteem and their sense of being backed up by a historical and traditional poetic identity.

Gender and genre were thus crucial components in the formation of what Jerome McGann has labelled 'Romantic ideology', the novel becoming associated, by way of a recurrent and quite tenacious habit of caricature, with all that was anathema to traditional poetic values. Used as the signifier of novelty (fashionable, fickle, and feminine) rather than originality (serious, manly, destined for survival), it was also figured as dangerous by virtue of its connections with a proactive and levelling capacity for sympathy which had strongly revolutionary overtones. Furthermore, as we saw in Chapter 1, the specifically feminine associations of the novel—its largely female authorship and reception—were connected with a reproductive capacity which had got out of control. The fear of doubling which manifested itself subtly and guardedly in Romantic criticism was played out, in castigations of contemporary novels, as an outright hostility towards excessive reproduction.

By the same token, the fact that reading practices were frequently seen as mirror images of creative processes in this period is suggestive of the very doubling that Romantic writers feared. Novels, because of their

---

[54] *The Contours of Masculine Desire: Romanticism and the Rise of Poetry* (Oxford: Oxford University Press, 1989), 25.
[55] Ibid. 49, 23.

rapid turnover (and the subscription rules in circulating libraries), were believed to encourage the hasty reading and forgetting of large amounts of repetitive material. The recurrence with which they circulated reflected back on their content, in such a way as to confuse the method of circulation with the product itself, so that, just as 'Authors of novels are supposed to be the greatest plunderers in the world, stealing a bit here and a bit there, and thus vamping up a book by any means',[56] their readers too were figured as indiscriminate ingesters of material they had seen numerous times before. When Mary Alcock, in her satirical poem, 'A Receipt for Writing a Novel' (1799), complained that the formulaic content of contemporary novels rendered them readily reproducible, her emphasis fell on the unhealthy complicity between production and consumption in circulating stale and repetitive material: 'These stores supply the female pen, | Which writes them o'er and o'er again, | And readers likewise may be found | To circulate them round and round.'[57] Conversely, the assumption that the novel as a genre had become worn out through overuse was confirmed by the physical state of the duodecimo volumes themselves, as battered material objects bearing the marks of successive readers. Subscribers to circulating-libraries were, Taylor informs us, 'especially inclined toward making marginal notations, sometimes in writing, sometimes with the mark of thumb or fingernail.... Pages over which an enthusiast had rejoiced or suffered were returned to the bookseller in a particularly bad state'.[58]

The position of novels relative to poetry in the Romantic hierarchy of genres had important repercussions for the role and status of nonfictional prose. Newspapers, with their rapid and immediate coverage of events, allowed no time for the reader to reflect; reviews, which 'reinforced received wisdom and illustrated axioms with a multitude of examples and parallels'[59] encouraged slothful reading; periodical essays, whose 'natural life is only six weeks', and were 'not expected to be highly finished' or even to sustain a continuous thread of argument,[60] caused the author, in Lee Erickson's words 'to chop up his thought into

---

[56] Henry Siddons, *Virtuous Poverty* (London, 1804), iii. 2; quoted in Taylor, *Early Opposition to the English Novel*, 44.

[57] ll. 69–72, in Roger Lonsdale (ed.), *Eighteenth Century Women Poets: An Oxford Anthology* (Oxford: Oxford University Press, 1989), 468.

[58] *Early Opposition to the English Novel*, 10–11.

[59] Lee Erickson, *The Economy of Literary Form: English Literature and the Industrialization of Publishing, 1800–1850* (Baltimore: Johns Hopkins University Press, 1996), 73.

[60] *The Letters of Thomas Babington Macaulay*, ed. Thomas Pinney (6 vols., Cambridge: Cambridge University Press, 1974–81), iv. 40; quoted in Erickson, *Economy of Literary Form*, 94.

pieces'[61] and the reader to do likewise; while magazines and miscellanies, because they thrived on the profitable practice of publishing works in parts rather than as wholes, gave rise to what Coleridge called 'the general taste for unconnected writing'.[62] Although not always identified with women-writers, all these genres—by virtue of their novelty and accessibility—acquired associations with femininity. Like the novel, they were accused of encouraging habits of passive consumption on the part of the reader, as opposed to habits of active reception. The vocabulary used to describe them was culinary and appetitive, frequently combining metaphors of chopping up, recycling, and rendering down with ideas of hunger and lack of refinement, in ways that were unflattering both to the producer and the consumer. As Bergk put it, readers 'who devour one insipid dish after another in an effort to escape an intolerable mental vaccuum. . . . watch events appear and disappear as in a magic mirror, each one more absurd than the last one. . . . All mental activity is stifled by the mass of impressions'.[63] But equally, this passivity and secondariness reflected back on those who concocted the dishes in the first place: the *Critical* in 1764 expressed surprise that a recipe book for 'romance cookery' did not exist, since the process was so well known;[64] and on another occasion remarked that 'All the difference between [novels] lies in the skill of the cook; for, after all, the dish is but cow-heel.'[65]

If the figures of cookery and eating implied the compulsively repetitive interlocking of supply and demand, another recurrent metaphor (perhaps most familiar to us from Wordsworth's reference to 'gross and

---

[61] Erickson is paraphrasing Carlyle's chapter on 'Editorial Difficulties' in *Sartor Resartus*. See *Economy of Literary Form*, 109.

[62] Coleridge, writing to Poole in Jan. 1810, traces this habit of reading back to Addison, who was, he claims, its unwitting progenitor: 'the love of Reading, as a refined pleasure weaning the mind from grosser enjoyments, which it was one of the Spectator's chief Objects to awaken, has by that work, & those that followed . . . but still more, by Newspapers, Magazines, and Novels, been carried into excess: and the Spectator itself has innocently contributed to the general taste for unconnected writing—just as if 'Reading made easy' should act to give men an aversion to words of more than two syllables, instead of drawing them *thro'* those words into the power of reading Books in general.' (Griggs, iii. 281.)

[63] Quoted by Woodmansee, *The Author, Art, and the Market*, 97.

[64] *Critical Review*, 17 (June 1764), 478. Taylor discusses this passage, but also refers to a suggestion made in *Monthly Review*, 5 (1791), that a machine might be made for composing new books by revising old ones. For this early idea of mass-production, see *Early Opposition to the English Novel*, 43.

[65] *Critical Review*, 17 (June 1764), 478. Taylor, *Early Opposition to the English Novel*, 45. The same vocabulary is used by Hazlitt, in his essay 'On Reading Old Books', to explain his preference for the old over the modern: 'New-fangled books are . . . like made-dishes in this respect, that they are generally little else than hashs and *rifaccimentos* of what has been served up entire and in a more natural state at other times.' *The Plain Speaker*, essay xx (Howe, xii. 221).

violent stimulants') was that of addiction. Again, both producers and consumers were implicated in habits of passive dependency. Coleridge, for instance—an expert in such matters—claimed that

> where the reading of novels prevails as a habit, it occasions in time the entire destruction of the powers of the mind: it is such an utter loss to the reader, that it is not so much to be called pass-time as kill-time.... *it produces no improvement of the intellect*, but fills the mind with a mawkish and morbid sensibility, which is directly hostile to the cultivation, invigoration, and enlargement of the nobler faculties of understanding.[66]

If the vocabulary here ('prevails as a habit', 'entire destruction of the powers of mind') is redolent of the effects of opium, a connection is suggested between what opium supplies—short-term stimulation; long-term lassitude—and what is provided by novels pandering to the 'mawkish and morbid sensibility' of their readers. Kant lamented, in his essay 'What is Enlightenment?', that 'Reading is supposed to be an educational tool of independence, and most people use it like sleeping pills; it is supposed to make us free and mature, and how many does it serve merely as a way of passing time and as a way of remaining in a condition of eternal immaturity!',[67] while this curious passage from Thomas Clarkson's *Portraiture of Quakerism* (1806) associates the excesses of female sensibility with the torpor and debility of the addict:

> I have been told by a physician of the first eminence that music and novels have done more to produce the sickly countenances and nervous habits of our highly educated females, than any other causes that can be assigned. The excess of stimulus on the mind from the interesting and melting tales, that are peculiar to novels, affects the organs of the body, and relaxes the tone of the nerves, in the same manner as the melting tones of music have been described to act upon the constitution.[68]

---

[66] Collier's text of Lecture I in the 1811–12 series (*Lectures*, ii. 463). See also Coleridge's earlier comments in the 1808 'Lectures on Principles of Poetry': 'I may not compliment their Pastime, or rather *Kill-time*, with the name of *Reading*. Call it rather a sort of beggarly Day-dreaming, in which ... the mind furnishes for itself only laziness and a little mawkish sensibility, while the whole *Stuff* and Furniture of the Doze is supplied *ab extra* by a sort of spiritual Camera Obscura' (*Lectures* i. 124). In the eleventh of his 'Lectures on European Literature' (1818) he refers to novels as encouraging 'that love of sloth' which is 'inherent in the mind': 'they afford excitement without producing reaction' (*Lectures* ii. 194).

[67] Quoted by Woodmansee, *The Author, Art and the Market*, 29.

[68] *A Portraiture of Quakerism* (New York, 1806), i. 129–36; quoted in Taylor, *Early Opposition to the English Novel*, 107–8. Notice the erotic metaphors used to describe the effect of this 'drug' on the female body.

Poetry, in opposition to these discourses of imitation, derivativeness, passivity, consumption, and addiction, was seen as a source of end-lessly renewable pleasure, whose intensity and depth repaid concen-trated effort and increased with reperusal. Implicitly advocating this kind of reading, Schlegel complained in 1797 that 'People read vora-ciously, but how and what? How many readers are there after all who, once the fascination of novelty has worn off, can return again and again to a work that deserves it—not to kill time or obtain infor-mation on this or that subject, but to clarify its impression through repetition and to appropriate completely what is best in it?'[69] In *Bio-graphia Literaria*, Coleridge asserts that it is 'not the poem which we have *read*, but that to which we *return*, with the greatest pleasure', that 'possesses the genuine power, and claims the name of *essential poetry*', and in this sense, poems shared some of the characteristics of the Scriptures themselves, whose significance (as described in *The Statesman's Manual*) consisted not in novelty but in recoverable depth.[70] Again Coleridge was in accord with Bergk, who sought—as Martha Wood-mansee has shown—to intensify reading by reviving the older strategies familiar at the beginning of the eighteenth century, when readers 'had little choice but to return again and again to the handful of sacred and devotional texts available to them'.[71] Poetry, increasingly figured as an antidote to the fragmentation associated with the novel and news, thus became identified as a discourse of reflectiveness, depth, and wholeness. It was viewed as a means of challenging the stimulus-hunting reading-practices of modernity, and of reawakening a devo-tional or spiritual dimension in reader-response. The notion of genius as something that resisted novelty (retaining its own integrity no matter how many times it is reread) combined with the canonization of poets such as Milton and Shakespeare, to reinforce this Romantic hierarchy of genres.

The most striking evidence of the symbolic hold that generic hier-archies had over critical discourse occurred when the genius of either Shakespeare or Milton was perceived to come under threat from con-temporary habits of reception. It was here that late eighteenth- and early nineteenth-century anxieties were at their most acute. Hannah More,

---

[69] Quoted in Woodmansee, *The Author, Art, and the Market*, 87.

[70] *BL* i. 23; *SM* 25. See my discussion of this passage in the text and n. 46 of Ch. 2.

[71] *The Author, Art, and the Market*, 99. Interestingly, for our context, Woodmansee describes the reading-method advocated by Coleridge and Bergk as 'a kind of creation in reverse'.

writing to her sister in 1775, observed 'We have been reading a treatise on the morality of Shakespeare':

it is a happy and easy way of filling a book, that the present race of authors have arrived at—that of criticising the works of some eminent poet; with monstrous extracts, and short remarks. It is a species of cookery I begin to grow tired of; they cut up their authors into chops, and by adding a little crumbled bread of their own, and tossing it up a little, they present it as a fresh dish: you are to dine upon the poet;—the critic supplies the garnish; yet, has the credit, as well as the profit, of the whole entertainment.[72]

More had an almost visceral abhorrence for what she saw as a modern tendency to fragment past authors for the purposes of readerly consumption. Contemporary criticism of Shakespeare provided a special instance of the widely prevalent phenomenon of readerly cannibalism which More identified as the spirit of the age. When she condemned the contemporary taste for anthologies, abridgements, and compendiums in her *Strictures on Female Education*, it was ostensibly to discourage the easy commodification of culture, which pandered to idleness and passivity rather than reflection. But a deeper fear—of the fragmentation and attenuation of authorial identity—may be read between the lines of More's critique:

A few fine passages from the poets (passages perhaps which derived their chief beauty from their position and connection) are huddled together by some extract-maker, whose brief and disconnected patches of broken and discordant materials, while they inflame young readers with the vanity of reciting, neither fill the mind nor form the taste: and it is not difficult to trace back to their shallow sources the hackney'd quotations of certain *accomplished* young ladies, who will be frequently found not to have come legitimately by any thing they know.... the taste, thus pampered with delicious morsels, is early vitiated. The young reader of these *clustered beauties* conceives a disrelish for every thing which is plain.[73]

More attacks not only anthologists for their preparation of such 'delicious morsels' but the age of criticism for enjoying so inauthentic and secondary a culinary experience. Amongst the many volumes she had in mind, Wollstonecraft's *The Female Reader* would almost certainly have featured as an example—its title alone suggesting a slippage between the reader as a personal entity and the reader as an anthology of quotations.

---

[72] *Selected Writings of Hannah More*, ed. Robert Hole (London: William Pickering, 1996), 5.
[73] *Strictures on Female Education*, i. 174–6.

There is a striking (albeit anachronistic) resemblance between More's fear of fragmentation and the anxiety voiced by John Locke, a century earlier, regarding the division of the text of the Bible into chapter and verse. For Locke, this division had risked obliterating the seamless coherence of the Word of God: '*Not only Common People take the Verses usually for distinct Aphorisms*', he complained, with respect to the Epistle of St Paul, '*but even Men of more advanc'd knowledge in reading them, lose very much of the strength and force of the Coherence and the Light that depends on it*'. When printed correctly, the Bible's sacred authority was conveyed to the reader '*in continued Discourse where the Argument is continued*', not in '*loose sentences and Scripture crumbled into Verses, which quickly turn into independent Aphorism*'. Locke defended not only the coherence of the biblical text, here, but the powerful hegemony of Church and State: the danger of aphorism was that it could be adapted to sectarian purposes, allowing an unorthodox reader to make '*immediately strong and irrefragable Arguments for his Opinion*'.[74]

If there is a culinary association in Locke's metaphor of Scripture 'crumbled into verses' which anticipates Hannah More, an even more arresting connection works the other way round, in More's implicit parallel between the spirit of poetry and the sacred text of the Bible. In the first of the passages by More quoted above, it is the authority of Shakespeare as cherished national bard which is threatened by consumerist habits of reading; in the second passage, this authority is applied by extension to poetry in general, whose organic unity (here the carrier of a distinctly patriarchal charge of significance) was under threat from anthologists pandering to the tastes of female readers. In both cases, the language of victimization is applied to poets, not to authors in general: a coincidence which reminds us that the division between poetry and prose was frequently used to encode choices between hermeneutic models, in much the same way that the pairing of Shakespeare and Milton sustained logocentrism alongside secularism.

Charles Lamb, recalling with mock horror the first occasion when he looked at the manuscript of 'Lycidas', voiced a similar fidelity to the

---

[74] See the discussions of this passage from Locke in D. F. McKenzie, *Bibliography and the Sociology of Texts* (Panizzi Lectures, 1985) (London: British Library, 1986), 46–7; and Roger Chartier, 'Labourers and Voyagers' in Andrew Bennett (ed.), *Readers and Reading* (London: Longman, 1995), 139–40. Chartier refers to 'the opening up of the page through the multiplication of paragraphs that broke the uninterrupted continuity of the text common in the Renaissance.... A new reading of the same works or genres was consequently suggested by their new publishers—a reading that fragments texts into small and separate units'. This textual segmentation is known in French as *decoupage*.

sacralized concept of genius, this time as it was embodied in Milton. Significantly—given that the most recent developments in hermeneutic theory were emphasizing the historical life of texts, their contingency and temporality—Lamb's reaction is presented in terms of a resistance to the discovery that Milton was, like any other human being, fallible and changeable; that his creative process did not have univocal finality. Significantly, too, that resistance turns on the symbolically charged opposition between handwriting and print:

There is something to me repugnant, at any time, in written hand. The text never seems determinate. Print settles it. I had thought of the Lycidas as of a full-grown beauty—as springing up with all its parts absolute—till, in evil hour, I was shown the original written copy of it.... How it staggered me to see the fine things in their ore! interlined, corrected! as if their words were mortal, alterable, displaceable at pleasure! as if they might have been otherwise, and just as good! as if inspiration were made up of parts, and those fluctuating, successive, indifferent![75]

Like More, Lamb registers a resistance to modernity in its contemporary form (on the Continent, the fragment was officially inaugurated by Schlegel as a modish literary genre), and he evidently shares with Wordsworth and De Quincey a terror of futurity. ('He evades the present, he mocks the future', Hazlitt observed in *The Spirit of the Age*.)[76] But it is as if, looking ahead knowingly to an age in which it will be accepted that words are 'mortal, alterable, displaceable at pleasure', he accepts the pathos of his own resistance to change. The uncertainty of direction in his ironic voice tells a double story—on the one hand playfully debunking the expectation that the poet's authority must always be fixed, mysterious, and hermetic; on the other lamenting the discovery that there might be an openness in poetic discourse which admits of reconstruction. How to celebrate the transforming power of reading without implicitly conceding the provisionality of writing (and the demise, therefore, of its authority) is the question his irony poses—a question which points back to the precarious condition of the writing–reading subject in the age of criticism, and to a fear of engulfment which threatened the divided self.

In a letter to Samuel Rogers, written in 1833, the vulnerability of literary authority (its openness to interpretation, its potential subjugation

---

[75] 'Oxford in the Vacation', *London Magazine*, 3 (Oct. 1820), 367. See my discussion of this passage in 'Aesthetics of Indeterminacy', 232.

[76] Howe, xi. 180. 'Mr. Lamb has a distaste to new faces, to new books, to new buildings, to new customs', Hazlitt observes: '...His affections revert to, and settle on the past, but then, even this must have something personal and local in it to interest him deeply and thoroughly'.

to the changing tastes of its readers) are again acknowledged. Lamb is lamenting the fashion for literary galleries, of the kind exemplified by Boydell, because he sees the visual representation of poetry as a reduction of its sublimity. Arguing that the combination of the sister arts is counter-productive, and that they should be allowed to 'sparkle apart', he enters into a mock-diatribe against painters, in which the tones of self-irony and equivocation are apparent:

What injury (short of the Theatres) did not Boydell's Shakspeare Gallery do me with Shakspeare? to have Opie's Shakspeare, Northcote's Shakspeare, light-headed Fuselis' [*sic*] Shakespear, heavy-headed Romney's Shakspeare, wooden-headed West's Shakspeare... deaf-headed Reynolds's Shakspeare, instead of my, and every body's Shakspeare, To be tied down to an authentic face of Juliet! To have Imogen's portrait! to confine the illimitable![77]

As when, on a different occasion, he claimed that *King Lear* was unactable (thus protecting Shakespeare from the encroachments of popular theatrical representation) Lamb is objecting, here, to the fashion for spectacle.[78] What appears to be at stake is the notion of genius as something removed from temporality—an ideal and harmonious consciousness, at once 'illimitable' and available to all. Just as, in the case of *King Lear*'s sublimity, this ideal is destroyed when it becomes subject to the 'tyranny of the eye', so the gallery exhibits fragmented versions of a poetic spirit which is potentially (that is, imaginatively) universal.

As always, however, Lamb's tone of voice is hard to read. Working against the consensual and elitist drive towards ideality, his use of epithet—'wooden-headed', 'deaf-headed'—betrays a deep affection for human beings, with all their fallible and eccentric limitations. The Shakespeare whose genius is open to multiple interpretation is available to all precisely in so far as he passes into the popular imagination. Lamb acknowledges the paradoxical nature of his genius, not just in the counterpointing of pronouns ('my, and every body's Shakespeare'), but in the evident delight with which he runs through the variety of Shakespeares available for public consumption. His concluding exclamation, 'To be tied down to an authentic face of Juliet! To have Imogen's portrait! to confine the illimitable!', takes on a force that is directly comparable, in its *faux naïveté*, to the exclamations against

---

[77] To Samuel Rogers, 21 Dec. 1833, in *Letters of Charles and Mary Lamb, 1821–1842* ed. E. V. Lucas (2 vols.; London: Methuen, 1912), ii. 985. Excerpted by Roy Park, and included in *Lamb as Critic* (London: Routledge, 1980), 348.

[78] See 'Aesthetics of Indeterminacy', 231.

Milton's handwriting: 'as if their words were mortal, alterable, displace-able at pleasure! as if they might have been otherwise, and just as good!' In both cases, irony so unsettles his apparent resistance to modernity that one wonders if, after all, modernity is not cause for celebration.

Lamb's ambivalent response to the competing claims of wholeness and fragmentation, openness and closure—and, implicitly, creativity and criticism—reminds us of the extremes between which a Romantic poetics of reception mediated. If, at one end, the author was figured as univocal, authoritative, sealed off from readerly transformations, at the other end, he was seen as relinquishing the desire for authority, becoming a 'thoroughfare' for the voices of others. This ideal of creativity, in which the poet 'has no identity', moved writing over to a position of receptivity that closely resembles reading, apparently wel-coming the merging of one activity into the other. In this discourse, reading was figured as sympathetic completion; and the fear of frag-mentation was replaced by a range of rhetorical and formal strategies designed precisely to *accentuate* the contingency and openness of writing. That the second model of reception should have coexisted alongside its opposite bears witness, once again, to the paradox implicit in the Romantic concept of genius. In being both 'everything and nothing', genius mediated between the desire for self-possession and the desire for self-dispersal. As Drummond Bone puts it:

The post-Romantic association of genius with uniqueness or at a lower level eccentricity constantly hovers over its opposite—that genius is the dissolution of the merely personal into the universal, and that in a merely personal world, the universal will inevitably appear as the *reductio ad absurdum* of personality.[79]

An insight into the ways in which this paradox underpinned hermen-eutics helps us to understand the survival of a dual focus at the centre of Romantic literary theory and its subsequent reception. But as the com-plexity of Lamb's prose suggests, it is not a paradox which worked smoothly and continuously, as a synthesis of opposites; nor did the dichotomies it negotiated fall neatly on either side of gender- or genre-divides. The chameleon rhetoric of Romanticism is irregular, sometimes uncomfortable; and its dialectical structure is often incomplete.

---

[79] See 'The Emptiness of Genius: Aspects of Romanticism' in Murray (ed.), *Genius: The History of an Idea*, 122. The same paradox allows Jonathan Bate to claim, first that Shakespeare is for the Romantics symbolic of individuality; and later that he is 'the archetype of community...He lived—and lives—in a communality of artists' ('Shakespeare and Original Genius', 94).

CHAPTER 9

Reading Aloud: An 'Ambiguous Accompaniment'

They who are great talkers in company, have never been any talkers by themselves.

Shaftesbury, *Advice to an Author*, 1711

The habit of speaking is the habit of being heard, and of wanting to be heard; the habit of writing is the habit of thinking aloud, but without the help of an echo. The orator sees his subject in the eager looks of his auditors; and feels doubly conscious, doubly impressed with it in the glow of their sympathy; the author can only look for encouragement in a blank piece of paper.

Hazlitt, 'On the Difference between Writing and Speaking', 1826

I. 1798: HAZLITT ON PREACHING, CHANTING, AND SPEAKING

'It seemed to me, who was then young, as if the sounds had echoed from the bottom of the human heart, and as if that prayer might have floated in solemn silence through the universe.' The year of writing is 1823. Hazlitt (at 45 the most distinguished journalist and critic in Britain) is recalling his first encounter with Coleridge, which took place in the small Unitarian chapel at Shrewsbury, one Sunday morning in 1798. It was a year he retrospectively associated with youthful idealism, the birth of a new poetic spirit, and, crucially, the emergence of his own creative voice. Preaching a Unitarian sermon, Coleridge had the 'long pendulous hair... peculiar to enthusiasts', and in the dim light of the chapel, 'a strange wildness in his aspect, a dusky obscurity'. Passionate with the eloquence of gratitude, Hazlitt remembers listening to him as the experience of a lifetime:

my heart, shut up in the prison-house of this rude clay, has never found, nor will it ever find, a heart to speak to; but that my understanding also did not remain dumb and brutish, or at length found a language to express itself, I owe to Coleridge. (Howe, xvii. 107–9)

In his many regretful and angry reproaches against this genius who deserted the radical cause, Coleridge the Unitarian preacher—a larger-than-life, more magnetic version of his own father—haunted Hazlitt's imagination in a form reminiscent of Milton's republican hero, the damaged archangel of *Paradise Lost*. 'The figures that composed' the date 1798 were etched in his memory as clearly as 'the dreaded name of Demogorgon'. Associatively recalling the momentous year of 1789, they conjured up the spirit of millennarian optimism, embodied in Coleridge, which first inspired him to write. Accompanying his moving tribute to the poet's 'strange power of speech', there was a longing that history might reverse itself (like the two last figures of 1798); that the shadows of a personal, political, and spiritual betrayal might be removed, and the 'primitive spirit of Christianity' with its progressive power restored.

'My First Acquaintance with Poets' is a deeply affectionate and elegiac essay, but not an uncritical one. It discloses the depth of Hazlitt's anger with respect to Coleridge's apostasy, and his regret that the political impetus behind *Lyrical Ballads* could not be sustained. Hazlitt's reception of the *Lay Sermon* and *The Statesman's Manual*, which can be traced in a sequence of reviews in the *Examiner* and the *Edinburgh* in 1816–17, is a key to understanding its allusive implications. In the infamous 'review by anticipation' published anonymously among the 'Literary Notices' in the *Examiner* on 8 September 1816, Coleridge had been accused of haunting the public imagination 'with obscure noises', keeping up 'the importance of his oracular communications, by letting them remain a profound secret both to himself and the world' (Howe, vii. 114). In the *Edinburgh Review* article which appeared in December of the same year, he was further reprimanded for muttering 'all unintelligible, and all impertinent things'; for speaking rhapsodically from a pulpit or rostrum that was 'high enthroned above all height' like the Satanic seat of Dullness in Pope's *Dunciad* (Howe, xvi. 113). In his spoof letter to the editor of the *Examiner*, dated 12 January 1817, Hazlitt adopted the persona of his own earlier self to eulogize Coleridge's sermon delivery in 1798 ('Poetry and Philosophy had met together. Truth and Genius had embraced, under the eye and with the sanction of Religion') then asked truculently how there came to be such a mismatch between the Coleridge he remem-

bered and the Coleridge whose 'Lay Sermon' had recently been reviewed: 'what I have to complain of is this, that from reading your
account of the "Lay-Sermon," I begin to suspect that my notions
formerly must have been little better than a deception. . . . Again, Sir, I
ask Mr. Coleridge, why, having preached such a sermon as I have
described, he has published such a sermon as you have described?
What right, Sir, has he or any man to make a fool of me or any man?'
(Howe, vii. 129). This letter formed the germ of 'My First Acquaintance',
and when Hazlitt requisitioned it in 1823, he was tacitly recalling two
very different contexts in which Coleridge had delivered sermons. In
1798, he had talked on 'peace and war; upon church and state—not [as
in 1816] their alliance, but their separation' (Howe, xvii. 108). A contemporary audience would have been more immediately aware than we
are of the troubled reception history packed into that single, glancing
remark.

The same density of topical allusion is apparent further on in the
narrative of 'My First Acquaintance'. Soon after his description of the
encounter with Coleridge in Shrewsbury chapel, Hazlitt moves to a
scene of reading that is altogether more homely. Describing his first
visit to see the Wordsworths at Alfoxden, he remembers how 'Coleridge
read aloud with a sonorous and musical voice, the ballad of *Betty Foy*'
(Howe, xvii. 117). The full resonance of those words 'sonorous and
musical' comes from their double associations—with the charged eloquence of Coleridge's earlier sermon delivery, and with the bardic orality
recently celebrated by such writers as Macpherson and Blair, and revived
in the collaborative venture of *Lyrical Ballads*. There is a touch of bathos
in the conjunction between registers, the idiomatic sounds of Wordsworth's 'Betty Foy' becoming slightly muffled in Coleridge's elevated
recital. Hazlitt hints, here, with the benefit of hindsight, at the 'radical
difference' between two theories of poetic language. It was a difference
that had emerged implicitly in the 1798 collaboration, and became
discernible in the Preface to *Lyrical Ballads* (1800). In subsequent statements by Coleridge in 1802 it was openly recognized, and by the time
Biographia Literaria was published it had become the focus for sustained
theoretical discussion.[1] It centred on whether poetry was or was not
inevitably more elevated than spoken language. Wordsworth in 1798
had wanted to take poetry as close as possible to the rhythms and

[1] See esp. *BL* chs. 17–19.

register of ordinary speech, while Coleridge by 1816 had concluded that poetic language was by definition extraordinary. This difference with respect to language was confirmed by other divergences of poetic temperament and subject-matter. Summarizing these in *Biographia Literaria*, Coleridge argued that a tacit division of labour had been agreed between the two poets, Wordsworth dealing with everyday concerns, while he himself focused on the supernatural. This *post hoc* rationalization of their disagreement helped to minimize the pain and mess to which it had given rise.

Hazlitt's hint that such differences were already apparent in 1798 is amplified two pages later in 'My First Acquaintance' when he describes how Wordsworth 'sat down and talked very naturally and freely, with a mixture of clear gushing accents in his voice, a deep gutteral intonation, and a strong tincture of the northern *burr*, like the crust on wine' (Howe, xvii. 118). The Rousseauian associations of 'naturally and freely' (implicitly contrasted with 'sonorous and musical') combine here with an enjoyment of regional accent and personal idiolect, themselves redolent of the vernacular liberties celebrated in *Lyrical Ballads*. Wordsworth's voice acquires what Hazlitt elsewhere calls 'gusto': its intensity and immediacy are those of 'manly' prose.[2] Familial and domestic, the meal around the kitchen table at Alfoxden both complements and contrasts with the dark chapel at Shrewsbury, where Coleridge had disclosed his affinities with seventeenth-century enthusiasm. There was, Hazlitt implies, a powerful convergence of eloquence and oratory on the one hand with idiomatic spontaneity on the other, which made the *Lyrical Ballads* a rich experiment in progressive discourse. But at the same time, this hybrid venture was shadowed from the outset by its bifurcation.

If the ironies and equivocations in Hazlitt's narrative show him to be retrospectively alert to incompatibilities between Wordsworth and Coleridge, pulling their linguistic theories in opposite directions, they also point to more troubling affinities in the two poets' attitudes to audience, which had complicated the reception of *Lyrical Ballads* and hampered

---

[2] See Tom Paulin, *The Day-Star of Liberty: William Hazlitt's Radical Style* (London: Faber and Faber, 1998), a book to which I am greatly indebted throughout this chapter; Paulin's discussion of intensity and immediacy occurs in ch. 3. For Coleridge's opposite views of what constitutes a 'masculine' syntax, see John Barrell, *Poetry, Language and Politics* (Manchester: Manchester University Press, 1988). For a less gendered characterization of radical prose style see Olivia Smith, *The Politics of Language, 1791–1819* (Oxford, Oxford University Press, 1984), esp. ch. 11.

their subsequent careers. A passing resemblance between Wordsworth's northern burr and the 'burr burr' of the idiot boy (unlikely to be accidental) at once celebrates and ironizes an aesthetic grounded in the sympathetic identification between a poet and his subject-matter. Hazlitt's irony, directed at the poet's lack of critical detachment, is confirmed a page further on, when he tells how 'Wordsworth read us the story of Peter Bell in the open air; and the comment upon it by his face and voice was very different from that of some later critics! Whatever might be thought of the poem, "his face was as a book where men might read strange matters"' (Howe, xvii. 118). As the focus of attention moves from the poet's performance of his poem among friends to its public reception by critics and reviewers, Hazlitt's sympathy gives way to sarcasm:

There is a *chaunt* in the recitation both of Coleridge and Wordsworth, which acts as a spell upon the hearer, and disarms the judgment. Perhaps they have deceived themselves by making habitual use of this ambiguous accompaniment. (Howe, xvii. 118)

The aside is brief but telling. Hazlitt plays on the phonetic and etymological links between 'chant' and 'enchantment' to drive home a critique of the poetics underpinning *Lyrical Ballads*. He suggests that, despite their underlying difference of opinion with respect to language and the supernatural, Coleridge and Wordsworth shared a desire to awaken in their readers a sense of mystery—to bring them under a spell. For Hazlitt, whose Dissenting origins put him on the side of rational enlightenment, this component of poetic language was suspect. It was this that made poetry 'fall in with the language of power', sometimes against its own intentions.

In showing how the two poets enchanted each other, Hazlitt begins to adumbrate the story of withdrawal and political apostasy which was to unfold in their subsequent careers. He seems to hold their collaboration responsible for each poet's relinquishment of an authentic radical voice. The 'chaunt' in which he remembers hearing them read their poems aloud sounds a hollow note after the passionate commitment of Coleridge's sermon and the rugged homeliness of Wordsworth's spoken idiom. It recalls a mode of delivery which flattened and homogenized their distinctive energies into a monotonous unity. Hazlitt's choice of the obsolete, poetic variant of the word 'chant' is redolent of 'The Ancient Mariner' 's archaic diction. 'Chaunt' is the word that Wordsworth chose

to replace 'speak' when he revised the passage in *The Prelude*, Book XIV
in which he nostalgically relived the 1798 collaboration: 'Thou in be-
witching words with happy heart | Didst chaunt the vision of that
Ancient Man, | The bright-eyed Mariner' (*Prelude, 1850*, xiv. 400–2).
And when Coleridge composed 'To William Wordsworth', 'on the night
after his recitation of a poem on the growth of an individual mind', he
returned Wordsworth's compliment with an apposite allusion. *The Pre-
lude*, he wrote, is 'An Orphic tale indeed, | A song divine of high and
passionate thoughts | *To their own music chaunted*'. The association of
'chaunting' with the highest of poetic registers (epic, heroic, traditional)
is confirmed by Hazlitt himself in his *Spirit of the Age* essay on Byron,
where it is used to describe the 'solemn measures' in which *Childe Harold*
'chaunts a hymn to fame', rekindling 'the earliest aspirations of the mind
after greatness and true glory' (Howe, xi. 73). The *Oxford English Dictionary* gives as its second and fourth definitions of the word, 'to sing,
utter musically' (often with notion of 'prolonged or drawling intonation'); and 'to recite musically, intone; to sing a chant, as the Psalms, etc.
in public worship'. The dimension of 'public worship' implied in chanting was out of place in the comparative safety (although always under
threat from informers) of Alfoxden. So too, the democratic agenda of
the *Lyrical Ballads* volume—the 'levelling muse' discerned by Hazlitt—
was at odds with an elevated and mystifying delivery.

Hazlitt's critique extends beyond the politics of style, into the politics
of reception. Mischievously applying Coleridge's idea of the 'suspension
of disbelief' to this private scene of reading, he suggests that the
Biographia's distinction between illusion and delusion is shaky, and that
this casts doubt on the quality of the material delivered.[3] Hearers who
succumbed to a spell might 'chuse to be deceived', but if their judgement
is disarmed in the process, how is it possible to distinguish between
'enchantment' and what Hugh Blair called 'blind and implicit veneration'?[4] Once again, the shadow context of December 1816 provides a
key to Hazlitt's meaning. 'In this state of voluntary self-delusion', he
lamented, in his review of *The Lay-Sermon*, Coleridge '... mistakes hallu-
cinations for truths ... It is in this sort of waking dream, this giddy maze

---

[3] See *BL* ii. 134; *Lectures*, i. 134 and ii. 266; and my discussion of this issue in 'Coleridge and
the Anxiety of Reception', *Romanticism*, 1/2 (1995), 225–6.

[4] Blair argues that the true function of criticism is to help us to guard against 'blind and
implicit veneration', and to teach us 'to admire and to blame with judgement, and not to follow
the crowd blindly'. See *Lectures on Rhetoric and Belles Lettres* (2 vols., London: W. Strachan and
T. Cadell, 1783), i. 9.

of opinions, started, and left, and resumed... that Mr. Coleridge's pleasure, and, we believe, his chief faculty, lies' (Howe, xvi. 101). Implied in Hazlitt's comments on 'reading aloud' was a critique which reflected more widely on coterie reading-circles, systems of private patronage, and mutual 'puffing', as they prevailed in late eighteenth-century Britain. Just as the magic exerted over an audience by the sing-song voice of a poet disarmed the judgement of both poets and listeners, so the mutual congratulation of poets who were each others' ideal audience was in danger of pre-empting the criticism poetry needed and deserved. 'Chaunting', in this context, begins to take on associations with the vanity of Chaucer's Chaunticleer.[5]

II. THE ORATOR'S SPEAKING BODY: FROM SHERIDAN TO THELWALL

To understand the full implications of Hazlitt's allusion to 'chaunting' in this late essay, we need to put it in the wider context of issues concerning the politics of language—and specifically of performative utterance—which had been actively debated in Britain from the mid-eighteenth century onward. Our knowledge of how reading aloud was understood both inside and outside the Dissenting tradition helps us to make clear discriminations between a bodily eloquence whose rhythms are those of everyday prose and an elevated, chanting delivery whose affiliations are to poetry. In practice, however, as we shall see, ideas that travelled down different conduits of influence could cross over and merge. When Hazlitt identified Wordsworth's and Coleridge's manner in reading aloud as 'an ambiguous accompaniment', he nicely caught the sense in which the *Lyrical Ballads* project straddled discursive preferences. Chanting had a complex linguistic significance, disclosing a range of possible inflections for oral discourse at this time. Its musicality could claim kinship with the ballad tradition, and with a distinctly progressive notion of primitivism. But it could also attach itself to the more oracular authority of the Anglican Church. Symbolically, the doubleness of these associations, as retrospectively detected by Hazlitt, accounts for the later divergence of Wordsworth's 'natural conversation of men under the influence of natural feelings' (*BL* ii. 42) from Coleridge's Aristotelian belief that 'poetry is essentially *ideal*' (*BL* ii. 45).

[5] See 'The Nun's Priest's Tale'.

Hazlitt's preference for the spoken idiom of prose over the sung idiom of poetry had its roots in an oratorical tradition, germane to the collaboration of 1798, in which chanting was condemned. The key contributors to this tradition were the Irish orator Thomas Sheridan (father of Richard Sheridan), who gave lecture courses all over Britain in the 1760s; James Burgh, who published a cheap and popular instruction manual, *The Art of Speaking* in 1763; Hugh Blair, whose *Lectures on Rhetoric and Belles Lettres* were delivered over a period of twenty-four years in Edinburgh; and Joseph Priestley, whose *Lectures on Oratory and Criticism*, given at the Dissenting academy of Warrington, were published in 1777. 'Some of our greatest men have been trying to do that with the pen, which can only be performed by the tongue; to produce effects by the dead letter, which can never be produced but by the living voice, with its accompaniments'.[6] These words are taken from the Preface to Sheridan's *Lectures on Elocution*, the single most important contribution to elocutionary theory in the eighteenth century. Published in 1762 with a subscription list of 1,700 names, 600 of them 'taken down at the door of the several places where the Lectures were delivered', this book represented the summation of a decade's thought, as it had been tried and tested on numerous audiences in Bristol, Oxford, Cambridge, and Edinburgh. W. Benzie, in his learned monograph, *The Dublin Orator*, informs us that Sheridan learnt the art of oral expression from Swift, his godfather, who made him read aloud two to three hours a day—a tradition later upheld, in the 'Attic Mornings' in Bath beginning in 1763, where Sheridan recited select passages from great authors.[7]

At the centre of Sheridan's theory of language was a belief that we have two kinds of language, spoken and written—'one... the gift of God; the other, the invention of man' (p. xiii)—and that the power which words acquire, 'when forcibly uttered by the living voice' (p. xiii),

---

[6] Thomas Sheridan, AM, *A Course of Lectures on Elocution: together with two Dissertations on Language, and some other Tracts relative to those Subjects* (London: W. Strachan, 1762), p. xii. Page refs. will be given in the text.

[7] W. Benzie, *The Dublin Orator* (Leeds: Scolar Press Ltd., 1972), pp. viii, 54. See also Linda Kelly, *Richard Brinsley Sheridan: A Life* (London: Sinclair Stevenson, 1997), 5 where she argues that 'It was from Swift that [Tom Sheridan] first acquired his passionate interest in oratory and the correct pronunciation of English—the task of establishing a general standard of pronunciation, along the lines laid down by the French Academy, was one that Swift had always hoped to carry out'. Sheridan in his turn, taught grammar and oratory to his sons, carrying on the tradition of reading aloud which he had learned from Swift (ibid. 22–3). Kelly describes the Attic Entertainments in Bath as 'combining recitations from the English poets with vocal and instrumental music' (ibid. 25).

is a power for good, creating sympathy between human beings through a universal language. In drawing attention to the gap between speaking and writing, Sheridan's focus narrowed on the act of reading, which 'must fall short of the power of speaking, in all articles which depend upon feeling' (p. 13). He lamented what he called 'a certain tone or chant in reading or reciting'. This, he claimed, was produced by the modern art of punctuation, 'not taken from the art of speaking' but from 'grammatical construction, often without reference to the pauses used in discourse' (p. 80). If punctuation had never been invented, there would be no such thing as the 'reading tones' or 'false pauses and rests of the voice' (p. 80):

Here then is to be found the true source of the bad manner of reading and speaking in public, that so generally prevails: which is, that we are taught to read in a different way, with different tones and cadences, from those which we use in speaking; and this artificial manner, is used instead of the natural one, in all recitals and repetitions at school, as well as in reading. (p. 4)[8]

No one, Sheridan argues, could deliver someone else's words with the same variety and force as his own, until they were 'so perfectly impressed on the memory, that the mind may be wholly at liberty to attend only to the delivery' (p. 11); and even the delivery of one's own words could be artificial. '[T]he most bookish men are generally remarkable for the worst delivery' (p. 8), he observed: a truth borne out, not only by Hazlitt's awkward early experience as a lecturer, but by his later theorizing on the subject of eloquence. 'An author is bound to write—well or ill, wisely or foolishly; it is his trade', he announced, in his 'On the Conversation of Authors'; but this did not guarantee that he would also be a good speaker: 'Reading, study, silence, thought, are a bad introduction to loquacity' (Howe, xii. 24). The same argument was amplified in his essay 'On the Difference between Writing and Speaking', where the fact of being a good speaker seemed almost to guarantee that one was a bad writer: 'Not only is it obvious that the two faculties do not always go together in the same proportions: but they are not unusually in direct opposition to each other' (Howe, xii. 262).

[8] This complaint is repeated in his *Rhetorical Grammar*, prefixed to his *Dictionary* (p. 57), where Sheridan claims that 'the usual fault of introducing sing-song notes, or a species of chanting, into poetical numbers, is disagreeable to every ear but that of the chanter himself'. The passage is quoted by Gilbert Austin in *Chironomia, or a Treatise on Rhetorical Delivery* (London: T. Cadell and W. Davies, 1806), 55.

Sheridan's solution to the gap between the spoken and the written discourse was twofold: first, he advocated a vocal eloquence, reinforced by 'expressive looks and significant gestures'—in short, a body language of articulate feeling; and second he designed a new form of notation, directing the vocal emphases and pauses of the speaker in oral delivery by accents placed over the relevant words. In *The Art of Reading*, published in 1775, this notation was used '*to serve as Lessons to practice on*',[9] and introduced so as to coincide with the political climax of Sheridan's argument—the moment at which a claim for eloquence became a claim for constitutional stability. In keeping with what Peter De Bolla calls 'the consensus politics of liberal humanism, the balanced economy of civic politesse',[10] Sheridan here made the commonplace link between the state of the language and the health of the nation:

Now if the minds of the inhabitants of this country were formed by a suitable education correspondent to the nature of the constitution... it would produce subjects worthy of so noble a form of government and capable of supporting it.[11]

The full force of Sheridan's vocal emphasis can be felt by comparing his pages with those from an exactly contemporary publication by the Cumbrian schoolmaster William Cockin, *The Art of Delivering Written Language; or, an Essay on Reading*, which was dedicated to the actor David Garrick. Cockin also advocated naturalness of spoken utterance in reading aloud; but his notation was graphocentric rather than phonocentric. In his text, all the emphases and modulations of the speaker's voice were directed by changes in font, paradoxically reinforcing the bondage of eye to text. Sheridan's was as near as one might get to a manual for reading aloud; Cockin's remained a visual representation of the voice reading.

James Burgh's *The Art of Speaking*, published in 1763, was associated with the 'mechanical' school of elocution, to which John Walker (author of three later works on elocution) also belonged. Burgh was of Scottish descent: the son of a Presbyterian minister in Perthshire, he abandoned his training for the ministry to become a businessman, but later set up an academy at Stoke Newington. From here, he published a number of

---

[9] Thomas Sheridan, *Lectures on the Art of Reading; First Part: Containing the Art of Reading Prose* (London: J. Dodsley et al., 1775), 286.

[10] 'Of the Gesture of the Orator: The Speaking Subject', in *The Discourse of the Sublime: Readings in History, Aesthetics and the Subject* (Oxford: Basil Blackwell, 1989).

[11] *Lectures on the Art of Reading*, 296–7.

important and strongly reformist works, including *Thoughts on Education* (1747) and *Political Disquisitions* (1774), a book that Hazlitt admired. Burgh's *The Art of Speaking* was designed 'To offer a help toward the improvement of youth in the useful and ornamental accomplishment of speaking properly their mother-tongue',[12] and its *'easy expence'* (p. 3) and readable format made it one of the most popular instruction manuals of its kind. Wordsworth, who (like many other schoolboys) owned a copy, would have been familiar with its words of warning against monotonous delivery in reading aloud:

Young readers are apt to get into a *rehearsing* kind of *monotony,* of which it is very difficult to break them. Monotony is holding one *uniform* humming sound through the whole discourse, without rising or falling. Cant, is, in speaking, as psalmody and ballad in music, a strain consisting of a few notes *rising* and *falling* without variation, like a peal of bells, let the *matter* change how it will. The chaunt, with which the prose psalms are half-sung, half-said, in cathedrals, is the same kind of absurdity. (p. 8)

Burgh's dismissal of three kinds of monotony—'chaunting in cathedrals, psalmody in parish churches, ballad-music put to a number of verses'—is intriguing in the light of the various registers discussed in 'My First Acquaintance with Poets'; as is the etymological connection between 'chaunt' and 'cant'.[13]

Burgh, like Sheridan, emphasized the naturalness of the spoken voice, which won out over the written or printed text in its immediacy and clarity. His ideal for 'reading aloud' was one in which the voice 'speaks' what the eye reads, as if no gap existed between reader and writer:

Young people must be taught to let their voice *fall* at the *ends* of sentences; and to read without any particular whine, cant, or drawl, and with the *natural*

---

[12] Burgh, *The Art of Speaking* (2nd edn., London: T. Longman and J. Buckland, 1768), 3. Page refs. will be given in the text.

[13] For Hazlitt, as for Byron, the word 'cant' has negative associations when used in its figurative sense: 'Of all the cants that ever were canted in this canting world, this is the worst!' he protests, in his *Examiner* review of *The Statesman's Manual* (Howe, vii. 121). Cant is also the word used in the 18th century to describe private languages, dialects, or idiolects. Hazlitt may be playing on this sense of the word 'cant' to suggest that Wordsworth and Coleridge speak to each other in a vocabulary that is inaccessible to those outside their circle. Compare his observation, in the first of his two essays 'On the Conversation of Authors', that 'There is a Free-masonry in all things. You can only speak to be understood, but this you cannot be, except by those who are in the secret.... C——is the only person who can talk to all sorts of people, on all sorts of subjects, without caring a farthing for their understanding a word of what he says—and *he* talks only for admiration and to be listened to, and accordingly the least interruption puts him out' (Howe, xii. 35).

inflections of voice, which they use in *speaking*. For *reading* is nothing but *speaking* what one sees in a book, as if he were expressing his *own* sentiments, as they rise in his mind. And no person reads well, till he comes to speak what he sees in the book before him in the same *natural* manner as he speaks the thoughts, which arise in his *own* mind. (p. 8)

Sheridan and Burgh were not alone in stressing the superiority of the living voice over the printed word. By the mid-eighteenth century, this preference had emerged as a distinctive feature of the primitivist poetic widely advocated in Britain and on the Continent. Hugh Blair (appointed to the newly created Chair in Rhetoric and Belles Lettres at Edinburgh University in 1760), was Scotland's counterpart to Rousseau in his commitment to the metaphysics of presence. As Fiona Stafford has argued, Blair saw 'the continuing value of speech even in modern society where written discourse had long been the medium of authority, and was rapidly becoming the main channel for intellectual traffic'.[14] His belief in the power of spoken utterance informed his enthusiasm about the discovery of Ossian, in whom he found his views on the connection between passion, primitive society, and great poetry confirmed. Blair mentioned Sheridan approvingly in the published text of his *Lectures* in 1783. His preference for spoken over written communication was grounded in a conviction that 'the voice of the living Speaker, makes an impression on the mind, much stronger than can be made by the perusal of any Writing'.[15] Voice preceded writing, in the same way that a natural language of gestures preceded sophisticated linguistic communication:

The tones of voice, the looks and gesture, which accompany discourse, and which no Writing can convey, render discourse, when it is well managed, infinitely more clear, and more expressive, than the most accurate Writing. For tones, looks, and gestures, are natural interpreters of the sentiments of the mind. They remove ambiguities; they enforce impressions; they operate on us by means of sympathy, which is one of the most powerful instruments of persuasion. Our sympathy is always awakened more, by hearing the Speaker, than by reading his works in our closet. (i. 136)

Blair acknowledged that writing had some advantages over speech: whereas speech was 'fugitive and passing', the written word gave readers

---

[14] 'Hugh Blair's Ossian, Romanticism and the Teaching of Literature', in Robert Crawford (ed.), *The Scottish Invention of English Literature* (Cambridge: Cambridge University Press, 1998), 68–88: 76.

[15] *Lectures on Rhetoric and Belles Lettres*, i. 136. Page refs. will be given in the text.

the freedom to 'arrest the sense of the writer'; to 'pause, and revolve, and compare, at their leisure, one passage with another' (i. 135–6). But despite this drawback, spoken language was superior to written language in its energy and force. The living voice, for Blair, was authentic in exactly the way that gestures were: 'It is that method of interpreting our mind, which nature has dictated to all, and which is understood by all; whereas, words are only arbitrary conventional symbols of our ideas' (ii. 204).

In his extensive discussion of eloquence, Blair underlined the distinction between voice as the vehicle of sympathy and the printed word as its empty signifier: 'a discourse that is read, moves us less than one that is spoken, as having less the appearance of coming warm from the heart', he said (ii. 7); and again: 'a Discourse read, is far inferior to an Oration spoken. It leads to a different sort of composition, as well as of delivery; and can never have an equal effect upon any audience' (ii. 43–4). Despite the fact that, at one point in his argument, Blair appeared to be praising the declamation of Greek and Roman orators because they approached 'the nature of recitative in music', the habit of sing-song delivery was condemned by him, as it was by Sheridan, for its suppression of the sense behind the words spoken:

If any one, in Public Speaking, shall have formed to himself a certain melody or tune, which requires rests and pauses of its own, distinct from those of the sense, he has, for certain, contracted one of the worst habits into which a Public Speaker can fall. (ii. 214)

The relation of print to voice was also important to Joseph Priestley, who acknowledged the influence of Sheridan in his *Lectures on Oratory and Criticism* published in 1777. For Priestley, the art of oratory was the art of persuasion. It did not consist in elevated diction and delivery, but rather in the use of 'an *unpremeditated discourse*, in which the sentiments are supposed to be natural and sincere, proceeding directly from the heart'.[16] Priestley used the history of the Dissenting tradition as proof of the power of extempore speaking: 'Can we imagine it possible that the primitive christians, the first reformers, and, I may add, the founders of our modern sects ... could ever have attained to so great a degree of popularity, without the talent of haranguing extempore?' (p. 112). His elocutionary ideal was modelled on enthusiasm, its communicative

---

[16] *A Course of Lectures on Oratory and Criticism* (London: Joseph Johnson, 1777), 111. Page refs. will be given in the text.

power consisting in an expressive immediacy which was universally legible. Oratory was persuasive in so far as it was egalitarian: just as pauses, hesitations, consulting the interlocutor created a bond of sympathy, on which the speaker's efficacy relied; so it was the informality of the spoken voice that rendered feelings powerfully: 'when the mind is agitated, the voice is interrupted, and a man expresses himself in short and broken sentences' (p. 293).

Priestley's discursive allegiances were summarized in a passage which was deeply germane to the concerns of Wordsworth and Coleridge in 1798, but even more so to Hazlitt, educated at the Dissenting academy in Hackney where Priestley taught after the Warrington Academy was dissolved in 1783:

Anciently, I believe, in all nations, mankind were so captivated with the charms of verse, that, in reciting poetry, no regard was paid to any thing but the metrical pause; which made the pronunciation of verse a kind of *singing* or *chanting*: and accordingly we never read of *poems* being *read*, but always of their being *sung* by them. Nor shall we wonder at this, if we consider that, even in our own age, all persons who have not been instructed in the true art of pronunciation (which is governed wholly by the *sense*) naturally pronounce verse in the same manner, and quite differently from their manner of pronouncing prose; so that it generally requires a good deal of pains to correct that vicious habit. (p. 300)

For Priestley, then, the art of correct pronunciation was one that disaffiliated 'reading aloud' from the poetic and musical end of the discursive spectrum, moving it securely into the domain of plain speaking. 'Let your primary regards be always to the *sense* and to *perspicuity*', he advised, 'and in every competition between harmony and these more valuable objects... let the harmony be sacrificed without hesitation' (p. 313). If it was a Priestleyan position that Hazlitt adopted when referring to the chanting delivery of 'The Idiot Boy' and 'Peter Bell', then some kind of sacrifice of sense to musical sound was no doubt the implication. Perhaps, too, a Priestleyan influence may be detected in Hazlitt's dismissive comments on the prose style of poets:

What is a little extraordinary, there is a want of *rhythmus* and cadence in what they [i.e. poets] write without the help of metrical rules. Like persons who have been accustomed to sing to music, they are at a loss in the absence of the habitual accompaniment and guide to their judgment.... The measured cadence and regular *sing-song* of rhyme or blank verse have destroyed, as it were, their natural ear for the mere [*sic*] characteristic harmony which ought to subsist between the sound and the sense. (Howe, xii. 5)

Crucial to Priestley's and Hazlitt's belief in the communicative power of the spoken voice was an emphasis on the natural eloquence of the body. We are reminded of this by Hazlitt's tongue-in-cheek portrait of Wordsworth reading 'Peter Bell', his face and voice providing a legible commentary on his feelings: 'Whatever might be thought of the poem', Hazlitt observed wryly, ' "his face was as a book where men may read strange matters" ' (Howe, xvii. 118). This emphasis on the transparency of facial and vocal expression is somewhat ironized here by Hazlitt's use of the book metaphor, which crops up again in his description of the painter Northcote in the *Plain Speaker* essay 'On the Conversation of Authors':

His look is a continual, ever-varying history-piece of what passes in his mind. His face is as a book. There need no marks of interjection or interrogation to what he says. (Howe, xii. 39)

But the same belief was expressed less knowingly by numerous eighteenth-century commentators, writing in the overlapping fields of elocution, oratory, and pulpit-delivery. John Mason, whose *Essay on Elocution and Pronunciation* was addressed to a Presbyterian audience (some of whom were entering the ministry), claimed in 1748 that an orator's or preacher's countenance was 'the Seat of the soul and the very Life of the Action'; that 'every Passion, whilst uttered with the tongue, should be painted in the face'; and that 'there is often more Eloquence in a Look than any Words can express':

The Language of the Eye is inexpressible. It is the Window of the Soul; from which sometimes the whole Heart looks out at once, and speaks more feelingly than all the warmest Strains of Oratory.[17]

Gilbert Austin, looking back on a century of treatises on rhetoric in his compendious *Chironomia* (1806), weighed the advantages of voice against facial and bodily expressions: 'The countenance and the gesture', he argued, 'address their mute language to the eye. The very name of eloquence is derived from the exertions of the voice, and where the voice fails, eloquence ceases to have living existence, and may be found only in the dead letter'.[18] But if voice was the prime organ of oratory, the

---

[17] *An Essay on Elocution, or, Punctuation, Intended chiefly for the assistance of those who instruct others in the Art of Reading. And of those who are often called upon to speak in Publick* (London: M. Cooper, 1748), 36.
[18] *Chironomia*, 29.

eye was its acutely sensitive monitor and receptor. Austin acknowledged this by quoting from John Lavater, whose *Essays on Physiognomy* (1789) were widely known. 'The eye at once receives and reflects the intelligence of thought, and the warmth of sensibility', wrote Lavater: 'it is the sense of the mind, the tongue of the understanding'.[19] Austin saw the eye as having uncanny, almost magical properties. When the orator used these to hold sway over his audience, his performance resembled a mesmeric spell: 'We seem to have the power, as it were, of touching each other by the sense of sight, and to be endued with something of that fascination of the eye which is attributed to other animals, and which the serpent is particularly said to possess.'[20] The connection Austin made between the eye and enchantment was one to which Coleridge himself recurred on more than one occasion. What interested these writers was that the language spoken through the eye connected human beings with their deep-buried, primitive origins. It revealed to them, in ways that could not be denied, their kinship with the animal world—a sometimes disturbing kinship, as the symbolic associations of the serpent suggest.

Just as the body was an expressive signifier of feelings—a 'supplement' to the speaking voice—so it was in the gaps and fissures of spoken discourse that genuine eloquence was to be found. This is why extempore utterance was thought to be more appropriate to the communication of powerful feeling than finished prose; and why there was a long-established association in the eighteenth century between extemporality, eloquence, and enthusiasm. James Fordyce's influential manual, *The Eloquence of the Pulpit* (1755), which contained tips on deportment and delivery, was intended to encourage the 'art' of sincerity by showing that theatrical skills are not incompatible with an evangelical purpose. Fordyce, a Presbyterian divine and poet, spent his early years in Scotland, before moving to London in 1760, where, as the minister of a congregation in Monkwell street, he became known as an inspiring and charismatic orator. Garrick was said to have heard him more than once, and to have spoken highly of his performances: he had, according to eyewitnesses, 'the natural advantages of a dignified presence and a piercing eye; his delivery and gestures were studied with great care'.[21] Fordyce condemned 'the sing-song voice, and the see-saw gestures' which epitomized artificial orations. He preferred a 'certain graceful

[19] Quoted by Austin, ibid. 116.   [20] Ibid. 102.
[21] See the entry in the *Dictionary of National Biography*.

easiness, a certain happy negligence' to a 'formal regularity of argument' or 'the constant glitter of shining phrases, and the endless string of rounded periods'.[22] 'Whatever [the preacher] advances', Fordyce advised his audience, should have 'a native air, a peculiar stamp of sincerity, that inexpressible kind of genuine look, which belongs to unaffected worth alone; which art may imitate, but cannot reach'.[23] The following were in his view among the rhetorical and stylistic features that enlivened extempore delivery:

exclamations quick and few, inspired and justified by the occasion; bold apostrophe's thrown out in an heat, but neither frequent nor long; sudden transitions; moving and home addresses to different sorts of men; abrupt sallies of devout affection, of virtuous indignation, of melting compassion, of pious zeal[24]

Austin, too, spoke on behalf of a clarity that came with immediacy and conviction. His emphasis fell on the streamlined efficiency of eloquence—its apparently effortless artistry. In 'just articulation', he said, words were

delivered out from the lips, as beautiful coins, newly issued from the mint, deeply and accurately impressed, perfectly finished, neatly struck by the proper organs, distinct, sharp, in due succession, and of due weight.[25]

One can see in Fordyce, Priestley, and Austin a prefiguration of the prose-style allegiances developed in Hazlitt and championed by Tom Paulin. Metaphors of heating, melting, coining—and even, at one point, electrical charge—bear witness to an excitement in the experimental possibilities of the speech-act: its volatile properties and verifiable effects. Extemporality became the conduit of 'a kind of sympathy between the heart of the speaker and the hearts of the hearers', which no outside interference could affect:

the religious passion darts and vibrates from one to the other; and a secret but powerful and instantaneous stroke is felt, which may be compared ... to the surprising effect produced by communication in the case of some late noted experiments [in electricity].[26]

[22] *The Eloquence of the Pulpit, an ordination-sermon, to which is added a charge* (4th edn., Glasgow: P. Banks, Stirling, 1755), 26.
[23] Ibid. 46.
[24] Ibid. 32–3.
[25] *Chironomia*, 38.
[26] Fordyce, *Eloquence of the Pulpit*, 46.

Priestley's preference for a delivery governed by spoken rather than written discourse was symptomatic of his loyalty to the clear-thinking tradition of Enlightenment Dissent, whose stylistic features and recurrent metaphors we have just sampled. That preference was, however, complicated by his acknowledgement that writing was permanent, speech transient, and that print made ideas accessible in ways that voice could not. This explains the occasional equivocations in his text as he weighed up the advantages and disadvantages of both media. For Peter De Bolla, these equivocations have a sharply political resonance: Priestley, he says, has 'a more complex view of the interrelation between speech and writing than Sheridan, one-time friend of Johnson and recipient of a state pension [because] his own experience of the distribution of "free speech" was marked by a profound recognition of the inequality perpetrated in its name'.[27] The inference one might draw fom this—that important connections existed between dissent, literacy, progress, and print culture—has important ramifications, both for the chronological plot I am tracing, and for Hazlitt's role within it. We should remember, though, that there was no equivocation in Priestley's belief that poetry was a less transparent medium of communication than prose.

The combined influence of Sheridan's and Priestley's elocutionary ideas on an entire generation of writer–readers cannot be overstated. Sheridan's was the wider audience: more diffuse as well as more diverse in its political and social complexion than the Dissenters who heard and perpetuated Priestley's teachings; and, as De Bolla reminds us, Sheridan was 'far from clear about the political ramifications' of his role, which wavered between 'democratic populist philosopher and speech master to the aspiring ruling classes'.[28] It was, however, Sheridan who made explicit the possibilities that might open up for women, as vernacular discourse gained in importance, edging out the primacy of the classics:

let the men take care of themselves for should they continue to rely upon their old weapon the pen to the neglect of speech and on their skill in the dead languages without cultivating their own they would find themselves over-

---

[27] 'Of the Gesture of the Orator: The Speaking Subject', in *The Discourse of the Sublime: Readings in History, Aesthetics and the Subject* (Oxford: Basil Blackwell, 1989), 176.

[28] Ibid. 163. Linda Kelly claims that it was thanks to the influence of Sheridan that Dr Johnson received a pension of £300 in 1762; but that when Sheridan himself received one shortly after, Johnson ungraciously exclaimed: 'What! Have they given *him* a pension? Then it is time for me to give up mine': *Richard Brinsley Sheridan: A Life*, 17.

matched in all topics of conversation and victory declare itself on the side of the ladies.[29]

It is interesting, in this context, to think that the young Hannah More, who heard Sheridan lecturing in Bristol in 1761 (and dared to show him a copy of her poems) may have had his lectures in mind when writing her poem 'The Bas Bleu; or Conversation' in 1787; and that in this respect she was linked by a strong affinity with Anna Barbauld—educated at the Warrington Academy, friend of Priestley—and the author of a poem which famously celebrated the prattle of women.[30] It was Barbauld who provided the epigraph for William Enfield's *The Speaker* (1774), a volume underpinned by Priestley's ideas, in which 'miscellaneous pieces, selected from the best English writers' were 'disposed under proper heads, with a view to facilitate the improvement of youth in reading and speaking'. Her poem on 'Warrington Academy' included further on in the body of the anthology, contained a moving tribute to Priestley's influence, celebrating a generation of Dissenters who, 'Love in their heart, persuasion in their tongue, | With words of peace shall charm the list'ning throng'.[31]

Enfield's anthology, in its turn, had a profound impact, popularizing for thousands the idea that oratory should be natural and prosaic, not artificial: 'If public speaking must be musical, let the words be set to music in recitative, that these melodious speakers may no longer lie open to the sarcasm; *Do you read or sing? If you sing, you sing very ill*' (p. xx). The practice of reading aloud (by oneself or in the company of friends) must involve removing the eye from the printed page if the words spoken were to have their full effect. Memory, Enfield insisted, therefore played a crucial part in ensuring the illusion of extempore delivery. Reciting by memory

---

[29] *Art of Reading; First Part*, 329. A generation later, the vernacular had succeeded to a considerable degree in edging the classics out. In an unfinished essay on prosody, Richard Brinsley Sheridan (son of Tom and Frances Sheridan), dismisses the idea of modelling English poetry on Greek and Latin verse: 'We have lost all knowledge of the antient accent', he says, 'we have lost their Pronunciation; —all puzzling about it is ridiculous and trying to find the melody of our own verse by theirs is still worse. We should have had all our own metres, if we had never heard a word of their language' (quoted by Linda Kelly, *Richard Brinsley Sheridan: A Life*, 23).

[30] I refer of course to Barbauld's poem 'Washing Day' which begins: 'The muses have turned gossips'. This poem is discussed in Ch. 4, Sect. IV, above.

[31] Included in William Enfield, *The Speaker: Or, Miscellaneous Pieces, Selected from the Best English Writers, and Disposed under Proper Heads, with a View to Facilitate the Improvement of Youth in Reading and Speaking. To which is Prefixed an Essay on Elocution* (London: Joseph Johnson, 1774), 272. Page refs. will be given in the text.

obliges the speaker to dwell upon the ideas which he is to express … And by taking off his eye from the book, it in part relieves him from the influence of the school-boy habit of reading in a different key and tone from that of conversation; and gives him greater liberty to attempt the expression of the countenance and gesture. (p. xxvii)

Enfield's belief in the body's integral relation to the mind stemmed from his Unitarian faith, as did his commitment to the energizing power of discourse—indeed, of breath itself, whose properties Priestley spent much of his career investigating. When Enfield lamented that 'a speaker without energy, is a lifeless statue' (p. ix), he invoked energy in this Priestleyan sense; just as when he gave instructions about the art of speaking, he focused on the work performed by the lungs in inhaling and exhaling oxygen, and thus on the body's potential for maximizing energy:

draw in as much air as your lungs can contain with ease, and to expel it with vehemence, in uttering those sounds which require an emphatical pronunciation; read aloud in the open air, and with all the exertion you can command; preserve your body in an erect attitude while you are speaking; let the consonant sounds be expressed with a full impulse or percussion of the breath, and a forcible action of the organs employed in forming them; and let all the vowel sounds have a full and bold utterance. (pp. ix–x)

With its Dissenting origins strongly stamped upon it, *The Speaker* formed British taste and reading-habits over at least three decades. Dorothy Wordsworth alluded to it in a journal entry of April 1802, as to a familiar companion;[32] and Barbauld imitated its title and format in *The Female Speaker; or, miscellaneous pieces in prose and verse selected from the best writers, and adapted to the use of young women* in 1811. Hazlitt, in his essay, 'On Patronage and Puffing' (*Table Talk*, 1821) remembered learning to recite one of the passages in Enfield—the speech from John Home's *Douglas*—'with good emphasis and discretion when at school' (Howe, viii. 294). In another essay he praised the same speech for 'the spirit of modest heroism, and conscious worth that breathes in it', comparing it with 'Othello's apology to the Senate, on which it is evidently modelled' (Howe, ix. 94). All readers familiar with Enfield would have recognized the appositeness of the Shakespearian comparison: in the section devoted to 'Narrative Pieces' in *The Speaker*, Othello's speech appears alongside the one from *Douglas*. Jane Austen made a similar, but less

---

[32] *The Journals of Dorothy Wordsworth*, ed. E. de Selincourt (2 vols., London: Macmillan and Co., 1941), i. 132.

exact comparison, in the reading-aloud scene which occurs in *Mansfield Park*. Tom Bertram, defending the plan for a play-recital by appealing to the authority of his absent father, reminds Edmund of their early oratorical upbringing: 'Nobody is fonder of the exercise of talent in young people, or promotes it more', he says:

> ... and for any thing of the acting, spouting reciting kind, I think he has always a decided taste. I am sure he encouraged it in us as boys. How many a time have we mourned over the dead body of Julius Cæsar and *to be'd* and *not to be'd*, in this very room, for his amusement! And I am sure *my name was Norval* every evening of my life through one Christmas holidays.[33]

Although the Norval passage from *Douglas* appeared also in *Elegant Extracts* (which has a more conservative inflection) many of Austen's readers would have associated it with *The Speaker*. Tom is mocking an oratorical tradition, here, which has some Dissenting affiliations, but is clearly distinguished—at least in Edmund's mind—from the kind of political subversion later to emerge in the choice and performance of *Lovers' Vows*.

Enfield's translation of Priestleyan ideas into an instruction manual, designed to teach the art of reading aloud, had an important parallel in the educational theory and practice of the radical writer John Thelwall—member of the London Corresponding Society, associate of Wordsworth and Coleridge, who was tried for treason in 1794. Thelwall delivered lectures on 'The Science and Practice of Elocution' in 1796, and supposedly 'withdrew' from politics in 1798; but found in his speech therapy and his lecture tours an alternative form of radical expression. At the Institution for the Correction of Speech Defects, which he set up and ran, his 'Plan and Object' was 'the removal of those defects, usually considered under the denomination of Impediments: but also ... the correction of Feebleness and Dissonance of Voice; Foreign and Provincial Accents, and every offensive peculiarity of Tone and Enunciation'.[34] Thelwall aimed to restore 'a completely intelligible

---

[33] *Mansfield Park*, ed. Tony Tanner (Harmondsworth, Middlesex: Penguin, 1966), 152. The 'Douglas' speech was clearly a set-piece used to test oratorical and acting skills. Hazlitt recounts how he saw Master Betty playing the part of Douglas, 'moving about gracefully, with all the flexibility of youth, and murmering AEolian sounds with plaintive tenderness.' He goes on to argue that 'Boys at that age can often read remarkably well, and certainly are not without natural grace and sweetness of voice' (Howe, viii. 294).

[34] *Plan and Objects of Mr Thelwall's Institution* (London: Lincoln's Inn Fields, 1813), 2. In Bodley's copy, the pamphlet is bound with *Results of Experience*.

distinctness'[35] to speech-patterns by encouraging 'the habits of clear and energetic enunciation' and the use of 'physical and harmonic rhythmus'.[36] In doing so, he drew consciously, not just on his own experience (the *Dictionary of National Biography* informs us that he himself had suffered originally from 'a marked hesitation of speech and even a slight lisp') but on a well-known classical precedent: the Athenian orator Demosthenes, who was often referred to by eighteenth-century elocutionists as a role model. Mason, in the *Essay on Elocution*, asserted that Demosthenes' innate 'weakness of voice' was cured by 'declaiming on the Sea-shore, amidst the Noise of Waves'; that his 'Shortness of Breath' was 'mended by repeating his Orations as he walked up a Hill', and that 'a thick mumbling Way of speaking' was overcome by 'declaiming with pebbles in his mouth'.[37] Gilbert Austin, too, referred to the 'extraordinary and successful perseverance' of Demosthenes in 'labouring against the natural imperfections of his voice and utterance'.[38] Late eighteenth-century experiments, of the kind undertaken by Thelwall, derived much of their optimism from this famous instance of education triumphing over circumstance to produce a model of oratorical perfection. Extensive documentary evidence, in the form of case histories, proved that Thelwall's own methods brought about a correspondingly dramatic improvement in his pupils' speech. What this signified was nothing less than that discourse was capable of progress; that individuals might empower themselves through the discovery of eloquence. In the process, they would contribute to what Thelwall calls 'the expanding undulations of virtuous sympathy' which characterized a truly progressive society.[39]

Far from 'discarding politics in favour of elocution',[40] Thelwall continued, through the model of discourse which he promulgated in his lectures, to maintain a strong connection with radical culture. Hazlitt referred to him in his essay 'On the Difference between Speech and Writing' as 'The most dashing orator I have ever heard . . . the model of a flashy, powerful demagogue—a madman blessed with a fit audience'

---

[35] *Plan and Objects*, 2.

[36] *Results of Experience in the Treatment of cases of Defective Utterance, from Deficiencies in the Roof of the Mouth, & other Imperfections & Mal-conformations of the Organs of Speech; with Observations on Cases of Amentia, and tardy & imperfect Development of the Faculties* (London: J. McCreery, 1814), 2, 43.

[37] *Essay on Elocution*, 10.   [38] *Chironomia*, 30.

[39] *Selections and Original Articles, for Mr Thelwall's Lectures on the Science and Practice of Elocution: together with the Introductory Discourse and Outlines* (Birmingham: J. Belcher & Son, 1806), 16.

[40] See *Dictionary of National Biography* entry.

(Howe, xii. 264). The paper-war he conducted in 1803–4 with Francis Jeffrey was instigated by an ugly incident which took place while he was on tour in Edinburgh. Here, his enthusiastic claims for the power of oratory met with a hostile reception, allegedly stage-managed by Jeffrey. It becomes quite clear, when one examines the lecture notes he later published as part of his defence, that it was the radical idealism of his message that his audience found unpalatable. Thelwall himself identified the following paragraph, which concerns the spread of sympathy through discourse, as the cause of the outcry against him:

Hence from the central throb of individual impulse, the feeling expands to the immediate circle of relative connections;—from relatives to friends and intimate associates; from intimate association to the neighbourhood where we reside—to the country for which we would bleed!—from the patriot community to civilized society—to the human race—to posterity—to the sentient universe: and wherever the throb of sensation can exist, the Virtuous find a motive for the regulation of their actions.[41]

It is ironic that the very passage in which Thelwall described the 'contagion' of sympathy, should have provoked an opposite contagion among the group of scoffers who, in his own account, were carefully distributed around the lecture hall. Their mockery, rippling out into the audience at large, produced a grotesque parody of the progressive discourse he was celebrating. On this historic occasion, the Dissenting tradition of oratory came face to face with the rise of criticism, and produced a classic instance of the anxiety of reception.

III. THE POLITICS OF READING ALOUD

Not only, as we have seen, was the practice of 'reading aloud' a thriving one at the end of the eighteenth century, but the debates surrounding it were deeply implicated in the politics of language. For Blair, Sheridan, Priestley, and Thelwall, there was a clear perceived connection between extempore delivery and enthusiasm: 'The sectaries and fanatics, before the Restoration', Blair argued, 'adopted a warm, zealous, and popular manner of preaching; and those who adhered to them, in after-times, continued to distinguish themselves by somewhat of the same manner'.[42] It was, he complained, the odium of these sects that 'drove

---

[41] *Mr Thelwall's Letter to Francis Jeffray, Esq* (London, 1804), 88–9.
[42] *Lectures on Rhetoric and Belles Lettres*, ii. 44.

the established church from that warmth which they were judged to have carried too far, into the opposite extreme of a studied coolness and composure of manner'[43]. The political point was driven home by Blair in a way that bore directly on the practice of reading aloud:

the practice of reading Sermons, is one of the greatest obstacles to the Eloquence of the Pulpit in Great Britain, where alone this practice prevails. No discourse, which is designed to be persuasive, can have the same force when read, as when spoken. The common people all feel this, and their prejudice against this practice is not without foundation in nature.[44]

This was a point later confirmed by Thelwall, who complained, in his *Selections and Original Articles . . . on the Science and Practice of Elocution* (1806), that 'the Dulness and Indolence of modern Elocutionists' had reduced 'almost all public speaking, but that of the stage, to one sympathetic monotomy [*sic*] of tone and look and attitude'; and that a hue and cry had been raised against 'all expression of attitude and feature'. But 'what is Oratory', he asked, 'if it does not awaken and influence and impel?'

when really actuated by any strong or genuine emotion, the tones become affected; the physiognomy assumes a sympathetic expression; and, bursting thro' the boundaries of fashion and the chains of unnatural torpor, each limb and muscle seems to swell and struggle with inspiring passion.[45]

In figuring the natural eloquence of the body in direct antithesis to the artificiality of a 'churchy' voice, Thelwall drew on the long tradition I have been tracing here, in which monotonous delivery was condemned. To understand the implications of that tradition for all forms of reading aloud—from sermon-delivery to schoolroom learning—we have only to glance back at John Mason's *Essay on the Action proper for the Pulpit*, published fifty years earlier, in which the author inveighed against the 'entirely uniform and ever-returning Tune or Cadence, employed alike on all occasions, for all purposes whatsoever', which he likened to 'a

---

[43]   Blair, *Lectures on Rhetoric and Belles Lettres*, 43.

[44]   Ibid. 118.

[45]   *Selections*, 11–12. Thelwall had earlier made comments on the connection between eloquence and animated oral delivery in a series of lectures whose content was clearly political, albeit in an ironically camouflaged way: 'the grand charm of oral eloquence consists not only in the correspondence of the tone of voice with the subject matter, but in that powerful harmony of feature and gesticulation—that electric animation of the eye, which, varying its expression with every transition of rising passion, prepares the minds of the audience for the sentiments about to be delivered.' See *Prospectus of a Course of Lectures to be delivered every Monday, Wednesday, and Friday, during the ensuing Lent, in strict conformity with the restrictions of Mr Pitt's Convention Act* (London: 1796), 3.

Chime of Bells, that clink continually upon the Ear, in one wearisome, unvaried, uninterrupted Tenour'.[46]

The damaging effect of 'sing-song' habits, as practised in the pulpit and encouraged in the schoolroom, later proved important in the dispute which took place between Andrew Bell and Joseph Lancaster over the respective merits of chanting and speaking. Bell was the author of *An Experiment in Education* (1797), an influential tract which outlined the advantages of the 'monitorial' system he had piloted while working as superintendent of an understaffed orphanage asylum in Madras. This serviceable and economic system involved the older children in teaching the younger ones (thus reducing the need for trained staff), and was swiftly adopted with modifications by Joseph Lancaster for use at a large Quaker school in Southwark. As the editors of the *Biographia* have noted,

Lancaster was given such enthusiastic support by the Nonconformists that the Church of England asked Bell to organize some schools in a similar way. Thereafter, especially because religious differences fanned it, the men were thrown into the position of rivals. (*BL* ii. 60 n.3)

Their competition centred on who had first patented or practised the monitorial system, and which version of that system was preferable, especially in respect of its attitudes to discipline and punishment. Coleridge and Southey, who both entered the debate, came down decisively on the side of Bell; one of their reasons for doing so being that they disliked the punishments allegedly used by Lancaster to correct 'sing-song' habits of recitation. In his essay on *The Origin, Nature, and Object of the New System of Education* (1812), Southey complained about the contempt and risibility that Lancaster's punishments provoked:

When a boy gets into a singing tone in reading, he is hung round with matches, ballads, or dying speeches, and marched round the school with some boys before him, crying 'matches, last dying speech, &c.—exactly imitating the dismal tones with which such things are hawked about the streets in London'.[47]

Southey's objections were echoed, a year later, in a lecture delivered by Coleridge in Bristol, when he complained that 'to load a boy with

---

[46] *An Essay on the Action proper for the Pulpit* (London: R. & J. Dodsley, 1753), 42.

[47] *The Origin, Nature, and Object of the New System of Education* (London: John Murray, 1812), 89. Southey is quoting from Lancaster's *Improvements in Education* (1808), 86–7: 'When a boy gets into a singing tone in reading, the best cure that I have hitherto found effectual, is by *force* of ridicule.—Decorate the offender with matches, ballads; (dying-speeches, *if needful;*) and, in this garb send him round the school, with some boys before him, crying matches, &c. exactly imitating the dismal tones with which such things are hawked about the streets in London.'

fetters ... to expose him to the sneers and insults of his peers, because forsooth he reads his lessons in a singsong tone, was a pitiful mockery of human nature'.[48] Later, when he writes in his *Biographia* footnote about the practice of reading aloud in the schoolroom, his preference is for an incantatory mode of delivery. Alluding to the Bell–Lancaster controversy, he again sides with Bell:

> It is no less an error in teachers, than a torment to the poor children, to inforce the necessity of reading as they would talk. In order to cure them of *singing* as it is called; that is of too great a difference, the child is made to repeat the words with his eyes from off the book.... But as soon as the eye is again directed to the printed page, the spell begins anew (*BL* ii. 60)

In its context, this note is used to reinforce his more general point, that poetry was distinct from prose, and that 'prose itself, at least, in all argumentative and consecutive works, differs, and ought to differ, from the language of conversation; even as reading ought to differ from talking' (*BL* ii. 60–1). The anti-democratic implications of Coleridge's thinking are underlined in his reference to the author as 'one far wiser' than the child himself, whose superiority is acknowledged in the elevated register he elicits from his spellbound readers. The idealizing properties of poetry are ascribed not only to their musical effects, but to the easy transference of their authorial spirit from powerful source to submissive recipient:

> an instinctive sense tells the child's feelings, that to utter its own momentary thoughts, and to recite the written thoughts of another, as of another, and a far wiser than himself, are two widely different things; and as the two acts are accompanied with widely different feelings, so must they justify different modes of enunciation. (*BL* ii. 60 n.)

Coleridge emphasizes the connection between music and poetry, suggesting that the capacity of words to convey emotion lies in their musicality. But the mesmeric power of words—their capacity to exert a spell over the reader—is seen to reside in visual not aural properties.

The Bell–Lancaster debate crystallizes around the opposition between Anglican and Dissenting traditions of eloquence—an opposition which helps to explain the underlying differences between Coleridge and Hazlitt. Although still a Unitarian when he preached his sermon at Shrewsbury, Coleridge's later career was marked by a steady movement

---

[48] Lecture 7, 18 Nov. 1813 in Bristol, in *Lectures*, ii. 588. (see also ibid. 286 n. 3).

towards the Anglican church. But Hazlitt hints in 'My First Acquaint-ance' at the possibility that Coleridge's Dissent was always comprom-ized by a tendency towards mystification. Whereas he himself remained democratically attuned to his audience, Coleridge was from the first destined to write in an abstract and elevated register, inspiring awe rather than communicating intelligibly.

Wordsworth—tacitly in agreement with Hazlitt—parodied the mesmeric aspect of Coleridge's poetics as early as 1798 in his anti-supernatural poem, 'Peter Bell':

> And Peter looks, and looks again,
> Just like a man whose brain is haunted.
> He looks, he cannot chuse but look,
> Like one that's reading in a book,
> A book that is enchanted.

> (ll. 546–50)

Wordsworth here translates the enchantment exerted by the Ancient Mariner's story into a form of ocular tyranny (the wedding guest 'cannot choose but hear' the mariner; Peter 'cannot chuse but look' into the lake), as though tracing an implicit analogy between the power of a printed text and the power of spoken utterance. Is it chance that the rhyme word we expect for 'haunted' is 'chaunted' rather than 'chanted', and that Wordsworth here recalls a similar rhyme in 'Kubla Khan': 'A savage place! as holy and enchanted | As e'er beneath a waning moon was haunted | By woman wailing for her demon-lover!' (ll. 13–15)? The conflation in Wordsworth's allusion of two Coleridgean sources, one stressing a visual spell, the other a form of oral enchantment, parallels Coleridge's own emphasis on the Mariner's 'glittering eye' and on print's capacity to exert a spellbinding effect on the child who is reading poetry aloud. 'As soon as the eye is again directed to the printed page, the spell begins anew', Coleridge observes (*BL* ii. 60): the visual and the aural work jointly, to ensure the reader's submission.

Coleridge's model of sympathetic reciprocity between author and reader had always been poetic rather than prosaic. As this predilection became more explicitly acknowledged, it acquired a sharper political significance, bearing out the truth of Hazlitt's claim, that 'The language of poetry naturally falls in with the language of power' (Howe, iv. 214–15). Enacted in *Biographia* was a set of preferences which indicated how far Coleridge had travelled from his early Dissenting affiliations, and it came as no surprise to Hazlitt that his one-time friend sided with Bell not Lancaster on the issue of reading aloud in school. In his *Examiner* review of *The Statesman's Manual*, where he discussed Coleridge's views on education, Hazlitt protested against the conservative repudiation of Lancaster's reforms which Coleridge shared with Southey. 'Learning', he wrote sarcastically, 'is an old University mistress, that [Coleridge] is not willing to part with, except for the use of the church of England; and he is sadly afraid she should be debauched by the "liberal ideas" of Joseph Lancaster!' (Howe, vii. 126). This comment, which appears in a paragraph addressed to the theory and practice of reading, meshes Hazlitt's political loyalties with his discursive tastes. In the same way, when Thelwall, in his 1806 *Selections*, contrasts an intelligible body language of enthusiasm with 'the usual Pedantic and Bell-man Styles of reading', he is using 'Bell' as shorthand for orthodox Anglicanism.[49] Implicitly, he thus expresses his preference for the conversational register in recitation advocated by Lancaster over the 'sing-song' delivery which Bell leaves unpunished. The very name 'Bell' was fortuitously connected with churchiness, with the 'entirely uniform and ever-returning Tune or cadence' condemned by writers such as Mason; and Thelwall plays on the associations provided by this pun. Similarly, when he writes about monotony in its various forms—the 'Barking or Schoolboy Style'; the 'Monotonous Level style', the 'Clerical Drawl', and the 'Cathedral Chaunt'[50]—he gives them an orthodox, Anglican inflection which contrasts with his own enthusiasm.

IV. SPEECH–WRITING, PROSE–POETRY, PUBLIC–PRIVATE

There were, as we have seen, important connections between 'reading aloud' and the progressive model of vocal and bodily eloquence to which Hazlitt claimed allegiance. These he celebrated both in 'My First Acquaintance' and elsewhere in his writings:

Horne Tooke, among other paradoxes, used to maintain, that no one could write a good style who was not in the habit of talking and hearing the sound of his own voice. He might as well have said that no one could relish a good style without reading it aloud, as we find common people do to assist their apprehension.... I agree that no style is good, that is not fit to be spoken or read

---

[49] *Selections*, 26.   [50] Ibid. 27–8.

aloud with effect. This holds true not only of emphasis and cadence, but also with regard to natural idiom and colloquial freedom. ('On the Conversation of Authors', in Howe, xii. 40)

But there were also some special features of reading aloud in the Wordsworth–Coleridge circle, which had more troubling implications. At a time when literature was establishing itself in the market place, and the reading-public was emerging as the final arbiter of its merit, writers must either welcome or resist the transition from a culture based on oral delivery and manuscript circulation into a culture centred on print. Hazlitt's observation of the coterie practice of 'chaunting' showed his awareness that a Romantic aesthetic grounded in orality might camouflage a hostility to the public sphere. That awareness helps bring into sharper focus the political animus which lay behind his attacks on Coleridge, even as it discloses an ambivalence in his own response to orality.

Something of this ambivalence (is the erosion of orality a gain or a loss?) was discernible in the preface which Hazlitt attached in 1807 to his *Eloquence of the British Senate*: a memorial to the great parliamentary addresses delivered by 'Those celebrated men of the last age... who filled the columns of the news-papers with their speeches, and every pot-house with their fame'. These men, Hazlitt wrote, who were 'the wisdom of the wise, and the strength of the strong, whose praises were inscribed on every window-shutter or brick-wall, or floated through the busy air, upborne by the shouts and huzzas of a giddy multitude' were now, like their orations, '... silent and forgotten; all that remains of them is consigned to oblivion in the musty records of Parliament, or lives only in the shadow of a name' (Howe, i. 139). Hazlitt's noble ambition was 'to revive what was forgotten, and embody what was permanent' (Howe, i. 140), but this was no easy task. He sensed that what was precious in these speeches could not be recovered, because each was a single, irreplaceable *performance*; but equally, that these irrecoverable elements might deserve their ephemerality, since the tastes of the 'giddy multitude' were not always to be trusted.

Hazlitt was consistently ambivalent about the craving for publicity which linked popular literature and demagoguery with what he diagnosed as personality disorders of the Coleridgean variety. In his essay 'On Novelty and Familiarity' he associates the desire for popularity with addiction: actors, he claims, 'live on applause, and drag on a laborious artificial existence by the administration of perpetual provocatives to their sympathy with the public gratification. . . . The excitement of public applause at last becomes a painful habit, and either in indolent or over-active temperaments produces a craving after privacy and leisure' (Howe, xii. 299–300). Similarly, 'On the Difference between Writing and Speaking' gives us the flip side of his concern to arrest the passage of time and restore the vanishing power of orality:

> The orator's vehemence of gesture, the loudness of the voice, the speaking eye, the conscious attitude, the inexplicable dumb shew and noise,—all 'those brave sublunary things that made his raptures clear,'—are no longer there, and without these he is nothing. (Howe, xii. 265)

In this essay, loquacity is figured as the obverse of profundity. Hazlitt identifies, not with the great speakers of the day, who courted popularity, but with the silent thinkers, who 'in revenge for being tongue-tyed' poured 'a torrent of words from their pens': 'What they would say (if they could) does not lie at the orifices of the mouth ready for delivery, but is wrapped in the folds of the heart and registered in the chambers of the brain' (Howe, xii. 278–9). For these deep-thinking *writers*, Hazlitt reserves his highest stylistic lexicon. There is something De Quinceyan, even Piranesian, in the spatial metaphors used to describe their hidden but durable profundity:

> The whole of a man's thoughts and feelings cannot lie upon the surface, made up for use; but the whole must be a greater quantity, a mightier power, if they could be got at, layer under layer, and brought into play by the levers of imagination and reflection. (Howe, xii. 279)

By comparison, *The Eloquence of the British Senate* is an act of loving restitution towards transient speech. But it still reflects Hazlitt's anxiety that oratory is superficial, stimulus-driven, habit-forming, as well as his longing that something might survive, beyond the ephemeral speech-act, of lasting value.

The complexity of Hazlitt's observations on speech and writing is everywhere apparent, and nowhere more so than in his many scattered comments on Coleridge, who became the symbolic focus for his mistrust of voice as the signifier of thoughts and feelings. This mistrust is not what one might expect of the Hazlitt who emerged from the Dissenting tradition, which placed its faith in elocution as a passport to intellectual and social standing; and believed that speech, in and of itself, had a progressive power. But it does tally with what we know about Hazlitt's temperament, and with what he sensed was a deep underlying difference between Coleridge and himself. Tongue-tied, as an adolescent, in the presence of his intellectual hero, Hazlitt was diffident always. Stanley Jones, drawing on Henry Crabb Robinson's *Diary*, gives a mortifying account of his first lecture (on Tuesday 14 January 1812) recited 'calamitously, despite the loyal encouragement of his friends' to a blur of faces:

He had never before stood at a lecturer's rostrum. He delivered himself in a low, monotonous, half-audible voice, kept his eyes glued to the manuscript, not once daring to look at his hearers, and read so rapidly that no one could follow.[51]

The next week, asked to repeat the first lecture, he 'stopped abruptly half way through' and 'could not be persuaded to continue'. This anecdote carries a special charge of irony in the light of Coleridge's legendary eloquence, recorded by Hazlitt over an entire writing career. ' "He talked far above singing" ', recalled the younger man, in 'On Going a Journey' (*Table Talk*, 1821): 'If I could so clothe my ideas in sounding and flowing words, I might perhaps wish to have some one with me to admire the swelling theme; or I could be more content, were it possible for me still to hear his echoing voice in the woods at All-Foxden' (Howe, viii. 183). The envy is as transparent in his touching generosity here as it is beneath his frustration and rage against wasted talent elsewhere. 'If Mr. Coleridge had not been the most impressive talker of his age, he would probably have been the finest writer' he remarked acidly in *The Spirit of the Age* (1825), 'but he lays down his pen to make sure of an auditor, and mortgages the admiration of posterity for the stare of an idler' (Howe, xi. 30). More painful in its bleakness of loss is this close-up of Coleridge's drugged face, twenty years on from the Shrewsbury sermon recollected in 'My First Acquaintance with Poets':

Look in C——'s face while he is talking. His words are such as might 'create a soul under the ribs of death.' His face is a blank. Which are we to consider as the true index of his mind? Pain, languor, shadowy remembrances are the uneasy inmates there: his lips move mechanically! ('On the Knowledge of Character', in Howe, viii. 305)

---

[51] *Hazlitt: A Life, from Winterslow to Frith Street* (Oxford: Clarendon Press, 1989), 66. See Robinson, *Diary, Reminiscences and Correspondence*, selected and ed. Thomas Sadler Ph.D. (3 vols., London: Macmillan and Crabbo, 1869), i. 368.

We have I think to be aware of what Tom Paulin has called the 'density of associative reference' in Hazlitt's writings, their 'self-allusive and autotelic' richness, if we are fully to understand the complexity of significance he invested in the figure of Coleridge the Talker.[52] As if suffering a bereavement that could not be accepted, he never entirely gave up on the memory of Coleridge the radical—or, for that matter, on the hope that Coleridge's gift for extempore enthusiasm might be made durable in writing. In his essay 'On Effeminacy of Character', the poet's dormant revolutionary spirit is reawakened and activated by this impassioned plea:

> oh thou! who didst lend me speech when I was dumb, to whom I owe it that I have not crept on my belly all the days of my life like the serpent, but sometimes lift my forked crest or tread the empyrean, wake thou out of thy mid-day slumbers! (Howe, viii. 251)

The allusive language, here, is charged with personal, poetic, and political significance. Remembering the central dramatic encounter between Satan and Eve in *Paradise Lost*, Book IX, Hazlitt likens himself to the serpent, 'created mute to all articulate sound', whose 'gentle dumb expression' gives way to eloquence when Satan inhabits his body. Eve's question, 'How camest thou speakable of mute?', implicitly addressed by Hazlitt to himself, is answered by way of his undying gratitude to Coleridge, whose early radical enthusiasm had not only inspired him but helped him realize his own potential as a writer. The passage owes its tremendous emotive charge to Hazlitt's identification with Milton's fallen republican hero, who appears again, in a similar context, in 'My First Acquaintance with Poets'. Describing the state of abject entrapment from which he was released by his first contact with genius, Hazlitt compares himself to a 'worm' (often used as a synonym for serpent) who is given wings and freedom through language. His moving tribute to Coleridge is darkened by the recent experience of obsessional, unrequited love, which gave an added bitterness to the 'longings infinite and unsatisfied' he shared with Satan and Eve:

> I was at that time dumb, inarticulate, helpless, like a worm by the way-side, crushed, bleeding, lifeless; but now, bursting from the deadly bands that 'bound

---

[52] *The Day-Star of Liberty*, 184. For discussion of Hazlitt on speech and writing, see also Timothy Clark, *The Theory of Inspiration: Composition as a Crisis of Subjectivity in Romantic and Post-Romantic Writing* (Manchester: Manchester University Press, 1997), 84–6; and Uttara Natarajan, *Hazlitt and the Reach of Sense, Criticism, Morals, and the Metaphysics of Power* (Oxford: Oxford University Press, 1998).

them . . . my ideas float on winged words, and as they expand their plumes, catch the golden light of other years. My soul has indeed remained in its original bondage, dark, obscure, with longings infinite and unsatisfied; my heart, shut up in the prison-house of this rude clay, has never found, nor will it ever find, a heart to speak to; but that my understanding also did not remain dumb and brutish, or at length found a language to express itself, I owe to Coleridge. (Howe, xvii. 107)

Linked by their common language of Miltonic allusion, the two passages from 'My First Acquaintance with Poets' and 'On Effeminacy of Character' draw attention to the republican legacy Coleridge shared with Hazlitt, and was by implication neglecting. Hazlitt yearned to reciprocate Coleridge's early influence on his own dormant creative potential by awakening the poet from his silent, unproductive sleep.

There was a time, Milton had claimed, when serpents were proud, upright, beautiful creatures. Hazlitt's reference in 'On Effeminacy of Character' to not 'creeping on [his] belly all the days of [his] life' reminds us of the snake's unfallen state, and of the glorious ambitions which ennoble him when he is moved by Satan's spirit:

> not with indented wave,
> Prone on the ground, as since, but on his rear,
> Circular base of rising folds, that towered
> Fold above fold a surging maze, his head
> Crested aloft, and carbuncle his eyes;
> With burnished neck of verdant gold, erect
> Amidst his circling spires, that on the grass
> Floated redundant . . .
>
> (*Paradise Lost*, ix. 496–503)

'Crest' is an image repeatedly associated by Milton with Satan. Hazlitt's image of his own 'forked crest' complicates Milton's 'head crested aloft' by conflating the devil's horned head with the serpent's forked tongue, to create a powerfully compressed symbol of aspiring eloquence. At the same time, there is here a typical Hazlittian ambivalence towards speech itself, which the wider Miltonic context reinforces. Hazlitt's ability to 'lift [his] head and sometimes tread the empyrean' may by inference be a borrowed gift, a false incarnation; just as Coleridge's infectious enthusiasm may be as empty as the speaking serpent's promise to Eve. Hazlitt's recognition of the debt he owed to Coleridge was one that carried with it a heavy freight of suspicion and regret. These negative feelings reflected back on his assessment of the role played by speech in public and political life.

Carried over from *Paradise Lost* into Hazlitt's thickly allusive prose there is an anxiety about the 'forked' duplicity of eloquence, not just as it was symbolized by Milton's handling of the temptation, but as it emerged in the influential role of politicians and public speakers. The authenticity of Coleridge's enthusiasm—and by extension, Hazlitt's dependent acquisition of eloquence, reason, imagination—are brought under question through a packed and coded allusion to the Fall, which spans a large section of *Paradise Lost*, Book IX. A little further into the encounter with Eve, Satan is compared by Milton to an Athenian or Roman orator, pleading a noble republican cause:

> The tempter, but with show of zeal and love
> To man, and indignation at his wrong,
> New part puts on, and as to passion moved,
> Fluctuates disturbed, yet comely and in act
> Raised, as of some great matter to begin.
> As when of old some orator renowned
> In Athens or free Rome, where eloquence
> Flourished, since mute, to some great cause addressed,
> Stood in himself collected, while each part,
> Motion, each act won audience ere the tongue,
> Sometimes in highth began . . .
>
> (*Paradise Lost*, ix. 665–75)

So complex, by this stage, is Milton's handling of Satan's disguise, that it is difficult for the reader to disentangle tenor from vehicle in the unfolding simile. Is this a case of Satan giving voice to Milton's republican ideals, and thus reminding us that he has 'not yet lost all his original brightness'? Or does Satan dissemble a republican virtue which, for Milton, is ideally embodied in Greek and Roman oratory? A third possibility, that there is an association in Milton's mind between oratory and play-acting, gives an added irony to Satan's impersonation. To understand how Hazlitt would have read this passage we should imagine him in a position somewhere between the credulous Eve and the better-informed narrator of *Paradise Lost*. He identified with the aspiration towards reason, knowledge, freedom of speech, and access to power, which Satan voices so persuasively in his temptation of Eve. He also emerged from and claimed allegiance to the republican and Dissenting traditions of oratory which Milton was here celebrating. But he none-theless shared with Milton a wariness towards the performative com-ponent of the speech-act, and the seductive body language which was its ambiguous accompaniment.

An even denser cluster of allusions goes on to complicate and enrich the Satanic parallel Hazlitt is drawing. Lamenting the decline of all that had once seemed heroic in Coleridge, he remembers two equally mo-mentous passages in Milton, both concerned with the public account-ability of heroes. He reassures Coleridge that his creative power will return to him, after its apparent stagnation, much as Milton reassures the English nation that, at the end of a long period of political quietism, freedom will be achieved. But this regeneration can only occur, Hazlitt warns, if Coleridge is prepared to exchange the transient, untrustworthy mobility of speech for the durable medium of writing:

wake thou out of thy mid-day slumbers! Shake off the heavy honey-dew of thy soul, no longer lulled with that Circean cup, drinking thy own thoughts with thy own ears, but start up in thy promised likeness, and shake the pillared rottenness of the world! Leave not thy sounding words in air, write them in marble, and teach the coming age heroic truths! Up, and wake the echoes of Time! (Howe, viii. 251)

Coleridge is here associated with Samson Agonistes, stirring himself out of his temporary lethargy into the courageous act of heroism that will liberate his people. But he is also linked—through a cognate Miltonic echo that Blake would have approved—with 'that noble and puissant Nation' in *Areopagitica*, 'rousing herself like a strong man after sleep, and shaking her invincible locks'.[53] This reference to the most famous of publications on the freedom of the press works tacitly as a rebuke to Coleridge for his stance against reviewers, periodicals, and the reading-public—a stance that Hazlitt had denounced openly on several occa-sions: 'For what have we been labouring for the last three hundred years?' he asked in 1816:

Would Mr. Coleridge, with impious hand, turn the world 'twice ten degrees askance,' and carry us back to the dark ages? Would he punish the *reading public*

---

[53] 'Methinks I see in my mind a noble and puissant Nation rousing herself like a strong man after sleep, and shaking her invincible locks: Methinks I see her as an Eagle muing her mighty youth, and kindling her undazl'd eyes at the full midday beam; purging and unscaling her long abused sight at the fountain it self of heav'nly radiance', *Complete Prose Works of John Milton* (gen. ed. D. Wolfe (8 vols. in 10, 1953–82), ii, ed. E. Sirluck (New Haven: Yale University Press, 1959), 557–8.

for their bad taste in reading periodical publications which he does not like, by suppressing the freedom of the press altogether, or destroying the art of printing? (Howe, xvi. 106)

Angry reproaches such as this one remind us of the intractable difference of ideology which persisted between these two writers. The connection Hazlitt observes between Coleridge's slowness to publish and his hostility to the press gives his analysis of the anxiety of reception a sharply political edge; as does his detection of an underlying irony in Coleridge's clinging to speech as an alternative to print. This irony is further enriched by Hazlitt's chiasmic figuration of their respective professional roles: Coleridge the conservative poet-critic, embattled and beleaguered in relation to the reading-public, is presented as a loquacious performer. Hazlitt the radical journalist, tongue-tied when it comes to speaking, is seen as welcoming and eagerly entering the world of publication. But although both writers recurred constantly to these public–private, speech–writing oppositions, neither in the end believed them to be valid, except as symbolic shorthand for more complex emotions and ideas. As Coleridge himself knew only too well (and Hazlitt was not slow to point out) a declared preference for private circulation and recitation was no guarantee of a safe retreat from the public demands and pressures of the literary market place; any more than emergence into the public sphere was inevitably the mark of bravery and candour.

1816 ought to have been a momentous year for Coleridge, in that it saw the poet's sudden re-emergence, after a long period of silence, into the world of print. It was not, however, primarily as a poet that Coleridge chose to re-emerge; but rather as an amalgam of sermon-izer-critic-politician-theologian-metaphysician; and for this Hazlitt never forgave him. It is possible that a touch of jealousy in his response to Coleridge's new status as prose writer coloured his reception of the poetry. (Prose was after all the single medium which Hazlitt had made his own; it was here that he had discovered himself able to 'lift his forked crest or tread the empyrean', much as Coleridge did when talking.) But it seems more likely that his disappointment in the later poetry intensified his disgust with the prose; and made Coleridge's claims to excellence in both media the harder to swallow. 'He might, we seriously think, have been a very considerable poet', Hazlitt lamented, in the review of the *Biographia* which appeared in the *Edinburgh* soon after the reviews of *Lay*

Sermons and *The Pains of Sleep*, '—instead of which he has chosen to be a bad philosopher and a worse politician. There is something, we suspect, in these studies that does not easily amalgamate' (Howe, xvi. 137).

All told, then, the years 1816–17 were, in Hazlitt's eyes, a fiasco: Coleridge had signally failed to 'rouse [him]self like a strong man after sleep, and shake [his] invincible locks'. Hazlitt did not write the withering review which appeared anonymously in the *Edinburgh* in September 1816; but he might just as well have done: 'forth steps Mr. Coleridge, like a giant refreshed with sleep,' sneers the reviewer, slipping in sideways the apposite and topical allusion to *Areopagitica*: 'and as if to redeem his character after so long a silence, ("his poetic powers having been, he says, from 1808 till very lately, in a state of suspended animation,") . . . breaks out in these precise words—" 'Tis the middle of the night by the castle clock" '.[54] As a judgement on the quality of Coleridge's writing, this bathetic quotation is left to speak for itself. The charge pressed home by the reviewer is that 'Christabel' has come to be overvalued as a result of its private circulation and oral delivery, but above all, as a result of its having been praised and advocated by Lord Byron:

we are a little inclined to doubt the value of the praise which one poet lends another. It seems now-a-days to be the practice of that once irritable race to laud each other without bounds; and one can hardly avoid suspecting, that what is thus lavishly advanced may be laid out with a view to being repaid with interest. Mr. Coleridge, however, must be judged by his own merits.[55]

In this acid remark, one hears an anticipation—faint, perhaps, but nonetheless significant—of the charge implicitly levelled by Hazlitt in 'My First Acquaintance' at another pair of writers, who back in 1798 had read their poems aloud in a chaunting voice. Were they not also in danger of 'lauding each other without bounds'? Did their dependence on coterie admiration not signify a defensive adherence to systems of

[54] Arnold Glover included the *Edinburgh Review* article of Sept. 1816 in his *Collected Works of William Hazlitt*, but relegated it to the notes because of its doubtful provenance. It has since been attributed to Tom Moore. Quotation from *The Collected Works of William Hazlitt*, ed. A. R. Walker and Arnold Glover, introd. W. E. Henley (London: J. M. Dent & co., 1902), x. 412.

[55] Ibid. The review ends with an even stronger condemnation of private patronage, including the following: 'Must we then be doomed to hear such a mixture of raving and driv'ling, extolled as the work of a "*wild and original*" genius, simply because Mr. Coleridge has now and then written fine verses, and a brother poet chooses, in his milder mood, to laud him from courtesy or from interest? And are such panegyrics to be echoed by the mean tools of a political faction, because they relate to one whose daily prose is understood to be dedicated to the support of all that courtiers think should be supported?' (ibid. 418).

patronage and puffing, which Hazlitt abhorred? And were they not guilty, also, of claiming to be aloof from the economic laws which governed the market place, even as they played the part of capitalists in the game of borrowing and lending praise?

The case for considering Hazlitt as the author of this review has long been closed. But it is not hard to see why Coleridge should have made the attribution. Connecting the *Edinburgh Review* article, the cluster of reviews of the *Lay Sermons*, the essay on 'Patronage and Puffing', and (more subtly) 'My First Acquaintance with Poets' was a consistent thread of criticism. Coleridge stood accused of a cowardly refusal to embrace the modernity and progress associated with print culture—a refusal which disguised itself as a commitment to the sociable diffusion associated with oral discourse. In his use of the practice and figure of 'reading aloud'—alluded to in the Preface to 'Christabel' and later in *Biographia*—he protected himself from the candid, disinterested criticism likely to be levelled at his published writings.

The politics of reception are inescapably linked to the politics of language and style. Even as early as 1798, Hazlitt seems to suggest in 'My First Acquaintance with Poets', Coleridge's defensive conservatism was symbolized by the ambiguous accompaniment, the kitsch orality, of 'chaunting'. Wordsworth too—for all his affinity with Blair, his professed allegiance in 1800 to the 'natural conversation of men', and his northern burr—was drawn under an Anglican spell when it came to reciting poetry. Hazlitt does not go so far as to say that this was a spell cast by Coleridge over his friend; but he does hint that of the two writers Coleridge had always been the one more inclined to reverence the act of enchantment that can take place between a poet and his listeners. The linkage between incantation, enchantment, and Anglicanism reveals what in Hazlitt's eyes seemed to be an attraction on Coleridge's part towards the elevated, mystificatory potential of all discourse, including conversation. In Wordsworth's case, it appeared indicative, rather, of the special category into which he placed poetry—his own in particular—despite all his assertions to the contrary in the 1800 Preface to *Lyrical Ballads*. The carefully poised ironies of Hazlitt's essay accuse both poets of an incipient political apostasy in their manner of reading poems aloud. Their collaboration, even as it is recognized for the inauguration of a new kind of poetry, is retrospectively seen as instigating their withdrawal into a private and self-protective world of mutual enchantment. From this safe haven, Hazlitt implies, the two poets went on in later life to consolidate their reputations as conservative members of the Anglican Church, addressing their readers in an increasingly exclusive language. Hazlitt, meanwhile, true to his Dissenting roots, continued to champion the cause of 'colloquial freedom' in the unambiguously public forum of the periodical press. His abiding commitment was to a republic of letters, founded on the principles of meritocracy; and his medium was always prose.

Bibliography

PRIMARY

Ashfield, Andrew (ed.), *Women Romantic Poets, 1770–1838: An Anthology* (2 vols., Manchester: Manchester University Press, 1995).

Austin, Gilbert, *Chironomia, or a Treatise on Rhetorical Delivery* (London: T. Cadell and W. Davies, 1806).

Barbauld, Anna Laetitia, *The Poems of Anna Letitia Barbauld*, ed. William McCarthy and Elizabeth Kraft (Athens, Ga.: University of Georgia Press, 1994).

—— *The Works of Anna Laetitia Barbauld* (2 vols., London: Longman, Hurst, Rees, Orme, Brown, and Green, 1825).

Blair, Hugh, *Lectures on Rhetoric and Belles Lettres* (2 vols., London: W. Strachan and T. Cadell, 1783).

Blake, William, *The Complete Writings of William Blake*, ed. Geoffrey Keynes (London: Oxford University Press, 1966).

—— *The Poetry and Prose of William Blake*, ed. David Erdman (4th edn. rev., New York: Doubleday, 1965).

Breen, Jennifer (ed.), *Women Romantic Poets, 1785–1832* (London: J. M. Dent and Sons, 1994).

Breton, Anna Letitia, *Memoir of Mrs Barbauld, Including Letters and Notices of her Family and Friends* (London: George Bell, 1874).

Bromwich, David (ed.), *Romantic Critical Essays* (Cambridge: Cambridge University Press, 1987).

Burgh, James, *The Art of Speaking* (2nd edn., London: T. Longman and J. Buckland, 1768).

Burke, Edmund, *Reflections on the Revolution in France*, ed. with introd. Connor Cruise O'Brien (Harmondsworth, Middlesex: Penguin, 1986).

—— *A Philosophical Enquiry into the Origin of Our Ideas of the Sublime and the Beautiful* ed. J. T. Boulton (Oxford: Oxford University Press, 1990).

Burton, J., *Lectures on Female Education and Manners* (New York: Samuel Campbell, 1794).

Byron, Lord George, *Letters and Journals*, ed. Leslie A. Marchand (12 vols. and suppl., London: William Clowes and Sons, 1975).

—— *The Complete Poetical Works*, ed. Jerome J. McGann (7 vols., 1980–93; Oxford: Clarendon Press, 1986).

Carlyle, Thomas, *The Collected Works of Thomas Carlyle*, ed. H. D. Traill (30 vols., London: Chapman and Hall, 1896–9).

Chapone, Hester, *Letters on the Improvement of Mind* (2 vols., London: H. Hughs, 1775).

—— *Miscellanies in Prose and Verse* (London: E. and C. Dilly, 1775).

Clare, John, *The Letters of John Clare*, ed. Mark Storey (Oxford: Clarendon Press, 1985).

Coleridge, S. T., *Lectures 1808–1819 On Literature*, ed. R. A. Foakes (Bollingen Series, 2 vols., Princeton: Princeton University Press, 1987).

—— *The Complete Poetical Works of Samuel Taylor Coleridge*, ed. Ernest Hartley Coleridge (2 vols.; Oxford: Clarendon Press, 1975).

—— *The Collected Letters of Samuel Taylor Coleridge*, ed. E. L. Griggs (6 vols.; Oxford: Oxford University Press, 1956–71).

—— *The Friend* (Bollingen Series; 2 vols., Princeton: Princeton University Press, 1969).

—— *The Notebooks of Samuel Taylor Coleridge*, ed. Kathleen Coburn (Bollingen series; Princeton: Princeton University Press, 1957–).

—— *Coleridge's Miscellaneous Criticism*, ed. Thomas Middleton Raysor (London: Constable, 1936).

Cooper, Anthony Ashley (Earl of Shaftesbury), *Soliloquy, or, Advice to an Author*, in *Characteristics of Men, Manners, Opinions, Times* (3 vols., London: J. J. Tourneisan and J. L. Legrand, 1711).

De Quincey, Thomas, *Confessions of an English Opium Eater and Other Writings*. ed. with introd., Grevel Lindop (Oxford: Oxford University Press, 1989).

—— *De Quincey's Collected Writings*, ed. David Masson (14 vols., Edinburgh: Adam and Charles Black, 1890).

—— *De Quincey's Art of Autobiography* (Edinburgh: Edinburgh University Press, 1990).

D'Israeli, Isaac, *An Essay on the Manners and Genius of the Literary Character* (London: T. Cadell and W. Davies, 1795).

—— *Literary Character of Men of Genius* (London: Frederick Wark and Co., 1846).

Enfield, William, *The Speaker: Or, Miscellaneous Pieces, Selected from the Best English Writers, and Disposed under Proper Heads, with a View to Facilitate the Improvement of Youth in Reading and Speaking. To which is Prefixed an essay on Elocution* (London: Joseph Johnson, 1774).

—— *Observations on Literary Property* (London: Joseph Johnson, 1774).

—— Feldman, Paula (ed.), *British Women Poets of the Romantic Era: An Anthology* (Baltimore: Johns Hopkins University Press, 1997).

Fordyce, James, *Sermons to Young Women* (London: printed for A. Millar and T. Cadell, J. Dodsley, and J. Rayne, 1766).

—— *The Eloquence of the Pulpit, an ordination-sermon, to which is added a charge* (4th edn., Glasgow: P. Banks, Stirling, 1755).

Godwin, William, *Political and Philosophical Writings of William Godwin*, gen. ed. Mark Philp (7 vols., London: William Pickering, 1993).

Hazlitt, William, *Complete Works*, ed. P. P. Howe (21 vols., London: J. M. Dent and Sons, 1930–4).

—— *The Collected Worths of William Hazlitt*, ed. A. R. Waller and Arnold Glover, introd. W. E. Henley (London: J. M. Dent & Co., 1902).

Hogg, James, *Selected Poems*, ed. Douglas S. Mack (Oxford: Clarendon Press, 1970).

Hunt, Leigh, *Leigh Hunt's Dramatic Criticism, 1808–1831*, ed. Lawrence Huston Houtchens and Carolyn Washburn Houtchens (London: Geoffrey Cumberledge; Oxford University Press, 1950).

—— *The Feast of the Poets* (London: James Cawthorn, 1814).

Jeffrey, Francis, *Jeffrey's Criticism: A Selection*, ed. with introd. Peter F. Morgan (Edinburgh: Scottish Academic Press, 1983).

Jewsbury, Maria Jane, *Phantasmagoria; or Sketches of Life and Literature* (London: Hurst, Robinson and Co., 1825).

Johnson, Samuel, *The Yale Edition of the Works of Samuel Johnson*, ed. W. J. Bate and Albrecht B. Strauss (New Haven: Yale University Press, 1969).

Keats, John, *Keats: The Complete Poems*, ed. Miriam Allott (London: Longman, 1970).

—— *Letters of John Keats, 1814–1821*, ed. H. E. Rollins (2 vols., Cambridge, Mass.: Harvard University Press, 1958).

Knox, Vicesimus, *Essays Moral and Literary* (London: Charles and Edward Dilly, 1778–9).

Lackington, James, *Memoirs of the Forty-Five First Years of the Life of James Lackington* (London: James Lackington, 1795).

Lamb, Charles, *Elia and The Last Essays of Elia*, ed. Jonathan Bate (Oxford: Oxford University Press, World's Classics, 1987).

—— *Lamb as Critic*, ed. Roy Park (London: Routledge, 1980).

—— and Mary, *The Letters of Charles and Mary Lamb*, ed. Edwin W. Marrs, Jr. (Ithaca, NY: Cornell University Press, 1975).

—— *Letters of Charles and Mary Lamb, 1821–1842*, ed. E. V. Lucas (2 vols., London: Methuen, 1912).

Lonsdale, Roger (ed.), *Eighteenth-Century Women Poets: An Oxford Anthology* (Oxford: Oxford University Press, 1989).

Macaulay, Catharine, *Letters on Education* (London: printed for C. Dilly, 1790).

—— *A Modest Plea for the Property of Copyright* (London: printed by R. Cruttwell, Bath, for C. Dilly, 1774).

Macpherson, C. B., *The Political Theory of Possessive Individualism: Hobbes to Locke* (Oxford: Clarendon Press, 1962).

Mason, John, *An Essay on Elocution, or, Punctuation, Intended chiefly for the assistance of those who instruct others in the Art of Reading. And of those who are often called upon to speak in Publick* (London: M. Cooper, 1748).

—— *An Essay on the Action proper for the Pulpit* (London: R. & J. Dodsley, 1753).

Milton, John, *The Complete Prose Works of John Milton*, gen. ed. D. Wolfe (8 vols. in 10, 1953–82), ii, ed. E. Sirluck (New Haven: Yale University Press, 1959).

More, Hannah, *Strictures on the Modern System of Female Education. With a view of the principles and conduct prevalent among women of rank and fortune* (2 vols., London: Cadell and Davies, 1799).

—— *A Search After Happiness: A Pastoral in Three Dialogues.* By a Young Lady (London: S. Farley, 1783).

—— *The Complete Works* (2 vols., New York: Harper and Brothers, 1835).

—— *Selected Writings of Hannah More*, ed. Robert Hole (London: William Pickering, 1996).

Paine, Thomas, *The Thomas Paine Reader*, ed. Michael Foot and Isaac Kramnick (Harmondsworth, Middlesex: Penguin, 1987).

Peacock, Thomas Love, *The Works of Thomas Love Peacock*, ed. H. F. B. Brett-Smith and C. E. Jones (10 vols., London: Constable and Co., New York: Gabriel Wells, 1934).

Polwhele, Richard, *The Unsex'd Females: A Poem, Addressed to the Author of the Pursuits of Literature* (London: Cadell and Davies, 1798).

Priestley, Joseph, *A Course of Lectures on Oratory and Criticism* (London: Joseph Johnson, 1777).

Ralph, James, *The Case of Authors by Profession or Trade. Stated with regard to Booksellers, the Stage, and the Public, No Matter by Whom* (London: R. Griffiths, 1758).

Rawnsley, Canon, *Reminiscences of Wordsworth among the Peasantry of Westmoreland* (London: Dillons, *c.*1968).

Redpath, Theodore (ed.), *The Young Romantics and Literary Opinion, 1807–1824* (London: George G. Harrap and Co., 1973).

Reiman, Donald H. (ed.), *The Romantics Reviewed: Contemporary Reviews of British Romantic Writers* (9 vols., New York: Garland, 1972).

Reynolds, John Hamilton, *Selected Prose of John Hamilton Reynolds*, ed. Leonidas M. Jones (Cambridge, Mass.: Harvard University Press, 1966).

Reynolds, Joshua, *Discourses on Art*, ed. Robert R. Wark (San Marino, Calif.: The Huntington Library, 1959).

Robinson, Henry Crabb, *Diary, Reminiscences and Correspondence*, selected and ed. Thomas Sadler Ph.D. (3 vols., London: Macmillan and co., 1869).

—— *The Correspondence of Henry Crabb Robinson with the Wordsworth Circle*, ed. Edith J. Morley (2 vols., Oxford: Clarendon Press, 1927).

—— *Henry Crabb Robinson on Books and their Writers*, ed. Edith J. Morley (London: J. M. Dent and sons, 1938).

Rousseau, Jean-Jacques, *Emile or Education*, trans. Allan Bloom (Harmondsworth, Middlesex: Penguin, 1979).

Schlegel, Friedrich, *Lucinde and the Fragments*, trans. Peter Firchow (Minneapolis: University of Minnesota Press, 1971).

Schlegel, Friedrich, *Dialogue on Poetry and Literary Aphorisms*, trans. and ed. Ernst Behler and Roman Struc (University Park, Penn.: Pennsylvania State University Press, 1968).

Schleiermacher, F. D., *Hermeneutics: The Handwritten Manuscripts*, ed. Heinz Kimmerle, trans. James Duke and Jack Forstman (Missoula, Mont.: Scholars Press, 1977).

Shaftesbury: *see* Cooper, Anthony Ashley.

Shelley, Mary, *The Novels and Selected Works of Mary Shelley*, gen. ed. Nora Crook, with Pamela Clemit; ii, ed. Pamela Clemit (London: William Pickering, 1996).

Shelley, Percy Bysshe, *Shelley's Poetry and Prose*, selected and ed. Donald H. Reiman and Sharon B. Powers (New York: Norton, 1977).

Sheridan, Frances, *The Discovery. A Comedy. As it is Performed At the Theatre-Royal, In Drury Lane*. Written by the Editor of Miss Sidney Bidulph (London: T. Davies, R. & J. Dodsley, G. Kearsley, J. Coote, and J. Walker, 1763).

Sheridan, Robert Brinsley, *Sheridaniana; or, Anecdotes of Robert Brinsley Sheridan; His Table-Talk, and Bon Mots* (London: Henry Colburn, 1826).

Sheridan, Thomas, AM, *A Course of Lectures on Elocution: together with two Dissertations on Language, and some other Tracts relative to those Subjects* (London: W. Strachan, 1762).

—— *Lectures on the Art of Reading: First Part: Containing the Art of Reading Prose* (London: J. Dodsley et al., 1775).

Simpson, David (ed.), *The Origins of Modern Critical Thought: German Aesthetic and Literary Criticism from Lessing to Hegel* (Cambridge: Cambridge University Press, 1988).

Southey, Robert, *The Origin, Nature, and Object of the New System of Education* (London: John Murray, 1812).

Stones, Graeme, and Strachan, John, *Parodies of the Romantic Age* (5 vols., London: Pickering and Chatto, 1999), ii. *Collected Verse Parody*, ed. John Strachan.

Talfourd, Thomas Noon, *Speech of Sergeant Talfourd on Literary Property* (18 May 1837) (London; Sherwood and Co., 1837).

Thelwall, John, *Plan and Objects of Mr Thelwall's Institution* (London: Lincoln's Inn Fields, 1813).

—— *Results of Experience in the Treatment of cases of Defective Utterance, from Deficiencies in the Roof of the Mouth, & other Imperfections & Mal-conformations of the Organs of Speech; with Observations on Cases of Amentia, and tardy & imperfect Development of the Faculties* (London: J. McCreery, 1814).

—— *Selections and Original Articles, for Mr Thelwall's Lectures on the Science and Practice of Elocution: together with the Introductory Discourse and Outlines* (Birmingham: J. Belcher & Son, 1806).

—— *Mr Thelwall's Letter to Francis Jeffray, Esq* (London, n. pub., 1804).

—— *Prospectus of a Course of Lectures to be delivered every Monday, Wednesday, and Friday, during the ensuing Lent, in strict conformity with the restrictions of Mr Pitt's Convention Act* (London: sold at the lecture-room, Beaufort-Buildings; at Symond's; Eaton's; and Smith's Feb 2. 1796).

Wilson, John, *The Recreations of Christopher North* (3 vols., Edinburgh and London: William Blackwood, 1842).

Wollstonecraft, Mary, *The Works of Mary Wollstonecraft*, ed. Janet Todd and Marilyn Butler (7 vols., London: William Pickering, 1989).

—— *A Vindication of the Rights of Woman*, ed. Carol H. Poston (New York: W. W. Norton and Co., 1975).

—— *The Collected Letters of Mary Wollstonecraft*, ed. Ralph M. Wardle (Ithaca, NY: Cornell University Press, 1979).

—— *Mary, a Fiction and the Wrongs of Woman*, ed. with introd., Gary Kelly (London: Oxford University Press, 1976).

Wordsworth, Dorothy, *Journals of Dorothy Wordsworth*, ed. E. de Selincourt (2 vols., London: Macmillan and Co., 1941).

Wordsworth, William, *The Prelude: The Four Texts (1798, 1799, 1805, 1850)*, ed. Jonathan Wordsworth (Harmondsworth, Middlesex: Penguin, 1995).

—— *The Prose Works of William Wordsworth*, ed. W. J. B. Owen and J. W. Smyser (3 vols., Oxford: Clarendon Press, 1974).

—— *William Wordsworth*, ed. Stephen Gill (Oxford: Oxford University Press (Oxford Authors series), 1984).

—— *Wordsworth's Poetical Works*, ed. E. de Selincourt (5 vols., Oxford: Clarendon Press, 1949).

—— *The Borderers*, ed. Robert Osborn (Ithaca, NY: Cornell University Press, 1982).

—— *Poems, in Two Volumes and Other Poems, 1800–1807*, ed. Jared Curtis (Ithaca, NY: Cornell University Press, 1983).

—— and Dorothy, *The Letters of William and Dorothy Wordsworth: The Early Years, 1787–1805*, ed. Ernest de Selincourt, 2nd edn. rev. Chester Shaver (Oxford: Clarendon Press, 1967).

—— *The Letters of William and Dorothy Wordsworth: The Middle Years, 1806–1811*, ed. Ernest de Selincourt, 2nd edn. rev. Chester Shaver (Oxford: Clarendon Press, 1967).

—— *The Letters of William and Dorothy Wordsworth: The Later Years 1821–1853*, ed. Ernest de Selincourt, rev. Alan G. Hill (4 vols., Oxford: Clarendon Press, 1978–88).

Young, Edward, *Love of Fame, the Universal Passion* (London: printed for J. and R. Tonson and S. Draper, 1752).

—— *Conjectures on Original Composition in a Letter to the Author of Sir Charles Grandison* (London: A. Millar and R. and R. Dodsley, 1759).

SECONDARY

Abrams, M. H., *The Mirror and the Lamp: Romantic Theory and the Critical Tradition* (Oxford: Oxford University Press, 1953).

—— *Natural Supernaturalism: Tradition and Revolution in Romantic Literature* (New York: Norton, 1971).

Altick, R. D., *The English Common Reader: A Social History of the Mass Reading Public, 1800–1900* (Chicago: University of Chicago Press, 1957).

Arac, Jonathan, *Critical Genealogies: Historical Situations for Postmodern Literary Studies* (New York: Columbia University Press, 1987).

Armour, R. W., and Howes, R. F. (eds.), *Coleridge The Talker* (New York: Cornell University Press, 1940).

Ashton, Rosemary, *The German Idea: Four English Writers and the Reception of German Thought, 1800–1860* (Cambridge: Cambridge University Press, 1980).

—— *The Life of Samuel Taylor Coleridge: A Critical Biography* (Oxford: Basil Blackwell, 1996).

Atkins, G. Douglas, *Geoffrey Hartman: Criticism as Answerable Style* (London: Routledge, 1990).

Bakhtin, *The Dialogic Imagination*, ed. Michael Holquist, trans. Caryl Emerson and Michael Holquist (Austin, Tex.: University of Texas Press, 1981).

Barker-Benfield, G. J., *The Culture of Sensibility* (Chicago: Chicago University Press, 1992).

Baron, Michael, *Language and Relationship in Wordsworth's Writing* (London: Longman, 1995).

Barrell, John, *Poetry, Language and Politics* (Manchester: Manchester University Press, 1988).

Bate, Jonathan, *Romantic Ecology: Wordsworth and the Environmental Tradition* (London: Routledge, 1991).

Baxter, Edmund, *De Quincey's Art of Autobiography* (Edinburgh: Edinburgh University Press, 1990).

Beer, John (ed.), *Questioning Romanticism* (Baltimore: Johns Hopkins University Press, 1995).

Bennett, Andrew (ed.), *Readers and Reading* (London: Longman, 1995).

—— *Keats, Narrative and Audience: The Posthumous Life of Writing* (Cambridge: Cambridge University Press, 1994).

—— *Romantic Poets and the Culture of Posterity* (Cambridge, Cambridge University Press, 1999).

Benzie, W., *The Dublin Orator* (Leeds: Scolar Press Ltd., 1972).

Bewell, Alan, ' "Jacobin Plants": Botany as Social Theory in the 1790's', *Wordsworth Circle*, 20/3 (summer 1989), 132–9.

Bialostosky, Don H., *Making Tales: The Poetics of Wordsworth's Narrative Experiments* (Chicago: Chicago University Press, 1984).

—— *Wordsworth, Dialogics, and the Practice of Criticism* (Cambridge: Cambridge University Press, 1992).

Blanchot, Maurice, *The Space of Literature*, trans. with introd. Ann Smock (Lincoln, Nebr.: University of Nebraska Press, 1982).

Bleich, David, *Readings and Feelings* (Champaign, Ill.: NCTE 1975).

—— *Subjective Criticism* (Baltimore: Johns Hopkins University Press, 1978).

Bloom, Harold, *The Anxiety of Influence: A Theory of Poetry* (London: Oxford University Press, 1973).

—— *Ruin the Sacred Truths: Poetry and Belief from the Bible to the Present* (Cambridge, Mass.: Harvard University Press, 1989).

—— *The Western Canon: The Books and School of the Ages* (New York: Harcourt Brace and Company, 1995).

—— et al., *Deconstruction and Criticism* (New York: Continuum, 1979).

Bromwich, David, *A Choice of Inheritance: Self and Community from Edmund Burke to Robert Frost* (Cambridge, Mass.: Harvard University Press, 1989).

—— *Hazlitt: The Mind of a Critic* (New York: Oxford University Press, 1983).

Butler, Marilyn, *Peacock Displayed: A Satirist in his Context* (London: Routledge and Kegan Paul, 1979).

Bygrave, Stephen, *Coleridge and the Self: Romantic Egotism* (Houndmills, Basingstoke: Macmillan, 1986).

Cafarelli, Annette Wheeler, *Prose in the Age of Poets: Romanticism and Biographical Narrative from Johnson to De Quincey* (Philadelphia: University of Pennsylvania Press, 1990).

Campbell, Colin, *The Romantic Ethic and the Spirit of Modern Consumerism* (Oxford: Basil Blackwell, 1987).

Caraher, Brian C., *Wordsworth's 'Slumber' and the Problematics of Interpretation* (University Park, Penn.: Pennsylvania State University Press, 1991).

Chandler, James, *Wordsworth's Second Nature* (Chicago: Chicago University Press, 1984).

Chartier, Roger, *The Order of Books: Readers, Authors and Libraries in Europe between the Fourteenth and Eighteenth Centuries*, trans. Lydia G. Cochrane (Cambridge: Polity, 1992).

Chase, Cynthia, *Decomposing Figures* (Baltimore: Johns Hopkins University Press, 1986).

Chodorow, Nancy, *The Reproduction of Mothering: Psychoanalysis and the Sociology of Gender* (Berkeley and Los Angeles: University of California Press, 1978).

Christensen, Jerome, *Coleridge's Blessed Machine of Language* (Ithaca, NY: Cornell University Press, 1981).

—— 'The Symbol's Errant Allegory: Coleridge and his Critics', *English Literary History*, 45 (1978), 640–59.

—— 'The Genius in *Biographia Literaria*', *Studies in Romanticism*, 17 (1978), 215–31.

Christensen, Jerome (cont.), *Lord Byron's Strength: Romantic Writing and Commercial Society* (Baltimore: Johns Hopkins University Press, 1993).

Clark, Timothy, *The Theory of Inspiration: Composition as a Crisis of Subjectivity in Romantic and Post-Romantic Writing* (Manchester: Manchester University Press, 1997).

Clarke, Norma, *Ambitious Heights: Writing, Friendship, Love—The Jewsbury Sisters, Felicia Hemans, and Jane Welsh Carlyle* (London: Routledge, 1990).

Cohen, Gillian, 'The Psychology of Reading', *New Literary History*, 4 (Autumn 1972), 75–90.

Collini, Stefan (ed.), *Interpretation and Over-Interpretation* (Cambridge: Cambridge University Press, 1992).

Collins, A. S., *The Profession of Letters: A Study of the Relation of Author to Patron, Publisher and Public, 1780–1832* (New York: E. P. Dutton, 1929).

Copley, Stephen, and Whale, John (eds.), *Beyond Romanticism* (London: Routledge, 1992).

Cox, Jeffrey, 'Keats in the Cockney School', *Romanticism*, 2/1 (1996), 27–39.

Cruttwell, Patrick, 'Wordsworth, The Public, and the People', *Sewanee Review*, 64 (1956).

Curtis, Jared, *Wordsworth's Experiments with Tradition: The Lyric Poems of 1802* (Ithaca, NY: Cornell University Press, 1971).

Davis, Philip (ed.), *Real Voices on Reading* (Houndmills, Basingstoke: Macmillan Press, 1997).

De Bolla, Peter, *The Discourse of the Sublime: Readings in History, Aesthetics, and the Subject* (Oxford: Blackwell, 1989).

De Certeau, Michel, *The Practice of Everyday Life* (Berkeley and Los Angeles: University of California Press, 1988).

De Man, Paul, *The Rhetoric of Romanticism* (New York: Columbia University Press, 1984).

——*Allegories of Reading: Figural Language in Rousseau, Nietzsche, Rilke and Proust* (New Haven: Yale University Press, 1979).

—— *Blindness and Insight: Essays in the Rhetoric of Contemporary Criticism* (2nd edn. rev., Minneapolis: University of Minnesota Press, 1983).

Demaria, Robert, 'The Ideal Reader: A Critical Fiction' *PMLA* 93 (1978), 463–74.

Derrida, Jacques, *Margins of Philosophy*, trans. with additional notes by Alan Bass (Brighton: Harvester, 1986).

Devlin, D. D., *Wordsworth and the Poetry of Epitaphs* (London and Basingstoke: Macmillan, 1980).

Dilthey, Wilhelm, *Selected Writings*, ed., transl., and introd. H. P. Robinson (Cambridge: Cambridge University Press, 1976).

Eagleton, Terry, *The Function of Criticism: From 'The Spectator' to Post-Structuralism* (London: Verso, 1984).

—— *The Ideology of The Aesthetic* (Oxford: Blackwell, 1990).

Eaves, Morris, 'Romantic Expressive Theory and Blake's Idea of the Audience', *PMLA* 95/5 (1980), 784–801.

—— and Fisher, Michael (eds.), *Romanticism and Contemporary Criticism* (Ithaca, NY: Cornell University Press, 1986).

Eco, Umberto, *The Role of the Reader: Explorations in the Semiotics of Texts* (London: Hutchinson, 1979).

Eilenberg, Susan, *Strange Power of Speech: Wordsworth, Coleridge and Literary Possession* (Oxford: Oxford University Press, 1992).

Eliot, T. S., 'Tradition and the Individual Talent', in *Selected Essays* (London: Faber and Faber, 1932).

Ellison, Julie, *Delicate Subjects: Romanticism, Gender, and the Ethics of Understanding* (Ithaca, NY: Cornell University Press, 1990).

Engell, James, *The Creative Imagination: Enlightenment to Romanticism* (Cambridge, Mass.: Harvard University Press, 1981).

—— *Framing the Critical Mind: Dryden to Coleridge* (Cambridge, Mass.: Harvard University Press, 1989).

Erickson, Lee, 'The Poet's Corner: The Impact of Technological Changes in Printing on English Poetry, 1800–1850', *ELH* 52 (1985), 894–9.

—— *The Economy of Literary Form: English Literature and the Industrialisation of Publishing, 1800–1850* (Baltimore: Johns Hopkins University Press, 1996).

Erskine-Hil, Howard, and McCabe, Richard (eds.), *Presenting Poetry: Composition, Publication, Reception* (Cambridge: Cambridge University Press, 1995).

Feldman, Paula, and Kelley, Theresa (eds.), *Romantic Women Writers: Voices and Counter-Voices* (Hanover, NH: University Press of New England, 1995).

Ferguson, Frances, *Solitude and the Sublime* (New York: Routledge, 1992).

Fetterley, Judith, *The Resisting Reader: A Feminist Approach to American Fiction* (Bloomington, Ind.: Indiana Press, 1978).

Fielding, Penny, *Writing and Orality: Nationality, Culture, and Nineteenth Century Scottish Fiction* (Oxford: Clarendon Press, 1996).

Fish, Stanley, *Surprised by Sin: The Reader in 'Paradise Lost'* (Berkeley and Los Angeles: University of California Press, 1967).

—— *Is there a Text in this Class? The Authority of Interpretive Communities* (Cambridge, Mass.: Harvard University Press, 1980).

Flint, Kate, *The Woman Reader: 1837–1914* (Oxford: Clarendon Press, 1993).

Flynn, Elizabeth, and Schweickart, Patricinio, *Gender and Reading: Essays on Readers, Texts, and Contexts* (Baltimore: Johns Hopkins University Press, 1986).

Foucault, M., *The Order of Things: An Archeology of the Human Sciences* (1970; London and New York: Tavistock/Routledge, 1989).

Freund, E., *The Return of the Reader: Reader Response Criticism* (London: Methuen, 1987).

Fulford, Tim, *Coleridge's Figurative Language* (Houndmills, Basingstoke: Macmillan, 1991).

—— 'Apocalyptic and Reactionary? Coleridge as Hermeneutist', *Modern Language Review*, 87 (1992), 18–31.

—— ' "Living Words": Coleridge, Christianity and National Renewal', *Prose Studies*, 15/2 (Aug. 1992), 187–207.

—— and Paley, Morton D. (eds.), *Coleridge's Visionary Languages: Essays in Honour of John Beer* (Cambridge: Boydell and Brewer, 1993).

Gadamer, Hans Georg, *Truth and Method* (2nd rev. ed.), trans. rev. Joel Weinsheimer and Donald G. Marshall (London: Sheed and Ward, 1975).

—— *Philosophical Hermeneutics*, trans. and ed. David E. Linge (Berkeley and Los Angeles: University of California Press, 1976).

Galperin, William H., *Revision and Authority in Wordsworth: The Interpretation of a Career* (Philadelphia: University of Pennsylvania Press, 1989).

Gardiner, Judith Kegan, 'On Female Identity and Writing by Women', *Critical Inquiry*, 8 (1981), 347–61.

Gellner, Ernest, *The Psychoanalytic Movement: The Cunning of Unreason* (2nd edn., Guernsey: Guernsey Press, 1993).

Gill, Stephen, 'Wordsworth's Poems: The Question of the Text', *Review of English Studies*, NS 34 (1983), 172–90.

—— ' "Affinities Preserved": Poetic Self-Reference in Wordsworth', *Studies in Romanticism*, 24 (1985), 531–49.

—— *William Wordsworth: A Life* (Oxford: Clarendon Press, 1989).

Gilligan, Carol, *In a Different Voice: Psychological Theory and Women's Development* (Cambridge, Mass.: Harvard University Press, 1982).

Glen, Heather, *Vision and Disenchantment: Blake's Songs and Wordsworth's Lyrical Ballads* (Cambridge: Cambridge University Press, 1983).

Gould, S. J., *Time's Arrow and Time's Cycle* (Harmondsworth, Middlesex: Penguin, 1988).

Gravil, Richard, and Lefebure, Molly, *The Coleridge Connection: Essays in Honour of Thomas McFarland* (Houndmills, Basingstoke: Macmillan, 1990).

—— Newlyn, Lucy, and Roe, Nicholas (eds.), *Coleridge's Imagination: Essays in Memory of Pete Laver* (Cambridge: Cambridge University Press, 1986).

Greer, Germaine, *Slip-Shod Sybils: Recognition, Rejection and the Woman Poet* (London: Viking, 1995).

Griffin, Dustin, *Rejoining Paradise: Milton and the Eighteenth Century* (Cambridge: Cambridge University Press, 1986).

Halmi, Nicholas, 'From Hierarchy to Opposition: Allegory and the Sublime', *Comparative Literature*, 4 (Fall 1992), 337–60.

Hamilton, Paul, *Coleridge's Poetics* (Oxford: Basil Blackwell, 1983).

—— *Historicism* (London: Routledge, 1996).

Harding, A. J., *Coleridge and the Inspired Word* (Montreal: McGill Queens University Press, 1985).

Hartman, Geoffrey, *Wordsworth's Poetry: 1787–1814* (1964; Cambridge, Mass.: Harvard University Press, 1987).

—— *Beyond Formalism: Literary Essays, 1958–1970* (New Haven: Yale University Press, 1970).

—— *The Fate of Reading* (Chicago: University of Chicago Press, 1975).

—— *Criticism in the Wilderness: The Study of Literature Today* (New Haven: Yale University Press, 1980).

—— *The Unremarkable Wordsworth* (London: Methuen, 1987).

Hayden, John O., *The Romantic Reviewers, 1802–1824* (London: Routledge and Kegan Paul, 1969).

Heinzelman, Kurt, *The Economics of the Imagination* (Amherst, Mass.: University of Massachusetts Press, 1980).

Hertz, Neil, *The End of the Line: Essays on Psychoanalysis and the Sublime* (New York: Columbia University Press, 1985).

Hewitt, Regina, 'Towards a Wordsworthian Phenomenology of Reading: "The Childless Father" and "Poor Susan" as Paradigms', *Essays in Literature*, 16 (1989), 188–202.

Hillis-Miller, J., 'The Stone and the Shell: The Problem of Poetic Form in Wordsworth's Dream of the Arab', in *Mouvements premiers: Études offertes a Georges Poulet* (Paris, 1972), 125–47.

Hirsch, E. D., Jr., *Validity in Interpretation* (New Haven: Yale University Press, 1967).

—— *The Aims of Interpretation* (Chicago: University of Chicago Press, 1976).

Hobsbawm, E., and Ranger, T., *The Invention of Tradition* (Cambridge: Cambridge University Press, 1983).

Holland, Norman N., *Poems in Persons* (New York: W.W. Norton, 1973).

—— *5 Readers Reading* (New Haven: Yale University Press, 1975).

—— *The Dynamics of Literary Response* (New York, 1975).

—— 'Literary Interpretation and the Three Phases of Psychoanalysis', *Critical Inquiry*, 3 (1976) 221–33.

Holub, R. C., *Reception Theory: A Critical Introduction* (London: Methuen, 1984).

Homans, Margaret, *Women Writers and Poetic Identity: Dorothy Wordsworth, Emily Bronte, and Emily Dickinson* (Princeton: Princeton University Press, 1980).

—— *Bearing the Word: Language and Female Experience in Nineteenth Century Women's Writing* (Chicago: Chicago University Press, 1986).

—— 'Women Reading Keats, Keats Reading Women', *Studies in Romanticism*, 29/3 (Fall, 1990), 341–70.

Iser, Wolfgang, *The Act of Reading: A Theory of Aesthetic Response* (Baltimore: Johns Hopkins University Press, 1978).

Iser, Wolfgang (cont.), *The Implied Reader: Patterns of Communication in Prose Fiction from Bunyan to Beckett* (Baltimore: Johns Hopkins University Press, 1974).

—— *Laurence Sterne: Tristram Shandy* (Cambridge: Cambridge University Press, 1988).

Jackson, J. R. de J., *Method and Imagination in Coleridge's Criticism* (London: Routledge and Kegan Paul, 1969).

Jacobus, Mary, *Romanticism, Writing and Sexual Difference* (Oxford: Clarendon Press, 1989).

Jauss, H. R., *Toward an Aesthetic of Reception*, trans. T. Bahti, introd. Paul de Man (Minnesota, Minn.: University of Minnesota Press, 1982).

Jay, Paul, *Being in the Text: Self-Representation from Wordsworth to Barthes* (Ithaca, NY: Cornell University Press, 1984).

Johnson, Claudia L., *Equivocal Beings: Politics, Gender, and Sentimentality in the 1790's: Wollstonecraft, Radcliffe, Burney, Austen* (Chicago: University of Chicago Press, 1995).

Jones, M. G., *Hannah More* (Cambridge: Cambridge University Press, 1952).

Jones, Stanley, *Hazlitt: A Life, from Winterslow to Frith Street* (Oxford: Clarendon Press, 1989).

Keach, William, 'A Regency Prophecy and the End of Anna Barbauld's Career', *Studies in Romanticism*, 33/4 (Winter 1994), 569–77.

Kelly, Linda, *Richard Brinsley Sheridan: A Life* (London: Sinclair-Stevenson, 1997).

Kitson, Peter, and Corns, Thomas (eds.), *Coleridge and the Armoury of the Human Mind: Essays on his Prose Writings* (London: Frank Cass, 1991).

Klancher, Jon P., *The Making of English Reading Audiences, 1790–1832* (Madison, Wisc.: University of Wisconsin Press, 1987).

Koelb, Clayton, *The Incredulous Reader: Literature and the Function of Disbelief* (Ithaca, NY: Cornell University Press, 1984).

Kowaleski-Wallace, Elizabeth, *Their Fathers' Daughters: Hannah More, Maria Edgeworth and Patriarchal Complicity* (New York: Oxford University Press, 1991).

Kramnick, Jonathan Brody, *Making the English Canon: Print-Capitalism and the Cultural Past, 1700–1770* (Cambridge: Cambridge University Press, 1998).

Kucich, Greg, 'Gendering the Canons of Romanticism: Past and Present', *Wordsworth Circle*, 27/2 (Spring 1996), 95–102.

Laing, R. D., *The Divided Self: An Existential Study in Sanity and Madness* (Harmondsworth, Middlesex: Penguin, 1959).

—— *The Politics of Experience* (Harmondsworth, Middlesex: Penguin, 1967).

Landow, George P., *Hypertext: The Convergence of Contemporary Critical Theory and Technology* (Baltimore: Johns Hopkins University Press, 1992).

Leask, Nigel, *The Politics of Imagination in Coleridge's Critical Thought* (Houndmills, Basingstoke: Macmillan, 1988).

Levin, Susan M., *Dorothy Wordsworth and Romanticism* (New Brunswick: Rutgers University Press, 1987).

Levinson, Marjorie, *The Romantic Fragment Poem; A Critique of a Form* (Chapel Hill, NC: University of North Carolina Press, 1986).

—— *Wordsworth's Great Period Poems: Four Essays* (Cambridge: Cambridge University Press, 1986).

—— with Butler, Marilyn, McGann, Jerome, and Hamilton, Paul, *Rethinking Historicism: Critical Readings in Romantic History* (Oxford: Blackwell, 1989).

Lodge, David, *Modern Criticism and Theory: A Reader* (London: Longman, 1988).

McFarland, Thomas, *Romanticism and the Forms of Ruin: Wordsworth, Coleridge, and Modalities of Fragmentation* (Princeton, NJ: 1981).

—— *Originality and Imagination* (Baltimore: Johns Hopkins University Press, 1985).

McGann, Jerome J., *The Romantic Ideology: A Critical Investigation* (Chicago: University of Chicago Press, 1983).

—— *Social Values and Poetic Acts: The Historical Judgment of Literary Works* (Cambridge, Mass.: Harvard University Press, 1988).

McKenzie, D. F., *Bibliography and the Sociology of Texts* (Panizzi Lectures, 1985) (London: British Library, 1986).

Macpherson, C. B., *The Political Theory of Possessive Individualism: Hobbes to Locke* (Oxford: Oxford University Press, 1962).

Meisenhelder, Susan Edwards, *Wordsworth's Informed Reader: Structures of Experience in his Poetry* (Nashville, Tenn.: Vanderbilt University Press, 1988).

Mellor, A. K., *English Romantic Irony* (Cambridge, Mass.: Harvard University Press, 1969).

—— (ed.), *Romanticism and Feminism* (Bloomington, Ind.: Indiana University Press, 1988).

—— *Romanticism and Gender* (New York: Routledge, 1993).

Mileur, Jean-Pierre, *Vision and Revision: Coleridge's Art of Immanence* (Berkeley and Los Angeles: University of California Press, 1982).

Modiano, Raimonda, 'The Ethics of Gift Exchange and Literary Ownership: Coleridge and Wordsworth', *Wordsworth Circle*, 22 (Spring 1989), 113–20.

Morgan, Peter F., *Literary Critics and Reviewers in Early 19th-Century Britain* (London: Croom Helm, 1983).

Murray, Penelope, *Genius: The History of an Idea* (Oxford: Basil Blackwell, 1989).

Myers, Sylvia, *The Bluestocking Circle: Women, Friendship, and the Life of the Mind in Eighteenth-Century England* (Oxford: Clarendon Press, 1990).

Nabholtz, John R., *'My Reader My Fellow Labourer': A Study of English Romantic Prose* (Columbia, Mo.: University of Missouri Press, 1986).

Natarajan, Uttara, *Hazlitt and the Reach of Sense, Criticism, Morals, and the Metaphysics of Power* (Oxford: Oxford University Press, 1998).

Nelson, Lowry, 'The Fictive Reader: Aesthetic and Social Aspects of Literary Performance', *Comparative Literature Studies*, 15 (June 1978).

Newlyn, Lucy, *Coleridge, Wordsworth, and the Language of Allusion* (Oxford: Clarendon Press, 1986).

——*'Paradise Lost' and the Romantic Reader* (Oxford: Clarendon Press, 1993).

—— ' "Reading After", The Anxiety of the Writing Subject', In *Essays in Honor of Geoffrey Hartman*, special issue of *Studies in Romanticism*, 35/4 (Winter 1996), 609–28.

—— 'Coleridge and the Anxiety of Reception', *Romanticism*, 1/2 (1995), 206–38.

Norris, Christopher, *Deconstruction: Theory and Practice* (London: Methuen, 1982).

O'Brien, P., *Warrington Academy, 1757–1786: Its Predecessors and Successors* (Wigan, Lancs.: Owl Books, 1989).

Ong, Walter J., *Orality and Literacy: The Technologizing of the Word* (London: Routledge, 1982).

Palmer, R. E., *Hermeneutics: Interpretation Theory in Schleiermacher, Dilthey, Heidegger and Gadamer* (Evanston, Ill.: North-Western University Press, 1969).

Paulin, Tom, *Minotaur: Poetry and the Nation State* (London: Faber and Faber, 1992).

—— *The Day-Star of Liberty: William Hazlitt's Radical Style* (London: Faber and Faber, 1998).

Paulson, Ronald, *Representations of Revolution* (New Haven: Yale University Press, 1983).

Pirie, David (ed.), *The Penguin History of the Romantic Period* (Harmondsworth, Middlesex: Penguin, 1994).

Poovey, Mary, *The Proper Lady and the Woman Writer: Ideology as Style in the Works of Mary Wollstonecraft, Mary Shelley, and Jane Austen* (Chicago: Chicago University Press, 1984).

Poulet, Georges, 'Phenomenology of Reading', *New Literary History*, 1/1 (Fall, 1969), 53–68.

—— *Studies in Human Time*, trans. E. Coleman (Baltimore: Johns Hopkins University Press, 1956).

Preston, John, *The Created Self: The Reader's Role in 18th Century Fiction* (London: Heinemann, 1970).

Prickett, Stephen, *Words and the Word: Language, Poetics, and Biblical Interpretation* (Cambridge: Cambridge University Press, 1986).

Rajan, Ballachandra, *The Form of the Unfinished* (Princeton: Princeton University Press, 1985).

Rajan, Tilottama, *Dark Interpreter: The Discourse of Romanticism* (Ithaca, NY: Cornell University Press, 1980).

—— *The Supplement of Reading: Figures of Understanding in Romantic Theory and Practice* (Ithaca, NY: Cornell University Press, 1990).

—— 'Displacing Poststructuralism: Romanticism after Paul de Man', *Studies in Romanticism*, 24 (Winter, 1985), 451–74.

Raven, James, Small, Helen, and Tadmor, Naomi, (eds.), *The Practice and Representation of Reading in England* (Cambridge: Cambridge University Press, 1996).

Rich, Adrienne, 'Vesuvius at Home: The Power of Emily Dickinson', in *On Lies, Secrets and Silence: Selected Prose, 1966–1978* (New York: Norton, 1979).

Richardson, Alan, *Literature, Education, and Romanticism: Reading as Social Practice 1780–1832* (Cambridge: Cambridge University Press, 1994).

Riede, David, *Oracles and Hierophants: Constructions of Romantic Authority* (Ithaca, NY: Cornell University Press, 1991).

Riffaterre, Michael, 'Interpretation and Descriptive Poetry', *New Literary History*, 4 (1972–3), 229–56.

Robinson, Daniel, 'From "mingled measure" to "Ecstatic Measures": Mary Robinson's Poetic Reading of "Kubla Khan"', *Wordsworth Circle*, 26/1, (Winter, 1995), 4–7.

Rodgers, Betsy, *Georgian Chronicle: Mrs Barbauld and her Family* (London: Methuen and Co., 1958).

Roe, Nicholas (ed.), *Keats and History* (Cambridge: Cambridge University Press, 1995).

——*John Keats and the Culture of Dissent* (Oxford: Clarendon Press, 1998).

Rose, Mark, *Authors and Owners: The Invention of Copyright* (Cambridge, Mass.: Harvard University Press, 1993).

Rosenblatt, Louise, *The Reader, The Text, The Poem* (Carbondale, Ill.: Southern Illinois University Press, 1978).

Ross, Marlon B., *The Contours of Masculine Desire: Romanticism and the Rise of Poetry* (Oxford: Oxford University Press, 1989).

Ross, Trevor, 'The Emergence of "Literature": Making and Reading the English Canon in the Eighteenth Century', *ELH* 63 (1996), 397–422.

Royle, Nicholas, *Telepathy and Literature: Essays on the Reading Mind* (Oxford: Blackwell, 1990).

Rzepka, Charles, *The Self as Mind: Vision and Identity in Wordsworth, Coleridge, and Keats* (Cambridge, Mass.: Harvard University Press, 1986).

Sage, Lorna, *Peacock: The Satirical Novels* (London: Macmillan, Anchor Press, 1976).

Shaffer, Elinor, *'Kubla Khan' and the Fall of Jerusalem: The Mythological School in Biblical Criticism and Secular Literature, 1770–1880* (Cambridge: Cambridge University Press, 1975).

Sharpe, Lesley, *Friedrich Schiller: Drama, Thought and Politics* (Cambridge: Cambridge University Press, 1991).

Simpson, David (ed.), *The Origins of Modern Critical Thought: German Aesthetic and Literary Criticism from Lessing to Hegel* (Cambridge: Cambridge University Press, 1988).

—— *Irony and Authority in Romantic Poetry* (London: Macmillan, 1979).

—— *Wordsworth's Historical Imagination: The Poetry of Displacement* (London: Methuen, 1987).

Siskin, Clifford, *The Historicity of Romantic Discourse* (New York: Oxford University Press, 1988).

Slatoff, Walter, *With Respect to Readers* (Ithaca, NY: Cornell University Press, 1970).

Smith, Olivia, *The Politics of Language, 1791–1819* (Oxford: Oxford University Press, 1984).

Sontag, Susan, *Against Interpretation and Other Essays* (London: Eyre and Spottiswoode, 1966).

Spivak, Gayatri, *In Other Worlds: Essays in Cultural Politics* (London: Routledge, 1987).

Stafford, Fiona, *The Last of the Race: The Growth of a Myth from Milton to Darwin* (Oxford: Clarendon Press, 1994).

—— 'Hugh Blair's Ossian, Romanticism and the Teaching of Literature', in Robert Crawford (ed.), *The Scottish Invention of English Literature* (Cambridge: Cambridge University Press, 1998), 68–88.

Suleiman, Susan R., and Crosman, Inge, *The Reader in the Text: Essays on Audience and Interpretation* (Princeton: Princeton University Press, 1980).

Swartz, Richard G., 'Wordsworth, Copyright, and the Commodities of Genius', *Modern Philology*, 89 (1992), 482–509.

Taylor, Archer, and Mosher, Frederick J., *The Bibliographical History of Anonyma and Pseudonyma* (Chicago: University of Chicago Press, 1951).

Taylor, John Tinnon, *Early Opposition to the English Novel: The Popular Reaction from 1760–1830* (1943; New York: King's Crown Press, 1970).

Terry, Richard (ed.), *James Thomson: Essays for the Tercentenary* (Liverpool: Liverpool University Press, 1999).

Tompkins, Jane P. (ed.), *Reader-Response Criticism* (Baltimore: Johns Hopkins University Press, 1980).

Vargo, Lisa, 'The Claims of Real Life and Manners: Coleridge and Mary Robinson', *Wordsworth Circle*, 26/3 (Summer 1995), 134–7.

Wallace, C. M., *The Design of Biographia Literaria* (London: Allan and Unwin, 1983).

Weiskel, Thomas, *The Romantic Sublime: Studies in the Structure and Psychology of Transcendence* (Baltimore: Johns Hopkins University Press, 1976).

Wheeler, Kathleen, *Sources, Processes and Methods in Coleridge's Biographia Literaria* (Cambridge: Cambridge University Press, 1980).

—— *The Creative Mind in Coleridge's Poetry* (London: Heinemann, 1981).

—— *Romanticism, Pragmatism and Deconstruction* (Oxford: Blackwell, 1993).

Whitrow, G., *Time in History* (Oxford: Oxford University Press, 1988).

Wilson, Carol Shiner, and Haefner, Joel (eds.), *Re-Visioning Romanticism: British Women Writers, 1776–1837* (Philadelphia: University of Pennsylvania Press, 1994).

Wolfson, Susan J., *The Questioning Presence: Wordsworth, Keats, and the Interrogative Mode in Romantic Poetry* (Ithaca, NY: Cornell University Press, 1986).

Woodmansee, Martha, *The Author, Art, and the Market: Rereading the History of Aesthetics* (New York: Columbia University Press, 1994).

Wordsworth, Jonathan, *William Wordsworth: The Borders of Vision* (Oxford: Clarendon Press, 1982).

Worton, M., and Still, J., *Intertextuality: Theories and Practices* (Manchester: Manchester University Press, 1990).

Zall, Paul M., 'The Cool World of Samual Taylor Coleridge: Mrs Barbauld and the Building of a Mass Reading Audience', *Wordsworth Circle*, 2/3 (Spring 1971), 74–9.

—— 'Wordsworth and the Copyright Act of 1842', *PMLA* 70 (1955).

Index